D0205611

About the Series:

In Their Own Words chronicles landmark events in American history through original source documents and narratives. Next in this compelling series is **Warriors and Pioneers,** the story of westward expansion and the conquest of the American frontier, coming soon from Perigee Books.

About the Author:

T. J. Stiles is a writer and historian living in New York City. His books include *The Citizen's Handbook: Essential Documents and Speeches from American History* and *Jesse James.*

About the Introducer:

Gary W. Gallagher is head of the Department of History at Pennsylvania State University. His publications on the Civil War include *Stephen Dodson Ramseur: Lee's Gallant General; Fighting for the Confederacy: The Personal Recollections of General Edward Porter Alexander;* and *The Third Day at Gettysburg and Beyond.*

IN THEIR OWN WORDS

CIVIL WAR COMMANDERS

Collected and Edited by

T. J. Stiles

With an Introduction by Gary W. Gallagher

A PERIGEE BOOK

A Perigee Book
Published by The Berkley Publishing Group
200 Madison Avenue
New York, NY 10016

Copyright © 1995 by T. J. Stiles.
Book design by Irving Perkins Associates
Cover design by James R. Harris
Cover photograph: Officers of the 80th New York (NYSM 20th),
Culpepper, Virginia, September 1863; photograph by Matthew Brady.
(Reproduced from the Collections of the Library of Congress.)

First edition: April 1995

Published simultaneously in Canada.

Library of Congress Cataloging-in-Publication Data

In their own words : Civil War commanders / [collected] by
T. J. Stiles.—1st ed.
p.   cm.
"A Perigee book."
ISBN 0-399-51909-2 (paper : acid-free)
1. United States—History—Civil War, 1861–1865—Campaigns.
2. United States—History—Civil War, 1861–1865—Sources.
I. Stiles, T. J.
E470.I5   1995   94-27322
                                      CIP

Printed in the United States of America

10 9 8 7 6 5 4 3 2 1

This book is printed on acid-free paper.

CONTENTS

List of Maps   ix

Preface   xi

Sources   xiii

The Writers and Their Positions at the Time   xv

Introduction by Gary W. Gallagher   xvii

I. The High Tide of the Confederacy
FROM BULL RUN TO ANTIETAM   1

1. The Battle of Bull Run   3
    Prelude and Battle: General P. G. T. Beauregard
    Impressions of the Battle and the Union Retreat: General William T.
      Sherman
2. The Peninsula Campaign   23
    The Confederate Strategic Quandary: General Joseph E. Johnston
    The Army of the Potomac Creeps Ahead: General George B. McClellan
    Lee Takes Command: General James Longstreet
    The Seven Days' Battles: General George B. McClellan
3. The Second Battle of Bull Run   39
    The Second Battle of Bull Run: General James Longstreet
4. The Battle of Antietam   51
    The Battle of Antietam: General George B. McClellan

II. Ironclads and Rivers
THE FIRST NAVAL BATTLES   65

5. Duel of the Ironclads   67
    In the Monitor's *Turret: S. Dana Greene*
6. The Fight for New Orleans   77
    The Opening of the Lower Mississippi: Admiral David D. Porter

III. The Union Breakthrough
FROM SHILOH TO VICKSBURG   91

7. The Battle of Shiloh   93
    The Battle of Shiloh: General U. S. Grant
8. The Invasion of Kentucky   109
    The Invasion of Kentucky and the Battle of Perryville:
    General Philip H. Sheridan
9. The Struggle for Vicksburg   119
    Grant's First Failure: General Joseph E. Johnston
    The Second Vicksburg Campaign: General U. S. Grant

IV. The Great Turning Point
GETTYSBURG   145

10. The Gettysburg Campaign   147
    The Battle of Gettysburg: General James Longstreet

V. The Guerrilla War   175

11. Mosby's Confederacy   177
    The Capture of General Stoughton: Colonel John S. Mosby
12. The Missouri Bushwhackers   183
    The Lawrence Massacre: John McCorkle
    The Massacre and Battle of Centralia: John McCorkle

VI. Decision in the West
FROM CHATTANOOGA TO ATLANTA   191

13. The Battle of Chattanooga   193
    Up Missionary Ridge: General Philip H. Sheridan
14. Grant's Grand Strategy   201
    The Plans for 1864: General U. S. Grant
15. The Atlanta Campaign   205
    From Dalton to Cassville: General William T. Sherman
    Aborted Counterattack: General Joseph E. Johnston
    To the Gates of Atlanta: General William T. Sherman
    Counterattack: From Peachtree Creek to the Battle of Atlanta:
        General John B. Hood
    The Capture of Atlanta: General William T. Sherman

VII. "Damn the Torpedoes"
THE FINAL NAVAL BATTLES 247

16. The Confederate Cruisers 249
    The Cruise of the C.S.S. Alabama: *John McIntosh Kell*
17. The Battle of Mobile Bay 257
    Detailed Report on the Battle of Mobile Bay:
    Admiral David Glasgow Farragut

VIII. Grant Goes East
THE LAST CAMPAIGNS 265

18. From the Wilderness to Petersburg 267
    From the Wilderness to Petersburg: General U. S. Grant
19. Sheridan in the Valley 297
    The Shenandoah Campaign: General Philip H. Sheridan
20. The Appomattox Campaign 311
    From Five Forks to Lee's Surrender: General U. S. Grant

MAPS

1. The Eastern Theater   6
2. Topographical map of the Bull Run battlefield   11
3. Plan of the Bull Run battlefield   14
4. The Peninsula   27
5. The Battle of Mechanicsville (Beaver Dam Creek), June 26, 1862   31
6. The Battle of Gaines's Mill, June 27, 1862   35
7. Lee's march around Pope's right flank, as of August 27, 1862   41
8. The Second Battle of Bull Run, August 29, 1862   46
9. The Battle of Antietam, September 17, 1862   55
10. The blockade of Confederate ports   66
11. The battle between the *Merrimack* (or *Virginia*) and the *Monitor*, Hampton Roads, March 9, 1862   69
12. The lower Mississippi, 1862   78
13. The Confederate defenses below New Orleans   83
14. The Western Theater, early 1862   92
15. Region of the Shiloh Campaign, March and April 1862   96
16. The Battle of Shiloh: initial Union positions and routes of reinforcements, April 6–7, 1862   99
17. The Confederate invasion of Kentucky and the Union pursuit, August to October 1862   111
18. The Battle of Perryville, October 8, 1862   115
19. The lower Mississippi valley, region of the two Vicksburg campaigns, December 1862 to July 1863   120
20. Operations in the rear of Vicksburg, May 1863   132
21. The march to Gettysburg, June 1863   151
22. The first day at Gettysburg, 6:00 P.M., July 1, 1863   156
23. The second day at Gettysburg, 3:30 P.M., July 2, 1863   160
24. The third day at Gettysburg, July 3, 1863   166
25. The Battle of Chattanooga, November 23–25, 1863   196
26. The Atlanta Campaign, May to September 1864   206
27. The Atlanta Campaign: the movement against Resaca   210
28. The Atlanta Campaign: the aborted Confederate counterattack at Cassville   215
29. The Atlanta Campaign: from Cassville to Marietta   218
30. The Siege of Atlanta, July to September 1864   228

31. The cruise of the C.S.S. *Alabama*, August 1862 to June 1864   251
32. The Battle of Mobile Bay, August 5, 1864   259
33. The Eastern Theater   269
34. The Battle of the Wilderness, May 5–6, 1864   272
35. The Battle of Spotsylvania, May 1864   281
36. The Battle of Cold Harbor, June 3, 1864   289
37. The Siege of Petersburg, June 1864 to March 1865   293
38. The Battle of Fisher's Hill, September 22, 1864   301
39. The Battle of Cedar Creek, October 19, 1864   306
40. The region of the Appomattox Campaign, April 1865   313

All maps are from *Battles and Leaders of the Civil War* (New York: Century Co., 1884–1886).

PREFACE

Civil War Commanders is the first book in a series entitled *In Their Own Words*, which aims to bring the drama of first-person accounts of American history into the hands of today's readers. This book begins the series by focusing on the supreme test of our nation's life, the massive, bloody, tragic war over unity and slavery.

Perhaps the most exciting and pleasurable part of the historian's work lies in reading firsthand accounts by people who shaped the past. The words of the actual historical actors, as they share their thoughts and observations, make historical events personal, immediate, and real. This fascination is hardly new: in the late nineteenth century, book publishers and magazine editors competed to print the stories told by generals and privates alike, and many of the memoirs that resulted are still available in reprint in many bookstores. But this book brings together a group of carefully selected and edited writings by commanders from both North and South, ranging from the first battle to the last, giving the general reader a chronological history of the war in the words of those who fought it.

Civil War Commanders is far more than a simple anthology. Everything has been done to make this a true narrative history of the war, brought to life by the voices of the actual commanders but resting in a firm chronological and critical framework. To keep the book from running on to thousands of pages, I have had to limit the number and scope of these selections—but I have bridged the gaps with detailed descriptions of the intervening events, allowing the reader to follow the war from beginning to end. Be warned: as Gary Gallagher reminds us in his excellent introduction, the generals may have left us vivid accounts of their actions, but they also tended to slant their stories to cast a more favorable light on themselves. With a healthy dose of skepticism, however, and careful attention to Professor Gallagher's comments on the worst offenders, reading these writings provides an enjoyable way of following the history of the Civil War.

I should also briefly explain the logic behind the selections made for this book. First, I have obviously focused on the military side of the Civil War. As

Professor Gallagher also mentions, recent historiography has given us rich studies of every possible aspect of the war: the role of African Americans, the economics and politics of the struggle, the diplomatic maneuvering, the place of women, and many others. In fact, in recent decades historians wrote as if events on the battlefield were either irrelevant or predestined by the disproportionate weight of men, soldiers, and morale. Recently, however, the centrality of the clash of arms has again attracted the attention of scholars. As James McPherson has deftly pointed out, many a nation has won defensive wars of independence despite long material odds; key victories at key moments gave the North the political will to press on and win.

A second question concerns the particular events I have chosen for first-person retelling. Those already familiar with the war will ask, where are the accounts of Pea Ridge? Chancellorsville? Chickamauga? Sherman's march to the sea? Alas, not everything could be included. I decided to choose accounts based primarily on the decisiveness of the events, the importance of the writer, and the literary quality of the story. Because of these criteria, for example, the tactically crushing Confederate victory of Chancellorsville dropped out, but the tactically drawn battle of Perryville stayed in. Chancellorsville served in the end as a prelude to the more important Gettysburg campaign, whereas the battle of Perryville forced the retreat of General Bragg from Kentucky and the end of one of the most important Confederate counterattacks in the West. And Sherman's march, while central to the Southern collapse, was basically just a march, if a destructive one; with limited space, I chose to concentrate on his Atlanta campaign, a much more closely run endeavor that made Sherman's later raids possible.

I must acknowledge those who were critical to the making of this book. First, my editor and friend John Schline has made this series a possibility through his tireless devotion to serious—but interesting—history. His tremendous enthusiasm has brought this worthwhile idea to life, bringing out accounts that otherwise would sit in ancient volumes in libraries, or on the shelves of bookstores in unedited, unhelpful reprints of memoirs. Another important figure in the making of this book was Professor Gary Gallagher, who agreed to help out a little-known writer by providing an outstanding introduction and very helpful comments on the manuscript. I am in debt to John Parras of Columbia University, a literature scholar and a man of great dignity and generosity who greatly helped with the research for this series. I am also very grateful to Dana Lowell and Stephanie Schaich, who read the manuscript and offered helpful comments.

T. J. Stiles

SOURCES

Battles and Leaders of the Civil War, edited by Robert Underwood Johnson and Clarence Clough Buel, 4 vols. (New York: Century Co., 1884–
1886)
   Articles:
      Beauregard, P. G. T., "The Battle of Bull Run"
      Kell, John McIntosh, "The Cruise and Combats of the C.S.S.
      Alabama"
      Greene, S. Dana, "In the *Monitor*'s Turret"

Farragut, Loyall, *The Life of David Glasgow Farragut, First Admiral of the
United States Navy, Embodying his Journal and Letters, by his Son* (New
York: D. Appleton & Co., 1879)

Grant, Ulysses S., *Personal Memoirs of U. S. Grant* (New York: C. L. Webster, 1886)

Hood, John Bell, *Advance and Retreat: Personal Experiences in the United
States and Confederate States Armies* (New Orleans: G. T. Beauregard,
1880)

Johnston, Joseph Eggleston, *Narrative of Military Operations Directed
During the Late War Between the States* (New York: D. Appleton & Co.,
1874)

Longstreet, James, *From Manassas to Appomattox: Memoirs of the Civil
War in America*, 2nd edition (Philadelphia: J. B. Lippincott Co., 1908)

McClellan, George Brinton, *Report on the Organization and Campaigns
of the Army of the Potomac* (New York: Sheldon & Co., 1864)

McCorkle, John, *Three Years with Quantrell* [sic]: *A True Story, Told by
his Scout, John McCorkle, Written by O. S. Barton* (Armstrong, Mo.:
Armstrong Herald Print, 1914)

Mosby, John Singleton, *The Memoirs of Colonel John S. Mosby*, edited by
Charles Wells Russell (Boston: Little, Brown, and Co., 1917)

Sheridan, Philip Henry, *Personal Memoirs of P. H. Sheridan* (New York: C. L. Webster & Co., 1888)

Sherman, William Tecumseh, *Memoirs of General William T. Sherman*, 2nd edition (New York: D. Appleton, 1889)

THE WRITERS AND THEIR POSITIONS AT THE TIME

Union

George B. McClellan, commander of the Army of the Potomac (1862)
U. S. Grant, commander of the Army of the Tennessee and later commander-in-chief of the Union armies
William T. Sherman, commander of a brigade at First Bull Run and later commander-in-chief in the West
Philip H. Sheridan, commander of an infantry division and later commander-in-chief of the cavalry of the Army of the Potomac
David D. Porter, second-in-command to Farragut at New Orleans
David G. Farragut, commander of the Gulf blockade squadron
S. Dana Greene, executive officer (second-in-command) on the U.S.S. *Monitor*

Confederate

P. G. T. Beauregard, commander of the Confederate army at Manassas
Joseph E. Johnston, commander-in-chief in Northern Virginia, later commander-in-chief in the West during the Vicksburg Campaign, and commander of the Army of Tennessee during the Atlanta Campaign
James Longstreet, commander of a division and later a corps under Robert E. Lee in the Army of Northern Virginia
John B. Hood, commander of the Army of Tennessee after Johnston
John S. Mosby, commander of the Partisan Rangers in Virginia
John McCorkle, scout for William C. Quantrill and later squad leader under guerrilla George Todd in Missouri
John McIntosh Kell, executive officer (second-in-command) under Captain Raphael Semmes on the C.S.S. *Alabama*

INTRODUCTION

The Civil War was one of the most complex and decisive moments in American history. A cluster of issues related to the institution of slavery had divided the nation through the antebellum decades, reaching a point by November 1860 where the election of Abraham Lincoln sent tremors through much of the South. Discounting Lincoln's pledge to respect the "peculiar institution" where it existed, many southerners concentrated instead on the Republican Party's promise to bar slavery from all federal territories. Between December 20, 1860, and February 1, 1861, seven states of the lower South seceded and quickly formed a new government. Tensions heightened during the spring of 1861, as citizens on both sides of the Potomac turned their eyes toward Charleston, South Carolina, where a small garrison held one of the few remaining United States installations in the seceded states. The Confederate decision to fire on Fort Sumter on April 12 triggered Lincoln's call for 75,000 volunteers to suppress the rebellion, which in turn prompted four states of the upper South to join the fledgling southern nation.

Americans thus embarked on a course that would bring profound changes in their government and their society. Before peace returned four years later, more than 2,100,000 men fought for the Union and approximately 800,000 for the Confederacy. They met in combat and died in staggering numbers at thousands of places across the American landscape. Disease claimed twice as many lives as the battlefield, and scores of thousands of men returned home with scars that would last their lifetimes. This horrific bloodletting settled two great issues. Never again would a state seriously threaten secession. The American nation emerged from the war, as Lincoln had insisted it must, a powerful democratic example for others around the world to emulate. Equally as important, the war liberated four million people from bondage, thereby removing a stain that had mocked the Declaration of Independence for almost nine decades. The future of the freed men and women remained uncertain, but they would face it unhindered by the shackles of slavery.

At no time in American history were more profound issues at stake, nor does any other period surpass the Civil War in terms of sheer drama or impact on subsequent generations. For these reasons, the conflict has drawn the attention of innumerable writers, beginning with thousands of participants who wrote of their own experiences. No one can estimate with precision the number of books and pamphlets on the subject, though the total certainly runs to more than 60,000. Americans continue to be drawn to the war because they find that it illuminates both their past and present circumstances. Increasingly, historians have turned away from famous personalities and battles to focus on the common folk. Why did men on either side fight? How did their time in the army affect them? What social, political, and economic changes occurred on the respective home fronts? How were the lives of women altered? As such questions receive additional attention, modern readers can better grasp the meaning of a war that too often has been presented as little more than a succession of bloody encounters between huge armies.

Yet a sense of the ebb and flow on the battlefield remains essential to any study of the Civil War. Citizens on both sides followed news from the fighting fronts carefully. Political decisions reflected concern with the military situation, and Union and Confederate morale rose and fell according to the fortunes of the armies. In the summer of 1864, for example, stalemates outside Richmond and Atlanta caused northern civilian morale to plummet; indeed, Lincoln detected so much war weariness in the North during late August that he prophesied his defeat in the November elections. Stunning triumphs at Atlanta and in the Shenandoah Valley during September and October reversed this trend. Lincoln and the Republicans swept to victory in November 1864, and any realistic Confederate hope for a negotiated settlement short of total Union victory evaporated. Throughout this crucial period, as at many other points in the preceding three years, the armies had shaped the context of the war to a remarkable extent.

Because the forces they headed wielded such influence, the war's principal military leaders remain critical witnesses. Their testimony resides in the massive corpus of memoirs, reminiscences, and accounts of battles that swelled the literature from the immediate postwar years through the early twentieth century. In forums such as the Century Company's *Battles and Leaders of the Civil War* and the Southern Historical Society's *Papers*, as well as in thick volumes written by Ulysses S. Grant, William Tecumseh Sherman, George B. McClellan, James Longstreet, and many others, Civil War commanders reexamined old campaigns, burnished their own reputations, and took revenge on enemies in blue and gray. Their writings, however flawed by special pleading, constitute a valuable and enjoyable introduction to the operations that helped decide the outcome of the conflict.

The roster of authors in *Civil War Commanders* includes virtually all of the most important Union and Confederate military figures. The obvious omission is Robert E. Lee, who towered above other southern officers but published nothing about his wartime role. Among other noteworthy leaders who survived the war but never wrote about it were Braxton Bragg, architect of a string of defeats in the Western Theater as head of the Confederacy's Army of Tennessee, and George Henry Thomas, a Virginian who remained loyal to the Union and compiled an enviable record in Tennessee and Georgia. But these individuals are the exceptions. Grant and Sherman have their say in the text that follows. Between them, they planned and executed the campaigns that doomed the Confederacy—with Grant the unquestioned senior partner and Sherman the devoted subordinate. Philip H. Sheridan, like Sherman a protégé of Grant's, rose to preeminence in the last year of the war by virtue of his success in the Shenandoah Valley against Confederate General Jubal A. Early. At sea and on the Mississippi River, David G. Farragut and David Dixon Porter formed the naval equivalent of Grant and Sherman. Their exploits often are slighted relative to those of their comrades in the Union army, but their contribution to the Confederate defeat was signal.

The most controversial of the Union soldiers represented in the narrative in this book was George B. McClellan. A fascinating combination of talent and profound flaws, McClellan bestrode the war in the Eastern Theater like a slothful colossus through most of 1861 and 1862. He built a magnificent army and won its devotion but lacked the moral courage to risk his creation in combat. At the Seven Days and again during the 1862 Maryland Campaign, McClellan's resolve withered in the face of Lee's superior confidence and daring. His greatest failure came on September 17–18 along the banks of Antietam Creek, where in refusing to mount an all-out effort to crush Lee's vulnerable Army of Northern Virginia he frittered away the best opportunity presented to any commander during the entire war. A Democrat at odds with Republican policies on emancipation, McClellan hoped to defeat the Confederacy with minimal disruption of the structure of prewar society—a manifest impossibility by the summer of 1862. He saw political enemies in the rear, wildly overestimated Southern military strength, and always found a reason not to press the war vigorously. In the end, Lincoln removed McClellan, though a year and a half would pass before the president found in Grant a man who would apply a firm hand to the helm of affairs in the Eastern Theater.

Postwar controversy clung to the four principal Confederate authors in this volume. P. G. T. Beauregard and Joseph E. Johnston, both of whom had feuded constantly with Jefferson Davis during the war, worked diligently to leave a written record that would justify their wartime actions. Each possessed considerable talent as a soldier but exhibited even larger shortcomings. Beauregard could not resist planning strategic concentrations that looked grand on paper and impressed civilians at social gatherings but stood scant chance of successful application in the field. A creole from Louisiana who consciously emulated Napoleon, Beauregard never lived up to his early fame as the hero of Sumter and First Manassas. Johnston, a Virginian and a contemporary of Lee's, had an obsession with rank (he stood fourth on the list of senior Confederate officers; he believed he should have been first) and a good bit of McClellan's aversion to battles. He never understood that the Confederate populace craved battlefield victories and would not tolerate indefinitely a general who retreated too far and too often. After giving up all the ground between Chattanooga and Atlanta to Sherman in the early summer of 1864, he found himself at odds with Davis and much of the Confederate citizenry and lost command of the Army of Tennessee to John Bell Hood.

Hood is one of the tragic figures of the Confederacy. A robust young man at the beginning of the war, he won a reputation as a hard-fighting brigade and division leader in Lee's army. Always ready to attack, he often achieved results at the cost of very high casualties—and in the process received a permanently disabling wound in an arm at Gettysburg and lost a leg at Chickamauga. Promoted beyond his capacities at a time when Confederate resources of command had entered a serious decline, he eventually presided over the loss of Atlanta and a disastrous campaign that virtually wrecked the Army of Tennessee at the battles of Franklin and Nashville in November and December 1864. Often pilloried because of his aggressive tactics at Atlanta, Hood was only responding to the wishes of his government and numerous others in the Confederacy who had tired of Johnston's Fabian strategy. But he lacked the intellectual capacity to command an army, exhibited a willingness to undercut superiors, and shamelessly exploited political connections in Richmond to gain advancement. Broken and embittered by the war, Hood often is used as a metaphor for the Confederate nation.

James Longstreet gained the most notoriety among this Confederate quartet. Undeniably a gifted corps commander, he served throughout the war as Lee's senior subordinate. Lee dubbed him "my old war horse" after the endless day of combat at Antietam on September 17, 1862, and relied on the dour Georgian on many fields. More committed than his chief to the tactical defensive, Longstreet urged Lee not to attack at Gettysburg on July 2 and 3 and probably was happy to leave Virginia with two-thirds of his corps to reinforce the Army of Tennessee in September 1863. He returned to Virginia in the spring of 1864 after a miserable winter in East Tennessee and served under Lee through Appomattox. Longstreet's postwar troubles began when he criticized Lee's generalship in public forums. He also became a Republican and urged reconciliation with the North. Many former Confederates shunned him, and it became a common view in the South that Longstreet's refusal to attack with fervor at Gettysburg had cost Lee that battle and the Confederacy its independence. Longstreet defended himself ineptly, writing numerous accounts that differed with one another and making intemperate comments about Lee. A huge volume of writing centered on the question of his role in the defeat at Gettysburg, and he remains today an often-maligned figure.

Readers should keep two things in mind as they traverse the pages of this book. The first is that they are privileged to read about famous events in the words of several central actors. There is no substitute for firsthand knowledge, and the fourteen authors in this collection possessed that in abundance. But readers also should know that what follows was filtered through the individual prisms of men who were writing to establish a record that would place their actions in the best possible light.

This leads to some interesting distortions, a few examples of which will suffice to make the point. In his report on Antietam, McClellan excused his failure to employ the troops of William B. Franklin and Fitz John Porter as necessary to guard against Confederate counterattacks; in truth, there were no prospective Southern attacks, and McClellan's decision to keep these two corps out of the battle wasted a wonderful opening to exploit Union successes. McClellan also dissembled about the time of his order instructing Burnside to attack on the morning of September 17, placing it at 8:00 A.M. when in fact it was dispatched at 9:10 and reached Burnside at about 10 o'clock. By claiming the earlier time, McClellan sought to shift responsibility for the failure to drive Lee from the field to Burnside's shoulders. Sheridan's discussion of relative strengths during the 1864 Valley Campaign contains the wonderfully self-serving statement that various factors "almost canceled" his advantage in numbers, when he actually enjoyed an edge of two and a half or three to one at Third Winchester, Fisher's Hill, and Cedar Creek. Finally, Longstreet's treatment of the preparations for Confederate assaults on the second day at Gettysburg gives no hint of his sloth in getting his two divisions into position; indeed, he unfairly blames "the conduct of the reconnoitering officer" for the fact that it took most of the day to make the march.

Such distortions are to be expected in firsthand accounts of any historical event. Armed with an awareness that the authors leave much out and adjust some facts to suit their purposes, readers can enjoy these narratives as the sometimes passionate words of participants who had painted broad strokes on the canvas of the nation's supreme moment of testing.

—Gary W. Gallagher

I

THE HIGH TIDE OF THE CONFEDERACY

FROM BULL RUN TO ANTIETAM

1
THE BATTLE OF BULL RUN
July 21, 1861

At 4:30 in the morning on April 12, 1861, an ominous sound rang out across the harbor of Charleston, South Carolina. It was the booming report of cannons aimed at Fort Sumter, the last bastion of Federal power in the first Southern state to secede. The battle was a brief one; less than thirty-six hours after those first shots, the commander of the island fort surrendered to General P. G. T. Beauregard, of the new Confederate States of America. But the aftermath would shake the continent for the next four years: for the South had thrown down a challenge to the Union, declaring its willingness to fight for independence.

For decades the fault line between the slave-owning South and free North had threatened to split the United States; the rise of the Republican Party in the 1850s, with its strong abolitionist support, and increasingly aggressive efforts by the South to preserve slavery by extending it, made the wound fresher and deeper. When the Republicans gained the White House with Lincoln's election in 1860, Southern states responded by seceding, and it seemed as though events had reached an inevitable climax. And yet, despite the years of anticipation, the Confederacy came into the world ill equipped to defend its existence, and the Federal government stood almost equally unprepared to snuff it out.

Of course, if the United States *had* possessed a powerful military, the South might never have attempted to break away. Instead, it had only a tiny regular army, stationed almost entirely in the wilderness of the West to keep an eye on the Indians. In the navy it had a fine professional force, but one far too small to control the thousands of miles of the Confederacy's shores—and ships took time to build and man. In the South, of course, Jefferson Davis took office as president of a new government with no military whatsoever. So North and South were forced to create armies where none had existed before, filling their ranks with volunteer regiments, armed and recruited by the state governments. In building armies

3

out of virtually nothing, however, both sides drew on the same institution: West Point, the United States Military Academy.

Both Lincoln and Davis, of course, needed more officers than West Point alumni could provide, and they had to use many men with no military experience: some were elected by their units, some appointed by state governors because of their prestige or wealth, some appointed by the respective presidents because of their political influence. Not all were untalented; in fact, some of the men on both sides with no previous experience turned out to be outstanding commanders—including a few political generals. But at the heart of the officer corps on both sides were the graduates of West Point.

It was the professionalism provided at the U.S. Military Academy that shaped the military institutions of the Civil War. There the key officers on both sides had learned not only elements of strategy and tactics, but also military organization, logistics, communications, and other aspects of war often overlooked by the battle-obsessed public. The North, with its far larger population, had the lion's share of West Pointers—but the South drew upon a sizeable number as well, allowing it to create an effective military establishment in a surprisingly brief period. This meant not only that the armies strongly resembled each other in organization and methods, but often opposing commanders knew each other quite well from their years together at West Point and in the U.S. Army. They knew something of each other's character and intelligence, and this knowledge shaped the plans they made.

But if the armies were much alike, the two presidents were worlds apart. Jefferson Davis was a plantation owner from Mississippi, a former senator and secretary of war, and himself a West Point graduate: intelligent, un-yielding, harshly critical of his commanders yet strongly loyal to his friends (including more than one controversial general). He both gave the Con-federacy a fierce will to win and interfered repeatedly with the army's operations (with mixed results). Lincoln, on the other hand, is legendary for his eloquence, his political skills, and his many character strengths—strengths that overcame his obscure background and limited education. Lincoln had no real military experience, and he tended to step into military affairs only when he thought it was necessary to drive the war effort ahead. In the end (after some stumbling), he proved to be an able supreme commander, with a clear vision of both the political and military necessities involved in crushing the Southern rebellion.

The North's advantage in men and materiel, Lincoln knew, would work to good effect only if the Union pressed its attacks at numerous points simultaneously. The South would be forced either to concentrate its limited forces at a few points, allowing breakthroughs somewhere, or to thinly distribute its men at all points, possibly allowing breakthroughs everywhere. Because of the uneven quality of Northern army commanders, this strategy worked only sporadically through the first years of the war—and when it did work, it was largely because Jefferson Davis was driven by political considerations to try to defend the Confederacy's borders *everywhere*. Despite Davis's initial preference for avoiding battles to preserve his armies (much as Washington had done in the Revolution), public pressure forced him to try at first to maintain the South's territorial integrity, in a brittle static defense all along the borders and coastlines.

Political considerations were most obvious in one particular theater: the forest-and-stream-clogged land between Washington and Richmond. Here the Union fought to decapitate the rebellious South, and the Confederacy struggled to preserve its capital city, placed so precariously close to that of the Yankee enemy. Here the world's attention remained focused through four years of war, as what would become two of the finest armies in existence—the Confederate Army of Northern Virginia, under Robert E. Lee, and the Union Army of the Potomac, under a succession of generals—fought a fierce duel, punctuated by epic battles and brilliant maneuvering.

In July 1861, however, these armies were just coming into existence, and Robert E. Lee was on assignment in western Virginia. Tens of thousands of short-term Union volunteers (most had signed up for only three months), with no experience and often no training, assembled near Washington under the command of General Irvin McDowell. McDowell had been a staff officer under the aging (and soon to retire) commander-in-chief General Winfield Scott, and he had been selected by Lincoln to capture Richmond and shut down the rebellion with one quick blow. Facing him was a Confederate force under General P. G. T. Beauregard, the Creole commander from Louisiana who had won fame by presiding over the attack on Fort Sumter in April. Beauregard held a position at an outpost called Manassas Junction, on a stream known as Bull Run. In the Shenandoah Valley to the west was another Confederate force under General Joseph E. Johnston, the overall commander for northern Virginia. Beauregard was outnumbered by the advancing Union army, and his troops were just as inexperienced as their opponents. But he knew he had to prevail: to lose the first battle might well doom the entire Confederacy to an immediate grave.

JACKSON AT HARPER'S FERRY IN 1861.

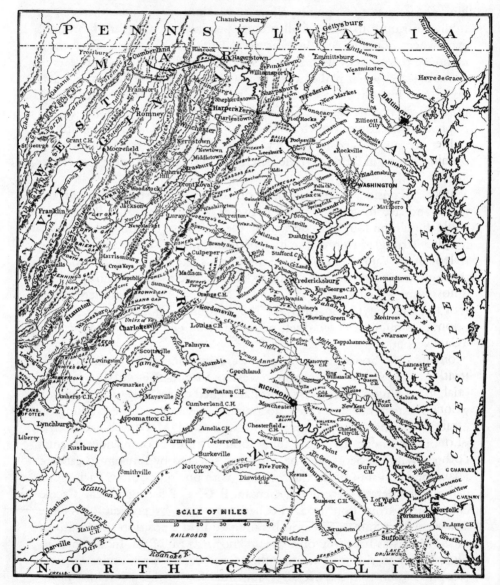

The Eastern Theater (note Bull Run, due west of Alexandria)

Prelude and Battle
By General P.G.T. Beauregard

Soon after the first conflict between the authorities of the Federal Union and the Confederate States had occurred in Charleston Harbor, by the bombardment of Fort Sumter . . . I was called to Richmond, which by that time had become the Confederate seat of government, and directed to "assume command of the Confederate troops on the Alexandria line." Arriving at Manassas Junction, I took command on the 2nd of June, forty-nine days after the evacuation of Fort Sumter by Major Anderson [the Union commander who had surrendered the fort to Beauregard].

Although the position at the time was strategically of commanding importance to the Confederates, the mere *terrain* was not only without natural defensive advantages, but on the contrary, was positively unfavorable. Its strategic value was that, with close proximity to the Federal capital, it held in observation their chief Federal army then being assembled in the quarter of Arlington by General McDowell, under the immediate eye of the commander-in-chief, General Scott, for an offensive movement on Richmond; and while it had a railway approach in the rear for the easy accumulation of reinforcements and all the necessary munitions of war from the southward, at the same time another (the Manassas Gap) railway, diverging laterally to the left from that point, gave rapid communications with the fertile valley of the Shenandoah, then teeming with livestock and cereal substances, as well as with other resources essential to the Confederates. There was this further value in the position to the Confederate army: that during the period of accumulation, seasoning, and training, it might be fed from the fat fields, pastures, and garners of Loudoun, Fauquier, and the lower Shenandoah Valley counties, which otherwise must have fallen into the hands of the enemy. But, on the other hand, Bull Run, a petty stream, was of little or no defensive strength, for it abounded in fords, and although for the most part its banks were rocky and abrupt, the side from which it would be approached offensively was in most places the higher, and therefore commanded the opposite ground.

At the time of my arrival at Manassas, a Confederate army under General Joseph E. Johnston was in occupation of the lower Shenandoah Valley along the line of the upper Potomac, chiefly of Harper's Ferry, which was regarded as the gateway of that valley and of one of the possible approaches to Richmond; a position from which he was speedily forced to retire, however, by a flank movement by a Federal army under the veteran General Patterson, thrown across the Potomac at about Martinsburg. On my other or right flank, so to speak, a Confederate force of some twenty-five hundred men under General Holmes occupied the position of the Aquia Creek on the lower Potomac, upon the line of approach to Richmond from that direction through Fredericksburg. The other approach, that by way of the James River, was held by Confederate troops under Generals Huger and Magruder. Establishing small outposts at Leesburg to observe the crossings of the Potomac in that quarter, and at Fairfax Court House in observation of Arlington, with other detachments in advance of Manassas, toward Alexandria on the south side of the railroad, from the very outset I was anxiously aware that the sole military advantage at the moment to the Confederates was that of holding the *interior lines*. On the Federal or hostile side were all material advantages, including superior numbers, largely drawn from the old militia organizations of the great cities of the North, decidedly better armed and equipped than the troops under me, and strengthened by a small but incomparable body of regular infantry, as well as a number of batteries of regular field artillery of the highest class, and a very large and thoroughly organized staff corps, besides a numerous body of professionally educated officers in command of volunteer regiments—all precious military elements at such a juncture; add to this the immensely superior industrial and mechanical resources and an unrestrictable commercial access to the markets and workshops of Europe, with all the accumulated wealth of the Northern people to draw upon.

Happily, through the foresight of Colonel Thomas Jordan—whom General Lee had placed as the Adjutant-General of the forces there assembled before my arrival—arrangements were made which enabled me to receive regularly, from private persons at the Federal capital, most accurate information, of which politicians high in council, as well as War Department clerks, were the unconscious ducts. Moreover, my enterprising, intelligent pickets were watchfully kept in the closest possible proximity to General McDowell's headquarters, and by a stroke of good fortune on the fourth of July, happened upon and captured a sergeant and soldier of the regulars, who were leisurely riding for recreation not far outside their lines. . . .

In these several ways, therefore, I was almost as well advised of the strength of the hostile army in my front as its commander, who, I may mention, had been a classmate of mine at West Point. Under these circumstances I had become convinced that a well-equipped, well-constituted Federal army at least fifty thousand strong, of all arms, confronted me at or about Arlington, ready and on the very eve of an offensive operation against me, and to meet which I could muster barely eighteen thousand men and twenty-nine field guns.

Previously, indeed, or as early as the middle of June, it had become apparent to my mind that through only one course of action could there be a well-grounded hope of ability on the part of the Confederates to encounter successfully the offensive operations . . . ; this course was to make the most enterprising, warlike use of the interior lines which we possessed, for the swift concentration at the critical instant of every available Confederate force upon the menaced position, at the risk, if need were, of sacrificing all minor places to the one clearly of major military value—then to meet our adversary so offensively as to overwhelm him, under circumstances that must assure immediate ability to assume the general offensive even upon the territory of the adversary, and thus conquer an early peace by a few well-delivered blows. . . .

This plan was rejected by Mr. Davis and his military advisers (Adjutant-General Cooper and General Lee), who characterized it as "brilliant and comprehensive" but essentially impracticable. . . .

Just before Colonel Chesnut was dispatched [to convey Beauregard's plans to Richmond], a former clerk in one of the departments at Washington, well known to him, had volunteered to return thither and bring back the latest information, from our most trusted friends, of the military and political situations. . . . He was at once sent across the Potomac, below Alexandria by our agencies in that quarter, merely accredited by a small scrap of paper bearing in Colonel Jordan's cipher the two words, "Trust bearer," with which he was to call at a certain house in a certain street in Washington within easy rifle range of the White House, and ask for the lady of the house, and present it only to her. This delicate mission was as fortunately as it was deftly executed. . . . With no more delay than was necessary for a hurried breakfast and the writing in cipher by Mrs. G— of the words, "Order issued for McDowell to march upon Manassas to-night," my agent was placed in communication with another friend, who carried him in a buggy with a relay of horses as swiftly as possible down the east shore of the Potomac to our regular ferry across that river. . . . Within half an hour my outpost commanders were advised of what was impending. . . . Having thus cleared my decks for action, I next acquainted Mr. Davis with the situation, and ventured once more to suggest that the Army of the Shenandoah, with the brigade at Fredericksburg or Aquia Creek, should be ordered to reenforce me—suggestions that were at once heeded so far that General Holmes was ordered to carry his command to my aid, and General Johnston was given directions to do likewise. . . .

It seemed, however, as though the deferred attempt at concentration was to go for naught, for on the morning of the 18th [of July] the Federal forces were massed around Centreville, but three miles from Mitchell's ford, and soon were seen advancing upon the roads leading to that and Blackburn's ford. . . . The Federals, after several attempts to force a passage, met a final repulse and retreated. . . .

Our success in this limited collision was of special prestige to my army of new troops, and moreover, of decisive importance by so increasing General McDowell's caution as to give time for the arrival of some of General Johnston's forces. . . . General Johnston brought 6,000 men from the Shenandoah Valley, with 20 guns, and General Holmes 1,265 rank and file, with six pieces of artillery from Aquia Creek. As these forces arrived (most of them in the afternoon of the 20th), I placed them chiefly so as to strengthen my center and left, the latter being weak from lack of available troops. . . .

There was much in this decisive conflict about to open, not involved in any after battle, which pervaded the two armies and the people behind them and colored the responsibility of the respective commanders. The political hostilities of a generation were now face to face with weapons instead of words. Defeat to either side would be a deep mortification, but defeat to the South must turn its claim of independence into an empty vaunt. . . .

General Johnston was the ranking officer, and entitled, therefore, to assume command of the united forces, but as the extensive field of operations was one which I had occupied since the beginning of June . . . General Johnston, in view of the gravity of the impending issue, preferred not to assume the responsibilities of the chief direction of the forces during the battle, but to assist me upon the field. Thereupon, I explained my plans and purposes, to which he agreed.

Sunday, July 21st, bearing the fate of the new-born Confederacy, broke brightly over the fields and woods that held the hostile forces. My scouts, thrown out in the night toward Centreville, along the Warrenton turnpike, had reported that the enemy was concentrating along the latter. This fact, together with the failure of the Federals in their attack upon my center at Mitchell's and Blackburn's fords, had caused me to apprehend that they would attempt my left flank at the Stone Bridge, and orders were accordingly issued by half-past four o'clock to the brigade commanders to hold their forces in readiness to move at a moment's notice, together with the

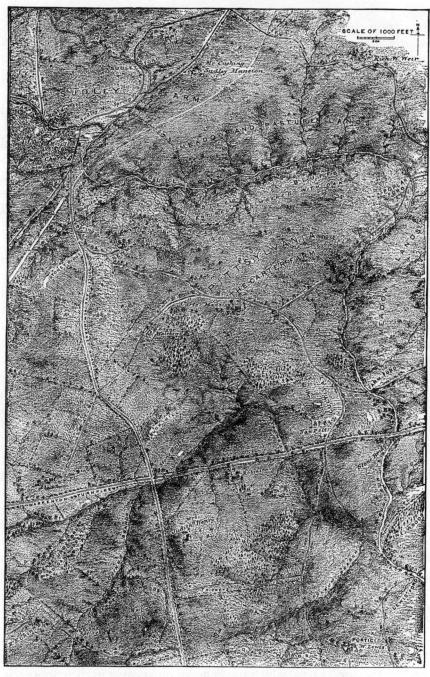

Topographical map of the Bull Run battlefield

suggestion that the Federal attack might be expected in that quarter. Shortly afterward the Federals were reported to be advancing from Centreville on the Warrenton turnpike, and at half-past five o'clock as deploying a force in front of Evans. As their movement against my left developed the opportunity I desired, I immediately sent orders to the brigade commanders, both front and reserves, on my right and center to advance and vigorously attack the Federal left flank and rear at Centreville, while my left, under Cocke and Evans with their supports, would sustain the Federal attack in the quarter of the Stone Bridge, which they were directed to do to the last extremity. . . . About half-past eight o'clock I set out with General Johnston for a convenient position—a hill in rear of Mitchell's ford—where we waited the opening of the attack on our right, from which I expected a decisive victory by mid-day, with the result of cutting off the Federal army from retreat upon Washington.

Meanwhile, about half-past five o'clock, the peal of a heavy rifled gun was heard in front of the Stone Bridge, its second shot striking through the tent of my signal officer, Captain E.P. Alexander; and at six o'clock a full rifled battery opened against Evans and then against Cocke, to which our artillery remained dumb, as it had not sufficient range to reply. But later, as the Federal skirmish line advanced, it was engaged by ours, thrown well forward on the other side of the Run. A scattering of musketry fire followed, and meanwhile, about seven o'clock, I ordered Jackson's brigade, with Imboden's and five guns of Walton's battery, to the left, with orders to support Cocke as well as Bonham, and the brigades of Bee and Bartow, under the command of the former, who also sent to the support of the left.

At half-past eight o'clock, Evans, seeing that the Federal attack did not increase in boldness and vigor, and observing a lengthening line of dust above the trees to the left of the Warrenton turnpike, became satisfied that the attack in his front was but a feint, and that a column of the enemy was moving around through the woods to fall on his flank from the direction of Sudley ford. Informing his immediate commander, Cocke, of the enemy's movement, and of his own dispositions to meet it, he left four companies under cover at the Stone Bridge and led the remainder of his force, six companies of Stoan's Fourth South Carolina and Wheat's battalion of Louisiana Tigers, with two six-pounder howitzers, across the valley of Young's Branch to the high ground beyond it. Resting his left on the Sudley road, he distributed his troops on each side of a small copse, with such cover as the ground afforded, and looking over the open fields and a reach of the Sudley road which the Federals must cover in their approach.

His two howitzers were placed one at each end of his position, and here he silently awaited the masses of the enemy now drawing near.

The Federal turning column, almost eighteen thousand strong, with twenty-four pieces of artillery, had moved down from Centreville by the Warrenton turnpike, and after passing Cub Run had struck to the right by a forest road to cross Bull Run at Sudley ford, about three miles above the Stone Bridge, moving by a long circuit for the purpose of attacking my left flank. The head of the column, Burnside's brigade of Hunter's division, at about 9:45 A.M. debouched from the woods into the open fields in front of Evans. Wheat at once engaged their skirmishers, and as the Second Rhode Island regiment advanced, supported by its splendid battery of six rifled guns, the fronting thicket held by Evans's South Carolinians poured forth its sudden volleys, while the two howitzers flung their grape shot into the attacking line, which was soon shattered and driven back into the woods behind. . . . The contest here lasted fully an hour; meanwhile Wheat's battalion, having lost its leader, had gradually lost its organization, and Evans, though still opposing the heavy odds with undiminished firmness, sought reinforcements from the troops in his rear.

General Bee, of South Carolina, a man of marked character, whose command lay in reserve in rear of Cocke, near the Stone Bridge, intelligently applying the general order given to the reserves, had already moved toward the neighboring point of conflict, and taken a position with his own and Bartow's brigades on the high plateau which stands in rear of Bull Run in the quarter of the Stone Bridge, and overlooking the scene of engagement in the stretch of high ground from which it was separated by the valley of Young's Branch. This plateau is inclosed on three sides by two small watercourses, which empty into Bull Run within a few yards of each other, a half mile to the south of the Stone Bridge. Rising to an elevation of quite one hundred feet above the level of Bull Run at the Bridge, it falls off on three sides to the level of the inclosing streams in gentle slopes, but furrowed by ravines of irregular directions and length, and studded with clumps and patches of young pines and oaks. . . . On the northwestern brow, overlooking Young's Branch, and near the Sudley road, as the latter climbs over the plateau, stood the house of the widow Henry. . . . Around the eastern and southern brow of the plateau an almost unbroken fringe of second-growth pines gave excellent shelter for our marksmen, who availed themselves of it with most satisfactory skill. To the west, adjoining the fields that surrounded the houses mentioned, a broad belt of oaks extends directly across the crest on both sides of the Sudley road, in which, during the battle, the hostile forces contended for the mastery. General Bee, with a soldier's eye to the situation, skillfully disposed his forces. His two brigades on either side of Imboden's battery—which he had borrowed from his neighboring reserve, Jackson's brigade—were placed in a small depression of the plateau in advance of the Henry house, whence he had a full view of the contest on the opposite height across the valley of Young's Branch. Opening with his artillery upon the Federal batteries, he answered Evans's request by advising him to withdraw to his own position on the height; but Evans, full of the spirit that would not retreat, renewed his appeal that the forces in rear would come to help him hold his ground. The newly arrived forces had given the Federals such superiority at this point as to dwarf Evans's means of resistance, and General Bee generously yielding his own better judgment to Evans's persistence, led the two brigades across the valley and under the fire of the enemy's artillery and threw them into action. . . .

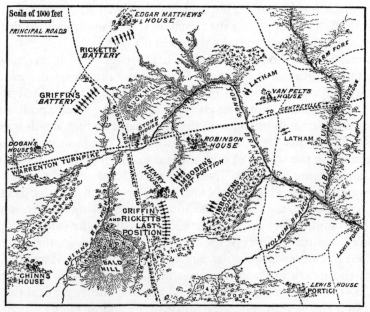

Plan of the Bull Run battlefield

The Federal infantry, though still in superior numbers, failed to make any headway against this sturdy van, notwithstanding, Bee's whole line was hammered also by the enemy's powerful batteries, until Heinzelman's division of two strong brigades, arriving from Sudley ford, extended the fire on the Federal right, while its battery of six ten-pounder rifled guns took an immediately effective part from a position behind the Sudley road. Against these odds the Confederate force was still endeavoring to hold its ground, when a new enemy came into the field upon its right. Major Wheat, with characteristic daring and restlessness, had crossed Bull Run alone by a small ford above the Stone Bridge in order to reconnoiter, when he and Evans had first moved to the left, and falling on some Federal scouts, had shouted a taunting defiance and withdrawn, not, however, without his place of crossing having been observed.[1] This disclosure was now utilized by Sherman's (W.T.) and Keyes's brigades of Tyler's division; crossing at this point, they appeared over the high bank of the stream and moved into position on the Federal left. There was no choice now for Bee but to retire—a movement, however, to be accomplished under different circumstances than when urged by him upon Evans. The three leaders endeavored to preserve the steadiness of the ranks as they withdrew over the open fields, aided by the fire of Imboden's guns on the plateau and the retiring howitzers; but the troops were thrown into confusion, and the greater part soon fell into rout across Young's Branch and around the base of the height in the rear of the Stone Bridge.

Meanwhile, in rear of Mitchell's ford, I had been waiting with General Johnston for the sound of conflict to open in the quarter of Centreville upon the Federal left flank and rear (making allowance, however, for the delays possible to commands unused to battle), when I was chagrined to hear from General D.E. Jones that, while he had been long ready for the movement upon Centreville, General Ewell had not come up to form on his right. . . . I dispatched an immediate order to Ewell to advance; but . . . the firing on the left began to increase so intensely as to indicate a severe attack, whereupon General Johnston said that he would go personally to that quarter.

After weighing attentively the firing, which seemed rapidly and heavily increasing, it appeared to me that the troops on the right would be unable to get into position before the Federal offensive should have made too much progress on our left, and that it would be better to abandon it altogether, maintaining only a strong demonstration so as to detain the enemy in front of our right and center, and hurry up all available reinforcements—including the reserves that were to have moved upon Centreville—to our left and fight the battle out in that quarter. . . .

---

[1] William T. Sherman himself observed Wheat cross at this point, and he led his men across the newly discovered ford.

General Johnston and I now set out at full speed for the point of conflict. We arrived there just as Bee's troops, after giving way, were fleeing in disorder behind the height in rear of Stone Bridge. They had come round between the base of the hill and the Stone Bridge into a shallow ravine which ran up to a point on the crest where Jackson had already formed his brigade along the edge of the woods. We found the commanders resolutely stemming the farther flight of the routed forces, but vainly endeavoring to restore order, and our own efforts were as futile. Every segment of line we succeeded in forming was again dissolved while another was being formed; more than two thousand men were shouting each some suggestion to his neighbor, their voices mingling with the noise of the shells hurtling through the trees overhead, and all words of command drowned in the confusion and uproar. It was at this moment that General Bee used the famous expression, "Look at Jackson's brigade! It stands there like a stone wall"—a name passed from the brigade to its immortal commander. The disorder seemed irretrievable, but happily the thought came to me that if their colors were planted out to the front the men might rally on them, and I gave the order to carry the standards forward some forty yards, which was promptly executed by the regimental officers, thus drawing the common eye of the troops. They now received easily the orders to advance and form on the line of their colors, which they obeyed with a general movement; and as General Johnston and myself rode forward shortly after with the colors of the Fourth Alabama by our side, the line that had fought all morning, and had fled, routed and disordered, now advanced again into position as steadily as veterans. . . . We had come none too soon, as the enemy's forces, flushed with the belief of accomplished victory, were already advancing across the valley of Young's Branch and up the slope, where they had encountered for a while the fire of the Hampton Legion, which had been led forward to the Robinson house and the turnpike in front, covering the retreat and helping materially to check the panic of Bee's routed forces.

As soon as order was restored I requested General Johnston to go back to Portici (the Lewis house), and from that point—which I considered most favorable for the purpose—forward me the reinforcements as they would come from the Bull Run lines below and those that were expected to arrive from Manassas. . . .

As General Johnston departed for Portici, I hastened to form our line of battle against the oncoming enemy. I ordered up the Forty-ninth and the Eighth Virginia regiments from Cocke's neighboring brigade in the Bull Run lines. Gartrell's Seventh Georgia I placed in position on the left of

Jackson's brigade, along the belt of pines occupied by the latter, on the eastern rim of the plateau. . . . I placed the Forty-ninth Virginia in position on the extreme left next to Gartrell, and as I paused to say a few words to Jackson, while hurrying back to the right, my horse was killed under me by a bursting shell, a fragment of which carried away part of the heel of my boot. The Hampton Legion, which had suffered greatly, was placed on the right of Jackson's brigade, and Hunton's Eighth Virginia, as it arrived, upon the right of Hampton: the two latter being drawn somewhat to the rear as to form with Jackson's right regiment a reserve, and be ready likewise to make defense against any advance from the direction of Stone Bridge, whence there was imminent peril from the enemy's heavy forces, as I had just stripped that position almost entirely of troops to meet the active crisis on the plateau, leaving this quarter now covered only by a few men, whose defense was otherwise assisted solely by the construction of an abatis.

With six thousand five hundred men and thirteen pieces of artillery, I now awaited the onset of the enemy, who were pressing forward twenty thousand strong, with twenty-four pieces of superior artillery and seven companies of regular cavalry. They soon appeared over the farther rim of the plateau, seizing the Robinson house on my right and the Henry house opposite my left center. Near the latter they placed in position two power-ful batteries of Rickett and Griffin of the regular army, and pushed forward up the Sudley road, the slope of which was cut so deep below the adjacent ground as to afford a covered way up to the plateau. Supported by the formidable files of Federal musketry, these two batteries lost no time in making themselves felt, while three more batteries in rear on the high ground beyond the Sudley and Warrenton cross-roads swelled the shower of shell that fell among our ranks.

Our own batteries . . . (their disadvantage being reduced by the short-ness of range), swept the surface of the plateau from their position on the eastern rim. I felt that, after the accidents of the morning, much depended on maintaining the steadiness of the troops against the first heavy on-slaught, and rode along the lines encouraging the men to unflinching behavior, meeting, as I passed each command, a cheering response. The steady fire of their musketry told severely on the Federal ranks, and the splendid action of our batteries was fit preface to the marked skill exhibited by our artillerists during the war. The enemy suffered particularly from the musketry on our left, now further reinforced by the Second Mississippi— the troops in this quarter confronting each other at very short range. Here two companies of Stuart's cavalry charged through the Federal ranks that filled the Sudley road, increasing the disorder wrought upon that flank of the enemy. . . . Although the enemy were held well at bay, their pressure became so strong that I resolved to take the offensive, and ordered a charge on my right for the purpose of recovering the plateau. The move-ment, made with alacrity and force by the commands of Bee, Bartow, Evans, and Hampton, thrilled the entire line, Jackson's brigade piercing the enemy's center, and the left of the line under Gartrell and Smith following up the charge, also, in that quarter, so that the whole of the open surface of the plateau was swept clear of Federals.

Apart from its impression on the enemy, the effect of this brilliant onset was to give a short breathing spell to our troops from the immediate strain of conflict, and to encourage them in withstanding the still more strenuous offensive that was to soon bear upon them. I prepared to meet the new attack which the enemy were about to make, largely reenforced by the fresh troops of Howard's brigade, newly arrived on the field. The Federals again pushed up the slope, the face of which partially afforded good cover from the numerous ravines that scored it and the clumps of young pines and oaks with which it was studded, while the sunken Sudley road formed a good ditch and parapet for their aggressive advance upon my left flank and rear. Gradually they pressed our lines back and regained possession of their lost ground and guns. With the Henry and Robinson houses once more in their possession, they resumed the offensive, urged forward by their com-manders with conspicuous gallantry.

The conflict now became very severe for the final possession of this position, which was the key to victory. The Federal numbers enabled them to extend their lines through the woods beyond the Sudley road so as to outreach my left flank, which I was compelled to throw back so as to meet the attack from that quarter; meanwhile, their numbers equally enabled them to outflank my right in the direction of the Stone Bridge, imposing anxious watchfulness in that direction. I knew that I was safe if I could hold out till the arrival of reinforcements, which was but a matter of time; and, with the full sense of my own responsibility, I was determined to hold the line of the plateau, even if surrounded on all sides, until assistance should come, unless my forces were sooner overtaken with annihilation. It was now between half-past two and three o'clock, a scorching sun increased the oppression of the troops, exhausted from incessant fighting against such heavy odds, many having been engaged since the morning. Fearing lest the Federal offensive should secure too firm a grip, and knowing the fatal result that might spring from any grave infraction of my line, I determined to make another effort for the recovery of the plateau, and ordered a charge of the entire line of battle, including the reserves, which at the crisis I myself led into action. The movement of the several commands was made with such keeping and dash that the whole surface of the plateau was swept clear of the enemy, who were driven down the slope and across the turnpike on our right and the valley of Young's Branch on our left, leaving in our final possession the Robinson and Henry houses, with most of Rickett's and Griffin's batteries, the men of which were mostly shot down where they bravely stood by their guns. . . . This handsome work, which broke the Federal fortunes of the day, was done, however, at severe cost. The soldierly Bee, and the gallant, impetuous Bartow, whose day of strong deeds was about to close with such credit, fell a few rods back of the Henry house, near the very spot whence in the morning they had first looked forth upon Evans's struggle with the enemy. . . .

Meanwhile, the enemy had formed a line of battle of formidable proportions on the opposite height, and stretching in crescent outline, with flanks advanced. . . . They offered a fine spectacle as they threw forward a cloud of skirmishers down the opposite slope, preparatory to a new assault against the line of the plateau. But their right was now severely pressed by the troops that had successively arrived, the force in the southwest angle of the Sudley and Warrenton cross-roads were driven from their position, and as Early's brigade, which, by direction of General Johnston, had swept around by the rear of the woods through which Elzey [another late-arriving brigade commander] had passed, appeared on the field, his line of march bore upon the flank of the enemy, as he was now retiring in that quarter.

The movement upon my extreme left was masked by the trend of the woods from many of our forces upon the plateau; and hearing those of my staff and escort around me raise a loud cheer, I dispatched the information to the several commands, with orders to go forward in a common charge. Before the full advance of the Confederate ranks the enemy's whole line, whose right was already yielding, irretrievably broke, fleeing across Bull Run by every available direction. Major Sykes's regulars, aided by Sherman's brigade, made a steady and handsome withdrawal, protecting the rear of the routed forces, and enabling them to escape by the Stone Bridge. Having ordered in pursuit all the troops on the field, I went to the Lewis house, and, the battle being ended, turned over the command to General Johnston.

Impressions of the Battle and the Union Retreat
By General William T. Sherman

[My after-battle] report, which I had not read probably since its date till now, recalls to me vividly the whole scene of the affair at Blackburn's Ford,[2] when for the first time in my life I saw cannonballs strike men and crash through the trees and saplings above and around us, and realized the always sickening confusion as one approaches a fight from the rear; then the night march from Centreville, on the Warrenton road, standing for hours wondering what was meant; the deployment along the edge of the field that sloped down to Bull Run, and waiting for Hunter's approach on the other side from the direction of Sudley Springs, away off to our right; the terrible scare of a poor negro who was caught between our lines; the crossing of Bull Run, and the fear lest we should be fired on by our own men; the killing of Lieutenant-Colonel Haggerty, which occurred in plain sight; and the first scenes of a field strewed with dead men and horses. . . . After I had put in each of my regiments, and had them driven back to the cover of the road, I had no idea that we were beaten, but reformed the regiments in line in their proper order, and only wanted a little rest, when I found that my brigade was almost alone, except Sykes's regulars. . . . I then realized that the whole army was "in retreat," and that my own men were individually making back for the stone bridge. Corcoran and I formed the brigade into an irregular square, but it fell to pieces; and, along with a crowd, disorganized but not much scared, the brigade got back to Centreville to our former camps. . . .

[The next day] a slow, mizzling rain had set in, and probably a more gloomy day never presented itself. All organization seemed to be at an end; but I and my staff labored hard to collect our men into their proper companies and into their former camps. . . . One morning, after reveille . . . I found myself in a crowd of men; among them was an officer, who said: "Colonel, I am going to New York today. What can I do for you?" I answered: "How can you go to New York? I do not remember to have signed a leave for you." He said, No; he did not want a leave. He had engaged to serve three months, and had already served more than that time. . . . I noticed that a good many of the soldiers had paused about us to listen, and knew that, if this officer could defy me, they also would. So I turned on him sharp, and said: "Captain, this question of your term of service has been submitted to the rightful authority, and the decision has

---

[2] This was a skirmish shortly before the battle, mentioned by Beauregard above.

been published in orders. You are a soldier, and must submit to orders till you are properly discharged. If you attempt to leave without orders, it will be mutiny, and I will shoot you like a dog! Go back into the fort *now*, instantly, and don't dare to leave without my consent." . . .

That same day, which must have been about July 26th, I was near the riverbank . . . when I saw a carriage coming by the road that crossed the Potomac River at Georgetown by a ferry. I thought I recognized in the carriage the person of President Lincoln. . . . I was in uniform, with a sword on, and was recognized by Mr. Lincoln and Mr. Seward, who rode side by side in an open back. I inquired if they were going to my camps, and Mr. Lincoln said: "Yes; we hear that you had got over the big scare, and we thought we would come over and see the 'boys.' " . . .

At last we reached Fort Corcoran [Sherman's camp]. The carriage could not enter, so I ordered the regiment, without arms, to come outside, and gather about Mr. Lincoln, who would speak to them. . . . In the crowd I saw the officer with whom I had the passage at reveille that morning. His face was pale, and lips compressed. . . . This officer forced his way through the crowd to the carriage, and said: "Mr. President, I have cause of grievance. This morning I went to speak to Colonel Sherman, and he threatened to shoot me." Mr. Lincoln, who was still standing, said, "Threatened to shoot you?" "Yes, sir, he threatened to shoot me." Mr. Lincoln looked at him, then at me, and stooping his tall, spare form toward the officer, said to him in a loud stage-whisper, easily heard for some yards around: "Well, if I were you, and he threatened to shoot, I would not trust him, for I believe he would do it." The officer turned about and disappeared, and the men laughed at him. . . . I explained the facts to the President, who answered, "Of course I don't know anything about it, but I thought you knew your own business best."

2
THE PENINSULA CAMPAIGN

Lincoln's sure hand with the men of Sherman's regiment might have raised their morale after the defeat of Bull Run, but it did little to ease the North's new difficulties. It seemed now that the defeat of the rebellion would be a great deal more difficult—and costly—than had been first hoped. Lincoln did what he could: he issued a call for three-year volunteers to supplant the three-month men who gave Sherman so much trouble; he ordered an expansion of the navy and declared a blockade of Confederate ports (which led to new problems, as the legal language used implied a recognition of Southern independence); and he gave supreme army command to one of the most admired men in the U.S. military, George B. McClellan.

McClellan was only in his early thirties when the Civil War broke out, but he was already considered one of the finest officers in the army— rivaled only, perhaps, by Robert E. Lee, who followed his native Virginia into the Confederacy. McClellan was extremely intelligent, confident, with a record of success in early fighting in West Virginia. Unfortunately, his intelligence later proved to be loaded with an excess of imagination, particularly when it came to his estimates of enemy strength; his confidence was mainly pure arrogance; and his successes had been won largely by more enterprising subordinates. But in 1861 he seemed the logical choice for commanding general of the Army of the Potomac.

The new commander proved his worth by immediately reinvigorating his defeated army. The diminutive McClellan demonstrated immense organizational talents by reorganizing, reequipping, and training his men until the Army of the Potomac was truly a mighty force. His problems appeared when the time came to use that force; McClellan dickered away months skirmishing with undermanned Confederate outposts along the Potomac, until Lincoln insisted he move against Richmond. The general answered the call with a potentially decisive plan—to move an entire army, over 100,000 strong, by sea to Fort Monroe, at the end of a peninsula east of Richmond, between the York and James rivers. Cooperating with a corps commanded by General Irvin McDowell to the north of Richmond, he would then march west and lay siege to the Confederate capital.

Meanwhile, the Southern command faced a dilemma. After the victory at Bull Run, General Beauregard had been transferred to serve under General Albert Sidney Johnston in the West, leaving General Joseph E. Johnston in charge in northern Virginia. Joseph Johnston was a widely respected veteran of the U.S. Army, a highly professional, if cautious, commander who well understood the crisis caused by his lack of troops. Confederate President Jefferson Davis wanted to hold the Yankees back everywhere; Southern troops were stationed in Missouri, in Kentucky, along the Atlantic coast—everywhere, practically, except where Joseph Johnston felt they were needed most, near Richmond. The overriding priority, Johnston knew, was to stop McClellan, who could use his advantage in numbers to strike almost anywhere. But to beat the Army of the Potomac, he first had to see through the Union strategy—and cope with his own interfering president.

The Confederate Strategic Quandary, *March through June 1862*
By General Joseph E. Johnston

We had to regard four routes to Richmond as practicable for the Federal army: that chosen the previous July [from Centreville through Manassas]; another east of the Potomac to the mouth of Potomac Creek, and thence by Fredericksburg; the third and fourth by water, the one to the Lower Rappahannock, the other to Fort Monroe; and from those points respective by direct roads. . . .

On the eighteenth [of March] it had become evident that the activity reported in Maryland, two weeks before, was connected with no advance of the enemy on the Fredericksburg route. This made the selection of one of the eastern routes by the Federal general seem to me more probable than I had before thought it. The army was, therefore, ordered to move to the south side of the Rapidan [River], where it was in better position to unite with the Confederate forces between Richmond and the invading army. . . .

From the twenty-fifth to the twenty-ninth of the month, our scouts, observing the Potomac, reported steam transports, loaded with Federal troops and military materiel, passing down the river continually. By their estimates of the number of men carried by each boat and their count of the number of trips, an army of one hundred and forty thousand men was conveyed in this way to some point beyond the mouth of the Potomac, probably Fort Monroe, as no reports of such vessels entering the Rappahannock were received. . . .

The President was uncertain whether this army was destined for Fort Monroe, to invade Virginia by the peninsula, or for the invasion of North Carolina. . . .

When it was ascertained, about the fifth of April, that the Federal army was marching from Fort Monroe toward Yorktown, D.H. Hill's, D.R. Jones's, and Early's divisions were transferred from the Army of Northern Virginia to that of the peninsula. The force was thus reduced to four divisions: Jackson's at Mount Jackson, Ewell's on the Rappahannock, Longstreet's at Orange Court-House, and G.W. Smith's at Fredericksburg.

Before the tenth, the President was convinced, by Major-General Magruder's reports, that the entire army just brought down the Potomac from Alexandria, by General McClellan, was then on the peninsula, to move upon Richmond by that route. He therefore directed me to make such defensive arrangements as might be necessary in the Department of Northern Virginia, and put my remaining troops in march for Richmond, and then to report for further instructions. In obedience to these orders, Major-General Ewell was left with his division and a regiment of cavalry, in observation on the upper Rappahannock; and Major-General Longstreet was directed to march with his to Richmond. Major-General Jackson was left in the [Shenandoah] Valley to oppose greatly superior Federal forces, and authorized to call Ewell's division to his assistance in case of necessity. . . . Major-General Smith was instructed to leave a mixed force, equal to a brigade, in front of Fredericksburg, and move toward Richmond with all his remaining troops. . . .

I went to the peninsula as soon as possible, reaching General Magruder's headquarters early in the morning; and passed the day in examining his works. . . .

That officer had estimated the importance of at least *delaying* the invaders until an army capable of coping with them could be formed; and opposed them with about a tenth of their number, on a line of which Yorktown, entrenched, made the left flank. This boldness imposed upon the Federal general, and made him halt to besiege instead of assailing the Confederate position. This resolute and judicious course on the part of General Magruder was of incalculable value. It saved Richmond, and gave the Confederate Government time to swell that officer's handful to an army. . . .

Before nightfall I was convinced that we could do no more on the peninsula than delay General McClellan's progress toward Richmond. . . . I thought it of great importance that a different plan of operations should be adopted without delay; and, leaving General Magruder's headquarters at nightfall, I hastened back to Richmond to suggest such a one, and arrived early enough to see the President in his office as soon as he entered it. . . .

Instead of only delaying the Federal army in its approach, I proposed that it should be encountered in front of Richmond by one quite as numerous, formed by uniting there all the available forces of the Confederacy in North Carolina, South Carolina, and Georgia, with those at Norfolk, on the peninsula, and then near Richmond, including Smith's and Longstreet's divisions, which had arrived. The great army thus formed, surprising that of the United States by an attack when it was expecting to besiege Richmond, would be almost certain to win; and the enemy, defeated a hundred miles from Fort Monroe, their place of refuge, could scarcely escape destruction. Such a victory would decide not only the campaign, but the war, while the present plan could produce no decisive result.

The President, who had heard me with apparent interest, replied that the question was so important that he would hear it fully discussed before making his decision, and desired me to meet General Randolph (Secretary of War) and General Lee, in his office, at an appointed time, for the purpose; at my suggestion, he authorized me to invite Major-Generals Smith and Longstreet to the conference. . . .

In the discussion that followed, General Randolph, who had been a naval officer, objected to the plan proposed, because it included at least the temporary abandonment of Norfolk, which would involve the probable loss of the materials for many vessels-of-war, contained in the navy-yard there. General Lee opposed it, because he thought that the withdrawal from South Carolina and Georgia of any considerable number of troops would expose the important seaport of Charleston and South Carolina to the danger of capture.[3] He thought, too, that the peninsula had excellent fields of battle for a small army contending with a great one, and that we should for that reason make the contest with McClellan's army there. . . .

At six o'clock the conference was adjourned by the President, to meet in his house at seven. The discussion was continued there, although languidly, until 1 A.M., when it ceased, and the President, who previously had

[3] At this time Lee was in charge of coastal defense.

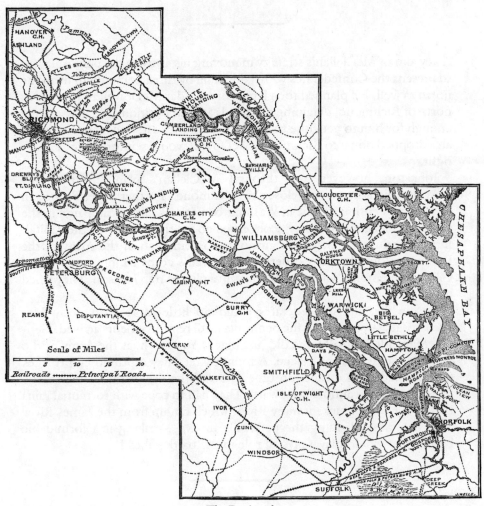

The Peninsula

expressed no opinion on the question, announced his decision in favor of General Lee's opinion, and directed that Smith's and Longstreet's divisions should join the Army of the Peninsula, and ordered me to go there and take command. . . .

The belief that events on the peninsula would soon compel the Confederate Government to adopt my method of opposing the Federal army reconciled me somewhat to the necessity of obeying the President's order.

A key aim of McClellan's strategy in moving his army to the peninsula was to present the Confederates with a dilemma by threatening them from the north as well. He planned for a large corps under McDowell to hover well north of Richmond, detaining the rebels at their position at Manassas long enough for him to get close to that city from the east; once the Confederates dropped down to Richmond, McDowell would reinforce McClellan's right.

Johnston, however, saw through McClellan's plan and promptly marched his army down closer to Richmond. Furthermore, Stonewall Jackson was raising a panic in Washington with a brilliant campaign in the strategic Shenandoah Valley. Concerned about the security of the capital, Lincoln reduced McClellan's authority to command of the Army of the Potomac alone; he then ordered McDowell's corps to join units under Generals Fremont, Shields, and Banks in a plan to trap Jackson. They failed utterly.

Meanwhile, the Confederates could do little more than delay McClellan's massive army on the peninsula until reinforcements arrived. General Magruder's small force did just that at Yorktown, as the Army of the Potomac settled in for a siege. A month later, they captured empty lines (the Confederates escaped in time to avoid the fire of the massive siege guns) and crept cautiously forward. They had to cope with torrential rains that swelled the Chickahominy River, which ran up from the James River and then west, dividing the peninsula in two—making it a formidable barrier that would play a pivotal role in the battles ahead.

The Army of the Potomac Creeps Ahead
By General George B. McClellan

[The] information that McDowell's corps would march for Fredericksburg on the following Monday [the twenty-sixth of May], and that he would be under my command . . . was cheering news, and I now felt confident that we would, on his arrival, be sufficiently strong to overpower the large army confronting us.

At a later hour on the same day I received the following:

MAY 24, 1862
FROM WASHINGTON, 4 P.M.
MAJ.-GEN. GEO. B. MCCLELLAN,

In consequence of General Banks's critical position, I have been compelled to suspend General McDowell's movements to join you. The enemy [under Stonewall Jackson] are making a desperate push upon Harper's Ferry, and we are trying to throw General Fremont's force and part of General McDowell's in their rear.

A. LINCOLN,
PRESIDENT

From which it will be seen that I could not expect General McDowell to join me in time to participate in immediate operations in front of Richmond, and on the same evening I replied to the President that I would make my calculations accordingly.

It then only remained for me to make the best use of the forces at my disposal, and to avail myself of all artificial auxiliaries, to compensate as much as possible for the inadequacy of men. I concurred fully with the President in the injunction contained in his telegram of the 24th, that it was necessary with my limited force to move "cautiously and safely." In view of the peculiar character of the Chickahominy, and the liability of its bottom-lands to sudden inundation, it became necessary to construct between Bottom's Bridge and Mechanicsville eleven new bridges, all long and difficult, with extensive log-way approaches.

The entire army could probably have been thrown across the Chickahominy immediately after our arrival, but this would have left no force on the left [north] bank to guard our communications, or to protect our right and rear. If the communication with our supply depot had been cut by the enemy, with our army concentrated on the right [south] bank of the Chickahominy, and the stage of water as it was for many days after our arrival . . . the troops must have gone without rations, and the animals without forage; the army would have been paralyzed.

It is true, I might have abandoned my communications and pushed forward towards Richmond, trusting to the speedy defeat of the enemy and the consequent fall of the city, for a renewal of supplies; but the approaches were fortified, and the town itself was surrounded with a strong line of entrenchments requiring a greater length of time to reduce than our troops could have dispensed with rations.

Under these circumstances, I decided to retain a portion of the army on the left bank of the river until our bridges were completed.

McClellan inched forward, easing his army across the Chickahominy bridges in preparation for a siege of Richmond. He was bitter about being denied McDowell's aid because of Stonewall Jackson's presence in the Shenandoah Valley; but even with the addition of McDowell's corps, it is doubtful McClellan would have been any more aggressive.

Meanwhile, Jefferson Davis demanded a counterattack from his commander, Joseph E. Johnston. On May 31, Johnston saw his chance. The Army of the Potomac was still divided by the raging Chickahominy; if Johnston attacked with maximum force on the south side, he might overwhelm the left wing of the Union army. In the ensuing Battle of Fair Oaks (Seven Pines to the Confederates)[4], the Southern troops made some initial gains in uncoordinated attacks, only to be driven back by Union troops.

The battle, however, only increased McClellan's extreme caution. He took a month to move his army across the Chickahominy for a move on Richmond, leaving the 5th Corps under General Fitz-John Porter behind, isolated and vulnerable. Though he mistakenly believed he was outnumbered, he faced an enemy commander almost as cautious as he was—until the Battle of Fair Oaks, that is. Johnston, who never got along with Davis anyway, was wounded in the fighting, and the Confederate president replaced him with his chief military adviser, General Robert E. Lee. It was one of the most momentous events in the history of the war—though not even division commander James Longstreet knew it at the time.

Lee Takes Command
By General James Longstreet

The assignment of General Lee to command the Army of Northern Virginia was far from reconciling the troops to the loss of our beloved chief, Joseph E. Johnston, with whom the army had been closely connected since

---

[4] This volume will generally use Northern names for battles (and for the warship *Merrimack*, renamed by the Confederates the *Virginia* after it was rebuilt as an ironclad), except where Southern usage appears within the selections.

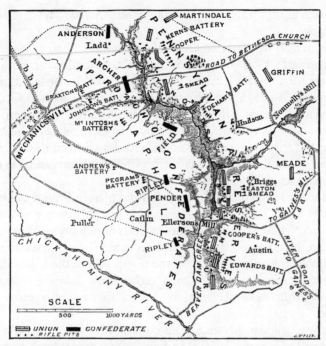

The Battle of Mechanicsville (Beaver Dam Creek), June 26, 1862

its earliest active life. All hearts had learned to lean upon him with confidence, and to love him dearly. General Lee's experience in active field work was limited to his West Virginia campaign against General Rosecrans, which was not successful. . . . There were, therefore, some misgivings as to the power and skill for field service of the new commander. The change was accepted, however, as a happy relief from the existing policy of the late temporary commander [of repeated retreats]. . . .

During the first week of his authority he called his general officers to meet him on the Nine Miles road for a general talk. This novelty was not reassuring, as experience had told that secrecy in war was an essential element of success; that public discussion and secrecy were incompatible. As he disclosed nothing, those of serious thought became hopeful, and followed his wise example. . . .

The day after the conference on the Nine Miles road, availing myself of General Lee's invitation to free interchange of ideas, I rode over to his headquarters, and renewed my suggestion of a move against General McClellan's right flank, which rested behind Beaver Dam Creek. . . . He received me pleasantly and gave a patient hearing to the suggestions, without indicating approval and disapproval. A few days later he wrote General Jackson. . . .

As indicated in his letter to General Jackson, General Lee's plan was a simultaneous attack on General McClellan's front and rear. Following his instructions for General Jackson, on the same day he ordered his cavalry, under General Stuart, upon a forced reconnaissance around General Mc-Clellan's army to learn if the ground behind his army was open. . . .[5]

The day after Stuart's return I rode over to General Lee's headquarters and suggested that General Jackson be withdrawn from the Valley to take position on our left, to march against McClellan's right, and was informed that the order for Jackson was sent. . . .

Then it was that General Lee revealed the plan indicated in his instructions of the 11th, for General Jackson to march down and attack Mc-Clellan's rear, while he made a simultaneous attack on his front. . . . After deliberation, he changed the plan and accepted the suggestion in favor of combining his fighting columns on the north side of the Chickahominy in echelon march against McClellan's right flank, leaving troops in the trenches in front of McClellan to defend in case of a move towards Richmond. . . .

Jackson was called in advance of his command to meet the Hills [division commanders D.H. and A.P. Hill] and myself at General Lee's headquarters for conference on the execution. On the forenoon of the twenty-third of June we were advised of his approach, and called to headquarters to meet him. He was there before us, having ridden fifty miles by relay of horses since midnight. We were together in a few minutes after his arrival, in General Lee's private office. The general explained the plan briefly: Jackson to march from Ashland between the Chickahominy and Pamunkey, turning and dislodging the Federal right, thus clearing the way for the march of troops to move on his right; A.P. Hill to cross the upper Chickahominy and march for Mechanicsville, in echelon to Jackson; the Mechanicsville Bridge being clear, D.H. Hill's division and mine to cross, the former to reinforce Jackson's column, the latter to file to the right and march down the river in right echelon to A.P. Hill's direct march through Mechanicsville to Gaines's Mill. . . .

Before sunrise on the twenty-sixth of June the division of A.P. Hill was in

---

[5] Stuart's ride, which completely circled the Union army, was one of the great feats of the war; the information he brought back told Lee that McClellan had only one corps north of the Chickahominy, with an unprotected right flank.

position at Meadow Bridge . . . all awaiting the approach of the initial column. Not anticipating delay, the division had no special cause to conceal their presence, nor did the lay of the ground offer good cover. Morning came, noon passed. . . .

At three o'clock, General A.P. Hill, hearing nothing from Jackson or his brigade under Branch, decided to cross the river and make his move without reference to Jackson or Branch. . . .

A.P. Hill's battle soon became firm, but he waited a little for Jackson before giving it full force. Jackson came up, marched by the fight without giving attention, and went into camp at Hundley's Corner, half a mile in rear of the enemy's position of contention. A.P. Hill put his force in severe battle and was repulsed. As D.H. Hill approached, he was called into the fray by the commanding general, then by the President. He sent Ripley's brigade and five batteries, which made the battle strong and hot along the line. . . . The battle was in close conflict till nine o'clock at night, when Hill was obliged to give over till morning.

———

Lee's counterattack on McClellan's exposed right flank was known as the battle of Mechanicsville or Beaver Dam Creek; it launched a series of Confederate attacks that were known as the Seven Days' battles. The attack at Mechanicsville was a complete failure; Jackson, for reasons still unknown, failed to attack the open flank all day, and A.P. Hill and D.H. Hill threw their men in futile headlong attacks against the Union front. But Lee had gained an important psychological advantage over McClellan, who believed against all reason that he was heavily outnumbered. Jackson's poor performance, so unlike his actions in the Shenandoah and during the rest of the war, persisted throughout the Seven Days, but McClellan continued to retreat. The Seven Days marked the start of a new strategy for the South: the offensive defensive, using bold, aggressive moves to force back the invading Union army. These battles also marked the start of Lee's long string of battlefield successes.

In the passage that follows, McClellan picks up precisely where Longstreet left off, describing key moments from the Seven Days and his reasons for continually withdrawing (despite only one tactical defeat in all of the Seven Days).

———

The Seven Days' Battles, *June 26 to July 1, 1862*
By General George B. McClellan

The firing ceased and the enemy retired about 9 P.M., the action having lasted six hours, with entire success to our arms. But few, if any, of Jackson's troops were engaged on this day; the portion of the enemy encountered were chiefly from the troops on the right bank of the river, who crossed near Meadow Bridge and at Mechanicsville. The information in my possession soon after the close of this action convinced me that Jackson was really approaching in large force. The position on Beaver Dam Creek, although so successfully defended, had its right flank too much in the air, and was too far from the main army to make it advisable to retain it longer. I therefore determined . . . to withdraw the corps itself to a position stretching around the bridges, where its flanks would be reasonably secure, and it would be within supporting distance of the main army. General Porter [the corps commander] carried out my orders to that effect. It was not advisable at that time, even had it been practicable, to withdraw the 5th Corps to the right [south] bank of the Chickahominy. Such a movement would have exposed the rear of the army, placed us between two fires, and enabled Jackson's fresh troops[6] to interrupt the movement to the James River, by crossing the Chickahominy in the vicinity of Jones Bridge before we could reach Malvern Hill with our trains. I determined, then, to resist Jackson with the 5th Corps, reinforced by all our disposable troops, in the new position near the bridgeheads, in order to cover the withdrawal of the trains and heavy guns, and to give time for the arrangements to secure the adoption of the James River as our line of supplies in lieu of the Pamunkey. The greater part of the heavy guns and wagons having been removed to the right bank of the Chickahominy, the delicate operation of withdrawing the troops from Beaver Dam Creek was commenced shortly before daylight, and successfully executed. . . .

The new position of the 5th Corps [at Gaines's Mill, on the twenty-seventh of June] was about an arc of a circle, covering the approaches to the bridges which connected our right wing with the troops on the opposite side of the river. . . .

Shortly after noon the enemy were discovered approaching in force, and it soon became evident that the entire position was to be attacked. His skirmishers advanced rapidly, and soon the fire became heavy along our

---

[6] Jackson and his troops, in fact, were exhausted from their long trip from the Valley, where they had marched and fought frantically for weeks. Exhaustion is perhaps the most accepted answer for Jackson's inaction in the Seven Days.

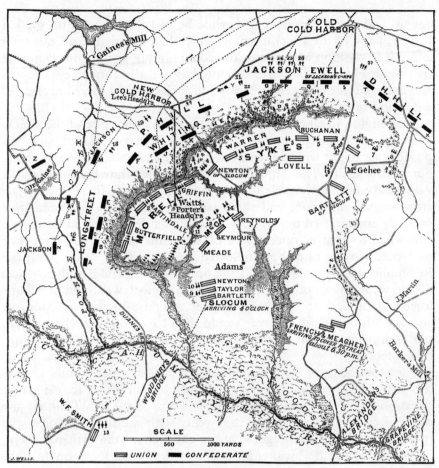

The Battle of Gaines's Mill, June 27, 1862

whole front. . . . By 3 P.M. the engagement had become so severe, and the enemy were so greatly superior in numbers, that the entire second line and reserves moved forward to sustain the first line against repeated and desperate assaults along the whole front. . . . About 7 P.M., they threw fresh troops against General Porter with still greater fury, and finally gained the woods held by our left. This reverse, aided by the confusion that followed an unsuccessful charge by five companies of the 5th Cavalry, and followed, as it was, by more determined assaults on the remainder of our lines, now outflanked, caused a general retreat from our position, to the hill in rear, overlooking the bridge. . . .

The operations of this day proved the numerical superiority of the enemy, and made it evident that while he had a large army on the left [north] bank of the Chickahominy, which had already turned our right and was in position to intercept the communications with our depots at the White House [McClellan's supply base on the Pamunkey], he was also in large force between our army and Richmond.[7] I therefore effected a junction of our forces.

This might probably have been executed on either side of the Chickahominy, and if the concentration had been effected on the left bank, it is possible we might with our entire force have defeated the enemy there; but at that time they held the roads leading to the White House, so that it would have been impossible to have sent supply trains in advance of the army in that direction, and the guarding of these trains would have seriously embarrassed our operations in the battle. We would have been compelled to fight if concentrated on that bank of the river. Moreover, we would have at once been followed by the enemy's forces upon the Richmond side of the river operating upon our rear, and if in the chances of war, we had been ourselves defeated in the effort, we would have been forced to fall back to the White House, and probably to Fort Monroe; and as both our flanks and rear would then have been entirely exposed, our entire supply train, if not the greater part of the army itself might have been lost.

The movements of the enemy showed that they expected this, as they themselves acknowledged, they were prepared to cut off our retreat in that direction. I therefore concentrated all our forces on the right [south] bank of the river during the night of the twenty-sixth and the morning of the twenty-seventh, all our wagons, heavy guns, etc., were gathered there.

It might be asked, why, after the concentration of our forces on the right [south] bank of the Chickahominy, with a large part of the enemy drawn away from Richmond, upon the opposite side, I did not, instead of striking for the James River fifteen miles below that place, at once march directly on Richmond.

It will be remembered that at this juncture the enemy was on our rear, and there was every reason to believe that he would sever our communications with our supply depot. . . .

The battles which continued day after day, in the progress of our flank movement to the James, with the exception of the one at Gaines's Mill, were successes to our arms, and the close engagement at Malvern

---

[7] Only a few thousand troops held Lee's fortified lines on the south side of the river. Lee's army—still smaller than McClellan's—was almost entirely to the north.

Hill [the final battle of the Seven Days, on the James River on July 1] was the most decisive of all. . . .

Although the result of the battle of Malvern was a complete victory, it was nevertheless necessary to fall back still further, in order to reach a point where our supplies could be brought to us with certainty.

THE SECOND BATTLE OF BULL RUN
August 1862

McClellan's *Report*, written before the war's end, deftly rationalizes his timid retreat. Unfortunately, his reasons were based on completely faulty information. He had far more troops, and far better equipment and supplies, than Lee had. Furthermore, McClellan was right in saying that he had won every fight except Gaines's Mill (in which a brigade under the command of John Bell Hood drove home a costly but victorious assault on Porter's left). Lee, who had just taken command, had trouble coordinating his divisions, and Jackson continued his inactivity.

Why, then, did McClellan retreat instead of following up his successes? His own writing begs the question—he could indeed have marched straight into Richmond, which was protected by a token force under Magruder, who had fooled McClellan once before at Yorktown. But McClellan was convinced he was outnumbered, and he could only think of the consequences of defeat. *If* he failed in his assault, he *might* be cut off from his base: such fears drove him more surely to retreat than the enemy's attacks did.

Lee sensed that he had immobilized McClellan at Harrison's Landing. He then reorganized his army into two corps, under Stonewall Jackson and James Longstreet, and shifted his operations to the north of Richmond, where the new Union Army of Virginia had been formed under the command of General John Pope. Lee sparred warily with the bombastic and arrogant Pope, then carried out perhaps his most perfect campaign, culminating in the climactic Second Battle of Bull Run.

The Second Battle of Bull Run
By General James Longstreet

The Federals had by this time organized the Army of Virginia from the independent forces in the State—the First Corps under General Sigel, the Second under General Banks, the Third under General McDowell—commanded by Major-General John Pope, brought from the West for that object and appointed June 26. This army reported July 31, 46,858 strong, for field service. . . .

The quiet of General McClellan's army at Harrison's Landing assured General Lee of his opportunity for attention to the movements of the army under General Pope, working towards Richmond by the Orange and Alexandria railway. On the thirteenth of July he ordered General Jackson, with his own and Ewell's division, to Gordonsville, to have a watch upon the Federal force operating in that quarter, promising reinforcements as soon as occasion should call for them. . . .

Just as a digression from following the operations of the armies of Lee and Pope, it should be remarked that the latter, by injudicious and unsoldierly attitude assumed at the outstart of his campaign, intensely incensed the people of Virginia and the South generally, the Confederate army to a man, and probably to a considerable degree discomfited the most considerate and thoughtful of his own officers and the authorities behind him. . . .

On the ninth [of August], Jackson advanced and found the enemy [under General Banks] in strong position at Cedar Run. His division under Ewell was posted on the northeast slope of Slaughter Mountain, his own division under Winder formed to the left. The engagement was pitched and soon became severe. While yet posting his troops, Winder was mortally struck by a fragment of shell. Banks, gaining confidence in his battle, moved forward to closer and severe fight and held it an hour, at points putting Jackson's troops in disorder. Jackson, reinforced by A.P. Hill's brigades, recovered his lost ground, advanced and renewed attack, and drove the enemy back. . . .[8]

That this was only a partial success—coming on the heels of the cruel orders of the Federal commander [Pope]—was gratifying to the Confederates, and encouraging as well.

Inaction of the Army of the Potomac gave General Lee opportunity for movement of his troops towards Washington and the army under General Pope. On the fifteenth [of July] I was ordered to Gordonsville by the Central Railroad with ten brigades. Two others under Hood at Hanover Junction were ordered to join me. . . .

Lee and Pope spent the next two weeks maneuvering along the Rappahannock River, each looking to turn the other's flank as heavy rains turned

[8] This fight is known as the Battle of Cedar Mountain.

roads to mud and the river to a torrent. Then Lee received word that forces from McClellan's army were coming to aid Pope. The news moved him to make his most daring thrust yet, as he gambled that he could crush Pope before the reinforcements arrived. His instrument: the "foot cavalry" of General Stonewall Jackson.

The Second Battle of Bull Run, *continued*
By General James Longstreet

On the twenty-fifth [of August], Jackson was ordered to pull away from our main force with the left wing, march by the crossings of the upper tributaries through Thoroughfare Gap, and strike the railway in the enemy's rear at Manassas Junction, his supply depot. Stuart's cavalry was ordered to follow during the night.

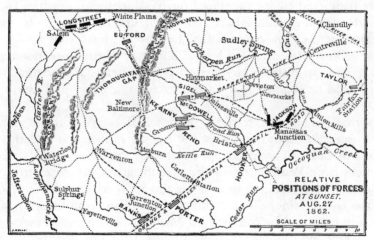

Lee's march around Pope's right flank, as of August 27, 1862

By a rapid march Jackson crossed the fords of the upper streams and made his bivouac near Salem. Forcing his march on the twenty-sixth, he passed Thoroughfare Gap to Gainesville, where Stuart joined him with all his cavalry. From Gainesville he inclined to the right for Bristoe Station, the cavalry holding the curtain between his column and Pope's. A little after sunset he reached the Orange and Alexandria Railroad, a march of thirty miles . . . . Two trains and a number of prisoners were taken, the greater part of the [Union] detachment at the station making a safe retreat. His plans against General Lee's right cut off by the high water, General Pope extended his right, under Sigel, Banks, and Reno, in search of Jackson up the river, who meanwhile had spirited himself away looking towards Pope's rear. . . .

Although the night of the twenty-sixth was very dark, and his troops severely worn, to be sure of his opportunity, Jackson sent a detachment to Manassas Junction (seven miles). The gallant Trimble, with five hundred of his men, volunteered for the service, and set out at once on the march. Stuart was afterwards ordered to join Trimble with his cavalry, and as ranking officer to command the operations of the entire force. The infantry advanced and attacked the enemy as soon as it could be formed for work, captured three hundred prisoners, an eight-gun battery complete, and immense quantities of army supplies.

Feeling the main force of his adversary in his front awaiting opportunity, General Pope became anxious about his left and rear, and was further hampered by instructions from Washington authorities to hold his Fredericksburg connections and "fight like the devil." (It may be fortunate for the Confederates that he was not instructed to *fight like Jackson.*) On the twenty-third he was informed of strong reinforcements to reach him at Warrenton Junction on the next day, and that larger forces would be shipped him on the twenty-fourth, to join him on the twenty-fifth.

Nevertheless, he began to realize, as he felt Jackson's march to his right, that he must abandon the line of the Rappahannock and attend to the movements of that command gone astray by the mountains. . . . Under assurances from Washington of the prompt arrival of forces from [the direction of Manassas], he looked for the approach of Franklin [with a corps] as far as Gainesville, marching by the Warrenton turnpike, and a division to reinforce the command at Manassas, so that when Jackson cut in on his rear and captured the detachment at the Junction, he was not a little surprised. He was in a position for grand tactics, however, midway between the right and left wings of his adversary's forces, that in his rear worn by severe marches and some fighting, that in his front behind a river, the crossing of which was difficult, and the lines of march to bring the distant wings to cooperation over routes that could be defended by small commands.

Communication with Washington being severed, the forces at and near Alexandria were thrown in the dark. To move by rail they were liable to run into the wrong camps, and the rapid change by water [from the peninsula] to the new position left them short of land transportation.

Pope stood on the evening of the twenty-seventh: McDowell's corps, including Reynolds's division, 15,500; Sigel's corps, 9,000; Banks's, 5,000; Reno's, 7,000; Heintzelman's and Porter's corps, 18,000—in all 54,500 men, with 4,000 cavalry. In his rear was Jackson, 20,000; in front on the Rappahannock was my 25,000; R.H. Anderson's reserve division, 5,000; total, 50,000, with 3,000 of cavalry under Stuart. . . .

On the twenty-seventh, Jackson marched at daylight to Manassas Junction with his own division, under Taliaferro, and A.P. Hill's, leaving Ewell's at Bristoe Station, with orders to withdraw if severely pressed. . . . Then a brigade of infantry under General Taylor, of New Jersey, just landed from the cars from Alexandria, advanced and made a desperate effort to recover the lost position and equipage at Manassas Junction. . . . It was driven back after a fierce struggle, General Taylor, commanding, mortally wounded. . . . The spoils were then quietly divided, such as could be consumed or hauled off, and the balance given to the torch.

[As Pope moved his army north, seeking to trap Jackson,] I marched from the Rappahannock, following on Jackson's trail, and camped at White Plains. . . .

General McClellan reached Alexandria, Virginia, on the twenty-seventh. On the twenty-eighth, Jackson was first to move at 12:20 A.M. He applied the torch to the stores of provisions and marched with his division, under Taliaferro, by the New Market Sudley Springs road across the Warrenton turnpike, and pitched bivouac on a line from near Groveton, towards Sudley Mills, on the field of first Manassas [First Bull Run], at daylight.

At one A.M., A.P. Hill marched from Manassas Junction, crossed at Bull Run, and halted at Centreville. Ewell followed at daylight towards Centreville, crossed Bull Run, marched up some distance, recrossed, and joined Jackson, forming on Taliaferro's left. After the morning fires of the bivouac burned out, Jackson's position could not be seen except upon near approach. He was hid away under the cuts and embankments of an unfinished railroad. . . .

At twelve o'clock [noon], General Pope reached Manassas Junction. Misled by the movements of A.P. Hill and Ewell, he ordered Reno's corps and Kearny's and Hooker's divisions of the Third to Centreville, in search of Jackson, while the latter was little more than a league from him, resting quietly in his hiding place, and his detached divisions had doubled on their courses and were marching to join him. . . .

The head of my column reached Thoroughfare Gap early in the afternoon. Reports from General Jackson were that he was resting quietly on the flank of the enemy, and between him and Washington.

[Longstreet proceeded to fight his way through Thoroughfare Gap, defeating a small force left there by McDowell. Meanwhile, the Union forces continued to march for Centreville, where Pope intended to concentrate his army in his search for Jackson.]

As King's [Union] division was marching by, Jackson thought to come out from his lurking-place to learn the meaning of the march. The direction of the move again impressed him that Pope was retreating, and that his escape to the north side of Bull Run would put his army in a position of safety before General Lee could join him. It was late, the sun had set, but Jackson was moved to prompt action, as the only means of arresting and holding Pope for General Lee's arrival. He was in plain view of the white smoke of the rifles of my infantry [fighting through Thoroughfare Gap] as they climbed over Bull Run Mountain, seven miles away, and in hearing of our artillery as the boom of the big guns, resounding along the rock-faced cliffs, gathered volume to offer salutations and greetings for the union of comrades and commands. . . .

General Jackson reported, "The conflict [against McDowell's marching columns] was firm and sanguinary." He fails to give his number lost, but acknowledges his severe loss in the division commanders, General Ewell losing a leg, and Taliaferro severely wounded.

During the night the Federal commander reported to his subordinates that McDowell had "intercepted the retreat of Jackson, and ordered concentration of the army against him," whereas it was, of course, Jackson who had intercepted McDowell's march. He seems to have been under the impression that he was about to capture Jackson, and inclined to lead his subordinates to the same opinion. . . .

Jackson moved his forces at daylight, and reestablished his line behind the unfinished railroad, his own division under General Stark, Ewell's under General Lawton, with A.P. Hill on his left.

General Pope's orders for the night directed the march of Kearny's division from Centreville by the turnpike at one A.M., to reinforce the troops against Jackson; the other division of Heintzelman's corps (Hooker's) to march by the same route at daylight, and to be followed by the corps under Reno. These orders were urgent, and directed that the commands should move promptly, leaving fragments behind if all could not be got together in time; Kearny to attack at daylight, to be supported by Hooker. . . .

As soon as advised of the withdrawal of King's division from the ground of the twenty-eighth, General Pope sent as substitutes for his orders of the early morning that General Porter should push forward with his corps and King's division of McDowell's command to Gainesville, to cooperate with his movements along the Warrenton turnpike. . . .

General Pope at daylight sent orders to General Sigel's corps, with Reynolds's division, to attack as soon as it was light enough to see, and bring the enemy to a stand if possible. At the same time orders were sent to Heintzelman and Reno for their corps to hurry along the turnpike and join on the right of Sigel. The batteries opened in irregular combat on the left, center, and right a little after eight o'clock, and drew from Jackson a monotonous but resolute response. And thus early upon the twenty-ninth of August was begun the second battle upon this classic and fateful field.

I marched at daylight and filed to the left at Gainesville at nine o'clock. As the head of the column approached Gainesville the fire of artillery became more lively, and its volume swelled to proportions indicating near approach to battle. The men involuntarily quickened step, filed down the turnpike, and in twenty minutes came upon the battle as it began to press upon Jackson's right, their left battery partially turning his right. His battle, as before stated, stood upon its original line of the unfinished railroad.

As my columns approached, the batteries of the leading brigades were thrown forward to ground of superior sweep. This display and the deploy of the infantry were so threatening to the enemy's left batteries that he thought prudent to change the front of that end of his line more to his left and rear. . . . As formed, my line made an obtuse angle forward of Jackson's, till it approached Manassas Gap Railroad, where D.R. Jones's division was broken in echelon to the rear. At twelve o'clock we were formed for battle. . . .

When I reported my troops in order for battle, General Lee was inclined to engage as soon as practicable, but did not order. All troops that he could hope to have were up except R.H. Anderson's division, which was near enough to come in when the battle was in progress. I asked him to be allowed to make a reconnaissance of the enemy's ground, and along his left. After an hour's work, mounted and afoot, under the August sun, I returned and reported adversely as to attack, especially in view of the easy approach of the troops reported at Manassas against my right in the event of severe contention. We knew of Rickett's division in that quarter, and of a considerable force at Manassas Junction, which indicated one corps. . . .

At one time the enemy broke through [Jackson's] line, cutting off the

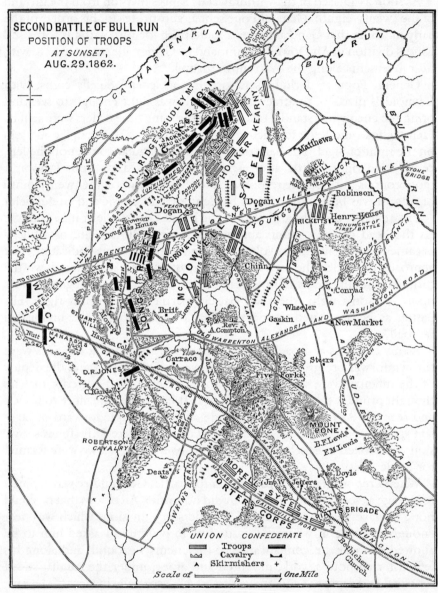

The Second Battle of Bull Run, August 29, 1862

extreme left brigade, and gained position on the railroad cut; but Jackson and A.P. Hill reinforced against that attack, and were in time to push it back and recover the lost ground.

Their attacks were too much in detail to hold even the ground gained, but they held firmly to the battle and their line until after night, when they withdrew to await orders for the next day.

Though this fight opened at two o'clock, and was fiercely contested till near night, no account of it came from headquarters to my command, nor did General Jackson think to send word of it. General Lee, not entirely satisfied with the report of my reconnaissance, was thinking of sending some of the engineers for more critical survey of his right front, when his chief of cavalry sent to inform him of the approach of a formidable column of infantry and artillery threatening his right. Wilcox's division was changed to supporting position of our right, under Jones, and I rode to look at this new force, its strength, and the ground of its approach. It was the column of McDowell's and Porter's corps, marching under the joint order. . . .

We saw nothing of McDowell's corps, and our cavalry had not been able to get far enough towards their rear to know of its presence or force. He afterwards drew off from Porter's column and marched by the Sudley Springs road to join the main force on the turnpike. I rode back and reported to General Lee that the column was hardly strong enough to mean aggressive work from that quarter, and at the same time reported a dust along the New Market road which seemed to indicate the movement of other troops from Manassas.

General Stuart rode up, making similar report, and asked for orders. As our chief was not ready with his orders at the moment, Stuart was asked to wait. The latter threw himself on the grass, put a large stone under his head, asked the general to have him called when his orders were ready for him, and went sound asleep.

Our chief now returned to his first plan of attack by his right down the turnpike. Though more than anxious to meet his wishes, and anticipating his orders, I suggested, as the day was far spent, that a reconnaissance in force be made at nightfall to the immediate front of the enemy, and if an opening was found for an entering wedge, that we have all things in readiness at daylight for a good day's work. After a moment's hesitation he assented, and orders were given for the advance at early twilight.

This gave General Stuart half an hour *siesta*. When called, he sprang to his feet, received his orders, swung into his saddle, and at a lope, singing,

"If you want to have a good time, jine the cavalry," his banjo-player, Sweeny, on the jump behind him, rode to his troopers. . . .

Meanwhile, General Pope had sent orders to General Porter, dated 4:30 P.M., to attack [Jackson's] right flank, but the order was not received until it was too late for battle. . . . The 4:30 order was issued under the impression that my troops, or the greater part of them, were still at Thoroughfare Gap, and General Pope said, in his official report—

> I believe, in fact I am positive, that at five o'clock in the afternoon of
> the twenty-ninth, General Porter had in his front no considerable
> body of the enemy. I believed then, as I am very sure now, that it was
> easily practicable for him to have turned the right flank of Jackson and
> to have fallen upon his rear. . . .

After night, Porter's column marched by its right to follow the route of McDowell.

The morning of the thirtieth broke fair, and for the Federal commander bright with anticipations for the day. He wired the Washington authorities of success, that "the enemy was retreating to the mountains. . . ."

About one o'clock in the afternoon, General Pope ordered an attack against Jackson's front by the corps under General Porter, supported by King's division, Heintzelman and Reno to move forward and attack Jackson's left, and to turn it and strike down against the flank, Rickett's division in support of it. . . .

During the early part of this severe battle not a gun was fired by my troops. . . .

Developments appearing unfavorable for a general engagement, General Lee had settled upon a move by Sudley Springs, to cross Bull Run during the night and try to again reach Pope's rear, this time with his army.

About three P.M. I rode to the front to prepare to make a diversion a little before dark, to cover the proposed night march. . . . Passing by and beyond my lines, a message came from General Jackson reporting his lines heavily pressed, and asking to be reinforced. Riding forward a few rods to an open, which gave a view of Jackson's field, I came in sight of Porter's battle, piling up against Jackson's right, center, and left. At the same time an order came from General Lee for a division to be sent to General Jackson. Porter's masses were in almost direct line from the point at which I stood, and in enfilade fire. It was evident that they could not stand fifteen minutes under the fire of batteries planted at that point, while a division marching back and across the field to aid Jackson could not reach him in an hour, more time probably than he could stand under the heavy weights then bearing down upon him. Boldness was prudence! Prompt work by the wing and batteries could relieve the battle. Reinforcements might not be in time, so I called for my nearest batteries. Ready, anticipating call, they sprang to their places and drove at speed, saw the opportunity before it could be pointed out, and went into action. The first fire was by Chapman's battery, followed in rolling practice by Boyce's and Reilly's. Almost immediately the wounded began to drop from Porter's ranks; the number seemed to increase with every shot; the masses began to waver, swinging back and forth, showing signs of discomfiture along the left and left center.

In ten or fifteen minutes it crumbled into disorder and turned towards the rear. Although the batteries seemed to hasten the movements of the discomfited, the fire was less effective upon broken ranks, which gave them courage, and they made brave efforts to rally; but as the new lines formed they had to breast against Jackson's standing line, and make a new and favorable target for the batteries, which again drove them to disruption and retreat. Not satisfied, they made a third effort to rally and fight the battle through, but by that time they had fallen back far enough to open the field to the fire of S.D. Lee's artillery battalion. As the line began to take shape, this fearful fire was added to that under which they had tried so ineffectually to fight. The combination tore the line to pieces, and as it broke the third time the charge was ordered. The heavy fumes of gunpowder hanging about our ranks, as stimulating as sparkling wine, charged the atmosphere with the light and splendor of battle. Time was culminating under a flowing tide. The noble horses took the spirit of the riders sitting lightly in their saddles. As orders were given, the staff, their limbs already closed to the horses' flanks, pressed their spurs, but the electric current overleaped their speedy strides, and twenty-five thousand braves moved in line as by a single impulse. . . .

Leaving the broken ranks for Jackson, our fight was made against the lines near my front. As the plain along Hood's front was more favorable for the tread of soldiers, he was ordered, as the column of direction, to push for the plateau at the Henry House, in order to cut off retreat at the crossings by Young's Branch. . . .

At the first sound of the charge, General Lee sent to revoke his call in favor of Jackson, asked me to push the battle, ordered R.H. Anderson's division up, and rode himself to join me. . . .

General Pope drew Rickett's division from his right to brace his left, then Reno's command to aid in checking our march, but its progress, furiously resisted, was steady, though much delayed. Piatt's brigade was also put against us. This made time for Porter to gather his forces. His regulars of Sykes's division, particularly, made desperate resistance, that could only be overcome by our overreaching lines threatening their rear.

When the last guns were fired the thickening twilight concealed the lines of friend and foe, so that the danger of friend firing against friend became imminent. The hill of the Henry House was reached in good time, but darkness coming on earlier because of thickening clouds hovering over us, and a gentle fall of rain closely following, the plateau was shut off from view, and its ascent only found by groping through the darkening rainfall. As long as the enemy held the plateau, he covered the line of retreat by the turnpike and the bridge at Young's Branch. As he retired, heavy darkness gave safe-conduct to such of his columns as could find their way through the weird mists.

4

THE BATTLE OF ANTIETAM

September 17, 1862

Within three months of taking command of the Army of Northern Virginia, Robert E. Lee had achieved an astonishing victory against massive (and better equipped) enemy forces. He had driven back McClellan's Army of the Potomac when it was at Richmond's doorstep, then turned and smashed the Army of Virginia under General John Pope. His maneuvers before the Second Battle of Bull Run remain a classic example of the strategic turning movement—threatening his opponent's rear with the detachment under Jackson, forcing him to fall back. In the battle that followed, the Union lost an estimated 16,000 out of 65,000 men; the Confederates lost only 9,000 out of 55,000—another stunning achievement in an age when attacking forces in battle usually suffered the heaviest losses in both absolute and relative terms.[9]

As the Yankees retreated to Washington, Lee tried to strike them one more time with a wheeling march by Jackson's men; the Northern troops managed to hold them off at Chantilly on September 1. The Union, however, had been badly beaten, and a heavy gloom settled across the North. The Confederates felt invincible in their euphoria; there was nothing, it seemed, that Lee and his men could not do—and nothing that the timid McClellan[10] could stop them from doing.

It was in this atmosphere of exaggerated confidence that Lee made one of the gravest mistakes of his career. Confident in his lieutenants and his men, sure of McClellan's extreme caution, he decided to make yet another turning movement, on a far larger scale. Shifting his troops to the

[9] This fact stemmed from the great range and killing power of the rifled musket, in widespread use by 1861, which forced charging troops to cross hundreds of yards in the face of deadly fire in order to close with the enemy.

[10] After the defeat at Second Bull Run, Lincoln removed Pope from command, incorporating his forces into the Army of the Potomac, with McClellan back in full command in the theater.

Shenandoah Valley, Lee crossed the Potomac and marched into Maryland, leaving Jackson in his wake to besiege the Federal arsenal at Harper's Ferry. Northern Virginia had suffered greatly during the last year of campaigning, Lee reasoned; in Maryland his men could live off the land, relieving his home state of the burden of supporting them. Furthermore, his advance would draw the Union forces farther away from Richmond, though he was certain that McClellan would not press him too hard. Perhaps his stay in Maryland would draw that slave state into the Confederacy as well, or even win French and English recognition of the new nation. Triumphant confidence reigned in the Army of Northern Virginia; Longstreet later wrote, "As our columns approached Leesburg, 'Maryland, my Maryland' was in the air, and on the lips of every man from General Lee down to the youngest drummer."

Unfortunately for Lee, McClellan moved with unusual speed to pin Lee down and then eject him from Maryland. As the Confederate commander waited for Jackson to seize Harper's Ferry and come forward, the Union commander captured a copy of the Confederate orders, which he used to locate the Southern army. After a brisk battle at South Mountain between the Army of the Potomac and a Confederate delaying force, the two armies met near Sharpsburg along the banks of Antietam Creek, where, on September 17, 1862, they endured the bloodiest day of fighting in American history.

The Battle of Antietam
By General George B. McClellan

On the 3rd [of September] the enemy disappeared from the front of Washington, and the information which I received induced me to believe that he intended to cross the upper Potomac into Maryland. This materially changed the aspect of affairs and enlarged the sphere of operations, for, in case of a crossing in force, an active campaign would be necessary to cover Baltimore, prevent the invasion of Pennsylvania, and clear Maryland. . . .

All the necessary arrangements for the defense of the city, under the new condition of things, had been made, and General Banks was left in command, having received his instructions from me.

I left Washington on the 7th of September. At this time it was known that the mass of the rebel army had passed up the south side of the Potomac in the direction of Leesburg, and that a portion of that army had crossed into Maryland; but whether it was their intention to cross their whole force, with a view to turn Washington by a flank movement down the north bank of the Potomac, to move on Baltimore, or to invade Pennsylvania, were questions which at that time we had no means of determining. This uncertainty as to the intentions of the enemy obliged me, up to the 13th of September, to march cautiously, and to advance the army in such order as to continually keep Washington and Baltimore covered, and at the same time to hold the troops well in hand, so as to be able to concentrate and follow rapidly if the enemy took the direction of Pennsylvania, or to return to the defense of Washington if, as was greatly feared by the authorities, the enemy should be merely making a feint with a small force to draw off our army, while with their main forces they stood ready to seize the first favorable opportunity to attack the capital.

In the meantime the process of reorganization rendered necessary after the demoralizing effects of the disastrous campaign upon the other side of the Potomac was rapidly progressing, the troops were regaining confidence, and their former soldierly appearance and discipline were fast returning. My cavalry was pushed out continually in all directions, and all possible steps taken to learn the positions and movements of the enemy. . . .

On the 10th of September, I received from my scouts information which rendered it quite probable that General Lee's army was in the vicinity of Frederick [Maryland], but whether his intention was to move towards Baltimore or Pennsylvania was not then known. . . .

On the 12th a portion of the right wing [of the Army of the Potomac] entered Frederick, after a brisk skirmish at the outskirts of the city and in the streets. On the 13th the main bodies of the right wing and center passed through Frederick.

It was soon ascertained that the main body of the enemy's forces had marched out of the city on the two previous days, taking the roads to Boonsboro and Harper's Ferry, thereby rendering it necessary to force the passes through the Catoctin and South Mountain ridges, and gain possession of Boonsboro and Rohrersville before any relief could be extended to Col. Miles at Harper's Ferry.

On the 13th, an order fell into my hands issued by General Lee, which fully disclosed his plans, and I immediately gave orders for a rapid and vigorous forward movement. . . .

Col. Miles surrendered Harper's Ferry at 8 A.M. on the 15th, as the cessation of the firing indicated, and Gen. Franklin was ordered to remain where he was, to watch the large force in front of him,[11] and protect our left and rear, until the night of the 16th, when he was ordered to join the main body of the army. . . .

While the events which have just been described were taking place at Crampton's Gap, the troops of the center and right wing, which had united at Frederick on the 13th, were engaged in the contest for the possession of Turner's Gap [of South Mountain ridge]. . . .

On the next day [after the fight began at Turner's Gap] I had the honor to receive the following very kind dispatch from his Excellency the President:

WASHINGTON, SEPT. 15, 1862. 2:45 PM

Your dispatch of today received. God bless you, and all with you. Destroy the rebel army if possible.

A. LINCOLN

On the night of the battle of South Mountain, orders were given to the corps commanders to press forward their pickets at early dawn. This advance revealed the fact that the enemy had left his positions, and an immediate pursuit was ordered. . . .

General Richardson's division of the 2d Corps, pressing the rear guard of the enemy with vigor, passed Boonsboro and Keedysville, and came upon the main body of the enemy, occupying in large force a strong position a few miles beyond the latter place. . . .

The enemy occupied a strong position on the heights, on the west side of Antietam Creek, displaying a large force of infantry and cavalry, with numerous batteries of artillery, which opened on our columns as they appeared in sight on the Keedysville and Sharpsburg turnpike. . . .

Antietam Creek, in this vicinity, is crossed by four stone bridges, the upper one on the Keedysville and Williamsport road; the second on the Keedysville and Sharpsburg turnpike, some two and a half miles below; the third about a mile below the second, on the Rohrersville and Sharpsburg road; and the fourth near the mouth of Antietam Creek, on the road leading from Harper's Ferry to Sharpsburg, some three miles below the third. The stream is sluggish, with few and difficult fords.

---

[11] Franklin had been ordered to Harper's Ferry to save the garrison. In a move worthy of McClellan himself, Franklin let his entire corps be stopped by three enemy brigades.

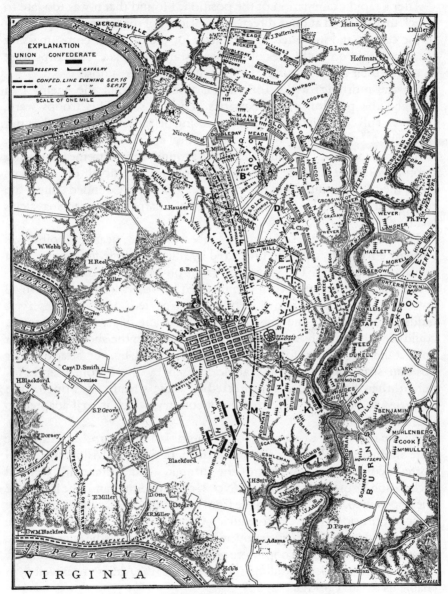

The Battle of Antietam, September 17, 1862

After a rapid examination of the position, I found that it was too late to attack that day, and at once directed the placing of the batteries in position in the center, and indicated the bivouacs for the different corps, massing them near and on both sides of the Sharpsburg turnpike. The corps were not all in their positions until the next morning after sunrise.

On the morning of the 16th it was discovered that the enemy had changed the position of his batteries. The masses of his troops were, however, still concealed behind the opposing heights. Their left and center were upon and in front of the Sharpsburg and Hagerstown turnpike, hidden by woods and irregularities of the ground; their extreme left resting upon a wooded eminence near the crossroads to the north of J. Miller's farm, their left resting upon the Potomac. Their line extended south, the right resting upon the hills to the south of Sharpsburg, near Snaveley's farm.

The bridge over the Antietam, described as No. 3, near this point, was strongly covered by riflemen protected by rifle pits, stone fences, etc., and enfiladed by artillery. The ground in front of this line consisted of undulating hills, their crests in turn commanded by others in their rear. On all favorable points the enemy's artillery was posted, and their reserves, hidden from view by the hills on which their line of battle was formed, could maneuver unobserved by our army, and from the shortness of their line, could rapidly reinforce any point threatened by our attack. Their position stretching across the angle formed by the Potomac and Antietam, their flanks and rear protected by these streams, was one of the strongest to be found in this region of country, which is well adapted to defensive warfare.

On the right near Keedysville, on both sides of the Sharpsburg turnpike were Sumner's and Hooker's corps. . . . General Sykes's division of General Porter's corps was on the left of the turnpike, and in line with General Richardson, protecting the bridge, No. 2, over the Antietam. The left of the line opposite to, and some distance from the bridge No. 3, was occupied by General Burnside's corps. Before giving General Hooker his orders to make the movement which will presently be described, I rode to the left of the line to satisfy myself that the troops were properly posted there to secure our left flank from any attack made along the left bank of the Antietam, as well as to enable us to carry bridge No. 3.[12]

_____

[12] This bridge became known as Burnside Bridge after the efforts made by Burnside to capture it during the battle.

I found it necessary to make considerable changes in the position of General Burnside's corps, and directed him to advance to a strong position in the immediate vicinity of the bridge, and to reconnoiter the approaches to the bridge carefully.

In the rear of Generals Sumner's and Hooker's corps, near Keedysville, General Mansfield's corps was massed. . . . General Franklin's corps, and General Couch's division held a position in Pleasant Valley, in front of Brownsville, with a strong force of the enemy in their front. . . .

It was afternoon [on September 16] before I could move the troops to their positions for attack, being compelled to spend the morning in reconnoitering the new position taken up by the enemy, examining the ground, finding fords and clearing their approaches, and hurrying up the ammunition and supply trains, which had been delayed by the rapid march of the troops over the few practicable fords from Frederick. . . .

My plan for the impending general engagement was to attack the enemy's left with the corps of Hooker and Mansfield, supported by Sumner's, and if necessary, Franklin's, and as soon as matters looked favorable there to move the corps of Gen. Burnside against the enemy's extreme right, upon the ridges running to the south and rear of Sharpsburg, and having carried their position to press along the crest towards our right; and whenever either of these flank movements should be successful to advance our center with all our forces then disposable.

About 2 P.M. General Hooker, with his corps consisting of General Rickett's, Meade's, and Doubleday's divisions was ordered to cross the Antietam at a ford, and at bridge No. 1, a short distance above, to attack, and if possible turn the enemy's left. General Sumner was ordered to cross the corps of General Mansfield (the 12th) during the night, and hold his own (the 2nd) ready to cross early the next morning. . . . The enemy was driven from the strip of woods where he was first met, the firing lasted until dark, when General Hooker's corps rested on their arms, on ground won from the enemy. . . .

At daylight, on the 17th, the action was commenced by the skirmishers of the Pennsylvania Reserves. The whole of General Hooker's corps was soon engaged, and drove the enemy from the open field in front of the first line of woods, into a second line of woods beyond, which runs to the eastward of and nearly parallel to the Sharpsburg and Hagerstown turnpike.

This contest became obstinate, and as the troops advanced the opposition became more determined, and the numbers of the enemy greater.

General Hooker then ordered up the corps of General Mansfield, which moved promptly towards the scene of action. . . .

The line of battle of this corps was formed and it became engaged at about 7 A.M., the attack being opened by Knapp's Pennsylvania, Cothran's New York, and Hampton's Pittsburg batteries. To meet this attack the enemy had pushed a strong column of troops into the open fields in front of the turnpike, while he occupied the woods on the west of the turnpike in strong force. The woods (as was found by subsequent observation) were traversed by the outcropping of ledges of rock. Several hundred yards to the right and rear was a line which commanded the debouch of the woods, and in the fields between was a long line of stone fences, continued by breastworks of rails, which covered the enemy's infantry from our musketry. The same woods formed a screen behind which his movements were concealed, and his batteries on the hill and the rifle works covered from the fire of our artillery in front.

For about two hours the battle raged with varied success, the enemy endeavoring to drive our troops into the second line of wood, and ours in turn trying to get possession of the line in front. Our troops ultimately succeeded in forcing the enemy back into the woods near the turnpike, General Green, with his two brigades, crossing into the woods to the left of the Dunker church. . . . General Green, being much exposed and applying for reinforcements, the 13th New York and 27th Indiana, and the 3rd Maryland were sent to his support with a section of Knapp's battery.

At about 9 o'clock A.M., General Sedgwick's division of General Sumner's corps arrived. Crossing by the ford previously mentioned, this division marched in three columns to the support of the attack on the enemy's left. On nearing the scene of the action the columns were halted, faced to the front, and established by General Sumner in three parallel lines by brigade, facing towards the south and west. . . .

The division was then put in motion, and moved upon the field of battle under fire from the enemy's concealed batteries on the hill beyond the woods, passing diagonally to the front across the open space, and to the front of the 1st division of General Williams's corps: this latter division withdrew.

Entering the woods on the west of the turnpike, and driving the enemy before them, the first line was met by a heavy fire of musketry and shell from the enemy's breastworks and the batteries on the hill commanding the exit from the woods. Meantime a heavy column of the enemy had succeeded in crowding back the troops of General Green's division, and appeared in the rear of the left of Sedgwick's division. By command of

General Sumner, General Howard faced the third line to the rear, preparatory to a change of front, to meet the column advancing on the left, but this line now suffering from the destructive fire in front and on its left, which it was unable to return, gave way towards the right and rear in considerable confusion, and was soon followed by the first and second lines. . . .

During General Sumner's attack, he ordered General Williams to support him. Brigadier-General Gordon, with a portion of his brigade, moved forward, but when he reached the woods the left of General Sedgwick's division had given way, and finding himself, as the smoke cleared up, opposed to the enemy in force, with his small command, he withdrew to the rear of the batteries at the second line of woods. As General Gordon's troops unmasked our batteries on the left, they opened with canister. . . . Unable to stand this deadly fire in front and the musketry fire from the right, the enemy again sought shelter in the woods and rocks beyond the turnpike. . . .

About the time of General Sedgwick's advance, General Hooker, while urging on his command, was seriously wounded in the foot and taken from the field. The repulse of the enemy offered opportunity to rearrange the lines and reorganize the commands on the right, now more or less in confusion.

While this conflict was so obstinately raging on the right, General French was pushing his division against the enemy still further to the left. This division crossed the Antietam at the same ford as General Sedgwick, and immediately in his rear. Passing over the stream in three columns, the division marched about a mile from the ford, then facing to the left, moved in three lines towards the enemy . . . The division was first assailed by a fire of artillery, but steadily advanced, driving the enemy's skirmishers, and encountered the infantry in some force at the group of houses on Roulette's farm. . . .

General French received orders from General Sumner, his corps commander, to push on with renewed vigor to make a diversion in favor of the attack on the right. Leaving the new troops . . . to form a reserve, he ordered the brigade of General Kimball to the front, passing to the left of General Weber. The enemy was pressed back to near the crest of the hill, where he was encountered in greater strength, posted in a sunken road running in a northwesterly direction and forming a natural rifle pit.[13] In a cornfield in rear of this road were also strong bodies of the enemy. As the

---

[13] This road became known as "Bloody Lane."

line reached the crest of the hill, a galling fire was opened on it from the sunken road and cornfield. Here a terrific fire of musketry burst from both lines, and the battle raged along the whole line with great slaughter. The enemy attempted to turn the left of the line. . . .

Foiled in this, the enemy made a determined assault on the front, but was met by a charge from our lines, which drove him back with severe loss, leaving in our hands some three hundred prisoners, and several stands of colors. The enemy having been repulsed by the terrible execution of the batteries, and the musketry fire on the extreme right, now attempted to assist the attack on General French's division by assailing him on his right, and endeavoring to turn his flank, but this attack was met and checked. . . . Having been under continuous fire for nearly four hours, and their ammunition nearly exhausted, this division now took position immediately below the crest of the heights on which they had so gallantly fought, the enemy making no attempt to regain their lost ground.

On the left of General French, General Richardson's division was hotly engaged. Having crossed the Antietam about 9:30 A.M. . . . it moved on a line nearly parallel to the Antietam, and formed in a ravine behind the high grounds overlooking Roulette's house. . . .

Meagher's brigade [of Richardson's division] advanced steadily, soon became engaged with the enemy posted to the left and in front of Roulette's house. It continued to advance under a heavy fire nearly to the crest of the hill overlooking Piper's house, the enemy being posted in a continuation of the sunken road, and cornfield, before referred to. Here the brave Irish brigade opened upon the enemy a terrific musketry fire. All of General Sumner's corps was now engaged, General Sedgwick's on the right, General French in the center, and General Richardson on the left. . . .

The ground over which General Richardson's and French's divisions were fighting was very irregular, intersected by numerous ravines, hills covered with growing corn, enclosed by stone walls, behind which the enemy could advance unobserved upon any exposed point of our lines. Taking advantage of this, the enemy attempted to gain the right of Richardson's position in the cornfield, near Roulette's house, where the division had become separated from that of General French. A change of front . . . drove the enemy from the cornfield, and restored the line.

The brigade of General Caldwell, with determined gallantry, pushed the enemy back opposite the left and center of this division, but sheltered in the sunken road they still held our forces on the right of Caldwell in check. Colonel Barlow . . . of Caldwell's brigade, seeing a favorable opportunity, advanced [his] regiments on the left, taking the line on the sunken road in flank, and compelled them to surrender, capturing over three hundred prisoners, and three stands of colors.

The whole of the brigade . . . now advanced with gallantry, driving the enemy before them in confusion into the cornfield beyond the sunken road. . . . Our troops on the left part of this line having driven the enemy far back, they, with reinforced numbers, made a determined attack directly in front. To meet this, Col. Barlow brought his two regiments to position in line, and drove the enemy through the cornfield into the orchard beyond. . . . This advance gave us possession of Piper's house, the strong point contended for by the enemy at this part of the line, it being a defensible building, several hundred yards in advance of the sunken road. . . .

Knowing the tried courage of the troops, General Hancock [who had taken command of Richardson's division after that officer fell mortally wounded] felt confident that he could hold his position, although suffering from the enemy's artillery, but was too weak to attack. . . .

To return to the incidents occurring still further to the right.

Between 12 and 1 P.M. General Franklin's corps arrived on the field of battle. . . . It was first intended to keep this corps in reserve on the east side of the Antietam, to operate on either flank or on the center, as circumstances might require. But, on nearing Keedysville, the strong opposition on the right, developed by the attacks of Hooker and Sumner, rendered it necessary to send this corps at once to the assistance of the right wing. . . .

The advance of General Franklin's corps was opportune. The attack of the enemy on the position, but for the timely arrival of his corps, must have been disastrous, had it succeeded in piercing the line between General Sedgwick's and French's divisions. . . .

General Porter's corps, consisting of General Sykes's division of regulars and volunteers, and General Morell's division of volunteers, occupied a position on the east side of Antietam creek, upon the main turnpike leading to Sharpsburg, and directly opposite the center of the enemy's line. This corps filled the interval between the right wing and General Burnside's command, and guarded the main approach from the enemy's position to our trains of supplies.

It was necessary to watch this part of our line with the utmost vigilance, lest the enemy should take advantage of the first exhibition of weakness here, to push upon us a vigorous assault for the purpose of piercing our center and turning our rear, as well as to capture or destroy our supply trains. Once having penetrated this line, the enemy's passage to our rear could have met but feeble resistance, as there were no reserves to reinforce or close up the gap.[14]

Towards the middle of the afternoon, proceeding to the right, I found that Sumner's, Hooker's, and Mansfield's corps had met with serious losses. Several general officers had been carried from the field severely wounded, and the aspect of affairs was anything but promising. At the risk of greatly exposing our center, I ordered two brigades from Porter's corps, the only available troops, to reinforce the right. . . .

General Sumner expressed the most decided opinion against another attempt during the day to assault the enemy's position in front, as portions of our troops were so much scattered and demoralized. In view of these circumstances, after making changes in the positions of some of the troops, I directed the different commanders to hold their positions, and, being satisfied that this could be done without the assistance of the two brigades from the center, I countermanded the order which was in course of execution. . . .

The troops of General Burnside held the left of the line opposite bridge No. 3. . . . Early on the morning of the 17th I ordered General Burnside to form his troops and hold them in readiness to assault the bridge in his front, and to await further orders.

At 8 o'clock an order was sent to him by Lieutenant Wilson, Topographical Engineers, to carry the bridge, then to gain possession of the heights beyond, and to advance along their crest upon Sharpsburg and its rear.

After some time had elapsed, not hearing from him, I dispatched an aide to ascertain what had been done. The aide returned with the information that but little progress had been made. I then sent him back an order to General Burnside to assault the bridge at once, and carry it at all hazards. The aide returned to me a second time, with the report that the bridge was still in the possession of the enemy. Whereupon I directed Colonel Sackett, Inspector-General, to deliver to General Burnside my positive order to push forward his troops without a moment's delay, and, if necessary, to carry the bridge at the point of the bayonet, and I ordered Colonel Sackett to remain with General Burnside and see that the order was executed promptly.

After these three hours' delay, the bridge was carried at 1 o'clock by a brilliant charge of the 51st New York and 51st Pennsylvania Volunteers.

[14] This paragraph seems to be a direct response to the most damaging criticism of McClellan's handling of the battle—that he failed to use Porter's unengaged corps to follow up the breakthrough at the sunken road in the center. His argument that *his* center could have been pierced is absurd.

Other troops were then thrown over and the opposite bank occupied, the enemy retreating to the heights beyond.

A halt was then made by General Burnside's advance until 3 P.M., upon hearing which I directed one of my aides—Col. Key—to inform General Burnside that I desired him to push forward his troops with the utmost vigor and carry the enemy's position on the heights, that the movement was vital to our success, that this was a time when we must not stop for loss of life if a great object could be thereby accomplished. . . . He replied that he would soon advance. . . . The advance was then gallantly resumed, the enemy driven from their guns, the heights handsomely carried, and a portion of the troops even reached the outskirts of Sharpsburg. By this time it was nearly dark, and strong reinforcements just then reaching the enemy from Harper's Ferry, attacked General Burnside's troops on their left flank, and forced them to retire to a lower line of hills nearer the bridge.

If this important movement had been consummated two hours earlier, a position would have been secured upon the heights from which our batteries might have enfiladed the greater part of the enemy's line, and turned their right and rear. Our victory might have been much more decisive. . . .

The night, however, brought with it grave responsibilities. Whether to renew the attack on the 18th, or to defer it, even with the risk of the enemy's retirement, was the question before me. After a night of anxious deliberations, and a full and careful survey of the situation and condition of our army, and the strength and position of the enemy, I concluded that the success of an attack on the 18th was not certain. I am aware of the fact, that under ordinary circumstances, a general is expected to risk a battle if he has a reasonable prospect of success; but at this critical juncture, I should have had a narrow view of the condition of the country, had I been willing to hazard another battle with less than an absolute assurance of success. At that moment—Virginia lost, Washington menaced, Maryland invaded—the national cause could afford no risks of defeat. One battle lost, and almost all would have been lost.

———

Afraid to risk any more than he already had, McClellan sat still on September 18, as Lee's battered and outnumbered army panted for breath. Perhaps he should not be judged too harshly: the savagery of the day before had taken more than 6,000 lives from the two armies, with 17,000 more lying wounded.

But despite the heavy Union casualties, the Army of Northern Virginia was in still worse shape. Lee's bitter losses (more deeply felt in his smaller force) were compounded by the gains Burnside had made (after much bumbling) on the Confederate right. But Lee remained in place as well, and McClellan refused to follow up his uncoordinated attacks of the 17th. The rebels could not remain long. On the evening of September 18, the Confederates slipped away from the battlefield, and McClellan was content to let them go unhindered by any serious pursuit. For the first time, the Army of Northern Virginia had been defeated—a narrow victory (if not a draw) on the battlefield, but a clear strategic success for the Union. Lee's invincible legions had been turned back at last.

II

IRONCLADS AND RIVERS

THE FIRST NAVAL BATTLES

The blockade of Confederate ports

5

DUEL OF THE IRONCLADS

March 9, 1862

Robert E. Lee's climactic victories during the Seven Days and the second Bull Run campaign won the admiration of the world, but they were almost stillborn. McClellan's intricate plan for shifting more than 100,000 men by sea to the peninsula—the move that set the stage for Lee's triumph—was nearly prevented by a single ship. That ship was the C.S.S. *Virginia*—better known as the *Merrimack*,[1] a U.S. Navy frigate hastily transformed by the rebels into a wheezing, unseaworthy, yet lethal ironclad.

The threat posed by the converted *Merrimack* underscored the importance of the war on the rivers and seacoasts. Though the land battles captured the public's attention, the authorities in both Washington and Richmond understood the need to control the Southern waterways. The major rivers, of course, formed essential arteries for ferrying goods, troops, and supplies—making them at least as important as the railroads. The South was also unusually dependent on oceangoing commerce, despite its weak maritime tradition. Its cotton-and-tobacco agricultural economy relied heavily on exports to Europe, and the Confederate armies needed to import weapons from the armories of England and France. And its hopes for recognition from those powers rested on transatlantic communication. It was possible that victory on the water would bring victory in the war as a whole.

Recognizing this, General Winfield Scott had proposed the famed Anaconda Plan to Lincoln at the beginning of the war—combining a blockade of the Confederacy with a campaign to seize its ports and capture the length of the Mississippi, aiming to split the South in two and squeeze it in a python's grip. Lincoln decided on a direct attack on Richmond, but as the war dragged on the Union proceeded to carry out Scott's plan with an ever-growing fleet of warships.

[1] The *Merrimack* is commonly misspelled with no final "k."

In 1861, however, barely forty Union naval vessels were in commission, and not even a dozen were available to patrol the Southern coasts. Secretary of the Navy Gideon Welles and his energetic Assistant Secretary Gustavus V. Fox acted quickly to buy and build new Union squadrons, but the process took time.

Meanwhile, Confederate Secretary of the Navy Stephen P. Mallory (who had long served as chairman of the Naval Affairs Committee in the U.S. Senate) performed miracles to create a navy where none had existed before. He encouraged the expansion of coastal fortifications, authorized ships to raid Yankee commerce, and began building the revolutionary new ironclad.

In the days before the war erupted, the *Merrimack* (a fairly new vessel) was stationed at the U.S. Navy base at Norfolk, Virginia, which the Confederates quickly captured from the inept commander. Along with hundreds of cannons and invaluable naval supplies, they retrieved the undamaged hull of the partially burned *Merrimack*. Under Mallory's direction, they began converting it to an armored warship, clad in great slabs of almost impenetrable iron. Welles and Fox knew there was not a single ship in the wooden Union fleet that could stand up to the ironclad *Merrimack*. Reluctantly, the naval establishment turned to a crusty Swedish inventor named John Ericsson for an even more advanced ship, one that could be completed in time to give battle to the enemy vessel. The ship's name was the U.S.S. *Monitor*.

As Ericsson drove ahead the construction of his new ship, the conversion of the *Merrimack* neared completion. To command it, Mallory turned to Franklin Buchanan, a hot-tempered former U.S. Navy officer with a remarkable record. He had commanded a warship in the Mexican War, joined Commodore Perry's expedition to Japan, and served as the first superintendent of the U.S. Naval Academy at Annapolis. A native of the border state of Maryland, Buchanan had locked horns with Gideon Welles at the outbreak of war and decided to go south. Now he was to command the *Merrimack*—a jury-rigged vessel with barely functioning engines but still the most powerful warship afloat.

On Saturday, March 8, 1862, Buchanan took the completed *Merrimack*, accompanied by a few wooden gunboats, out into Hampton Roads, the waters at the mouth of the James River east of Richmond. There he attacked five wooden ships of the Union blockade squadron, sinking two and damaging a third (the flagship *Minnesota*), which ran aground. The *Merrimack* retired for the day; it had suffered some damage from the skillful gunfire of the now-sunken *Cumberland*, and the wounded

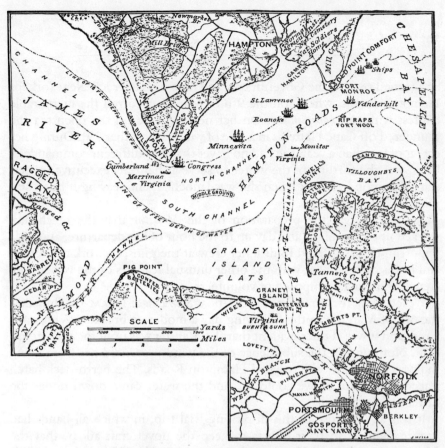

The battle between the Merrimack *(or* Virginia*)*
and the Monitor, *Hampton Roads, March 9, 1862*

Buchanan had to give up command. The next morning, it steamed out to complete the destruction of the Federal squadron. But the previous night, at midnight, the just-completed *Monitor* arrived after surviving a vicious storm. The battle was now between ironclads.

In the *Monitor's* Turret

By S. Dana Greene

The keel of the most famous vessel of modern times, Captain Ericsson's first ironclad, was laid in the shipyard of Thomas F. Rowland, at Greenpoint, Brooklyn, in October 1861, and on the 30th of January, 1862, the novel craft was launched. On the 25th of February, she was commissioned

69

and turned over to the Government, and nine days later left New York for Hampton Roads, where, on the 9th of March, occurred the memorable contest with the *Merrimack*. On her next venture on the open sea she foundered off Cape Hatteras in a gale of wind (December 29). During her career of less than a year, she had no fewer than five different commanders; but it was the fortune of the writer to serve as her only executive officer, standing upon her deck when she was launched, and leaving it but a few minutes before she sank.

So hurried was the preparation of the *Monitor* that the mechanics worked upon her night and day up to the hour of her departure, and little opportunity was offered to drill her crew at the guns, to work the turret, and to become familiar with the other unusual features of the vessel. The crew was, in fact, composed of volunteers. . . .[2]

We left New York in tow of the tug-boat *Seth Low* at 11 A.M. of Thursday, the 6th of March. On the following day a moderate breeze was encountered, and it was at once evident that the *Monitor* was unfit for a sea-going craft. Nothing but the subsidence of the wind prevented her from being shipwrecked before she reached Hampton Roads. The berth-deck hatch leaked in spite of all we could do, and the water came down under the turret like a waterfall. . . .

It was at the close of this dispiriting trial trip, in which all hands had been exhausted in their efforts to keep the novel craft afloat, that the *Monitor* passed Cape Henry at 4 P.M. on Saturday, March 8th. At this point was heard the distant booming of heavy guns, which our captain rightly judged to be an engagement with the *Merrimack*, twenty miles away. He at once ordered the vessel stripped of her sea rig, the turret keyed up, and every preparation made for battle. As we approached Hampton Roads we could see the fine old *Congress* burning brightly, and soon a pilot came on board and told of the arrival of the *Merrimack*, the disaster to the *Cumberland* and the *Congress*, and the dismay of the Union forces. The *Monitor* was pushed with all haste, and reached the *Roanoke* (Captain Marston), anchored in the Roads, at 9 P.M. Worden immediately reported his arrival to Captain Marston, who suggested he should go to the assistance of the *Minnesota*, then aground off Newport News. As no pilot was available, Captain Worden accepted the volunteer services of Acting Master Samuel Howard, who earnestly sought the

---

[2] The commander was Lieutenant John L. Worden, a forty-three-year-old veteran of the navy who had recently run a secret mission through the South to the Federal fleet at Pensacola.

duty. An atmosphere of gloom pervaded the fleet, and the pygmy aspect of the newcomer did not inspire confidence among those who had witnessed the destruction of the day before. Skillfully piloted by Howard, we proceeded on our way, our path illumined by the blaze of the *Congress*. Reaching the *Minnesota*, hard and fast aground, near midnight, we anchored, and Worden reported to Captain Van Brunt. Between 1 and 2 A.M. the *Congress* blew up. . . .

The dreary night dragged slowly on; the officers and crew were up and alert, as to be ready for any emergency. At daylight on Sunday the *Merrimack* and her consorts were discovered at anchor near Sewell's Point. At about half-past seven o'clock the enemy's vessels got under way and steered in the direction of the *Minnesota*. At the same time, the *Monitor* got under way, and her officers and crew took their stations for battle. . . .

The pilot-house of the *Monitor* was situated well forward, near the bow; it was a wrought iron structure, built of logs of iron nine inches thick, bolted through the corners, and covered with an iron plate two inches thick, which was not fastened down, but was kept in place merely by its weight. The sight-holes or slits were made by inserting quarter-inch plates at the corners between the upper sets of logs and the next below. The structure projected four feet above the deck, and was barely large enough inside to hold three men, standing. It presented a flat surface on all sides and on top. The steering-wheel was secured to one of the logs on the front side. The position and shape of the structure should be carefully borne in mind.

Worden took his station in the pilot-house, and by his side were Howard, the pilot, and Peter Williams, quartermaster, who steered the vessel throughout the engagement. My place was in the turret, to work and fight the guns; with me were Stodder and Stimers and sixteen brawny men, eight to each gun. John Stocking, boatswain's mate, and Thomas Lochrane, seaman, were gun-captains. . . .

The physical condition of the officers and men of the two ships at this time was in striking contrast. The *Merrimack* had passed the night quietly near Sewell's Point, her people enjoying rest and sleep, elated by thoughts of the victory they had achieved that day, and cheered by the prospects of another easy victory on the morrow. The *Monitor* had barely escaped shipwreck twice within the last thirty-six hours, and since Friday morning, forty-eight hours before, few if any of those on board had closed their eyes in sleep or had anything to eat but hard bread, as cooking was impossible; she was surrounded by wrecks and disaster, and her efficiency in action had yet to be proved.

Worden lost no time in bringing it to test. Getting his ships under way, he steered direct for the enemy's vessels, in order to meet and engage them as far as possible from the *Minnesota*. As he approached, the wooden vessels quickly turned and left. Our captain, to the "astonishment" of Captain Van Brunt (as he states in his official report), made straight for the *Merrimack*, which had already commenced firing; and when he came within short range, he changed his course so as to come alongside of her, stopped the engine, and gave the order, "Commence firing!" I triced up the port, ran out the gun, and, taking deliberate aim, pulled the lockstring. The *Merrimack* was quick to reply, returning a rattling broadside (for she had ten guns to our two), and the battle fairly began. The turret and other parts of the ship were heavily struck but the shots did not penetrate; the tower was intact, and it continued to revolve. A look of confidence passed over the men's faces, and we believed the *Merrimack* would not repeat the work she had accomplished the day before.

The fight continued with the exchange of broadsides as fast as the guns could be served and at very short range, the distance between the vessels frequently being not more than a few yards. Worden skillfully maneuvered his quick-turning vessel, trying to find some vulnerable point in his adversary. Once he made a dash at her stern, hoping to disable her screw, which he thinks he missed by not more than two feet. Our shots ripped the iron of the *Merrimack*, while the reverberation of her shots against the tower caused anything but a pleasant sensation. While Stodder, who was stationed at the machine which controlled the revolving motion of the turret, was incautiously leaning against the side of the tower, a large shot struck in the vicinity and disabled him. He left the turret and went below, and Stimers, who had assisted him, continued to do the work.

The drawbacks to the position of the pilot-house were soon realized. We could not fire ahead nor within several points of the bow, since the blast from our own guns would have injured the people in the pilot-house, only a few yards off. Keeler and Toffey passed the captain's orders and messages to me, and my inquiries and answers to him, the speaking-tube of the pilot-house to the turret having been broken early in the action. They performed their work with zeal and alacrity, but, both being landsmen, our technical communications sometimes miscarried. The situation was novel: a vessel of war was engaged in desperate combat with a powerful foe; the captain commanding and guiding all, was inclosed in one place, and the executive officer, working and fighting the guns, was shut up in another, and communication between them was difficult and uncertain. . . .

As the engagement continued, the working of the turret was not altogether satisfactory. It was difficult to start it revolving, or, when once started, to stop it, on account of the imperfections of the novel machinery, which was now undergoing its first trial. . . . My only view of the world outside of the tower was over the muzzles of the guns, which cleared the ports by a few inches only. When the guns were run in, the port holes were covered by heavy iron pendulums, pierced with small holes to allow the iron rammer and sponge handles to protrude when they were in use. To hoist these pendulums required the entire gun's crew and vastly increased the work inside the turret.

The effect upon one shut up in a revolving drum is perplexing, and it is not a simple matter to keep the bearings. White marks had been placed upon the stationary deck immediately below the turret to indicate the direction of the starboard and port sides, and the bow and stern, but these marks were obliterated early in the action. I would continually ask the captain, "How does the *Merrimack* bear?" He replied, "On the starboard beam," or "On the port quarter," as the case might be. Then the difficulty was to determine the direction of the starboard beam, or port quarter, or any other bearing. It finally resulted, that when a gun was ready for firing, the turret would be started on its revolving journey in search of the target, and when found it was taken "on the fly," because the turret could not be accurately controlled. Once the *Merrimack* tried to ram us; but Worden avoided the direct impact by the skillful use of the helm, and she struck a glancing blow, which did no damage. At the instant of collision I planted a solid one-hundred-and-eighty-pound solid shot fair and square upon the forward part of her casemate. Had the gun been loaded with thirty pounds of powder, which was the charge subsequently used with similar guns, it is probable that this shot would have penetrated her armor; but the charge being limited to fifteen pounds, in accordance with peremptory orders to that effect from the Navy Department,[3] the shot rebounded without doing any more damage than possibly to start some of the beams of her armor backing.

It is stated by Colonel Wood, of the *Merrimack*, that when the vessel rammed the *Cumberland* her iron ram, or beak, was broken off and left in that vessel. In a letter to me, about two years since, he described this ram as "of cast iron, wedge-shaped, about fifteen hundred pounds in weight, two feet under water, and projecting two and a half feet from the stem." A ram of this description, had it been intact, would have struck the *Monitor* at

[3] This order dated back to an accidental explosion of the earliest model of the guns used in the *Monitor*'s turret.

that part of the upper hull where the armor and backing were thickest. It is very doubtful if, under any headway that the *Merrimack* could have acquired at such short range, this ram could have done any injury to this part of the vessel. . . .

The battle continued at close quarters without apparent damage to either side. After a time, the supply of shot in the turret being exhausted, Worden hauled off for about fifteen minutes to replenish. The serving of the cartridges, weighing but fifteen pounds, was a matter of no difficulty; but the hoisting of the heavy shot was a slow and tedious operation. . . . Worden took advantage of the lull, and passed through the port hole upon the deck outside to get a better view of the situation. He soon renewed the attack, and the contest continued as before. . . .

Soon after noon a shell from the enemy's gun, the muzzle not ten yards distant, struck the forward side of the pilot-house directly in the sight-hole, or slit, and exploded, cracking the second iron log and partly lifting the top, leaving an opening. Worden was standing immediately behind this spot, and received in his face the force of the blow, which partly stunned him, and filling his eyes with powder, utterly blinded him. The injury was known only to those in the pilot-house and its immediate vicinity. The flood of light rushing though the top of the pilot-house, now partly open, caused Worden, blind as he was, to believe that the pilot-house was seriously injured, if not destroyed; he therefore gave orders to put the helm to starboard and "sheer off." Thus the *Monitor* retired temporarily from the action in order to ascertain the extent of the injuries she had received. At the same time Worden sent for me, and leaving Stimers the only officer in the turret, I went forward at once, and found him standing at the foot of the ladder leading to the pilot-house.

He was a ghastly sight, with his eyes closed and the blood apparently rushing from every pore in the upper part of his face. He told me that he was seriously wounded, and directed me to take command. I assisted in leading him to a sofa in his cabin, where he was tenderly cared for by Doctor Logue, and then I assumed command. Blind and suffering as he was, Worden's fortitude never forsook him; he frequently asked from his bed of pain of the progress of affairs, and when told that the *Minnesota* was saved, he said, "Then I can die happy."

When I reached my station in the pilot-house, I found the iron log was fractured and the top partly open; but the steering gear was still intact, and the pilot-house was not totally destroyed, as had been feared. In the confusion of the moment resulting from so serious an injury to the commanding officer, the *Monitor* had been moving without direction. Exactly how much time elapsed from the moment that Worden was wounded until I had reached the pilot-house and completed the examination of the injury at that point, and determined what course to pursue in the damaged condition of the vessel, it is impossible to state; but it could hardly have exceeded twenty minutes at the utmost. During this time the *Merrimack*, which was leaking badly, had started in the direction of the Elizabeth River; and, on taking my station in the pilot-house and turning the vessel's head in the direction of the *Merrimack*, I saw that she was already in retreat. A few shots were fired at the retiring vessel, and she continued on to Norfolk. I returned with the *Monitor* to the side of the *Minnesota*, where preparations were being made to abandon the ship, which was still aground. Shortly afterward Worden was transferred to a tug, and that night he was carried to Washington.

The fight was over. We of the *Monitor* thought, and still think, that we had gained a great victory. This the Confederates have denied. But it has never been denied that the object of the *Merrimack* on the 9th of March was to complete the destruction of the Union fleet in Hampton Roads, and that in this she was completely foiled and driven off by the *Monitor*, nor has it been denied that at the close of the engagement, the *Merrimack* retreated to Norfolk, leaving the *Monitor* in possession of the field.

6

THE FIGHT FOR NEW ORLEANS
April 1862

The battle between the U.S.S. *Monitor* and the old *Merrimack*, now the C.S.S. *Virginia*, was indeed a much-needed victory for the Union. By bottling up the *Merrimack* in Norfolk, the *Monitor* not only saved the *Minnesota* and the rest of the blockading squadron, it cleared the way for the Army of the Potomac to move to the peninsula by sea. McClellan soon captured the rebel base, forcing the Confederates to scuttle the proud ship.

The experience of the *Merrimack*, however, confirmed two things. One was the power of ironclads. Both sides now rushed ahead the construction of armored ships, or the conversion of old wooden ones; the North in particular began to build a fleet of turret-bearing vessels like the *Monitor*. Second, the *Merrimack*'s role in almost undoing McClellan's plans demonstrated the critical importance of controlling the South's waterways. Rivers and oceans, unlike railroads, could not be damaged by enemy raids; they formed permanent highways of transportation.

The most important river of all, of course, was the Mississippi. In the north, where the southern tip of Illinois meets Kentucky and Missouri, the Union army began a campaign to drive down the great river. At the other end, the Yankee navy launched a bold attack that sealed up the Mississippi and captured New Orleans, one of the leading cities (and ports) of the Confederacy. The assault was the brainchild of David D. Porter, and it was carried out under the command of one of the truly legendary officers of the U.S. Navy, David G. Farragut.

The Opening of the Lower Mississippi
By Admiral David D. Porter

The most important event of the War of the Rebellion, with the exception of the fall of Richmond, was the capture of New Orleans and the Forts

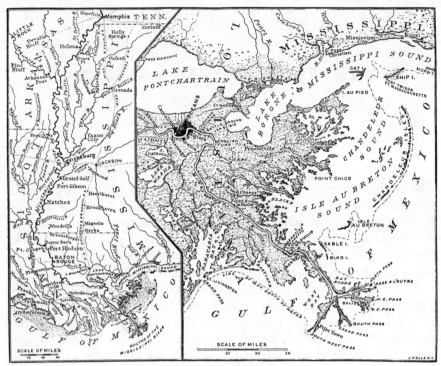

The lower Mississippi, 1862

Jackson and St. Philip, guarding the approach to that city. To appreciate the nature of this victory, it is necessary to have been an actor in it, and to be able to comprehend not only the immediate results to the Union cause, but the whole bearing of the fall of New Orleans on the Civil War. . . .

On the 9th of November, 1861, I arrived at New York with the *Powhatan* and was ordered to report to the Navy Department at Washington, which I did on the 12th. In those days it was not an easy matter for an officer, except one of high rank, to obtain access to the Secretary of the Navy, and I had been waiting nearly all the morning at the door of his office when Senators Grimes and Hale came along and entered into conversation with me concerning my service on the Gulf Coast. During the interview I told the senators of a plan I had formed for the capture of New Orleans, and when I had explained to them how easily it could be accomplished, they expressed surprise that no action had been taken in the matter, and took me in with them at once to see Secretary Welles. I then gave the Secretary, in as few words as possible, my opinion on the importance of capturing New Orleans and my plan for doing so. Mr. Welles listened to me attentively, and when I had finished what I had to say he remarked that the matter should be laid before the President at once; and we all went forthwith to the Executive Mansion, where we were received by Mr. Lincoln.

My plan, which I then stated, was as follows: To fit out a fleet of vessels of war, with which to attack the city, fast steamers drawing not more than eighteen feet of water and carrying about two hundred and fifty heavy guns; also a flotilla of mortar vessels, to be used in case it should be necessary to bombard Forts Jackson and St. Philip before the fleet should attempt to pass them. I also proposed that a body of troops should be kept along in transports to take possession of the city after it had been surrendered to the navy. When I had outlined the proposed movement the President remarked:

"This should have been done sooner. The Mississippi is the backbone of the Rebellion; it is the key to the whole situation. While the Confederates hold it they can obtain supplies of all kinds, and it is a barrier against our forces. . . ."

The Assistant Secretary of the Navy, Mr. G.V. Fox, selected the vessels for the expedition, and to me was assigned the duty of purchasing and fitting out a mortar flotilla, to be composed of twenty large schooners, each mounting one heavy thirteen-inch mortar and at least two long thirty-two pounders. . . .

By the latter part of January [1862] the mortar flotilla got off. In addition to the schooners, it included seven steamers (which were necessary to move the vessels about in the Mississippi River) and a store ship. Seven hundred picked men were enlisted, and twenty-one officers were to command the mortar schooners.

An important duty now devolved upon the Secretary of the Navy, viz. the selection of an officer to command the whole expedition. Mr. Fox and myself had often discussed the matter. He had in his mind several officers of high standing and unimpeachable loyalty, but, as I knew the officers of the navy better than he did, my advice was listened to, and the selection fell upon Captain David Glasgow Farragut.

I had known Farragut ever since I was five years old. He stood high in the navy as an officer and seaman, and possessed such undoubted courage and energy that no possible objection could be made to him. On the first sign of war Farragut, though a Southerner by birth and residence, had shown his loyalty in an outspoken manner. The Southern officers had used every argument to induce him to desert his flag, even going so far as to threaten to detain him by force. His answer to them has become historical: "Mind what I tell you: You fellows will catch the devil before you get through with this business." . . .

Flag-Officer Farragut did not arrive at Ship Island with the *Hartford* until the 20th of February, 1862, he having been detained for some time at Key West, where he commenced arranging his squadron for the difficult task that lay before him.

The vessels which had been assigned to his command soon began to arrive, and by the middle of March the following ships and gunboats had reported: *Hartford*, 25 guns, Commander Richard Wainwright; *Brooklyn*, 24 guns, Captain T.T. Craven; *Richmond*, 26 guns, Commander James Alden; *Mississippi*, 12 guns, Commander Melancton Smith; *Pensacola*, 24 guns, Captain H.W. Merrit; *Cayuga*, 6 guns, Lieutenant-commanding N.B. Harrison; *Oneida*, 9 guns, Commander S.P. Lee; *Varuna*, 10 guns, Commander Charles S. Boggs; *Katahden*, 4 guns, Lieutenant-commanding George N. Ransom; *Wissahickon*, 4 guns, Lieutenant-commanding A.N. Smith; *Winona*, 4 guns, Lieutenant-commanding F.T. Nichols; *Itasca*, 4 guns, Lieutenant-commanding C.H.B. Caldwell; *Pinola*, 4 guns, Lieutenant-commanding Pierce Crosby; *Kennebec*, 4 guns, Lieutenant-commanding John H. Russell; *Iroquois*, 9 guns, Commander John De Camp; *Sciota*, 4 guns, Lieutenant-commanding Edward Donaldson. Total guns, 177 [sic]. . . .

On the 18th of March all the mortar schooners crossed the [sand] bar at Pass a l'Outre, towed by the steamers *Harriet Lane*, *Owasco*, *Westfield*, and *Clifton*. They were ordered by Farragut to proceed to Southwest Pass.

As yet the only vessels that had crossed the bar were the *Hartford* and *Brooklyn*. The Navy Department had made a mistake in sending vessels of too great draught of water, such as the *Colorado*, *Pensacola*, and *Mississippi*. The two latter vessels succeeded in crossing with great difficulty, but the whole fleet was delayed at least twelve days.[4]

The first act of Farragut was to send Captain Henry H. Bell, his chief-of-staff, up the river with the steamers *Kennebec* and *Wissahickon*, to ascertain, if possible, what preparations had been made by the enemy to prevent the passage of the forts. This officer reported that "the obstructions seemed formidable. Eight hulks were moored in line across the river, with heavy chains extending from one to the other. Rafts of logs were also used, and the passage between the forts was thus entirely closed."

---

[4] Porter himself eventually directed operations for getting the ships over the sandbar at the river's mouth; he suspected the local pilots had intentionally failed.

The Confederates had lost no time in strengthening their defenses. They had been working night and day ever since the expedition was planned by the Federal Government. Forts Jackson and St. Philip were two strong defenses on each side of the river, the former on the west bank and the latter in the east. . . . Extending from [Fort Jackson] down the river was a water battery, containing two large rifled guns, one ten-inch and one nine-inch columbiad, and three thirty-two pounders on the outer curtain. This was a very formidable part of the defenses, its heavy guns having a commanding range down the river. . . .

In addition to the defenses of the forts, the Confederates had worked with great diligence to improvise a fleet of men-of-war, using for this purpose a number of heavy tugs, that had been employed in towing vessels up and down the river, and some merchant steamers. These, with the ram *Manassas* and the ironclad *Louisiana*, made in all twelve vessels. The whole naval force was nominally under the control of Commander John K. Mitchell, C.S.N.

The ironclad *Louisiana* mounted sixteen heavy guns, with a crew of two hundred men. She was a powerful vessel, almost impervious to shot, and was fitted with a shot-proof gallery from which her sharp shooters could fire at the enemy with great effect. Her machinery was not completed, however, and during the passage of the Union fleet she was secured to the riverbank and could only use the broadside and four of her stern guns. . . . Also the *McRae*, Lieutenant Thómas D. Huger, a sea-going steamer mounting six thirty-two pounders and one nine-inch shell gun; steamer *Jackson*, Lieutenant F. B. Renshaw, mounting two thirty-two pounders; ironclad ram *Manassas*, Lieutenant A.F. Warley, mounting one thirty-two pounder (in the bow); and two launches, mounting each one howitzer. Also, the following converted sea-steamers had been converted into Louisiana State gunboats, with pine and cotton barricades to protect the machinery and boilers: The *Governor Moore*, Commander Beverly Kennon, two thirty-two pounder rifled guns, and the *General Quitman*, Captain Grant, two thirty-two pounders. . . .

The Confederate fleet mounted, all told, thirty-nine guns, all but two of them being thirty-two pounders, and one fourth of these rifled.

It is thus seen that our wooden vessels, which passed the forts carrying 177 guns, had arrayed against them 128 guns in strongly built works, and 39 guns on board of partly armored vessels.

In addition to the above-mentioned defenses, Commodore Mitchell had at his command a number of fire rafts (long flatboats filled with pine knots, etc.) which were expected to do good service, either by throwing

the Union fleet into confusion or by furnishing light to the gunners in the
forts. On comparing the Confederate defenses with the attacking force of
the Union fleet, it will be seen that the odds were strongly in favor of the
former. It is generally conceded by military men that one gun in a fort is
about equal to five on board of a wooden ship, especially when, in this case,
the forces afloat are obliged to contend against a three-and-a-half-knot
current in a channel obstructed by chains and fire rafts. . . .

Having finished with the preliminary work, on the 10th of April Farragut
moved up with his fleet to within three miles of the forts, and informed me
that I could commence the bombardment as soon as I was ready. The ships
all anchored as they came up, but not in very good order, which led to
some complications.

The place which I had selected for the first and third divisions of the
mortar vessels was under the lee of a thick wood on the right bank of the
river, which presented in the direction of the fort an almost impenetrable
mass. The forts could be plainly seen from the mastheads of the mortar
schooners, which had been so covered with brush that the Confederate
gunners could not distinguish them from the trees. . . .

The vessels now being in position, the signal was given to open fire, and
on the morning of the 18th of April the bombardment fairly commenced,
each mortar vessel having orders to fire once in ten minutes.

The moment that the mortars belched forth their shells, both Jackson
and St. Philip replied with great fury; but it was some time before they
could obtain our range, as we were well concealed behind our natural
rampart. Their fire was rapid, and, finding that it was becoming rather hot,
I sent Lieutenant-commanding Guest up to the head of the line to open
fire on the forts with his eleven-inch pivot. This position he maintained for
one hour and fifty minutes, and only abandoned it to fill up with ammunition. In the meantime the mortars on the left bank were doing splendid
work, though suffering considerably from the enemy's fire. I went on
board the vessels of this division to see how they were getting on, and
found them so cut up that I considered it necessary to remove them, with
Farragut's permission, to the opposite shore, under cover of the trees, near
the other vessels, which had suffered but little. They held their position,
however, until sundown, when the enemy ceased firing.

At five o'clock in the evening Fort Jackson was seen to be on fire, and, as
the flames spread rapidly, the Confederates soon left their guns. There
were many conjectures among the officers of the fleet as to what was
burning. Some thought it was a fire raft, and I was inclined to this opinion
myself until I had pulled up the river in a boat and, by the aid of a night

glass, convinced myself that the fort itself was in flames. This fact was at once reported to Farragut.

At nightfall the crews of the mortar vessels were completely exhausted; but when it became known that every shell was falling inside of the fort, they redoubled their exertions and increased the rapidity of their fire to a shell every five minutes, or in all two hundred and forty shells an hour. During the night, in order to allow the men to rest, we slackened our fire, and only sent a shell once every half hour. That ended the first day's bombardment, which was more effective than that of any other day during the siege. Had the fleet been ready to move, it could have passed up at this time with little or no difficulty.

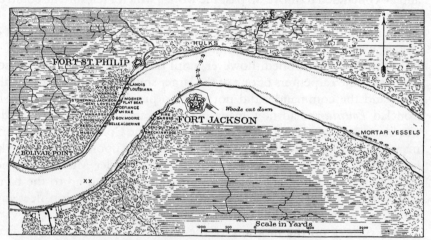

The Confederate defenses below New Orleans

Next morning the bombardment was renewed and continued night and day until the end. . . .

On the night of the 20th an expedition was fitted out for the purpose of breaking the chain which was supposed to extend from one shore to the other. Two steamers, the *Pinola*, Lieutenant Crosby, and *Itasca*, Lieutenant Caldwell, were detailed for the purpose, and placed under the direction of Captain Bell, chief-of-staff. Although the attempt was made under cover of darkness, the sharp eyes of the Confederate gunners soon discovered their enemies, and the whole fire of Fort Jackson was concentrated upon them. I had been informed of the intended movement by Farragut, so was ready to redouble the fire of the mortars at the proper time with good effect. In Farragut's words: "Commander Porter, however, kept up such a tremendous fire on them from the mortars that the enemy's shot did the gunboats no injury, and the cable was separated and their connection broken sufficiently to pass through on the left bank of the river."

The work of the mortar fleet was now nearly over. We had kept up a heavy fire night and day for nearly five days—about 2,800 shells every twenty-four hours; in all about 16,800 shells. The men were nearly worn out for want of sleep and rest. The ammunition was giving out, one of the schooners was sunk, and although the rest had received little actual damage from the enemy's shot, they were badly shaken up by the concussion of the mortars.

On the 23d instant I represented the state of affairs to the flag-officer and he concluded to move on past the works, which I felt sure he could do with but little loss to his squadron. He recognized the importance of making an immediate attack, and called a council of the commanders of vessels, which resulted in a determination to pass the forts that night. The movement was postponed, however, until the next morning, the reason being that the carpenters of one of the larger ships were at work down the river, and the commander did not want to proceed without them. The ironclad *Louisiana* had now made her appearance, and her commander was being strongly urged by General Duncan [the Confederate land commander] to sail down below the forts and open fire upon the fleet with his heavy rifled guns. . . . Fortunately for us, Commander Mitchell was not equal to the occasion, and the *Louisiana* remained tied up to the bank, where she could not obstruct the river or throw the Union fleet into confusion while passing the forts. . . .

Two o'clock on the morning of the 24th [of April] instant was fixed upon as the time for the fleet to start, and Flag-Officer Farragut had previously given the necessary orders to the commanders of vessels, instructing them to prepare their ships for action by sending down their light spars, painting their hulls mud-color, etc.; also to hang their chain cables over the sides abreast the engines, as a protection against the enemy's shot. . . .

Farragut's first plan was to lead the fleet with his flagship, the *Hartford*, to be closely followed by the *Brooklyn*, *Richmond*, *Pensacola*, and *Mississippi*, thinking it well to have his heavy vessels in the van where they could immediately crush any naval force that might appear against them. This plan was a better one than that afterwards adopted [to have the smaller gunboats lead], but he was induced to change the order of his column by the senior commanders of the fleet, who represented to him that it was unwise for the commander-in-chief to take the brunt of the battle. . . .

The mortar flotilla steamers under my command were directed to move up before the fleet weighed anchor, and to be ready to engage the water batteries of Fort Jackson as the fleet massed. These batteries mounted some of the heaviest guns in the Confederate defenses, and were depended upon to do efficient work. . . .

At two o'clock on the morning of April 24th all the Union vessels began to heave up their anchors. It was a still, clear night, and the click of the capstans, with the grating of the chain cables, as they passed through the hawse holes, made a great noise, which we feared would serve as a warning to our enemies. This conjecture proved to be correct, for the Confederates were on the alert as far as circumstances would admit, to meet the invaders. One fact only was in our favor, and this was the division of their forces under three different heads, which prevented the unanimity of action. In every other respect the odds were against us. . . .

The entire fleet did not get fully under way until half-past two A.M. The current was strong, and although the ships proceeded as rapidly as their steam power would permit, our leading vessel, the *Cayuga*, did not get under fire until a quarter of three o'clock, when both Jackson and St. Philip opened on her at the same moment. Five steamers of the mortar flotilla took their position below the water battery of Fort Jackson, at a distance of less than two hundred yards, and, pouring in grape, canister, and shrapnel, kept down the fire of that battery. The mortars opened at the same moment with great fury, and the action commenced in earnest.

Captain Bailey, in the *Cayuga*, followed by the other vessels of his division in compact order, passed the line of obstructions without difficulty. He had no sooner attained this point, however, than he was obliged to face the guns of Fort St. Philip, which did him some damage before he was able to fire a shot in return. He kept steadily on, however, and, as soon as his guns could be brought to bear, poured in grape and canister with good effect and passed safely above. He was met by the enemy's gunboats, and, although he was beset by several large steamers at the same time, he succeeded in driving them off. The *Oneida* and *Varuna* came to the support of their leader, and by the rapid fire of their heavy guns soon dispersed the enemy's flotilla. This was more congenial work for our men and officers than that through which they had just passed, and it was soon evident that the coolness and discipline of our navy gave it a great advantage over the fleet of the enemy. Bailey dashed on up the river, followed by his division, firing into everything they met; and soon after the head of the flag-officer's division [the center division] had passed the forts, most of the river craft were disabled, and the battle was virtually won. This was evident even to [Confederate] Lieutenant-Colonel Higgins, who, when he saw our large ships pass by, exclaimed, "Better go to cover, boys; our cake is all dough!"

In the meantime the *Varuna* (Commander Boggs), being a swift vessel, passed ahead of the other ships in the division, and pushed on up the river after the fleeing enemy, until he found himself right in the midst of them. The Confederates, supposing in the dark that the *Varuna* was one of their own vessels, did not attack her until Commander Boggs made himself known by delivering his fire right and left. One shot exploded the boiler of a large steamer crowded with troops, and she drifted ashore; three other vessels were driven ashore in flames. At daylight the *Varuna* was attacked by the *Governor Moore*, a powerful steamer, fitted as a ram, and commanded by Lieutenant Beverly Kennon, late of the U.S. Navy. This vessel raked the *Varuna* with her bow gun along the port gangway, killing five or six men; and while the Union vessel was gallantly returning this fire, her side was pierced below the waterline by the iron prow of the ram *Stonewall Jackson*. The Confederate backed off and struck again in the same place, the *Varuna* at the same moment punished her severely with grape and canister from her eight-inch guns, and finally drove her out of action in a disabled condition and in flames. But the career of the *Varuna* was ended; she began to fill rapidly, and her gallant commander was obliged to run her into shoal water, where she soon went to the bottom. Captain Lee, of the *Oneida*, seeing that his companion needed assistance, went to his relief, and rescued the officers and men of the *Varuna*. The two Confederate rams were set on fire by their crews and abandoned. Great gallantry was displayed on both sides during the conflict of these smaller steamers, which really bore the brunt of the battle, and the Union commanders showed great skill in managing their vessels.

Bailey's division may be said to have swept everything before it. The *Pensacola*, with her heavy batteries, drove the men from the guns of Fort St. Philip, and made it easier for the ships astern to get by. Fort St. Philip had not been at all damaged by the mortars, as it was virtually beyond our reach, and it was from the guns of that work that our ships received the greatest injury.

As most of the vessels of Bailey's division swept past the turn above the forts, Farragut came upon the scene with the *Hartford* and *Brooklyn*. The other ship of Farragut's division, the *Richmond*, Commander James Alden, got out of the line and passed up on the west side of the river, near where I was engaged with the mortar steamers in silencing the water batteries of Fort Jackson. At this moment the Confederates in Fort Jackson had nearly all been driven from their guns by bombs from the mortar boats and the grape and canister from the steamers. I hailed Alden, and told him to pass close in the fort and in the eddy, and he would receive little damage. He followed this advice, and passed by very comfortably.

By this time the river had been illuminated by two fire rafts, and everything could be seen as by light of day. I could see every ship and gunboat as she passed up as plainly as possible, and noted all their positions.

It would be a difficult undertaking at any time to keep a long line of vessels in compact order when ascending a crooked channel against a three-and-a-half-knot current, and our commanders found it to be especially so under the present trying circumstances. One of them, the *Iroquois*, Commander De Camp, as gallant an officer as ever lived, got out of line and passed up ahead of her consorts; but De Camp made good use of his opportunity, by engaging and driving off the ram and the gunboat *McRae*, which attacked him as soon as he had passed Fort Jackson. The *McRae* was disabled, and her commander (Huger) mortally wounded. The *Iroquois* was much cut up by Fort St. Philip and the gunboats, but did not receive a single shot from Fort Jackson, although passing within fifty yards of it.

While the events above mentioned were taking place, Farragut had engaged Fort St. Philip at close quarters with his heavy ships, and driven the men away from their guns. He was passing on up the river, when his flagship was threatened by a new and formidable adversary. A fire raft in full blaze was seen coming down the river, guided towards the *Hartford* by a tugboat, the *Mosher*. It seemed impossible to avoid this danger, and as the helm was put to port in the attempt to do so, the flagship ran up on a shoal. While in this position the fire raft was pushed against her, and in a minute she was enveloped in flames half-way up to her tops, and was in a condition of great peril. The fire department was at once called away, and while the *Hartford*'s batteries kept up the fight with Fort St. Philip, the flames were extinguished and the vessel backed off the shoal into deep water—a result due to the coolness of her commander and the good discipline of her men. While the *Hartford* was in this perilous position, and her entire destruction threatened, Farragut showed all the qualities of a great commander. He walked up and down the poop as coolly as though on dress-parade, while Commander Wainwright directed the firemen in putting out the flames. At times the flames would rush through the ports, and almost drive the men away from the guns.

"Don't flinch from that fire, boys," sang out Farragut; "there's a hotter fire than that for those who don't do their duty! Give that rascally little tug a shot, and don't let her go off with a whole coat!"

While passing the forts the *Hartford* was struck thirty-two times in hull and rigging, and had three men killed and ten wounded.

The *Brooklyn*, Captain Thomas T. Craven, followed as close after the flagship as the blinding smoke from guns and fire rafts would admit, and the garrison of the fort was again driven to cover by the fire of her heavy battery. She passed on with severe punishment, and was immediately attacked by the most powerful vessel in the Confederate fleet, excepting the *Louisiana*—the ram *Manassas*, commanded by Lieutenant Warley, a gallant young officer, of the old service. The first blow that the *Manassas* struck the *Brooklyn* did but little apparent injury, and the ram backed off and struck her again in the same place; but the chain armor on the *Brooklyn*'s side received the blow, and her adversary slid off in the dark to seek other prey. (It must be remembered that these scenes were being enacted on a dark night, and in an atmosphere filled with a dense smoke through which our commanders had to grope their way, guided only by the flashes of the guns in the forts and the fitful light of burning vessels and rafts.) The *Brooklyn* was next attacked by a large steamer, which received her broadside at the distance of twenty yards, and drifted out of the action in flames. Notwithstanding the heavy fire which the *Brooklyn* had gone through, she was only struck seventeen times in the hull. She lost nine men killed and twenty-six wounded.

When our large ships had passed the forts, the affair was virtually over. Had they all been near the head of the column, the enemy would have been crushed at once, and the flagship would have passed up almost unhurt. As it was, the *Hartford* was more exposed and imperiled than any of her consorts, and that at a time when, if anything had happened to the commander-in-chief, the fleet would have been thrown into confusion.

The forts had been so thoroughly silenced by the ships' guns and mortars that when Captain Bell came along in the little *Sciota*, at the head of the third division, he passed by nearly unharmed. . . .

I must refer here[5] to a gallant affair which took place between the *Mississippi* and the ram *Manassas*. The latter vessel proved the most troublesome of the Confederate fleet. She had rammed the *Brooklyn*, the *Hartford*, and the *Mississippi* at different times during the action.

---

[5] This paragraph and the next two have been moved ahead of the last paragraph in this section for narrative continuity.

At early daylight, as the vessels approached the quarantine above the forts, the *Manassas* was seen coming up the river as rapidly as her steam would allow.

As she approached the fleet, Flag-Officer Farragut directed Commander Smith in the *Mississippi* to turn and run her down. The order was instantly obeyed by the *Mississippi*, turning and going at the ram at full speed; but when it was expected to see the *Manassas* annihilated, the vessels being within fifty yards of each other, the ram put her helm hard-a-port, dodged the *Mississippi*, and ran ashore, where her crew deserted her. Commander Smith set fire to her, and then so riddled her with shot that she was dislodged from the bank and drifted below the forts, where she blew up and was sunk. . . .

While engaged on [my] duty, I had an excellent opportunity of witnessing the movements of Farragut's fleet, and by the aid of powerful night glasses, I could almost distinguish persons on the vessels. The whole scene looked like a beautiful panorama. From almost perfect silence—the steamers moving slowly through the water like phantom ships—one incessant roar of heavy cannon commenced, the Confederate forts and gunboats opening together on the head of our line as it came within range. The Union vessels returned the fire as they came up, and soon the hundred and seventy guns of our fleet joined in the thunder, which seemed to shake the very earth. A lurid glare was thrown over the scene by the burning rafts, and, as the bombshells crossed each other and exploded in the air, it seemed as if a battle were taking place in the heavens as well as on the earth. It all ended as suddenly as it had commenced. In one hour and ten minutes after the vessels of the fleet had weighed anchor, the affair was virtually over, and Farragut was pushing on towards New Orleans, where he was soon to crush the last hope of rebellion in that quarter by opening the way for the advance of the Union army.

III

THE UNION BREAKTHROUGH

FROM SHILOH TO VICKSBURG

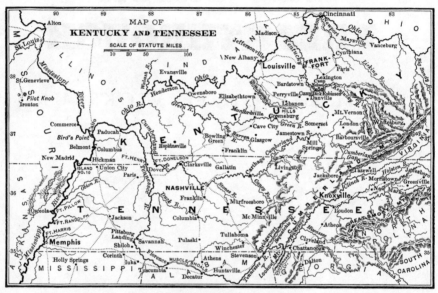

The Western Theater, early 1862

7

THE BATTLE OF SHILOH

April 6–7, 1862

One unavoidable fact of geography shaped the war in the West: the Mississippi River. From its junction with the Ohio at Cairo, Illinois, down to where it emptied into the Gulf, the Mississippi formed a vulnerable fault line running through the Confederacy, separating Texas, Arkansas, and western Louisiana from the rest of the South. David Farragut's victory below New Orleans hammered a wedge into this fissure; the central problem for the Union army, as it prepared to move south from Cairo, was how to crack it open all the way, and cut the Confederacy in two.

As in the East, however, Lincoln intervened in the military planning for political reasons. In the West, of course, the army had no capital to protect, or to capture; but there was a large pro-Union population in the mountains of east Tennessee, and Lincoln wanted them liberated. This meant the army had to fight two major campaigns simultaneously—one down the Mississippi, the other aimed at the rail junction of Chattanooga, in southeastern Tennessee. As 1862 began, this second effort was taken over by General Don Carlos Buell, whose subordinate General George H. Thomas barely managed to force the rebels out of Kentucky before winter shut down his campaign.

Meanwhile, the war in the Mississippi Valley took shape under the initiative of another set of subordinate generals—three of whom would rise to command of the key Union armies that brought the Confederacy to its knees at war's end: Ulysses S. Grant, William T. Sherman, and Philip H. Sheridan.

Of the three, only Sherman was known and respected in military circles when the war began—but even he had suffered humiliating failure as commander in Kentucky, where he was posted after First Bull Run. Grant, in particular, was almost unknown when the fighting broke out. After graduating from West Point in obscurity, he had won recognition as

93

a junior officer in Mexico, but later resigned from the army amid rumors of a drinking problem. His life between the Mexican and Civil Wars is hard to describe as better than a modest failure. But when he obtained a command in 1861, through the intervention of an influential friend, he soon proved to be precisely the man needed to lead the Union to victory.

Sherman was well-read, imaginative, the member of an influential family (his brother was a U.S. senator); Sheridan—who rose to prominence much later than the other two men—was a remarkable fighting leader, possessing unsurpassed battlefield charisma and energy; but Grant was a man frequently underestimated, both by contemporaries and historians. He eventually became famous for his quiet, unpretentious manner and the simple private's uniform he always wore (often spattered with mud), with only a pair of shoulder-straps to indicate his rank. Grant was no military scholar, unlike his friend Sherman, who had been head of a military academy in Louisiana. But he possessed profound common sense, deep insight into the condition of men in battle, an utterly calm disposition, and an overwhelming determination to see the war through to victory. As James McPherson has written, "He had discovered that his laconic, informal, commonsense manner inspired respect and obedience from his men. Unlike so many other commanders, Grant rarely clamored for reinforcements, rarely complained, rarely quarreled with associates, but went ahead and did the job with the resources at hand."

Grant's laconic manner concealed profound gifts of generalship. No matter how great the crisis, he always maintained a complete grip on command and a keen understanding of events amid the chaos of the battlefield. Military historian John Keegan, in a study of Grant's leadership at the battle of Shiloh, points out a telling trait that Grant shared with many other great commanders in history: his written orders and messages in combat possessed an almost perfect clarity and simplicity. Such qualities are easily overlooked, but they reveal a calm, sharp mind and a confidence lacking in McClellan and so many others. Given the chance, Grant would outshine every other Union general the war produced.

His chance came in February 1862. At the time, McClellan sat motionless with the Army of the Potomac; Buell was frozen in by the mountain winter; and in Arkansas, the Confederates were preparing to invade Union-held Missouri. Grant, however, joined forces with Flag-Officer Andrew H. Foote (of the navy's western riverboat flotilla) to break open the Confederate defensive line in west Tennessee.

Apart from the Mississippi itself, which was strongly guarded, the Tennessee and Cumberland rivers offered the key strategic routes for the Union army to follow as it drove south. Near the Kentucky border, where these two streams draw close together, the Confederates had built Forts Henry and Donelson to control these critical rivers. Grant, then a brigadier general, took advantage of the indecisive leadership of Confederate General Albert Sidney Johnston, and captured the forts (and tens of thousands of prisoners) with the aid of Foote's gunboats. This double victory opened the Tennessee River to the Union army and navy, offering a highway down to the northern borders of Mississippi and Alabama, and threatening to unhinge several Confederate strongpoints on the Mississippi.

Grant's commanding officer, General Henry W. Halleck (a balding scholar of military science and history nicknamed "Old Brains"), wasted no time in reaping the glory of the victory. To follow it up, he ordered Grant to take his force, the Army of the Tennessee, down the Tennessee River to Pittsburg Landing, not far below the town of Savannah. There Grant was to unite with Buell's army, then marching southwest through Nashville and central Tennessee. Once the armies were united, Halleck wanted to personally take command and capture the critical railway junction of Corinth, Mississippi.

The Confederates, however, had other ideas. Under a plan drawn up by General P. G. T. Beauregard (transferred to the West by Jefferson Davis, who disliked him), Albert Sidney Johnston ordered some 42,000 men from three distant detachments to unite at Corinth. With this newly concentrated army, the rebels planned to smash Grant's force at Pittsburg Landing before Buell could arrive. The plan had great promise, taking advantage of the Confederates' interior lines and the temporary division in the Union forces. Johnson and Beauregard had other factors in their favor as well: most men of the Army of the Tennessee were utterly inexperienced in military ways, let alone fighting; in addition, Grant and his divisional commanders had failed to order the troops to build defensive trenches and breastworks, which later became standard practice for an army at rest. At this point in the war, however, common soldiers did not understand the importance of fieldworks, and they carelessly pitched their tents near a log church called Shiloh, not far from where the rebels were assembling for their attack. But the Confederates faced one tremendous obstacle in the approaching battle: the unshakeable generalship of U. S. Grant, whose calm determination would turn the initial tragedy into a signal victory for the Union army.

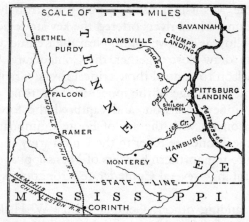

Region of the Shiloh Campaign, March and April 1862

The Battle of Shiloh
By General U.S. Grant

When I reassumed command on the seventeenth of March[1] I found the army divided, while one division was at Crump's Landing on the west bank about four miles higher up, and the remainder at Pittsburg Landing five miles above [south or upriver of] Crump's. The enemy was in force at Corinth, the junction of the two most important railroads in the Mississippi valley—one connecting Memphis and the Mississippi River with the East, and the other leading south to all the cotton states. Still another railroad connects Corinth with Jackson, in west Tennessee. If we obtained possession of Corinth the enemy would have no railroad for the transportation of armies or supplies until that running east from Vicksburg was reached. It was the great strategic position at the West between the Tennessee and the Mississippi rivers and between Nashville and Vicksburg.

I at once put all the troops at Savannah in motion for Pittsburg Landing, knowing that the enemy was fortifying at Corinth and collecting an army there under Johnston. It was my expectation to march against that army as soon as Buell, who had been ordered to reinforce me with the Army of the

[1] Grant writes that Halleck had telegraphed him, asking for a report on his troop strength; but Grant did not get the message, so Halleck presumed insubordination and suspended his command.

Ohio, should arrive; and the west bank of the river was the place to start from. Pittsburg is only about twenty miles from Corinth, and Hamburg Landing, four miles further up the river, is a mile or two nearer. I had not been in command long before I selected Hamburg as the place to put the Army of the Ohio when it arrived. The roads from Pittsburg and Hamburg to Corinth converge some eight miles out. This disposition of the troops would have given additional roads to march over when the advance commenced, within supporting distance of each other.

On the seventeenth of March the army on the Tennessee River consisted of five divisions, commanded respectively by Generals C.F. Smith, McClernand, L. Wallace, Hurlbut, and Sherman. General W.H.L. Wallace was temporarily in command of Smith's division, General Smith . . . being confined to his bed. Reinforcements were arriving daily and as they came up they were organized, first into brigades, and then into a division, and the command went to General Prentiss, who had been ordered to report to me. General Buell was on his way from Nashville with 40,000 veterans. On the nineteenth of March he was at Columbia, Tennessee, eighty-five miles from Pittsburg. When all reinforcements should have arrived I expected to take the initiative by marching on Corinth, and had no expectation of needing fortifications, though this subject came into consideration. McPherson, my only military engineer, was directed to lay out a line to entrench. He did so, but reported that it would have to be made in rear of the line of encampment as it then ran. The new line, while it would be nearer the river, was yet too far away from the Tennessee, or even from the creeks, to be easily supplied with water, and in case of attack these creeks would be in the hands of the enemy. The fact is, I regarded the campaign we were engaged in as an offensive one and had no idea that the enemy would leave strong entrenchments to take the initiative when he knew he would be attacked where he was if he remained. This view, however, did not prevent every precaution being taken and every effort made to keep advised of all movements of the enemy.

Johnston's cavalry meanwhile had been well out towards our front, and occasional encounters occurred between it and our outposts. On the first of April this cavalry became bold and approached our lines, showing that an advance of some kind was contemplated. On the second Johnson left Corinth in force to attack my army. On the fourth his cavalry dashed down and captured a small picket guard of six or seven men, stationed some five miles out from Pittsburg on the Corinth road. Colonel Buckland sent relief to the guard at once and soon followed with an entire regiment, and General Sherman followed Buckland taking the remainder of the brigade.

The pursuit was kept up for some three miles beyond the point where the picket guard had been captured, and after nightfall General Sherman returned to camp and reported to me by letter what had occurred.

At this time a large body of the enemy was hovering to the west of us, along the line of the Mobile and Ohio railroad. My apprehension was much greater for the safety of Crump's Landing than it was for Pittsburg. I had no apprehension that the enemy could really capture either place. But I feared that it was possible that he might make a rapid dash upon Crump's and destroy our transports and stores, most of which were kept at that point, and then retreat before Wallace could be reinforced. Lew. Wallace's position I regarded as so well chosen that he was not removed.

At this time I generally spent the day at Pittsburg and returned to Savannah in the evening. I was intending to remove my headquarters to Pittsburg, but Buell was expected daily and would come in at Savannah. I remained at this point, therefore, a few days longer than I otherwise should have done, in order to meet him on his arrival. The skirmishing in our front, however, had been so continuous from about the third of April that I did not leave Pittsburg each night until an hour when I felt there would be no further danger before the morning.

On Friday the fourth, the day of Buckland's advance, I was very much injured by my horse falling with me, and on me, while I was trying to get to the front where firing had been heard. The night was one of impenetrable darkness, with rain pouring down in torrents, nothing was visible to the eye except as revealed by the frequent flashes of lightning. Under these circumstances I had to trust to the horse, without guidance, to keep the road. I had not gone far, however, when I met General W.H.L. Wallace and Colonel (afterwards General) McPherson coming from the direction of the front. They said all was quiet so far as the enemy was concerned. On the way back to the boat my horse's feet slipped from under him, and he fell with my leg under his body. The extreme softness of the ground, from the excessive rains of the few preceding days, no doubt saved me from a severe injury and protracted lameness. As it was, my ankle was very much injured, so much so that my boot had to be cut off. For two or three days after I was unable to walk except with crutches.

On the fifth General Nelson, with a division of Buell's army, arrived at Savannah and I ordered him to move up the east bank of the river, to be in a position where he could be ferried over to Crump's Landing or Pittsburg as occasion required. I had learned that General Buell himself would be at Savannah the next day, and desired to meet me on his arrival. Affairs at Pittsburg Landing had been such for several days that I did not want to be away during the day. I determined, therefore, to take a very early breakfast and ride out to meet Buell, and thus save time. He had arrived on the evening of the fifth, but had not advised me of the fact and I was not aware of it until some time after. While I was at breakfast, however, heavy firing was heard in the direction of Pittsburg Landing, and I hastened there, sending a hurried note to Buell informing him of the reason why I could not meet him at Savannah. On the way up the river I directed the dispatch-boat to run in close to Crump's Landing, so that I could communicate with General Lew. Wallace. I found him waiting on a boat apparently expecting to see me, and I directed him to get his troops in line ready to execute any orders he might receive. He replied that his troops were already under arms and prepared to move.

Up to that time I had felt by no means certain that Crump's Landing might not be the point of attack. On reaching the front, however, about eight A.M., I found that the attack on Pittsburg was unmistakable, and that nothing more than a small guard, to protect our transports and stores, was needed at Crump's. Captain Baxter, a quartermaster on my staff, was accordingly directed to go back and order General Wallace to march

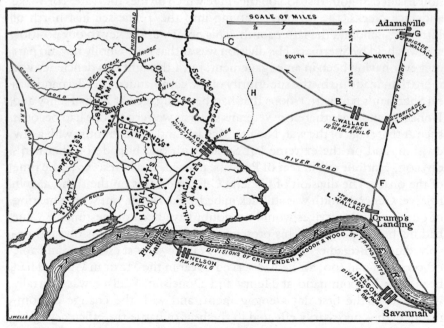

The Battle of Shiloh: initial Union positions and routes of reinforcements,
April 6–7, 1862

immediately to Pittsburg by the road nearest the river. Captain Baxter made a memorandum of the order. About 1 P.M., not hearing from Wallace and being much in need of reinforcements, I sent two more of my staff, Colonel McPherson and Captain Rowley, to bring him up with his division. They reported finding him marching towards Purdy, Bethel, or some point west from the river, and farther from Pittsburg by several miles than when he started. . . . Wallace did not arrive in time to take part in the first day's fight. General Wallace has since claimed that the order delivered to him by Captain Baxter was simply to join the right of the army, and that the road over which he marched would have taken him to the road from Pittsburg to Purdy where it crosses Owl Creek on the right of Sherman; but this is not where I had ordered him nor where I wanted him to go.

I never could see and do not see now why any order was necessary further than to direct him to come to Pittsburg Landing, without specifying by what route. His was one of three veteran divisions that had been in battle, and its absence was severely felt . . .

Some two or three miles from Pittsburg Landing was a log meeting house called Shiloh. It stood on the ridge which divides the waters of Snake and Lick creeks, the former emptying into the Tennessee just north of Pittsburg Landing, the latter south. This point was the key to our position and was held by Sherman. His division was at that time wholly raw, no part of it ever having been in an engagement; but I thought this deficiency was more than made up by the superiority of the commander. McClernand was on Sherman's left, with troops that had been engaged at Forts Henry and Donelson and were therefore veterans so far as western troops had become such at that stage of the war. Next to McClernand came Prentiss with a raw division, and on the extreme left Stuart with one brigade of Sherman's division. Hurlbut was in rear of Prentiss, massed, and in reserve at the time of the onset. The division of General C.F. Smith was on the right, also in reserve. General Smith was still sick in bed at Savannah, but within hearing of our guns. His services would no doubt have been of inestimable value had his health permitted his presence. The command of his division devolved upon Brigadier-General W.H.L. Wallace, a most estimable and able officer; a veteran too, for he had served a year in the Mexican War and had been with his command at Henry and Donelson. Wallace was mortally wounded in the first day's engagement, and with the change of commanders thus necessarily effected in the heat of battle the efficiency of his division was much weakened.

The position of our troops made a continuous line from Lick Creek on the left to Owl Creek, a branch of Snake Creek, on the right, facing nearly south and possibly a little west. The water in all these streams was very high at the time and contributed to protect our flanks. The enemy was compelled, therefore, to attack directly in our front. This he did with great vigor, inflicting heavy losses on the National side, but suffering much heavier on his own.

The Confederate assaults were made with such a disregard of losses on their own side that our line of tents soon fell into their hands. The ground on which the battle was fought was undulating, heavily timbered with scattered clearings, the woods giving some protection to the troops on both sides. There was also considerable underbrush. A number of attempts were made by the enemy to turn our right flank, where Sherman was posted, but every effort was repulsed with heavy loss. But the front attack was kept up so vigorously that, to prevent the success of these attempts to get on our flanks, the National troops were compelled, several times, to take positions to the rear nearer Pittsburg Landing. When the firing ceased at night the National line was all of a mile in rear of the position it had occupied in the morning.

In one of the backward moves, on the sixth, the division commanded by General Prentiss did not fall back with the others. This left his flanks exposed and enabled the enemy to capture him with about 2,200 of his officers and men. . . . I was with him, as I was with each of the division commanders that day, several times, and my recollection is that the last time I was with him was about half-past four, when his division was standing up firmly and the General was as cool as if expecting victory. But no matter whether it was four or later, the story that he and his command were surprised and captured in their tents is without any foundation whatever. If it had been true, as currently reported at the time and yet believed by thousands of people, that Prentiss and his division had been captured in their beds, there would not have been an all-day struggle, with the loss of thousands killed and wounded on the Confederate side.

With the single exception of a few minutes after the capture of Prentiss, a continuous and unbroken line was maintained all day from Snake Creek or its tributaries on the right to Lick Creek or the Tennessee on the left above Pittsburg. There was no hour during the day when there was not heavy firing and generally hard fighting at some point on the line, but seldom at all points at the same time. It was a case of Southern dash against Northern pluck and endurance. Three of the five divisions engaged on Sunday were entirely raw, and many of the men had only received their arms on the way from their States to the field. Many of them had arrived but a day or two before and were hardly able to load their muskets according to the manual. Their officers were equally ignorant of their duties. Under these circumstances it is not astonishing that many of the regiments broke at the first fire. In two cases, as I now remember, colonels led their regiments from the field on first hearing the whistle of the enemy's bullets. In these cases the colonels were constitutional cowards, unfit for any military position; but not so the officers and men led out of danger by them. Better troops never went upon a battlefield than many of these, officers and men, afterwards proved themselves to be, who fled panic-stricken at the first whistle of bullets and shell at Shiloh.

During the whole of Sunday [April 6] I was continuously engaged in passing from one part of the field to another, giving directions to division commanders. In thus moving along the line, however, I never deemed it important to stay long with Sherman. Although his troops were then under fire for the first time, their commander, by his constant presence with them, inspired a confidence in officers and men that enabled them to render services on that bloody battlefield worthy of the best of veterans. McClernand was next to Sherman, and the hardest fighting was in front of these two divisions. McClernand told me on that day, the sixth, that he profited much by having so able a commander supporting him. A casualty to Sherman that would have taken him from the field that day would have been a sad one for the troops engaged at Shiloh. And how near we came to this! On the sixth Sherman was shot twice, once in the hand, once in the shoulder, the ball cutting his coat and making a slight wound, and a third ball passed through his hat. In addition to this he had several horses shot during the day.

The nature of this battle was such that cavalry could not be used in front; I therefore formed ours into line in rear, to stop stragglers—of whom there were many. When there would be enough of them to make a show, and after they had recovered from their fright, they would be sent to reinforce some part of the line which needed support, without regard to their companies, regiments, or brigades.

On one occasion during the day I rode back as far as the river and met General Buell, who had just arrived; I do not remember the hour, but at that time there probably were as many as four or five thousand stragglers lying under cover of the river bluff, panic-stricken, most of whom would have been shot where they lay, without resistance, before they would have taken muskets and marched to the front to protect themselves. This meeting between General Buell and myself was on the dispatch boat used to run between the landing and Savannah. It was brief, and related specially to his getting troops over the river. As we left the boat together, Buell's attention was attracted by the men lying under cover of the river bank. I saw him berating them and trying to shame them into joining their regiments. He even threatened them with shells from the gunboats nearby. But it was all to no effect. Most of these men afterward proved themselves as gallant as any of those who saved the battle from which they had deserted. I have no doubt that this sight impressed General Buell with the idea that a line of retreat would be a good thing just then. If he had come in by the front instead of through the stragglers in the rear, he would have thought and felt differently. Could he have come through the Confederate rear, he would have witnessed there a scene similar to that at our own. The distant rear of an army engaged in battle is not the best place from which to judge correctly what is going on in front. Later in the war, while occupying the country between the Tennessee and the Mississippi, I learned the panic in the Confederate lines had not differed much from that within our own. . . .

The situation at the close of Sunday was as follows: along the top of the bluff just south of the log house which stood at Pittsburg Landing, Colonel J.D. Webster, of my staff, had arranged twenty or more pieces of artillery facing south or up the river. This line of artillery was on the crest of a hill overlooking a deep ravine opening into the Tennessee. Hurlbut with his division intact was on the right of this artillery, extending west and possibly a little north. McClernand came next in the general line, looking more to the west. His division was complete in its organization and ready for any duty. Sherman came next, his right extending to Snake Creek. His command, like the other two, was complete in its organization and ready, like its chief, for any service it might be called upon to render. All three divisions were, as a matter of course, more or less shattered and depleted in numbers from the terrible battle of the day. The division of W.H.L. Wallace, as much from the disorder arising from changes of division and brigade commanders, under heavy fire, as from any other cause, had lost its organization and did not occupy a place in the line as a division. Prentiss's command was gone as a division, many of its members having been killed, wounded, or captured; but it had rendered valiant services before its final dispersal, and had contributed a good share to the defense of Shiloh.

The right of my line rested near the bank of Snake Creek, a short distance above the bridge which had been built by the troops for the purpose of connecting Crump's Landing and Pittsburg Landing. Sherman had posted some troops in a log house and outbuildings which overlooked both the bridge over which Wallace was expected and the creek above that point. In this last position Sherman was frequently attacked before night, but held the point until he voluntarily abandoned it to advance in order to make room for Lew. Wallace, who came up after dark.

There was, as I have said, a deep ravine in front of our left. The Tennessee River was very high and there was water to a considerable depth in the ravine. Here the enemy made a last desperate effort to turn our flank, but was repelled. The gunboats *Tyler* and *Lexington*, Gwin and Shirk commanding, with the artillery under Webster, aided the army and effectually checked their further progress. Before any of Buell's troops had reached the west bank of the Tennessee, firing had almost entirely ceased; anything like an attempt on the part of the enemy to advance had absolutely ceased. There was some artillery firing from an unseen enemy, some of his shells passing beyond us; but I do not remember that there was the whistle of a single musket ball heard. As his troops arrived in the dusk General Buell marched several of his regiments part way down the face of the hill where they fired briskly for some minutes, but I do not think a single man engaged in this firing received an injury. The attack had spent its force.

General Lew. Wallace, with 5,000 effective men, arrived after the firing had ceased for the day, and was placed on the right. Thus night came, Wallace came, and the advance of Nelson's division came; but none—unless night—in time to be of material service to the gallant men who saved Shiloh on that first day against large odds. Buell's loss on the sixth of April was two men killed and one wounded, all members of the 36th Indiana infantry. The Army of the Tennessee lost on that day at least 7,000 men. The presence of two or three regiments of Buell's army on the west bank before the firing ceased had not the slightest effect in preventing the capture of Pittsburg Landing.

So confident was I before firing had ceased on the sixth that the next day would bring victory to our arms if we could only take the initiative, that I visited each division commander in person before any reinforcements had reached the field. I directed them to throw out heavy lines of skirmishers in the morning as soon as they could see, and push them forward until they found the enemy, following with their entire divisions in supporting distance, and to engage the enemy as soon as found. To Sherman I told the story of the assault at Fort Donelson, and said that the same tactics would win at Shiloh. Victory was assured when Wallace arrived, even if there had been no other support. I was glad, however, to see the reinforcements of Buell and credit them with doing all there was for them to do. During the night of the sixth the remainder of Nelson's division, [of] Buell's army, crossed the river and were ready to advance in the morning, forming the left wing. Two other divisions, Crittenden's and McCook's, came up the river from Savannah in the transports and were on the west bank early on the seventh. Buell commanded them in person. My command was thus nearly doubled in numbers and efficiency.

During the night rain fell in torrents and our troops were exposed to the storm without shelter. I made my headquarters under a tree a few hundred yards back from the river bank. My ankle was so much swollen from the fall of my horse the Friday night preceding, and the bruise was so painful, that I could get no rest. The drenching rain would have precluded the possibility of sleep without this additional cause. Some time after midnight, growing restive under the storm and the continuous pain, I moved back to the log house under the bank. This had been taken as a hospital, and all night wounded men were being brought in, their wounds dressed, a leg or an arm amputated as the case might require, and everything being done to save life or alleviate suffering. The sight was more unendurable than encountering the enemy's fire, and I returned to my tree in the rain.

The advance on the morning of the seventh developed[2] the enemy in the camps occupied by our troops before the battle began, more than a mile back from the most advanced position of the Confederates on the day before. It is known now that they had not yet learned of the arrival of Buell's command. Possibly they fell back so far to get the shelter of our tents during the rain, and also to get away from the shells that were dropped upon them by the gunboats every fifteen minutes during the night.

The position of the Union troops on the morning of the seventh was as follows: General Lew. Wallace on the right; Sherman on his left; then McClernand and then Hurlbut. Nelson, of Buell's army, was on our extreme left, next to the river. Crittenden was next in line after Nelson and on his right; McCook followed and formed the extreme right of Buell's command. My old command thus formed the right wing, while the troops directly under Buell constituted the left wing of the army. These relative positions were retained during the entire day, or until the enemy was driven from the field.

In a very short time the battle became general all along the line. This day everything was favorable to the Union side. We had now become the attacking party. The enemy was driven back all day, as we had been the day

---

[2] By "developed," Grant means something similar to "revealed."

before, until he beat a precipitate retreat. The last point held by him was near the road leading from the landing to Corinth, on the left of Sherman and right of McClernand. About three o'clock, being near that point and seeing that the enemy was giving way everywhere else, I gathered up a couple of regiments, or parts of regiments, from troops nearby, formed them in line of battle, and marched them forward, going in front myself to prevent premature or long-range firing. At this point there was a clearing between us and the enemy favorable for charging, although exposed. I knew the enemy were ready to break and only wanted a little encouragement from us to go quickly and join their friends who had started earlier. After marching to within musket-range I stopped and let the troops pass. The command, *Charge*, was given, and was executed with loud cheers and with a run; when the last of the enemy broke. . . .

After the rain of the night before and the frequent and heavy rains for some days previous, the roads were almost impassable. The enemy carrying his artillery and supply trains over them in his retreat, made them still worse for troops following. I wanted to pursue, but had not the heart to order the men who had fought desperately for two days, lying in the mud and rain whenever not fighting, and I did not feel disposed to positively order Buell, or any part of his command, to pursue. Although the senior in rank at the time I had been so only a few weeks. . . .

Shiloh was the severest battle fought at the West during the war, and but few in the East equaled it for hard, determined fighting. I saw an open field, in our possession on the second day, over which the Confederates had made repeated charges the day before, so covered with dead that it would have been possible to walk across the clearing, in any direction, stepping on dead bodies, without a foot touching the ground. On our side National and Confederate troops were mingled together in about equal proportions; but on the remainder of the field nearly all were Confederates. On one part, which had evidently not been plowed for several years, probably because the land was poor, bushes had grown up, some to the height of eight or ten feet. There was not one of these left standing unpierced by bullets. The smaller ones were all cut down.

Contrary to all my experience up to that time, and to the experience of the army I was then commanding, we were on the defensive. We were without entrenchments or defensive advantages of any sort, and more than half of the army engaged the first day was without experience or even drill as soldiers. The officers with them, except the division commanders and possibly two or three of the brigade commanders, were equally inexperienced in war. The result was a Union victory that gave the men who achieved it great confidence in themselves ever after.

The enemy fought bravely, but they started out to defeat and destroy an army and capture a position. They failed in both, with very heavy loss in killed and wounded, and must have gone back discouraged and convinced that the "Yankee" was not an enemy to be despised. . . .

Up to the battle of Shiloh I, as well as thousands of other citizens, believed that the rebellion against the Government would collapse suddenly and soon, if a decisive victory could be gained over any of its armies. Donelson and Henry were such victories. An army of more than 21,000 men was captured or destroyed. Bowling Green, Columbus, and Hickman, Kentucky, fell in consequence, and Clarksville and Nashville, Tennessee, the last two with an immense amount of stores, also fell into our hands. The Tennessee and Cumberland rivers, from their mouths to the head of navigation, were secured. But when Confederate armies were collected which not only attempted to hold a line farther south, from Memphis to Chattanooga, Knoxville, and on to the Atlantic, but assumed the offensive and made such a gallant effort to regain what had been lost, then, indeed, I gave up all idea of saving the Union except by complete conquest.

8

THE INVASION OF KENTUCKY

August–October 1862

Though Grant suffered severe criticism for letting his army be surprised, his victory was critical to the Union cause. It secured the great advance that had followed the capture of Forts Henry and Donelson, and left the Confederates with a slain commander and a shattered army. But the cost was grave, as seen in Grant's closing paragraphs. From two armies of about 45,000 each (plus Buell's 20,000 reinforcements), about 20,000 fell dead or wounded, making it the most costly battle of the war so far.

General Halleck, however, was slow to follow up the great success. Eager to win battlefield glory for himself, he arrived to take command of the combined Federal forces, totaling more than 100,000 after the arrival of further detachments. But Halleck was deeply imbued with military orthodoxy (he won his nickname "Old Brains" by translating French military texts into English), and he led his enormous force to Corinth at a creeping pace. Almost two months later, at the end of May, Halleck captured the town, but he had moved so slowly that Beauregard escaped unscathed with the entire Confederate army.

Meanwhile, Grant suffered the indignation of a meaningless post as second in command under Halleck, who was jealous of Grant's success. In fact, only Sherman's personal intervention prevented Grant from resigning his commission and returning to civilian life. After the capture of Corinth, he resumed an independent command, of the largely garrison forces holding the towns and railroads of west Tennessee and northern Mississippi. Grant did what he could with what he had, trying to trap the local Confederate forces as his subordinates sparred with them at Iuka and Corinth in September and October. Meanwhile, most of the mighty army was split off under Buell, who was ordered to march east toward Chattanooga, renewing Lincoln's cherished project of liberating east Tennessee.

As Buell started for Chattanooga in June and July 1862, two other factors combined to derail his offensive. The first was a series of Confederate raids behind Union lines, led by two men who were rapidly becoming legendary cavalry commanders: John Hunt Morgan and Nathan Bedford Forrest. Morgan and Forrest smashed up Union rail and telegraph lines and swooped down on isolated garrisons, cutting off supplies to Buell's Army of the Ohio. The second factor was the appointment of General Braxton Bragg to command of the Confederate Army of Tennessee.

Bragg was one of the most controversial commanders of the Civil War, a hot-tempered disciplinarian who was hated by his subordinates, a man who seemed to turn his every success into failure. Faced with Grant's presence near the Mississippi and Buell's campaign toward east Tennessee, Bragg decided in July to launch a bold offensive stroke aimed at forcing the Union army to fall all the way back to the Ohio River. Bragg split his forces, leaving 32,000 men behind to defend Vicksburg and Mississippi and leading the other 34,000 on an invasion of Kentucky. Traveling through Chattanooga and up into eastern Kentucky, he was joined in his invasion by Edmund Kirby Smith, who commanded a force of 18,000 men. Bragg hoped that his thrust around the Union flank would make Buell follow, opening most of Tennessee to recapture by the South.

Buell did indeed fall back, racing Bragg north to Louisville in August and September. There he warily faced the Confederate forces as Halleck bombarded him with telegraphed demands for action. Finally, after much hesitation and preparation, Buell moved to attack. In early October, he collided with Bragg at the town of Perryville. When the fighting broke out, Buell was unable to hear the firing from his command post, and the battle was conducted by his corps and division commanders.

One of those commanders was a short, combative, hard-driving officer named Philip H. Sheridan. Sheridan was barely thirty-one years old, a young West Point graduate who had been fighting Indians in the Northwest when the war broke out. Making his way east, he swiftly rose to ever higher commands, combining intense professionalism with tactical insight and sheer will to produce a long series of successes in combat. Sheridan saved the day at Perryville with his able front-line leadership. Though the battle itself seemed anticlimactic, it convinced Bragg that he could not maintain his presence in Kentucky in the face of much larger Union forces, and the Confederates quickly retreated back to Chattanooga, their invasion a failure.

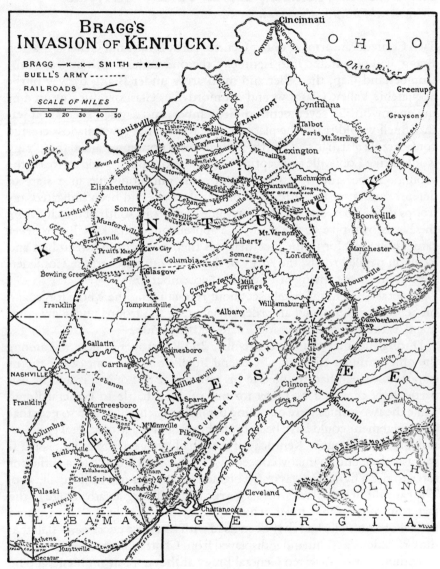

The Confederate invasion of Kentucky and the Union pursuit,
August to October 1862

The Invasion of Kentucky and the Battle of Perryville
By General Philip H. Sheridan

Two Confederate armies, under General Kirby Smith and General Braxton Bragg, had penetrated into Kentucky, the one under Smith by way of the Cumberland Gap, the other and main army under Bragg by way of the Sequatchie Valley, Glasgow, and Munfordville. Glasgow was captured by the enemy on the seventeenth of September, and as the expectation was that Buell would reach the place in time to save the town, its loss created considerable alarm in the North, for fears were now entertained that Bragg would strike Louisville and capture the city before Buell could arrive on the ground. It became necessary therefore to put Louisville in a state of defense, and after the cordon of principal works had been indicated, my troops threw up in one night a heavy line of rifle pits south of the city, from the Bardstown pike to the river. The apprehended attack by Bragg never came, however, for in the race that was then going on between him and Buell on parallel roads, the Army of the Ohio outmarched the Confederates, its advance arriving at Louisville September 25.

General Buell immediately set about reorganizing the whole force, and on September 29 issued an order designating the troops under my command as the Eleventh Division, Army of the Ohio. . . .

During the interval from September 25 till October 1 there was among the officers much criticism of General Buell's management of the recent campaign, which had resulted in his retirement to Louisville; and he was particularly censured by many for not offering battle to General Bragg while the two armies were marching parallel to each other, and so near that an engagement could have been brought on at any one of several points— notably so at Glasgow, Kentucky, if there had been a desire to join issue. It was asserted, and by many conceded, that General Buell had a sufficient force to risk a fight. He was much blamed for the loss of Munfordville also. The capture of this place with its garrison gave Bragg an advantage in the race toward the Ohio River, which odds would most likely have ensured the fall of Louisville had they been used with the same energy and skill that the Confederate commander displayed from Chattanooga to Glasgow; but something always diverted General Bragg at the supreme moment, and he failed to utilize the chances falling to him at this time, for, deflecting his march to the north toward Bardstown, he left open to Buell the direct road to Louisville by way of Elizabethtown.

At Bardstown Bragg's army was halted while he endeavored to establish a Confederate government in Kentucky by arranging for the installation of a provisional governor at Lexington. Bragg had been assured that the presence of a Confederate army in Kentucky would so encourage the secession element that the whole State could be forced into the rebellion and his army thereby largely increased; but he had been considerably misled, for he now found that though much latent sympathy existed for his cause, yet as far as giving active aid was concerned, the enthusiasm exhibited by the secessionists of Kentucky in the first year of the war was now replaced by apathy, or at best by lukewarmness. So the time thus spent in political machinations was wholly lost to Bragg; and so little reinforcement was added to his army that it may be said that the recruits gained were not enough to supply the deficiencies resulting from the recent toilsome marches of the campaign.

In the meanwhile Buell had arrived at Louisville, system had been substituted for the chaos which had previously been obtained there, and orders were issued for an advance upon the enemy with the purpose of attacking and the hope of destroying him within the limits of the "blue grass" region, and, failing in that, to drive him from Kentucky. The army moved October 1, 1862. . . . Bragg's troops retreated toward Perryville, only resisting sufficiently to enable the forces of General Kirby Smith to be drawn in closer—they having begun a concentration at Frankfort—so they could be used in a combined attack on Louisville as soon as the Confederate commander's political projects were perfected.

Much time was consumed by Buell's army in its march on Perryville, but we finally neared it on the evening of October 7. During the day, Brigadier-General Robert B. Mitchell's division of Gilbert's corps was in advance on the Springfield pike, but as the enemy developed [revealed] that he was in strong force on the opposite side of a small stream called Doctor's Creek, a tributary of Chaplin River, my division was brought up and passed to the front. It was very difficult to obtain water in this section of Kentucky, as a drought had prevailed for many weeks, and the troops were suffering so for water that it became absolutely necessary that we should gain possession of Doctor's Creek in order to relieve their distress. Consequently General Gilbert, during the night, directed me to push beyond Doctor's Creek early the next morning. At daylight on the eighth I moved out Colonel Dan McCook's brigade and Barnett's battery for the purpose, but after we had crossed the creek with some slight skirmishing, I found that we could not hold the ground unless we carried and occupied a range of hills, called Chaplin Heights, in front of the Chaplin River. As this would project my command in the direction of Perryville considerably beyond the troops that were on either flank, I brought up Laiboldt's brigade and Hescock's battery to strengthen Mc-Cook. Putting both brigades into line we quickly carried the Heights, much to the surprise of the enemy, I think, for he did not hold onto the valuable ground as strongly as he should have done. This success not only ensured us a good supply of water, but also, later in the day, had an important bearing on the battle of Perryville. After taking the heights, I brought up the rest of my division and entrenched, without much difficulty, by throwing up a strong line of rifle pits, although the enemy's sharpshooters annoyed us enough to make me order Laiboldt's brigade to drive them in on the main body. This was successfully done in a few minutes, but in pushing them back to Chaplin River, we discovered the Confederates forming a line of battle on the opposite bank, with the apparent purpose of an attack in force, so I withdrew the brigade to our entrenchments on the crest and awaited the assault.

While this skirmishing was going on, General Gilbert—the corps commander—whose headquarters were located on a hill about a mile distant to the rear, kept sending me messages by signal not to bring on an engagement. I replied to each message that I was not bringing on an engagement, but that the enemy evidently intended to do so, and that I believed I should shortly be attacked. Soon after returning to the crest and getting snugly fixed in the rifle pits, my attention was called to our left, the high ground we occupied affording me in that direction an unobstructed view. I then saw General A. McD. McCook's corps—the 1st—advancing toward the Chaplin River by the Mackville road, apparently unconscious that the Confederates were present in force behind the stream. I tried by the use of signal flags to get information of the situation to these troops, but my efforts failed, and the leading regiments seemed to approach the river indifferently prepared to meet the sudden attack that speedily followed, delivered as it was from the chosen position of the enemy. The fury of the Confederate assault soon halted this advance force, and in a short time threw it into confusion, pushed it back a considerable distance, and ultimately inflicted upon it such loss of men and guns as to seriously cripple McCook's corps, and prevent for the whole day further offensive movement on his part, though he stoutly resisted the enemy's assaults until four o'clock in the afternoon.

After seeing McCook so fiercely attacked, in order to aid him I advanced Hescock's battery, supported by six regiments, to a very good position in front of a belt of timber on my extreme left, where an enfilading fire could be opened on that portion of the enemy attacking the right of the 1st Corps, and also on his batteries across the Chaplin River. But at this

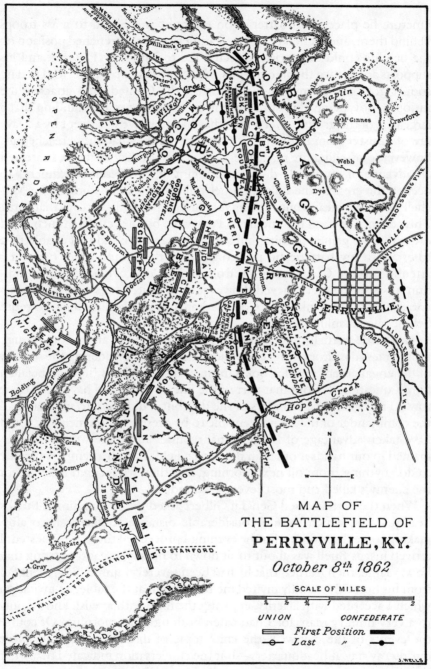

MAP OF
THE BATTLEFIELD OF
PERRYVILLE, KY.
October 8th 1862

SCALE OF MILES

UNION   CONFEDERATE
First Position
Last   "

The Battle of Perryville, October 8, 1862

juncture he placed two batteries on my right and began to mass troops behind them, and General Gilbert, fearing that my entrenched position on the heights could be carried, directed me to withdraw Hescock and his supports and return them to the pits. My recall was opportune, for I had no sooner got back to my original line than the Confederates attacked me furiously, advancing almost to my entrenchments, notwithstanding that a large part of the ground over which they had to move was swept by a heavy fire of canister from both my batteries. Before they had quite reached us, however, our telling fire made them recoil, and as they fell back, I directed an advance of my whole division, bringing up my reserve regiments to occupy the crest of the hills; Colonel William P. Carlin's brigade of Mitchell's division meanwhile moving forward on my right to cover that flank. This advance pressed the enemy to Perryville, but he retired in such good order that we gained nothing but some favorable ground that enabled me to establish my batteries in positions where they could again turn their attention to the Confederates in front of McCook, whose critical condition was shortly after relieved, however, by a united pressure of Gilbert's corps against the flank of McCook's assailants, compelling them to retire behind the Chaplin River.

The battle virtually ended about four o'clock in the afternoon, though more or less desultory firing continued until dark. Considering the severity of the engagement on McCook's front, and the reverses that had befallen him, I question if, from that part of the line, much could have been done toward retrieving the blunders of the day, but it did seem to me that, had the commander of the army been able to be present on the field, he could have taken advantage of Bragg's final repulse, and there would have remained in our hands more than the barren field. But no attempt was made to do anything more till next morning, and then we secured little except the enemy's killed and most severely wounded. . . .

When the battle ceased General Gilbert asked me to join him at Buell's headquarters, which were a considerable distance to the rear, so after making some dispositions for the evening I proceeded there as requested. I arrived just as Buell was about to sit down to his supper, and noticing that he was lame, then learned that he had been severely injured by a recent fall from his horse. He kindly invited me to join him at the table, an invitation which I accepted with alacrity, enjoying the meal with a relish known only to a very hungry man, for I had eaten nothing since morning. Of course the events of the day were the chief topic of discussion—as they were during my stay at headquarters—but the conversation indicated that what had occurred was not fully realized, and I returned to my troops impressed with the belief that General Buell and his staff officers were unconscious of the magnitude of the battle that had just been fought.

It had been expected by Buell that he would fight the enemy on the ninth of October, but the Confederates disposed of that proposition by attacking us on the eighth, thus disarranging a tactical conception which, with our superior numbers, would doubtless have proved successful had it not been anticipated by an enterprising foe. During the battle on the eighth the 2nd Corps, under General Thomas L. Crittenden, accompanied by General George H. Thomas, lay idle the whole day for want of orders, although it was near enough to the field to take an active part in the fight; and moreover, a large part of Gilbert's corps was unengaged during the pressure on McCook. Had these troops been put on the enemy's left at any time after he assaulted McCook, success would have been beyond question; but there was no one on the ground authorized to take advantage of the situation, and the battle of Perryville remains in history as an example of lost opportunities. . . .

Considering the number of troops actually engaged, the losses to Buell were severe, amounting to something over five thousand in killed, wounded, and missing. Among the killed were two brigade commanders of much promise—General James S. Jackson and General William R. Terrill. McCook's corps lost twelve guns, some of which were recovered the next day. The enemy's loss in killed and wounded we never learned, but it must have equaled ours; and about four thousand prisoners, consisting principally of sick and wounded, fell into our hands. . . .

The enemy retired from our front the night of the eighth, falling back on Harrodsburg to form a junction with Kirby Smith. . . .

Pursuit of the enemy was not continued in force beyond Crab Orchard, but some portions of the army kept at Bragg's heels until he crossed the Cumberland River, a part of his troops returning to Tennessee by way of the Cumberland Gap, but the major portion through Somerset. As the retreat of Bragg transferred the theater of operations back to Tennessee, orders were now issued for a concentration of Buell's army at Bowling Green, with a view to marching it to Nashville, and my division moved to that point without noteworthy incident. . . .

At Bowling Green General Buell was relieved, General W.S. Rosecrans succeeding him. The army as a whole did not manifest much regret at the change of commanders, for the campaign from Louisville was looked upon generally as a lamentable failure.

9

THE STRUGGLE FOR VICKSBURG
Winter–Spring, 1862–1863

Bragg's invasion of Kentucky, coming at the same time as Lee's move into Maryland, marked perhaps the highest high-water mark of the Confederate military effort. However, as military historian Archer Jones has noted, these invasions could never be more than raids, for the Confederates did not have enough troops to garrison and maintain the territory they captured. Lee and Bragg had to keep their troops fairly dispersed to gather supplies in the countryside; in the presence of Union armies, however, they had to concentrate their forces, limiting their ability to feed their armies. Even the inconclusive battles of Perryville and Antietam faced them with a choice between retreat or strangulation. Both Bragg and Lee chose to retreat, and Confederate hopes plunged as the armies fell back to secure territory farther south.

The next several months, however, failed to fulfill the promise of the Union successes in Kentucky and Maryland. In the East, Lincoln tired of McClellan's continued failure to drive south, and he appointed General Ambrose Burnside commander of the Army of the Potomac, over Burnside's own protests. On December 13, 1862, Burnside demonstrated how well founded his objections were with a suicidal attack on Lee's trenches at Fredericksburg. Back in the West, Grant had failed in an imaginative plan to trap the Confederate forces near Corinth, while the Union Army of the Ohio (with Rosecrans as the new commander) sat facing Bragg's Army of Tennessee in east central Tennessee.

From December 31, 1862, to January 2, 1863, Bragg attacked Rosecrans at the Battle of Stones River at Murfreesboro, Tennessee. Once again, Sheridan's astute, energetic leadership saved the day, and his division played a critical role in halting the Confederate assault. Though the battle was viciously fought by both sides, the result was even more indecisive than at Perryville; after the battle Bragg withdrew a distance along the Stones River, and the stalemate resumed as before.

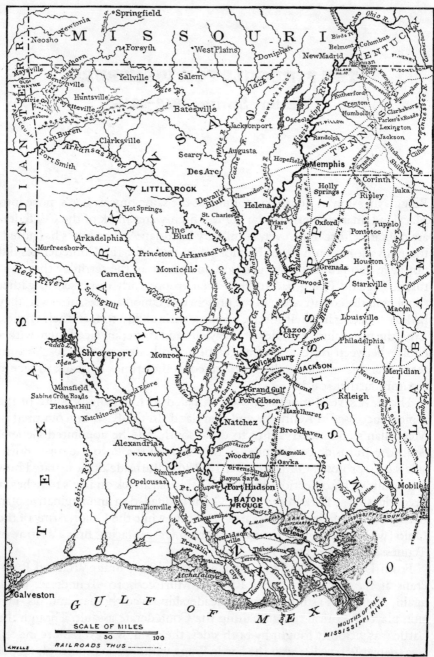

The lower Mississippi valley, region of the two Vicksburg campaigns,
December 1862 to July 1863

December also saw the failure of Grant's first campaign against Vicksburg, the key to the whole Mississippi River. As Grant described it, "It occupied the first high ground coming close to the river below Memphis. . . . Vicksburg was the only channel . . . connecting the parts of the Confederacy divided by the Mississippi. So long as it was held by the enemy, the frec navigation of the river was prevented. Hence its importance."

Grant planned a double swipe at the citadel. He himself was to jab with an army marching overland from his advanced base of supplies at Holly Springs, in northern Mississippi; after the Confederate garrison under Lieutenant-General John Pemberton moved north to fight Grant, Sherman was to descend on Vicksburg, with a powerful force landed from riverboats. General Joseph E. Johnston, supreme commander of the Confederate forces in the West, had the task of undoing Grant's plans—and of fighting divided lines of authority and repeated interference by President Jefferson Davis.

Grant's First Failure
By General Joseph E. Johnston

Without actual assignment, I was told . . . that the Government intended to place the Departments of Tennessee and Mississippi under my direction. This intimation justified me, I thought, in suggesting to the Secretary of War, General Randolph, that, as the Federal troops invading the Valley of the Mississippi were united under one commander, our armies for its defense should also be united, east of the Mississippi. By this junction, we should bring over seventy thousand men against 45,000 [under Grant], and secure all the chances of victory, and even the destruction of the Federal army; which, defeated so far from its base, could have little chance of escape. That success would enable us to overwhelm Rosecrans, by joining General Bragg with the victorious army, and transfer the war to the Ohio River, and to the state of Missouri, in which the best part of the population was friendly to us. I visited him in his office for this purpose, and began to explain myself. Before I had finished, he asked me, with a smile, to listen to a few lines on the subject; and, opening a large letter-book, he read me a letter to Lieutenant-General Holmes, in which he directed that officer to cross the Mississippi with his forces, and unite them with those of Lieutenant-General Pemberton [commanding at Vicksburg]. He then read me a note from the

President, directing him to countermand his instructions to Lieutenant-General Holmes. A day or two after this, General Randolph retired from the War Department, to the great injury of the Confederacy.

On the twenty-fourth, I received orders of that date, assigning me to command of the departments of General Bragg, Lieutenant-General E. Kirby Smith, and Lieutenant-General Pemberton. . . .

Several railroad accidents delayed me in my journey to Chattanooga—the location for my headquarters chosen by the War Department—so that I did not reach that place until the morning of the fourth of December.

A telegram from General Cooper, found there, informed me that Lieutenant-General Pemberton was falling back before superior forces [as Grant advanced from Holly Springs], and that Lieutenant-General Holmes had been "peremptorily ordered" to reinforce him; but that, as Lieutenant-General Holmes's troops might be too late, the President urged upon me the importance of sending a sufficient force from General Bragg's command to Lieutenant-General Pemberton's aid.

I replied immediately, by telegraph as well as by mail, that the troops near Little Rock could join General Pemberton sooner than those in middle Tennessee; and requested General Bragg, by telegraph, to detach a large body of cavalry to operate in General Grant's rear and cut his communications. . . .

On the twenty-seventh [of December] Major-General Loring, who was commanding at Grenada, reported that General Grant's army, which had been advancing, was retiring, and in a few hours the immediate cause became known—the destruction of the Federal depot at Holly Springs, by Major-General Van Dorn. That officer, with three thousand cavalry, surprised the garrison at daybreak, took two thousand prisoners, and destroyed the large stores of provision and ammunition, and six thousand muskets. . . .

Brigadier-General Forrest, who was detached by General Bragg to operate on Major-General Grant's rear, was very successful in breaking railroads in west Tennessee. After destroying large quantities of military stores also, and paroling twelve hundred prisoners, he was pressed back into middle Tennessee by weight of numbers. . . . [About this time, Bragg and Rosecrans fought the Battle of Stones River at Murfreesboro, Tennessee.]

While these events were occurring in middle Tennessee, Major-General Sherman was operating against Vicksburg.[3] He had embarked an army,

---

[3] Sherman was unaware that Grant's thrust—essential to Sherman's success—had been turned back by Van Dorn.

estimated at 30,000 men by Lieutenant-General Pemberton's scouts, on transports at Memphis, and, descending the Mississippi, ascended the Yazoo a few miles, and landed his troops on the southern shore on the twenty-sixth of December. Lieutenant-General Pemberton reported, the day after, that his lines had been attacked at four different points, and each attacking party handsomely repulsed. As his loss amounted to but five killed and fifteen wounded, these were probably reconnaissances rather than serious assaults. On the twenty-ninth, however, a real assault was made by a body of several thousand Federal troops, near Chickasaw Bayou, where Brigadier-General S.D. Lee commanded. That gallant soldier was successful in defeating the attempt with his brigade, inflicting a loss of eleven hundred upon the enemy, while his own was but a hundred and fifty.

On the second of January, General Sherman reembarked and ran up to Milliken's Bend. His fleet of transports disappeared soon after.

Mississippi was thus apparently free from invasion, General Grant's forces having already reached the northern border of the State [in retreat]. The condition of the country was such, too, as to make military operations on a large scale in it impracticable; and the most intelligent class of the inhabitants supposed that it would remain in that condition until the middle of the spring. In Tennessee, on the contrary, after the most effective fighting made by either party up to that time [at Stones River], our army had lost much ground, and was in danger of further disaster. For, while the United States government was sending such reinforcements as reestablished the strength of its army, the Confederate War Department made no answer to General Bragg's call for 20,000 additional troops. . . .

On the twenty-fourth [of January], a fleet of transports, bearing the united forces of Generals Grant and Sherman, descending the Mississippi from Memphis, appeared near Vicksburg. This army did not repeat the attack upon the place from the Yazoo, but landed on the west side of the river, and commenced the excavation of a canal through the point of land opposite the town. . . .

Until the end of [March] Lieutenant-General Pemberton's dispatches represented that General Grant's troops were at work industriously digging a canal opposite to Vicksburg; his design being, evidently, to turn the Confederate batteries in that way, and reach a landing-place below the town, to attack it from the south. On the third of April, however, he reported that the Federal army was preparing for reembarkation; the object of which, he thought, might be to reinforce General Rosecrans in middle Tennessee. . . .

On the eleventh, General Pemberton expressed the opinion that "most of General Grant's forces were being withdrawn to Memphis"; and said that he was assembling troops at Jackson; and was then ready to send 4,000 to Tennessee. . . .

On the sixteenth, however, General Pemberton expressed the belief that no large part of Grant's army would be sent away. . . .

The only activity apparent in either of the principal armies, before the end of March, was exhibited by that of General Grant, in his efforts to open a way by water around Vicksburg, to some point on the river below the town. But in the beginning of April this enterprise was abandoned, and General Grant decided that his troops should march to a point selected on the west bank of the Mississippi, and that the vessels-of-war and transports should run down to that point, passing the Confederate batteries at night. McClernand's corps (13th) led in the march, followed, at some distance, by McPherson's (17th). . . .

On the night of April 16th, the Federal fleet, of gunboats and three transports towing barges, passed the batteries of Vicksburg, and ran down to Hard Times [a landing on the west bank], where the land-forces were; and in the night of the twenty-second six more transports and barges followed. The whole effect of the artillery of the batteries [in Vicksburg] on the two occasions was the burning of one transport, sinking of another, and rendering six barges unserviceable.

General Grant's design seems to have been to take Grand Gulf by a combined military and naval attack, and operate against Vicksburg from that point. The squadron, under Admiral Porter, opened its fire upon the Confederate entrenchments at 8 A.M. on the twenty-ninth, and the 13th Corps was held in readiness to land and storm them as soon as their guns should be silenced. As that object had not been accomplished at six o'clock in the afternoon, General Grant abandoned the attempt, and determined to land at Bruinsburg. For this purpose the troops debarked at Hard Times, and marched to the plain below Grand Gulf; and the gunboats and transports, passing that place in the night, as they had done at Vicksburg, were in readiness at daybreak the next morning to ferry the troops to Bruinsburg, six miles. The number of vessels was sufficient to transport a division at a time.

General Pemberton reported to me, by telegraph, that day: "The enemy is at Hard Times in large force, with barges and transports, indicating a purpose to attack Grand Gulf, with a view to Vicksburg. Very heavy firing at Grand Gulf; enemy shelling our batteries from above and below."

At that time, according to General Pemberton's reports to me, more than twenty vessels, most of them gunboats, had passed the Confederate batteries, and were ready to aid the Federal army in its passage of the river.

Brigadier-General Bowen, who commanded at Grand Gulf, observing the movement of the Federal forces down the river, and their landing at Bruinsburg, placed Green's and Tracy's brigades on the route from that point into the interior, four miles in advance of Port Gibson. Here they encountered and [were] attacked early in the morning of the first of May, by the four divisions of McClernand's corps, which had crossed the river in the day and night of the thirtieth of April, and at once moved forward. . . .

While the troops were engaged, General Pemberton telegraphed to me: "A furious battle has been going on since daylight, just below Port Gibson. . . . General Bowen says he is outnumbered trebly. . . . Enemy can cross all his army from Hard Times to Bruinsburg. . . . I should have large reinforcements. . . . Enemy's success in passing our batteries has completely changed character of defense." In the reply, dispatched immediately, he was told: "If General Grant's army lands on this side of the river, the safety of the Mississippi depends on beating it. For that object you should unite your whole force."

Grant's move across the Mississippi, well below Vicksburg, startled not only the Confederate command but also Grant's own subordinate, Sherman. After the failure of the schemes to dig out a new channel for the Mississippi, out of range of Vicksburg's guns, Sherman argued that the army should fall all the way back to Memphis and reestablish a secure base. But after the collapse of the first campaign against Vicksburg, Grant decided there would be no turning back.

"At this time the North had become very much discouraged," he wrote. "Many strong Union men believed that the war must prove a failure. . . . It was my judgment at the time that to make a backward movement as long as that from Vicksburg to Memphis, would be interpreted, by many of those yet full of hope for the preservation of the Union, as a defeat. . . . There was nothing left to be done but to *go forward to a decisive victory*."

So it was that U. S. Grant ordered the navy to run past the batteries at Vicksburg, ferried his army across to Bruinsburg, and placed his army below the enemy stronghold, deep in Confederate territory, cut off from his own base. It was the beginning of his most famous campaign, widely considered one of the most daring and skillfull in history.

The Second Vicksburg Campaign
By General U.S. Grant

When the troops embarked on the evening of the twenty-ninth [of April], it was expected that we would have to go to Rodney, nine miles below, to find a landing; but that night a colored man came in who informed me that a good landing would be found at Bruinsburg, a few miles above Rodney, from which point there was a good road leading to Port Gibson some twelve miles in the interior. The information was correct, and our landing was effected without opposition.

Sherman had not left his position above Vicksburg yet. On the morning of the twenty-seventh, I ordered him to create a diversion by moving his corps up the Yazoo and threatening an attack on Haines's Bluff.

My object was to compel Pemberton to keep as much force about Vicksburg as I could, until I could secure a good footing on high land east of the river. The move was eminently successful and, as we afterwards learned, created great confusion about Vicksburg and doubts about our real design. Sherman moved the day of our attack on Grand Gulf, the twenty-ninth, with ten regiments of his command and eight gun-boats which Porter had left above Vicksburg.

He debarked his troops and apparently made every preparation to attack the enemy while the navy bombarded the main forts at Haines's Bluff. This move was made without a single casualty to either branch of the service. On the first of May Sherman received orders from me (sent from Hard Times the evening of the twenty-ninth of April) to withdraw from the front of Haines's Bluff and follow McPherson with two divisions as fast as he could. . . .

The embarkation below Grand Gulf took place at De Shroon's, Louisiana, six miles above Bruinsburg, Mississippi. Early on the morning of the thirtieth of April McClernand's corps and one division of McPherson's corps were speedily landed.

When this was effected I felt a degree of relief scarcely ever equaled since. Vicksburg was not yet taken it is true, nor were its defenders demoralized by any of our previous moves. But I was on dry ground on the same side of the river with the enemy. All the campaigns, labors, hardships, and exposures from the month of December previous to this time that had been made and endured, were for the accomplishment of this one object.

I had with me the 13th Corps, General McClernand commanding, and two brigades of Logan's division of the 17th Corps, General McPherson commanding—in all not more than 20,000 men to commence the campaign with. These were soon reinforced by the remaining brigade of Logan's division and Crocker's division of the 17th corps. On the seventh of May I was further reinforced by Sherman with two divisions of his, the 15th Corps. My total force was then about 33,000 men.

The enemy occupied Grand Gulf, Haines's Bluff, and Jackson with a force of nearly 60,000 men. Jackson is fifty miles east of Vicksburg and is connected with it by a railroad. My first problem was to capture Grand Gulf to use as a base.

Bruinsburg is two miles from high ground. The bottom at that point is higher than most of the low land in the valley of the Mississippi, and a good road leads to the bluff. It was natural to expect the garrison from Grand Gulf to come out to meet us and prevent, if they could, our reaching this solid base. Bayou Pierre enters the Mississippi just above Bruinsburg and, as it is a navigable stream and was high at the time, in order to intercept us they had to go by Port Gibson, the nearest point where there was a bridge to cross upon. This more than doubled the distance from Grand Gulf to the high land back of Bruinsburg. No time was to be lost in securing this foothold. Our transportation was not sufficient to move all the army across the river at one trip, or even two; but the landing of the 13th Corps and one division of the 17th was effected during the day, April 30th, and early evening. McClernand was advanced as soon as ammunition and two days' rations (to last five) could be issued to his men. The bluffs were reached an hour before sunset and McClernand was pushed on, hoping to reach Port Gibson and save the bridge spanning the Bayou Pierre before the enemy could get there; for crossing a stream in the presence of an enemy is always difficult. Port Gibson, too, is the starting point of roads to Grand Gulf, Vicksburg, and Jackson.

McClernand's advance met the enemy about five miles west of Port Gibson at Thompson's plantation. . . . The enemy had taken a strong natural position with most of the Grand Gulf garrison, numbering about seven or eight thousand men, under General Bowen. His hope was to hold me in check until reinforcements under Loring could reach him from Vicksburg; but Loring did not come in time to render much assistance south of Port Gibson. Two brigades of McPherson's corps followed Mc-Clernand as fast as rations and ammunition could be issued, and were ready to take position upon the battlefield whenever the 13th Corps could be got out of the way.

The country in this part of Mississippi stands on edge, as it were, the roads running along the ridges except when they occasionally pass from one ridge to another. Where there are no clearings the sides of the hills are covered with a very heavy growth of timber and with undergrowth, and the ravines are filled with vines and canebrakes, almost impenetrable. This makes it easy for an inferior force to delay, if not defeat, a far superior one.

Near the point selected by Bowen to defend, the road to Port Gibson divides, taking two ridges which do not diverge more than a mile or two at the widest point. These roads unite just outside the town. This made it necessary for McClernand to divide his force. It was not only divided, but it was separated by a deep ravine of the character above described. One flank could not reinforce the other except by marching back to the junction of the roads. McClernand put the divisions of Hovey, Carr, and A.J. Smith upon the right-hand branch and Osterhaus on the left. I was on the field by ten A.M., and inspected both flanks in person. On the right the enemy, if not being pressed back, was at least not repulsing our advance. On the left, however, Osterhaus was not faring so well. He had been repulsed with some loss. As soon as the road could be cleared of McClernand's troops I ordered up McPherson . . . with two brigades of Logan's division. This was about noon. I ordered him to send one brigade (General John E. Smith's was selected) to support Osterhaus, and to move to the left and flank the enemy out of his position. This movement carried the brigade over a deep ravine to a third ridge and, when Smith's troops were seen well through the ravine, Osterhaus was directed to renew his front attack. It was successful and unattended by heavy loss. The enemy was sent in full retreat on their right, and their left followed before sunset. While the movement to our left was going on, McClernand, who was with his right flank, sent me frequent requests for reinforcements, although the force with him was not being pressed. I had been upon the ground and knew it did not admit his engaging all the men he had. We followed up our victory until night overtook us about two miles from Port Gibson; then the troops went into bivouac for the night.

We started next morning for Port Gibson as soon as it was light enough to see the road. We were soon in the town, and I was delighted to find that the enemy had not stopped to contest our crossing further at the bridge, which he had burned. The troops were set to work at once to construct a bridge across the South Fork of the Bayou Pierre. . . . When it was finished the army crossed and marched eight miles beyond to the North Fork that day. . . . Before leaving Port Gibson we were reinforced by Crocker's division, [of] McPherson's corps, which had crossed the Mississippi at Bruinsburg and come up without stopping except to get two days' rations. McPherson still had one division west of the Mississippi River, guarding the road from Milliken's Bend to the river below until Sherman's command should relieve it. . . .

When the movement from Bruinsburg commenced we were without a wagon train. . . . My own horses, headquarters' transportation, servants, mess chest, and everything except what I had on, was with this train [across the Mississippi]. . . .

It was necessary to have transportation for ammunition. Provisions could be taken from the country; but all the ammunition that can be carried on the person is soon exhausted when there is much fighting. I directed, therefore, immediately on landing that all the vehicles and draft animals, whether horses, mules, or oxen, in the vicinity should be collected and loaded to their capacity with ammunition. Quite a train was collected during the thirtieth, and a motley train it was. In it could be found fine carriages, loaded nearly to the top with boxes of cartridges that had been pitched in promiscuously, drawn by mules with plow-harness, straw collars, rope-lines, etc. . . .

It was at Port Gibson I first heard through a Southern paper of the complete success of Colonel Grierson, who was making a raid through central Mississippi. He had started from La Grange [southwest Tennessee] April 17th with three regiments of about 1,700 men. On the twenty-first he detached Colonel Hatch with one regiment to destroy the railroad between Columbus and Macon and then return to La Grange. . . . Grierson continued his movement with about 1,000 men, breaking the Vicksburg and Meridian railroad and the New Orleans and Jackson railroad, arriving at Baton Rouge May 2nd. This raid was of great importance, for Grierson had attracted the attention of the enemy from the main movement against Vicksburg.

During the night of the second of May the bridge over the North Fork was repaired, and the troops commenced crossing at five the next morning. Before the leading brigade was over it was fired upon by the enemy from a commanding position; but they were soon driven off. It was evident that the enemy was covering a retreat from Grand Gulf to Vicksburg. Every commanding position from this crossing to Hankinson's ferry over the Big Black was occupied by the retreating foe to delay our progress.

McPherson, however, reached Hankinson's ferry before night, seized the ferry boat, and sent a detachment of his command across and several miles north on the road to Vicksburg. When the junction of the road going to Vicksburg with the road from Grand Gulf to Raymond and Jackson was reached, Logan with his division was turned to the left towards Grand Gulf. I went with him a short distance from this junction. McPherson had encountered the largest force yet met since the battle of Port Gibson and had a skirmish nearly approaching a battle; but the road Logan had taken enabled him to come up on the enemy's right flank, and they soon gave way. McPherson was ordered to hold Hankinson's ferry and the road back to Willow Springs with one division; McClernand, who was now in the rear, was to join in this as well as to guard the line back down the bayou. I did not want to take the chances of having an enemy lurking in our rear. . . .

When I reached Grand Gulf [now evacuated by the rebels] May 3rd I had not been with my baggage since the twenty-seventh of April and consequently had had no change of underclothing, no meal except such as I could pick up sometimes at other headquarters, and no tent to cover me. The first thing I did was to get a bath, borrow some fresh underclothing from one of the naval officers, and get a good meal on the flagship. I then wrote letters to the general-in-chief [Halleck, now in Washington, D.C.] informing him of our present position, dispatches to be telegraphed from Cairo, orders to General Sullivan commanding above Vicksburg, and gave orders to all my corps commanders. . . . While at Grand Gulf I heard from Banks, who was on the Red River, and who said that he could not be at Port Hudson before the tenth of May and then with only 15,000 men. Up to this time my intention had been to secure Grand Gulf as a base of supplies, detach McClernand's corps to Banks, and cooperate with him in the reduction of Port Hudson [the only other Confederate stronghold on the Mississippi, to the south].

The news from Banks forced upon me a different plan of campaign from the one intended. To wait for his cooperation would have detained me at least a month. . . . The enemy would have strengthened his position and been reinforced by more men than Banks could have brought. I therefore determined to move independently of Banks, cut loose from my base, destroy the rebel force in rear of Vicksburg, and invest or capture the city.

Grand Gulf was accordingly given up as a base and the authorities at Washington notified. I knew well that Halleck's caution would lead him to disapprove of this course; but it was the only one that gave any chance of success. . . . Even Sherman, who afterwards ignored bases of supplies other than what were afforded by the country while marching through four States of the Confederacy with an army more than twice as large as mine at this time, wrote me from Hankinson's ferry, advising me of the impossibility of supplying our army over a single road. He urged me to "stop all troops till your army is partially supplied with wagons . . ." To this I replied: "I do not calculate upon the possibility of supplying the army with full rations from Grand Gulf . . . What I do expect is to get up what rations of hard bread, coffee, and salt we can, and make the country furnish the balance."

McClernand's and McPherson's commands were kept substantially as they were on the night of the second, awaiting supplies sufficient to give them three days' rations in haversacks. Beef, mutton, poultry, and forage were found in abundance. . . .

While the troops were awaiting the arrival of rations I ordered reconnaissances made by McClernand and McPherson, with the view of leading the enemy to believe that we intended to cross the Big Black and attack the city at once.

On the sixth Sherman arrived at Grand Gulf and crossed his command that night and the next day. Three days' rations had been brought up from Grand Gulf for the advanced troops and were issued. Orders were given for a forward movement the next day. Sherman was directed to order up Blair, who had been left behind to guard the road from Milliken's Bend to Hard Times with two brigades. . . .

During the night of the sixth McPherson drew in his troops north of the Big Black and was off at an early hour on the road to Jackson, via Rocky Springs, Utica, and Raymond. . . .

After McPherson crossed the Big Black at Hankinson's ferry Vicksburg could have been approached and besieged by the south side. It is not probable, however, that Pemberton would have permitted a close besiegement. The broken nature of the ground would have enabled him to hold a strong defensible line from the river south of the city to the Big Black, retaining possession of the railroad back to that point. It was my plan, therefore, to get to the railroad east of Vicksburg, and approach from that direction. Accordingly, McPherson's troops that had crossed the Big Black were withdrawn and the movement east to Jackson commenced.

As has been stated before, the country is very much broken and the roads generally confined to the tops of the hills. The troops were moved one (and sometimes two) corps at a time to reach designated points out parallel to the railroad and only from six to ten miles from it. McClernand's corps was kept with its left flank on the Big Black guarding all the crossings. . . . McPherson was to the right of Sherman, extending to Raymond. The cavalry was used in this advance in reconnoitering to find the roads, to

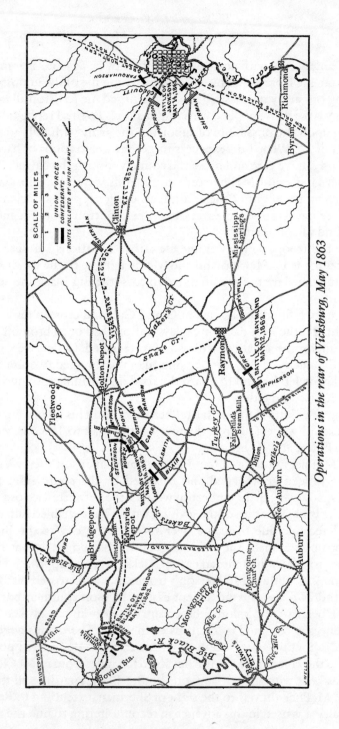

Operations in the rear of Vicksburg, May 1863

132

cover our advances, and to find the most practicable routes from one command to another so they could support each other in case of an attack. In making this move I estimated Pemberton's moveable force at Vicksburg at about 18,000 men, with smaller forces at Haines's Bluff and Jackson. It would not be possible for Pemberton to attack me with all his troops at one place, and I determined to throw my army between his and fight him in detail. This was done with success, but I found afterwards that I had entirely underestimated Pemberton's strength.

Up to this point our movements had been made without serious opposition. My line was nearly parallel with the Jackson and Vicksburg railroad and about seven miles south of it. The right was at Raymond eighteen miles from Jackson, McPherson commanding; Sherman in the center on Fourteen Mile creek, his advance thrown across; McClernand to the left, also on Fourteen Mile creek, advance across, and his pickets within two miles of Edward's Station, where the enemy had concentrated a considerable force and where they undoubtedly expected us to attack. McClernand's left was on the Big Black. In all our moves, up to this time, the left had hugged the Big Black closely, and all the ferries had been guarded to prevent the enemy throwing a force on our rear.

McPherson encountered the enemy, five thousand strong with two batteries under General Gregg, about two miles out of Raymond. This was about two P.M. Logan was in advance with one of his brigades. He deployed and moved up to engage the enemy. McPherson ordered the road in rear to be cleared of wagons, and the balance of Logan's division, and Crocker's, which was still farther in rear, to come forward with all dispatch. The order was obeyed with alacrity. Logan got his division in position for assault before Crocker could get up, and attacked with vigor, carrying the enemy's position easily, sending Gregg flying from the field not to appear against our front again until we met at Jackson.

In this battle McPherson lost sixty-six killed, 339 wounded, and thirty-seven missing—nearly or quite all from Logan's division. The enemy's loss was 100 killed, 305 wounded, besides 415 taken prisoner. . . .

When the news reached me of McPherson's victory at Raymond about sundown my position was with Sherman. I decided at once to turn the whole column towards Jackson and capture that place without delay.

Pemberton was now on my left, with, as I supposed, about 18,000 men; in fact, as I learned afterwards, with nearly 50,000. A force was also collecting on my right, at Jackson, the point where all the railroads communicating with Vicksburg connect. All the enemy's supplies of men and stores would come by that point. As I hoped in the end to besiege Vicksburg I must first destroy all possibility of aid. I therefore determined to move swiftly towards Jackson, destroy or drive any force in that direction, and then turn upon Pemberton. But by moving against Jackson, I uncovered my own communications. So I decided to have none—to cut loose altogether from my base and move my whole force eastward. I then had no fears for my communications, and if I moved quickly enough could turn upon Pemberton before he could attack me in the rear. . . .

General Joseph E. Johnston arrived at Jackson in the night of the thirteenth from Tennessee, and immediately assumed command of all the Confederate troops in Mississippi. I knew he was expecting reinforcements from the south and east. On the sixth I had written to General Halleck: "Information from the other side leaves me to believe the enemy are bringing forces from Tullahoma."

McPherson reached Clinton with the advance early on the thirteenth and immediately set to work destroying the railroad. Sherman's advance reached Raymond before the last of McPherson's command had got out of the town. McClernand withdrew from the front of the enemy, at Edward's Station, with much skill and without loss, and reached his position for the night in good order. On the night of the thirteenth, McPherson was ordered to march at early dawn upon Jackson, only fifteen miles away. Sherman was given the same order; but he was to move by the direct road from Raymond to Jackson, which is south of the road McPherson was on and does not approach within two miles of it at the point where it crossed the line of entrenchments which, at that time, defended the city. McClernand was ordered to move one division of his command to Clinton, one division a few miles beyond Mississippi Springs following Sherman's line, and a third to Raymond. . . . McClernand's position was an advantageous one in any event. With one division at Clinton he was in position to reinforce McPherson, at Jackson, rapidly if it became necessary; the division beyond Mississippi Springs was equally available to reinforce Sherman; the one at Raymond could take either road. He still had two other divisions farther back, now that Blair had come up, available within a day of Jackson. If this last command should not be wanted at Jackson, they were already one day's march from there on their way to Vicksburg and on three different roads leading to the latter city. But the most important consideration was to have a force confronting Pemberton if he should come out to attack my rear. This I expected him to do; as shown further on, he was directed by Johnston to make this very move.

I notified General Halleck that I should attack the State capital [Jackson] on the fourteenth. A courier carried the dispatch to Grand Gulf through an unprotected country.

Sherman and McPherson communicated with each other during the night and arranged to reach Jackson at about the same hour. It rained in torrents during the night of the thirteenth and the fore part of the day of the fourteenth. The roads were intolerable, and in some places on Sherman's line, where the land was low, they were covered more than a foot deep with water. But the troops never murmured. By nine o'clock Crocker, of McPherson's corps, who was now in advance, came upon the enemy's pickets and speedily drove them in upon the main body. They were outside the entrenchments in a strong position, and proved to be the troops that had been driven out of Raymond. Johnston had been reinforced during the night by Georgia and South Carolina regiments, so that his force amounted to 11,000 men, and he was expecting still more.

Sherman also came upon the rebel pickets some distance out from the town, but speedily drove them in. He was now on the south and southwest of Jackson confronting the Confederates behind their breastworks, while McPherson's right was nearly two miles north, occupying a line north and south across the Vicksburg railroad. Artillery was brought up and reconnaissances made preparatory to an assault. McPherson brought up Logan's division while he deployed Crocker's for the assault. Sherman made similar dispositions on the right. By 11 A.M. both were ready to attack. Crocker moved his division forward, preceded by a strong skirmish line. These troops at once encountered the enemy's advance and drove it back on the main body, when they returned to their proper regiment and the whole division charged, routing the enemy completely, and driving him into this main line. This stand by the enemy was made more than two miles outside of his main fortifications. McPherson followed up with his command until within range of the guns of the enemy from their entrenchments, when he halted to bring his troops into line and reconnoiter to determine the next move. It was now about noon.

While this was going on, Sherman was confronting a rebel battery which enfiladed the road on which he was marching—the Mississippi Springs road—and commanded a bridge spanning a stream over which he had to pass. By detaching right and left the stream was forced and the enemy flanked and speedily driven within the main line. This brought our whole line in front of the enemy's line of works, which was continuous on the north, west, and south sides of the Pearl River north of the city to the same river south. I was with Sherman. He was confronted by a force sufficient to hold us back. Appearances did not justify an assault where we were. I had directed Sherman to send a force to the right, and to reconnoiter as far as to the Pearl River. This force, Tuttle's division, on returning I rode to the right with my staff, and soon found that the enemy had left that part of the line. Tuttle's movement or McPherson's pressure had no doubt led Johnston to order a retreat, leaving only the men at the guns to retard us while he was getting away. . . . I rode immediately to the State House, where I was soon followed by Sherman. . . . Stevenson's brigade was sent to cut off the rebel retreat, but was too late or not expeditious enough.

Our loss in this engagement was: McPherson, thirty-seven killed, 228 wounded; Sherman, four killed and twenty-one wounded and missing. The enemy lost 845 killed, wounded, and captured. Seventeen guns fell into our hands, and the enemy destroyed by fire their storehouses, containing a large amount of commissary stores. . . .

I slept that night in the room that Johnston was said to have occupied the night before.

About four in the afternoon I sent for the corps commanders and directed the dispositions to be made of their troops. Sherman was to remain in Jackson until he destroyed that place as a railroad center and manufacturing city of military supplies. He did the work most effectually. . . .

On the night of the thirteenth Johnston sent the following dispatch to Pemberton at Edward's Station: "I have lately arrived, and learn that Major-General Sherman is between us with four divisions at Clinton. It is important to establish communication, that you may be reinforced. If practicable, come up in his rear at once. To beat such a detachment would be of immense value. All the troops you can quickly assemble should be brought. Time is all-important." . . .

Receiving this dispatch on the fourteenth, I ordered McPherson to move promptly in the morning back to Bolton, the nearest point where Johnston could reach the road. Bolton is about twenty miles west of Jackson. I also informed McClernand of the capture of Jackson and sent him the following order: "It is evidently the design of the enemy to get north of us and cross the Big Black, and beat us into Vicksburg. We must not allow them to do this. Turn all your forces toward Bolton Station, and make all dispatch in getting there. Move troops by the most direct road from wherever they may be on the receipt of this order." . . .

Johnston stopped on the Canton road only six miles north of Jackson, the night of the fourteenth. He sent from there to Pemberton dispatches announcing the loss of Jackson, and the following order:

"As soon as the reinforcements are all up, they must be united to the rest of the army. I am anxious to see a force assembled that may be able to inflict a heavy blow upon the enemy. Can Grant supply himself from the Mississippi? Can you not cut him off from it, and above all, should he be compelled to fall back for want of supplies, beat him."

The concentration of my troops was easy, considering the character of the country. McPherson moved along the road parallel with and near the railroad. . . . McClernand faced about and moved promptly. . . .

The night of the fifteenth Hovey was at Bolton; Carr and Osterhaus were about three miles south, but abreast, facing west; Smith was north of Raymond with Blair in his rear.[4]

McPherson's command, with Logan in front, had marched at seven o'clock, and by four reached Hovey and went into camp; Crocker bivouacked just in Hovey's rear on the Clinton road. Sherman, with two divisions, was in Jackson, completing the destruction of roads, bridges, and military factories. I rode in person out to Clinton. On my arrival I ordered McClernand to move early in the morning on Edward's Station, cautioning him to watch for the enemy and not bring on an engagement unless he felt very certain of success.

I naturally expected that Pemberton would endeavor to obey the orders of his superior, which I have shown were to attack us at Clinton. This indeed, I knew he could not do; but I felt sure he would make the attempt to reach that point. It turned out, however, that he had decided his superior's plans were impracticable, and consequently determined to move south from Edward's Station and get between me and my base. I, however, had no base, having abandoned it more than a week before. On the fifteenth Pemberton had actually marched south from Edward's Station, but the rains had swollen Baker's Creek, which he had to cross, so much that he could not ford it, and the bridges were washed away. This brought him back to the Jackson Road. . . . Receiving here early on the sixteenth a repetition of his order to join Johnston at Clinton, he concluded to obey. . . .

At five o'clock in the morning (sixteenth) two men, who had been employed on the Jackson and Vicksburg railroad, were brought to me. They reported that they had passed through Pemberton's army in the night, and that it was still marching east. They reported him to have eighty regiments of infantry and ten batteries; in all, about 25,000 men.

I had expected to leave Sherman at Jackson another day in order to

---

[4] All these men were division commanders.

complete his work; but getting the above information I sent him orders to move with all dispatch to Bolton, and to put one division with an ammunition train on the road at once, with directions to its commander to march with all possible speed until he came up to our rear. . . .

Smith's division on the most southern road was the first to encounter the enemy's pickets, who were speedily driven in. Osterhaus, on the middle road, hearing the firing, pushed his skirmishers forward, found the enemy's pickets and forced them back to the main line. About the same time Hovey encountered the enemy on the northern or direct wagon road from Jackson to Vicksburg. McPherson was hastening up to join Hovey, but was embarrassed by Hovey's trains occupying the roads. I was still back at Clinton. McPherson sent me word of the situation, and expressed the wish that I was up. By half-past seven I was on the road and proceeded rapidly to the front, ordering all trains that were in front of troops off the road. When I arrived Hovey's skirmishing had amounted almost to a battle.

McClernand was in person on the middle road and had a shorter distance to march to reach the enemy's position than McPherson. I sent him word by a staff officer to push forward and attack. These orders were repeated several times without apparently expediting McClernand's advance.

Champion's Hill, where Pemberton had chosen his position to receive us, whether taken by accident or design, was well selected. It is one of the highest points in that section, and commanded all the ground in range. On the east side of the ridge, which is quite precipitous, is a ravine running first north, then westerly, terminating in Baker's Creek. It was grown up thickly with large trees and undergrowth, making it difficult to penetrate with troops, even when not defended. The ridge occupied by the enemy terminated abruptly where the ravine turns westerly. The left of the enemy occupied the north end of this ridge. . . . There was, when we were there, a narrow belt of timber near the summit west of the road.

From Raymond there is a direct road to Edward's Station, some three miles west of Champion's Hill. There is one also to Bolton. From this latter road there is still another, leaving it about three and a half miles before reaching Bolton and leading directly to the same station. It was along these two roads that three divisions of McClernand's corps, and Blair of Sherman's, temporarily under McClernand, were moving. . . . Pemberton's lines covered all these roads, and faced east. Hovey's line, when it first drove in the enemy's pickets, was formed parallel to that of the enemy and confronted his left.

By eleven o'clock the skirmishing had grown into a hard-contested battle. Hovey alone, before other troops could be got to assist him, had captured a battery of the enemy. But he was not able to hold his position and had to abandon the artillery. McPherson brought up his troops as fast as possible, Logan in front, and posted them on the right of Hovey and across the flank of the enemy. Logan reinforced Hovey with one brigade of his division; with his other two he moved farther west to make room for Crocker, who was coming up as rapidly as the roads would admit. Hovey was still being heavily pressed, and was calling on me for more reinforcements. I ordered Crocker, who was now coming up, to send one brigade from his division. McPherson ordered two batteries to be stationed where they nearly enfiladed the enemy's line, and they did good execution.

From Logan's position now a direct forward movement carried him over open fields, in rear of the enemy and in a line parallel with them. He did make exactly this move, attacking, however, the enemy through a belt of woods covering the west slope of the hill for a short distance. Up to this time I had kept my position near Hovey where we were the most heavily pressed; but about noon I moved with a part of my staff by our right around, until I came up with Logan himself. I found him near the road leading down to Baker's creek. He was actually in command of the only road over which the enemy could retreat; Hovey, reinforced by two brigades from McPherson's command, confronted the enemy's left; Crocker, with two brigades, covered their left flank; McClernand two hours before, had been within two miles and a half of their center with two divisions, and the two divisions, Blair's and A.J. Smith's, were confronting the rebel right; Ransom, with a brigade of McArthur's division of the 17th Corps (McPherson's), had crossed the river at Grand Gulf a few days before, and was coming upon their right flank. Neither Logan nor I knew that we had cut off the retreat of the enemy. Just at this juncture a messenger came from Hovey, asking for more reinforcements. There were none to spare. I then gave an order to move McPherson's command by the left flank around to Hovey. This uncovered the rebel line of retreat, which was soon taken advantage of by the enemy.

During all this time, Hovey, reinforced as he was by a brigade from Logan and another from Crocker, and by Crocker gallantly coming up with two other brigades on his right, had made several assaults, the last one about the time the road was opened to the rear. The enemy fled precipitately. This was between three and four o'clock. . . . Hovey's division, and McPherson's two divisions with him, had marched and fought from early dawn, and were not in the best condition to follow the retreating foe. I sent orders to Osterhaus to pursue the enemy, and to Carr, whom I saw personally, I explained the situation and directed him to pursue vigorously as far as the Big Black, and to cross it if he could; Osterhaus to follow him. The pursuit was continued until after dark.

The battle of Champion's Hill lasted about four hours, hard fighting, preceded by two or three hours of skirmishing, some of which almost rose to the dignity of battle. Every man of Hovey's division and of McPherson's two divisions was engaged during the battle. No other part of my command was engaged at all, except that as described before. . . . McClernand, with two divisions, was within a few miles of the battlefield long before noon, and in easy hearing. I sent him repeated orders by staff officers fully competent to explain to him the situation. These traversed the wood separating us, without escort, but he did not come. . . .

Had McClernand come up with reasonable promptness, or had I known the ground as I did afterwards, I cannot see how Pemberton could have escaped with any organized force. As it was he lost over 3,000 killed and wounded and about 3,000 captured in battle and in pursuit. Loring's division, which was the right of Pemberton's line, was cut off from the retreating army and never got back into Vicksburg. Pemberton himself fell back that night to the Big Black River. . . .

We were now assured of our position between Johnston and Pemberton, without a possibility of a junction of their forces. Pemberton might have made a night march to the Big Black, crossed the bridge there, and, by moving north on the west side, have eluded us and finally returned to Johnston. But this would have given us Vicksburg. It would have been his proper move, however, and the one Johnston would have made had he been in Pemberton's place. In fact it would have been in conformity with Johnston's orders to Pemberton.

Sherman left Jackson with the last of his troops about noon on the sixteenth and reached Bolton, twenty miles west, before halting. . . . At Bolton he was informed of our victory. He was directed to commence the march early the next day, and to diverge from the road he was on to Bridgeport on the Big Black River, some eleven miles above the point where we expected to find the enemy. Blair was ordered to join him there with the pontoon train as early as possible.

This movement brought Sherman's corps together, and at a point where I hoped a crossing of the Big Black might be effected and Sherman's corps used to flank the enemy out of his position in our front, thus opening a crossing for the remainder of the army. I informed him that I would endeavor to hold the enemy in my front while he crossed the river.

The advance division, Carr's (McClernand's corps), resumed the pursuit

STORE: 0163   REG: 07/25   TRAN#: 0035
SALE   05/31/2001   EMP: 06268

KEN BURNS JAZZ - *Benny Goodman*
    6427571   CD T   11.99
INTRO TO GLENN MILLER - *His Best Recordings*
    1545910   CD T   15.99
WOODY HERMANS FINEST HOUR - *Woody Herman*
    6586361   CD T   11.99
C.W.Commanders - *In Their Own Words* -
    6434464   IR T   *Softcover* 2.99
NEWSPAPERS
    I B Q 5/31/01   NW N   1.00

              Subtotal   43.96
              COLORADO 3.7%   1.59
5 Items   Total   45.55
              DISCOVER   45.55
ACCT # /S 6011009247516
                 AUTH: 031798
NAME: CARLTON/GILBERT W

         CUSTOMER COPY

       05/31/2001 12:44PM

   THANK YOU FOR SHOPPING AT BORDERS
   PLEASE ASK ABOUT OUR SPECIAL EVENTS

Visit our website at www.borders.com!

BORDERS®

- Returns must be accompanied by the original receipt.
- Returns must be completed within 30 days.
- Merchandise must be in salable condition.
- Opened videos, discs and cassettes may be exchanged for replacement copies of the original items only.
- Periodicals and newspapers may not be returned.
- Items purchased by check may be returned for cash after 10 business days.
- All returned checks will incur a $15 service charge.
- All other refunds will be granted in the form of the original payment.

BORDERS®

- Returns must be accompanied by the original receipt.
- Returns must be completed within 30 days.
- Merchandise must be in salable condition.
- Opened videos, discs and cassettes may be exchanged for replacement copies of the original items only.
- Periodicals and newspapers may not be returned.
- Items purchased by check may be returned for cash after 10 business days.
- All returned checks will incur a $15 service charge.
- All other refunds will be granted in the form of the original payment.

BORDERS®

- Returns must be accompanied by the original receipt.
- Returns must be completed within 30 days.
- Merchandise must be in salable condition.
- Opened videos, discs and cassettes may be exchanged for replacement copies of the original items only.
- Periodicals and newspapers may not be returned.
- Items purchased by check may be returned for cash after 10 business days.
- All returned checks will incur a $15 service charge.
- All other refunds will be granted in the form of the original payment.

at half-past 3 A.M. on the seventeenth, followed closely by Osterhaus, McPherson bringing up the rear with his corps. As I expected, the enemy was found in position on the Big Black. The point was only six miles from that where my advance had rested for the night, and was reached at an early hour. Here the river makes a turn to the west, and has washed close up to the high land; the east side is a low bottom, sometimes overflowed at very high water, but was cleared and in cultivation. A bayou runs irregularly across this low land, the bottom of which, however, is above the surface of the Big Black at ordinary stages. . . . The rebels had constructed a parapet along the inner bank of this bayou by using cotton bales from the plantation close by and throwing dirt over them. The whole was thoroughly commanded from the height west of the river. . . . Carr's division was deployed on our right, Lawler's brigade forming his extreme right and reaching through these woods to the river above. . . .

While the troops were standing as here described an officer from Banks's staff came up and presented me with a letter from General Halleck, dated the eleventh of May. . . . It ordered me to return to Grand Gulf and to cooperate from there with Banks against Port Hudson, and then to return with our combined forces to besiege Vicksburg. I told the officer that the order came too late, and that Halleck would not give it now if he knew our position. The bearer of the dispatch insisted that I ought to obey the order, and was giving arguments to support his position when I heard great cheering to the right of our line and, looking in that direction, saw Lawler in his shirt sleeves leading a charge upon the enemy. I immediately mounted my horse and rode in the direction of the charge, and saw no more of the officer who delivered the dispatch; I think not even to this day.

The assault was successful. But little resistance was made. The enemy fled from the west bank of the river, burning the bridge behind him, and leaving the men and guns on the east side to fall into our hands. Many tried to escape by swimming the river. Some succeeded and some drowned in the attempt. Eighteen guns were captured and 1,751 prisoners. Our loss was thirty-nine killed, 237 wounded, and three missing. The enemy probably lost but few men except those captured and drowned. But for the successful and complete destruction of the bridge, I have but little doubt that we should have followed the enemy so closely as to prevent his occupying his defenses around Vicksburg. . . .

As soon as work could be commenced, orders were given for the construction of three bridges. . . . By eight o'clock in the morning of the eighteenth all three bridges were complete and the troops were crossing. . . .

On the eighteenth I moved along the Vicksburg road in advance of the troops and as soon as possible joined Sherman. My first anxiety was to secure a base of supplies on the Yazoo River above Vicksburg. Sherman's line of march led him to the very point on Walnut Hills occupied by the enemy the December before when he was repulsed. . . . Sherman had the pleasure of looking down from the spot coveted by him so much the December before on the ground where his command had lain so helpless for offensive action. He turned to me, saying that up to this minute he had felt no positive assurance of success. This, however, he said, was the end of one of the greatest campaigns in history and I ought to make a report of it at once. Vicksburg was not yet captured, and there was no telling what might happen before it was taken; but whether captured or not, this was a complete and successful campaign. . . .

McPherson, after crossing the Big Black, came into the Jackson and Vicksburg road which Sherman was on, but to his rear. He arrived at night near the lines of the enemy, and went into camp. McClernand moved by the direct road near the railroad to Mount Albans, and then turned to the left and put his troops on the road from Baldwin's ferry. . . . I now had my three corps up to the works built for the defense of Vicksburg, on three roads—one to the north, one to the east, and one to the southeast of the city. By the morning of the nineteenth, the investment was as complete as my limited number of troops would allow. . . .

The enemy had been much demoralized by his defeats at Champion's Hill and the Big Black, and I believed he would not make much effort to hold Vicksburg. Accordingly, at two o'clock [on the nineteenth] I ordered an assault. It resulted in securing more advanced positions for all our troops where they were fully covered by the fire of the enemy. . . .

I now determined on a second assault. Johnston was in my rear, only fifty miles away, with an army not much inferior in numbers to the one I had with me, and I knew he was being reinforced. There was danger of his coming to the assistance of Pemberton, and after all he might defeat my anticipations of capturing the garrison if, indeed, he did not prevent the capture of the city. The immediate capture of Vicksburg would save sending me the reinforcements which were much wanted elsewhere, and would set free the army under me to drive Johnston from the State. But the first consideration was—the troops believed they could carry the works in their front, and would not have worked so patiently in the trenches if allowed to try. . . .

The attack was gallant, and portions of each of the three corps succeeded in getting up to the very parapets of the enemy and in planting their battle flags upon them; but at no place were we able to enter. . . .

I now determined upon a regular siege—to "outcamp the enemy," as it were, and to incur no more losses. . . . With the navy holding the river, the investment of Vicksburg was complete.

After failing to capture Vicksburg by assault, Grant settled down to a regular siege. As Johnston hovered to the east with a small Southern army, Union engineers worked on blowing a hole in the Confederate lines with mines, and all the while starvation did the real work of the siege. Finally, after some negotiation, 30,000 Confederate soldiers surrendered on July 4, 1863. Grant paroled them, freeing them to return home and spread the demoralization of a beaten army. With news of Vicksburg's fall, the Confederate defenders of Port Hudson surrendered to General Banks, and the Mississippi River was in Union hands at last.

IV

THE GREAT TURNING POINT

GETTYSBURG

10

THE GETTYSBURG CAMPAIGN

June–July 1863

On November 19, 1863, Abraham Lincoln stood on the battlefield of Gettysburg to commemorate, in his most famous address, the Union soldiers who had died there four months before. "The world will little note, nor long remember what we say here," he predicted, "but it can never forget what they did here." He was wrong about the legacy of his own words, but his assessment of the battle's significance was exactly right—for Union victory at Gettysburg is still considered the great turning point of the Civil War.

As a turning point, the surrender of Vicksburg (just one day after the battle of Gettysburg) does seem more convincing. By taking that riverfront citadel, General Ulysses S. Grant captured an army of 30,000 men, a devastating blow to Southern arms; he also won control of the length of the Mississippi, permanently splitting the South in two. Vicksburg represented, as James McPherson has written, "the most important strategic victory of the war, perhaps meriting Grant's later assertion that 'the fate of the Confederacy was sealed when Vicksburg fell.' "

And yet, the significance of Gettysburg is impossible to deny, in both military and political terms. Regarding size alone, the battle was the most massive and bloody of the war, claiming 23,000 Union and 28,000 Confederate casualties. Gettysburg also marked the definitive failure of Lee's second raid into the North—a great gamble that he could conquer foreign recognition by winning a climactic victory deep in Union territory. But unlike the Antietam campaign (where Lee was forced to retreat as much from strategic conditions as from the drawn battle), the Army of Northern Virginia was clearly defeated in every sense—on the battlefield as well as in its larger aims.

Perhaps even more important was the moral and political effect of the Union victory in Pennsylvania. Before Gettysburg, Robert E. Lee and his army seemed unbeatable (a reputation only slightly tarnished by his failure at Antietam). The aura of invincibility was never greater than after the Battle of Chancellorsville, May 2–6, 1863. There, in an astonishingly daring maneuver, Lee split his forces as the Army of the Potomac moved around his left flank—and struck *its* flank, crushing the right wing with a surprise attack by Stonewall Jackson's corps. Though the Union troops (now under the command of General "Fighting Joe" Hooker) greatly outnumbered the rebels, Hooker himself was demoralized by Jackson's stroke, and he ordered his men to retreat. The only compensation for the North was the accidental fatal shooting of Jackson by his own troops.

After the rebel victory, Jefferson Davis and his generals debated what to do next; in particular, how to save Vicksburg, then besieged by Grant. The senior corps commander in the Army of Northern Virginia, James Longstreet (who with his troops had been away during Chancellorsville) proposed a move into Tennessee to draw Grant north. But Lee offered a bold vision of an invasion of the North—a grander version of the Antietam campaign. His reputation (at its peak after Chancellorsville) swept away all objections, and the Confederates set off on the road to disaster.

The Battle of Gettysburg
By General James Longstreet

Passing through Richmond [on the way to rejoin Lee][1], I called to report to Secretary of War Seddon, who referred to affairs in Mississippi, stating that the department was trying to collect an army at Jackson, under General Joseph E. Johnston, sufficient to push Grant away from his circling lines about Vicksburg. He spoke of the difficulty of feeding as well as collecting an army of that magnitude in Mississippi, and asked my views.

The Union army under Rosecrans [the Army of the Cumberland] was then facing the Confederate army under General Bragg in Tennessee, at Murfreesboro and Shelbyville.

I thought that General Grant had better facilities for collecting supplies and reinforcements on his new lines, and suggested that the only prospect of relieving Vicksburg that occurred to me was to send General Johnston and his troops about Jackson to reinforce General Bragg's army; at the same time send the two divisions of my command, then marching to join

[1] Longstreet, with two divisions, had just spent several weeks in southeast Virginia, warding off a threatened Union attack and collecting supplies.

General Lee, to the same point; that the commands moving on converging lines could have rapid transit and be thrown in overwhelming numbers on Rosecrans before he could have help, break up his army, and march for Cincinnati and the Ohio River; that Grant's was the only army that could be drawn to meet this move, and that the move must, therefore, relieve Vicksburg.

It was manifest before the war was accepted that the only way to equalize the contest was by skillful use of our interior lines, and this was so impressed by two years' experience that it seemed time to force it upon the Richmond authorities. But foreign intervention was the ruling idea with the President, and he preferred that as the easy solution of all problems.

The only objection offered by the Secretary was that Grant was such an obstinate fellow that he could only be induced to quit Vicksburg by terribly hard knocks.

On the contrary, I claimed that *he was a soldier*, and would obey the calls of his government, but was not lightly driven from his purpose.

My march continued, and we joined General Lee at Fredericksburg, where I found him in sadness, notwithstanding that he was contemplating his great achievement and brilliant victory at Chancellorsville, for he had met with great loss as well as great gains. The battle had cost heavily of his army, but his grief was over the severe wounding of his great lieutenant, General Thomas Jonathan Jackson, the head of the Second Corps of the Army of Northern Virginia; cut off, too, at a moment so much needed to finish his work in the battle so handsomely begun. With a brave heart, however, General Lee was getting his ranks together, and putting them in condition for other useful work. . . .

After reporting to General Lee, I offered the suggestion made to Secretary Seddon, in regard to the means that should be adopted for the relief of Vicksburg. . . .

He recognized the suggestion as of good combination, and giving strong assurance of success, but he was averse to having a part of his army so far beyond his reach. He reflected over the matter one or two days, and then fell upon the plan of invading the Northern soil, and so threatening Washington as to bring about the same hoped-for result [relieving Vicksburg]. To that end he bent his energies. . . . His confidence in making moves threatening Washington and the invasion of Maryland and Pennsylvania grew out of the known anxiety of the Washington authorities as to the safety of their capital and of the quiet within the Union lines. . . .

In the midst of his work of preparation came the announcement that General Jackson's trouble had taken an unfortunate turn, that he was thought to be sinking, and not many hours after that the news came that he had gone to rest. . . . General Jackson's death suggested to General Lee a reorganization of his army into three corps, and R.S. Ewell and A.P. Hill, appointed lieutenant-generals, were assigned to the Second and Third respectively. . . .[2]

INVASION OF PENNSYLVANIA

The Valley of the Shenandoah gave us firm, broad roads for the march north, curtained by the solid range of the Blue Ridge and South Mountains. There were some Federal troops occupying points in the Valley of Virginia, but not more than enough to give healthful employment to our leading columns as they advanced. . . .

The plan of campaign as projected was by the march of the Second Corps through the Valley of the Shenandoah to drive off or capture the Federal forces stationed along the Valley, and continue the march to Pennsylvania until further orders, meanwhile collecting supplies for the advance and for those who were to follow, Jenkins's brigade of cavalry working with the advance, and Imboden's on its left; the First Corps and the main force of cavalry to march near the east base of the Blue Ridge, threatening towards the rear line of the Army of the Potomac, and occupy the Blue Ridge, while the trains and other troops passed behind the mountains to follow the advance march. . . . In pursuance of the plan for the northern campaign our march was taken up on Wednesday, the third of June. . . .

On his march through the Valley, General Ewell took 4,000 prisoners and small arms, twenty-five cannon, eleven standards, 250 wagons, 400 horses, and large quantities of subsistence and quartermaster's stores, with a loss of 269 of all arms. He crossed the Potomac on the fifteenth, occupying Hagerstown and Sharpsburg, on the Maryland side, and sent the cavalry brigade, under Jenkins, north towards Chambersburg. . . .

After the First Corps was in position on the Blue Ridge, and while the Third was passing our rear down the Valley, it seems that General Lee so far modified the plan of march north as to authorize his cavalry chief [General James E.B. "Jeb" Stuart] to cross the Potomac with part of his command east of the Blue Ridge, and to change the march of the Third Corps by Hagerstown and Chambersburg. The point at which the cavalry force

[2] Longstreet commanded the First Corps.

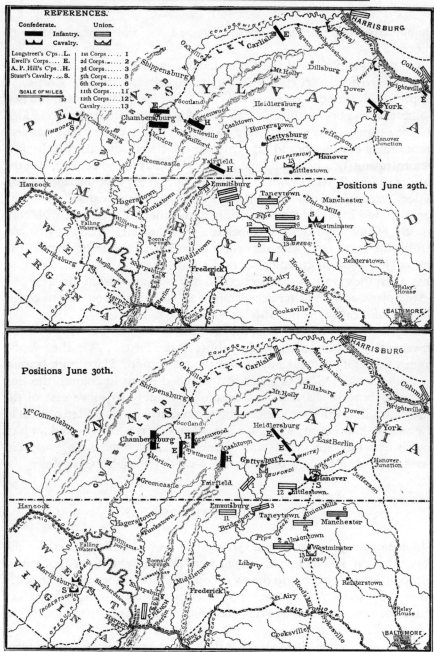

The march to Gettysburg, June 1863

should cross the river was not determined ... and I was ordered to choose. ...

On the twenty-second the Confederate commander sent unsealed instructions to his cavalry chief, through headquarters of the First Corps. ... As previously stated, I was to decide at the last moment between the two points that had been named. ... In the body of my note [to Stuart, added to Lee's instructions as they were forwarded to the cavalry commander] were orders that he should report to me of affairs along the cavalry line before leaving; that he should assign General Hampton to command of the cavalry to be left with us, with orders to report at my headquarters. These orders, emanating properly from the commander of the rear column of the army, should have not been questioned, but they were treated with contumely. He assigned General Robertson to command the cavalry that was left on the mountain, without orders to report at my headquarters; and though left there to guard passes of the Blue Ridge, he rode on a raid, so that when the cavalry was most needed it was far away from the army. ... So our plans, adopted after deep study, were suddenly given over to gratify the youthful cavalryman's wish for a nomadic ride. ...

On the twenty-third of June, the divisions of the Third Corps passed on towards the Potomac, followed by those of the First. ... On the twenty-eighth, General Lee issued orders for the march upon Harrisburg [capital of Pennsylvania]. General Ewell had marched his main column through Chambersburg to Carlisle. His column, intending to move east of the mountains through Emmitsburg and Gettysburg, had marched parallel to the main column as far as Greenwood, when orders were renewed for it to march east through Gettysburg. General Early, commanding, ordered Gordon's brigade and a detachment of cavalry through Gettysburg. ...

GETTYSBURG: THE FIRST DAY

The eve of the great battle was crowded with events. Movements for the concentration of the two vast armies went on in mighty force, but with a silence in strong contrast to the swift-coming commotion of their shock in conflict. It was the pent quiet of the gathering storm whose bursting was to shake the continent and suddenly command the startled attention of the world. ...

There were seven corps of the Army of the Potomac afield. We were informed on the twenty-eighth of the approximate positions of five of them—three near Frederick and two near the base of South Mountain.

The others, of which we had no definite information, we now know were the Sixth (Sedgwick's), south of Frederick and east of the Monocacy, and the Twelfth, towards Harper's Ferry.

On the twenty-sixth, General Hooker thought to use the Twelfth Corps and the garrison of Harper's Ferry to strike the line of our communication, but General Halleck forbade the use of the troops of that post, when General Hooker asked to be relieved of the responsibility of command, and was succeeded by General Meade on the night of the twenty-seventh. . . .

By the reports of [a] scout we found that the march of Ewell's east wing had failed of execution and of the effect designed, and that heavy columns of the enemy were hovering along the east base of the mountain. To remove this pressure towards our rear, General Lee concluded to make a more serious demonstration and force the enemy to look eastward. With this view he changed direction of the proposed march north, by counter-orders on the night of the twenty-eighth, calling concentration east of the mountains at Cashtown, and his troops began their march under the last orders on the twenty-ninth. . . .

General Hill decided to go beyond Cashtown on the first [of July] to ascertain as to the enemy reported at Gettysburg. He gave notice of his intentions to General Ewell, and sent back to the commanding general to have Anderson's division sent forward . . .

From Gettysburg roads diverge to the passes of the mountains, the borders of the Potomac and Susquehanna, and the cities of Baltimore and Washington; so that it was something of a strategic point. . . . North of Gettysburg the grounds are open and in fair fields. Directly south of it a bold ridge rises with rough and steep slopes. The prominent point of the south ridge is Cemetery Hill,[3] and east of this is Culp's Hill, from which the ridge turns sharply south half a mile, and drops off into low grounds. It was well wooded and its eastern ascent steep. East of it and flowing south is Rock Creek. From Cemetery Hill the ground is elevated, the ridge sloping south to the cropping out of Little Round Top, Devil's Den, the bolder Round Top, the latter about three miles south of the town. Cemetery Hill is nearly parallel to [and east of] Seminary Ridge, and is more elevated.

At five o'clock on the morning of July 1, General A.P. Hill marched towards Gettysburg with the divisions of Heth and Pender, and the battalions of artillery under Pegram and McIntosh, Heth's division and Pegram's artillery in advance. R.H. Anderson's division, with the reserve

[3] This feature is better known as Cemetery Ridge.

artillery left at Fayetteville, was ordered to march and halt at Cashtown. About ten o'clock Heth encountered Buford's [Union] cavalry. Archer's brigade, leading, engaged, and Davis's brigade came up on his left with part of Pegram's artillery. The cavalry was forced back till it passed Willoughby's Run.

On the thirtieth of June, General John F. Reynolds had been directed to resume command of the right wing of the Union army—First, Third, and Eleventh Corps. He was advised that day of the threatening movements of the Confederates on the Cashtown and Mummasburg roads. At the same time the indications from General Meade's headquarters pointed to Pipe Creek as the probable line of battle. Reynolds, however, prepared to support Buford's line of cavalry, and marched at eight o'clock on the first of July. . . .

As Reynolds approached Gettysburg, in hearing of the cavalry fight, he turned the head of his column to the left and marched through the fields towards the engagement. As the cavalry skirmish line retired and passed Willoughby's Run, he approached with his reinforcements. . . . During engagement on his right the advance of the Confederate infantry got in so close along the railroad cut that General Reynolds, in efforts to extricate his right, was shot, when the right, still under severe pressure, was forced to retire towards Seminary Ridge. . . .

The Confederates pushed rapidly on, particularly the fresher troops of Ewell, cleared the field, and followed on through the streets of Gettysburg at four o'clock. The retreat began and continued in good order. . . . As the troops retreated through Gettysburg, General Hancock rode upon the field, and under special assignment assumed [Union] command at three o'clock. . . .[4]

At Cashtown, General Lee found that General Hill had halted his division under R.H. Anderson and his reserve artillery. He had General Anderson called, who subsequently wrote me of the interview as follows:

> About twelve o'clock I received a message notifying me that General Lee desired to see me. I found General Lee intently listening to the fire of the guns, and very much disturbed and depressed. At length he said, more to himself than to me, "I cannot think what has become of Stuart. I ought to have heard from him long before now. . . . In

---

[4] During this part of the battle, the Union troops were forced east, past Seminary Ridge to Cemetery Ridge, where they were joined by the rest of the Army of the Potomac. General Reynolds's death was a heavy blow to the Union army, as he was one of its most able commanders.

absence of reports from him, I am in ignorance as to what we have in front of us here. It may be the whole Federal army, or it may be only a detachment. . . ."

He ordered Anderson forward, and rode on to Seminary Ridge in time to view the closing operations of the engagement. The Union troops were in disorder, climbing Cemetery heights, the Confederates following through the streets of Gettysburg. . . .

After a long wait I left orders for the troops to follow the trains of the Second Corps, and rode to find General Lee. His headquarters were on Seminary Ridge at the crossing of the Cashtown road. . . . Dismounting and passing the usual salutation, I drew my glasses and made a studied view of the position upon which the enemy was rallying his forces, and of the lay of the land surrounding. General Lee was engaged at the moment. He had announced beforehand [before the campaign began] that he would not make aggressive battle in the enemy's country. After the survey and in consideration of his plans—noting movements of detachments of the enemy on the Emmitsburg road, the relative positions for maneuver, the lofty perch of the enemy, the rocky slopes from it, all marking the position clearly defensive—I said, "We could not call the enemy to a position better suited to our plans. All that we have to do is file around his left and secure good ground between him and his capital." This, when said, was thought to be the opinion of my commander as much as my own. I was not a little surprised, therefore, at his impatience, as, striking the air with his closed hand, he said, "If he is there tomorrow I will attack him." . . .

When he rode away from me in the forenoon [when they had been on the march together] he made no mention of his absent cavalry, nor did he indicate that it was not within call. So I was at a loss to understand his nervous condition, and supported the suggestion so far as to say, "If he is there tomorrow it will be because he wants you to attack," and queried, "If that height has become the objective, why not take it at once? We have forty thousand men, less the casualties of the day; he cannot have more than twenty thousand." Then it was that I heard of the wanderings of the cavalry and the cause of his uneven temper. . . . His manner suggested to me that a little reflection would be better than further discussion, and right soon he suggested to the commander of the Second Corps to take Cemetery Hill if he thought it practicable, but the subordinate did not care to take upon himself a fight that his chief would not venture to order. . . .

Nothing coming from the center troops about Cemetery Hill, General Lee ordered the Second Corps, after night, from his left to his right, for

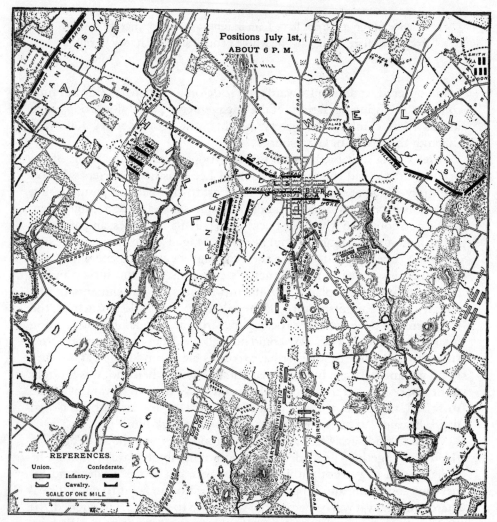

The first day at Gettysburg, 6:00 P.M., July 1, 1863

work in that direction, but General Ewell rode over and reported that another point—Culp's Hill—had been found on his left, which had commanding elevation over Cemetery Hill, from which the troops on the latter could be dislodged, by artillery, and was under the impression that his troops were in possession there. That was accredited as reported and approved, and the corps commander returned, and ordered the hill occupied if it had not been done. But the officer in charge had waited for specific orders, and when they were received he had made another reconnaissance. It was then twelve o'clock. By the reconnaissance it was found that the enemy was there, and it was thought that this should be reported, and further orders waited. . . .[5]

When I left General Lee, about seven o'clock in the evening, he had formed no plans beyond that of seizing Culp's Hill as his point from which to engage, nor given any orders for the next day, though his desperate mood was painfully evident, and gave rise to serious apprehensions. He had heard nothing of the movements of the enemy since his crossing the Potomac, except the report of his own scout. His own force on the field was the Second Corps, Rodes's, Early's, and E. Johnson's divisions from right to left through the streets of Gettysburg around towards Culp's Hill; on Rodes's right, Pender's division of the Third; on Seminary Ridge, R.H. Anderson's division of the Third (except Wilcox's brigade at Black Horse Tavern); behind Seminary Ridge, Heth's division of the Third; on the march between Cashtown and Greenwood, the First Corps.

THE SECOND DAY

The stars were shining brightly on the morning of the second when I reported at General Lee's headquarters and asked for orders. After a time Generals McLaws and Hood, with their staffs, rode up, and at sunrise their commands filed off the road to the right and rested. The Washington Artillery was with them, and about nine o'clock, after an all-out march, Alexander's batteries were up as far as Willoughby's Run, where he parked and fed, and rode to the headquarters to report.[6]

As indicated by these movements, General Lee was not ready with his plans. He had not heard from his cavalry, nor of the movements of the enemy further than the information from a dispatch captured during the night, that the Fifth Corps was in camp about five miles from Gettysburg, and the Twelfth Corps was reported near Culp's Hill. As soon as it was light enough to see, however, the enemy was found in position on his formidable heights awaiting us.

The result of the efforts during the night and early morning to secure Culp's Hill had not been reported, and General Lee sent Colonel Venable

[5] This commentary was a part of Longstreet's postwar criticism of Ewell for his tardy conduct; Longstreet believed that Ewell was most responsible for the defeat at Gettysburg (next to Lee himself).

[6] McLaws and Hood were divisional commanders in Longstreet's First Corps; much of the corps was still marching to the battlefield on the morning of the second day of battle.

of his staff to confer with the commander of the Second Corps as to opportunity to make the battle by his left. He was still in doubt whether it would be better to move to his far-off right. About nine o'clock he rode to his left to be assured of the position there, and of the general temper of affairs in that quarter. After viewing the field, he held conference with the corps and division commanders. They preferred to accept his judgment and orders, except General Early, who claimed to have learned of the topographical features of the country during his march towards York, and recommended the right of the line as the point at which the battle should be made. About ten o'clock General Lee returned to his headquarters, but his engineer who had been sent to reconnoiter on his right had not come back. To be on hand for orders, I remained with the troops at his headquarters. The infantry had arms stacked; the artillery was at rest.

The enemy occupied the commanding heights of the city cemetery, from which point, in irregular grade, the ridge slopes southward two miles and a half to a bold outcropping the height of three hundred feet called Little Round Top, and farther south half a mile ends in the greater elevation called Round Top. The former is covered from base to top by formidable boulders. From the cemetery to Little Round Top was the long main front of General Meade's position. At the cemetery his line turned to the northeast and east and southeast in an elliptical curve, with his right on Culp's Hill.

At an early hour of the second the Union army was posted: the Twelfth Corps at Culp's Hill, extending its left to Wadsworth's division of the First; on Wadsworth's left the Eleventh Corps; on the left of the Eleventh the other troops of the First; on their left the Second, and left of that to Little Round Top the Third Corps; the Fifth Corps stood in reserve across the bend from the right of the Twelfth to the left of the Second Corps. Thus there was formed a field of tremendous power upon a convex curve, which gave the benefit of rapid concentration at any point or points. The natural defenses had been improved during the night and early morning. The Sixth Corps was marching from Manchester, twenty-two miles from Gettysburg. . . . It was on the field at three o'clock in the afternoon—the Union cavalry under General Pleasonton in reach.

The Confederate left was covering the north and east curve of the enemy's line, Johnson's division near Culp's Hill, Early's and Rodes's extending the line to the right through Gettysburg; Pender's division on the right of Rodes's; the other divisions of the Third Corps resting on Seminary Ridge, with McLaws's division and Hood's three brigades near general headquarters; Pickett's brigades and Law's of Hood's division at Chambersburg and New Guildford, twenty-two and twenty-four miles away. Law had received orders to join his division, and was on the march. The cavalry was not yet heard from. The line was so extended and twisted about the rough ground that concentration at any point was not possible.

It was some little time after General Lee's return from his ride to the left before he received the reports of the reconnaissance ordered from his center to his right. His mind, previously settled to the purpose to fight where the enemy now stood, now accepted the explicit plan of making the opening on his right, and to have the engagement general. He ordered the commander of the Third Corps to extend the center by Anderson's division, McLaws's and Hood's divisions to extend the deployment to his right. Heth's division of the Third was drawn nearer the front, and notice of his plans was sent to the commander of the Second Corps. . . .

The battle was to be opened on the right by two divisions of the First Corps, supported on their left by four of the brigades of Anderson's division; the opening to be promptly followed on Lee's left by the Second Corps, and continued to real attack if the opportunity occurred; the Third (center) Corps to move to severe threatening and take advantage of opportunity to attack; the movements of the Second and Third Corps to be prompt, and in close, severe cooperation, so as to prevent concentration against the battle of the right. . . .

General Lee ordered his reconnoitering officer to lead the troops of the First Corps and conduct them by a route concealed from view of the enemy. . . . General Anderson marched by a route nearer the enemy's line, and was discovered by General Sickles, who commanded the Third Corps, the left of the Union line. A little uncomfortable at his retired position, and seeing that the battle was forming against him, General Sickles thought to put the Third Maine Regiment and the Berdan Sharpshooters on outpost in a bold woodland cover, to develop somewhat of the approaching battle, and presently threw his corps forward as far as the Peach Orchard, half a mile forward of the position assigned to it in the general line. . . .

Under the conduct of the reconnoitering officer, our march seemed slow—there were some halts and countermarches. To save time, I ordered the rear division to double on the front, and we were near the affair of Anderson's regiments with the outpost guard of Sickles. . . .[7]

General Hood was ordered to send his select scouts in advance, to go through the woodlands and act as vedettes, in the absence of cavalry, and give information of the enemy, if there. The double line marched up the slope and deployed—McLaws on the right of Anderson, Hood's division

[7] This comment forms part of Longstreet's postwar effort to explain away his tardy movement on July 2.

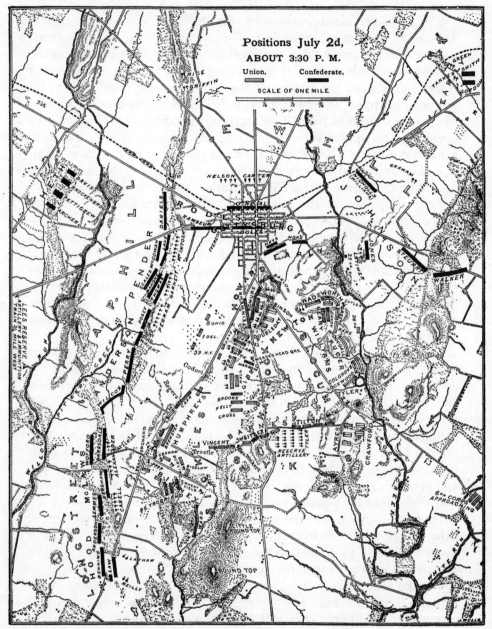

The second day at Gettysburg, 3:30 P.M., July 2, 1863

on his right, McLaws near the crest of the plateau in front of the Peach Orchard, Hood spreading and enveloping Sickles's left. The former was readily adjusted to ground from which to advance or defend. Hood's front was very rugged, with no field for artillery, and very rough for advance of infantry. As soon as he passed the Emmitsburg road, he sent to report of the great advantage of moving on by his right around to the enemy's rear. His scouting parties had reported that there was nothing between him and the enemy's trains. He was told that the move to the right had been proposed the day before and rejected; that General Lee's orders were to guide my left by the Emmitsburg road.

In our immediate front were the divisions of the [Union] Third Corps under Generals Humphreys and Birney, from right to left, with orders for support of the flanks by divisions of the Second and Fifth Corps. The ground on the left of Birney's division was so broken and obstructed by boulders that his left was dropped off to the rear, forming a broken line. In rear of the enemy, and between his lines and Little Round Top, was a very rough elevation of eighty feet formed by upheavals that left open passage deep down Devil's Den [as the boulders were known]. . . .

As McLaws's division came up on line, Barksdale's brigade was in front of a battery about six hundred yards off. He appealed for permission to charge and capture it, but was told to wait. On his right was Kershaw's brigade, and the brigades of Semmes and Wofford on the second line. Hood's division was in two lines—Law's and Robertson's brigades in front, G.T. Anderson's and Benning's in the second line. The batteries were with the divisions—four to the division. One of G.T. Anderson's regiments was put on picket down on the Emmitsburg road.

General Hood appealed again and again for the move to the right, but, to give more confidence to his attack, he was reminded that the move to the right had been carefully considered by our chief and rejected in favor of his present orders.

Four of the brigades of Anderson's division were ordered to advance in echelon in support of my left.

At three o'clock the artillery was ordered to open practice. General Meade was then with General Sickles discussing the feasibility of withdrawing his corps to the position from which it was originally assigned, but the opening admonished him that it was too late. . . .

Prompt to the order the combat opened, followed by artillery of the other corps, and our artillerists measured up to the better metal of the enemy by vigilant work. Hood's lines were not yet ready. After a little practice by the artillery, he was properly adjusted and ordered to bear down upon the enemy's left, but he was not prompt, and the order was repeated before he would strike down.

In his usual gallant style he led his troops through the rocky fastness against the strong lines of his earnest adversary, and encountered battle that called for all of his power and skill. The enemy was tenacious of his strong ground; his skillfully-handled batteries swept through the passes between the rocks; the more deadly fire of infantry concentrated as our men bore upon the angle of the enemy's line and stemmed the fiercest onset, until it became necessary to shorten their work by a desperate charge. This pressing struggle and the crossfire of our batteries broke in the salient angle, but the thickening fire, as the angle was pressed back, hurt Hood's left and held him in steady fight. His right brigade was drawn towards Round Top and by the heavy fire pouring from that quarter, Benning's brigade was pressed to the thickening line at the angle, and G.T. Anderson's was put in support of the battle growing against Hood's right.

I rode to McLaws, found him ready for his opportunity, and Barksdale chafing in his wait for the order to seize the battery in his front. Kershaw's brigade of his right first advanced and struck near the angle of the enemy's line where his forces were gathering strength. After additional caution to hold his ranks closed, McLaws ordered Barksdale in. With glorious bearing he sprang to his work, overriding obstacles and dangers. Without a pause to deliver a shot, he had the battery. Kershaw, joined by Semmes's brigade, responded, and Hood's men, feeling the impulsion of relief, resumed their bold fight, and presently the enemy's line was broken through its length. But his well-seasoned troops knew how to utilize the advantage of their grounds and put back their dreadful fires from rocks, depressions, and stone fences, as they went for shelter about Little Round Top.

That point had not been occupied by the enemy, nor marked as an important feature of the field. The broken ranks sought shelter under its rocks and defiles as birds fly to cover. General Hood fell seriously hurt, and General Law succeeded to command of his division, but the well-seasoned troops were not in need of a close guiding hand. The battle was on, and they knew how to press its hottest contention.

General Warren, chief engineer of the Federal army, was sent at the critical moment to Little Round Top, and found that it was the citadel of the field. He called for troops to occupy it. The Fifth Corps (Sykes's) was hurried to him, and General Hancock sent him Caldwell's division of the Second Corps. At the Brick House, General Sickles had a detachment that had been reinforced by General Hancock. This fire drew Anderson's brigade of direction (Wilcox) a little off from support of Barksdale's left.

General Humphreys, seeing the opportunity, rallied such of his troops as he could, and reinforced by Hays's division (Willard's brigade) of Hancock's corps, came against Barksdale's flank, but the latter moved bravely on, the guiding spirit of the battle. Wright's Georgia and Perry's Florida brigades were drawn in behind Wilcox and thrown against Humphreys, pushing him off and breaking him up.

The fighting had by this time become tremendous, and brave men and officers were stricken by hundreds. Posey and Wilcox dislodged the forces about the Brick House.

General Sickles was desperately wounded!

General Willard was dead!

General Semmes, of McLaws's division, was mortally wounded!

Our left relieved, the brigades of Anderson's division moved on with Barksdale's, passed the swale, and moved up the slope. Caldwell's division, and presently those of Ayres and Barnes of the Fifth Corps, met and held our strongest battle. While thus engaged, General Sykes succeeded in putting Vincent's and Weed's brigades and Hazlett's battery on the summit of Little Round Top, but presently we overreached Caldwell's division, broke it off, and pushed it from the field. Of his brigade commanders, Zook was killed, and Brooke and Cross were wounded, the latter mortally. General Hancock reported sixty percent of his men lost. On our side, Barksdale was down dying, and G.T. Anderson wounded.

We had carried Devil's Den, were at the Round Tops and the Wheat Field, but Ayres's division of regulars and Barnes's division were holding us in equal battle. The struggle throughout the field seemed at its tension. The brigades of R.H. Anderson's division could hold off other troops of Hancock's, but were not strong enough to step to the enemy's lines. When Caldwell's division was pushed away, Ayres's flank and the gorge at Little Round Top were covered only by a sharp line of picket men behind the boulders. If we could drive in the sharpshooters and strike Ayres's flank to advantage, we could dislodge his and Barnes's divisions, occupy the gorge behind Sykes's brigades on Round Top, force them to retreat, and lift our desperate fighters to the summit. I had one brigade—Wofford's—that had not been engaged in the hottest battle. To urge the troops to their reserve power in the precious moments, I rode with Wofford. The rugged field, the rough plunge of artillery fire, and the piercing musket shots delayed somewhat the march, but Alexander dashed up with his batteries and gave new spirit to the worn infantry ranks. By a fortunate strike upon Ayres's flank we broke his line and pushed him and Barnes so closely that they were obliged to use most strenuous efforts to get away without losing prisoners as well as their killed and wounded. We gained the Wheat Field, and were so close upon the gorge that our artillery could no longer venture their fire into it. We were on Little Round Top grappling for the crowning point. The brigade commanders there, Vincent and Wood, were killed, also the battery commander, Hazlett, and others, but their troops were holding to their work as firmly as the mighty boulders that helped them. General Meade thought that the Confederate army was working on my part of the field. He led some regiments of the Twelfth Corps and posted them against us, called a division of Newton's corps (First) from beyond Hancock's, and sent Crawford's division, the last of the Fifth Corps, splitting through the gorge, forming solid lines, in places behind stone fences, and making steady battle, as veterans fresh in action know so well how to make. While Meade's lines were growing my men were dropping; we had no others to call to their aid, and the weight against us was too heavy to carry. The extreme left of our lines was only about a mile across from the enemy's concentric position, which brought us within hearing of that battle, if engaged, and near enough to feel its swell, but nothing was heard or felt but the clear ring of the enemy's fresh metal as he came against us. No other part of our army had engaged! My seventeen thousand against the Army of the Potomac! The sun was down, and with it went down the severe battle. I ordered recall of the troops to the line of Plum Run and Devil's Den, leaving picket lines near the foot of the Round Tops. My loss was about six thousand, Meade's between twelve and fourteen thousand; but his loss in general and field officers was frightful. . . .[8]

General Stuart came down from Carlisle with his column of cavalry late in the afternoon of the second. As he approached he met a cavalry force of the enemy moving towards the Confederate left rear, and was successful in arresting it. He was posted with Jenkins's three thousand cavalry on the Confederate left.

Notwithstanding the supreme order of the day for general battle, and the reinforcement of the cavalry on our left, the Second and Third Corps remained idle during all of the severe battle of the Confederate right, except the artillery, and the part on the extreme left was only in practice long enough to feel the superior metal of the enemy, when it retired. . . .

At eight o'clock in the evening the division on our extreme left, E. Johnson's, advanced. . . . After brave attack and defense, part of the line was carried. . . .

General Lee ordered Johnson's division of his left, occupying part of the

---

[8] As always, casualty figures given by commanding generals need to be taken with a grain of salt. A more accurate estimate puts each side's casualties on July 2 at 9,000.

enemy's trenches about Culp's Hill, to be reinforced during the night of the second by two brigades of Rodes's division and one of Early's division. Why the other brigades of those divisions were not sent does not appear, but it does appear that there was a place for them on Johnson's left, in the trenches that were vacated by the Federal Twelfth Corps when called over to reinforce the battle of Meade's left. . . .

General Meade, after the battle of his left, ordered the divisions of his Twelfth Corps back to their trenches [on Culp's Hill], to recover the parts occupied by the Confederate left. It was night when the First Division approached. General Ruger, commanding, thought to feel his way through the dark by a line of skirmishers. He found the east end of his trenches, across the swale, unoccupied, and took possession. Pressing his adventure, he found the main line of his works occupied by the Confederates in force, and disposed his command to wait for daylight. . . .

During the night, General Meade held a council, which decided to fight it out. So it began to look as if the vicissitudes of the day had so worked as to call General Meade from defensive to aggressive battle for Culp's Hill. But the Confederates failed to see the opportunity and force the issue as it was presented. . . .[9]

THE THIRD DAY

In the absence of orders, I had scouting parties out during the night in search of a way by which we might strike the enemy's left, and push it down towards his center. I found a way that gave some promise of results, and was about to move the command, when [Lee] rode over after sunrise and gave his orders. His plan was to assault the enemy's left center by a column to be composed of McLaws's and Hood's divisions reinforced by Pickett's brigades. I thought that it would not do; that the point had been fully tested the day before, by more men, when all were fresh; that the enemy was there looking for us, as we heard him during the night putting up his defenses; that the divisions of McLaws and Hood were holding a mile along the right of my line against twenty thousand men, who would follow their withdrawal, strike the flank of the assaulting column, crush it, and get on our rear towards the Potomac River; that thirty thousand men was the minimum force necessary for the work; that even such force would need

[9] Here Longstreet again argues that the Confederates would have done better to maneuver so as to force the Federals to attack the rebel army (he preferred the tactical defensive).

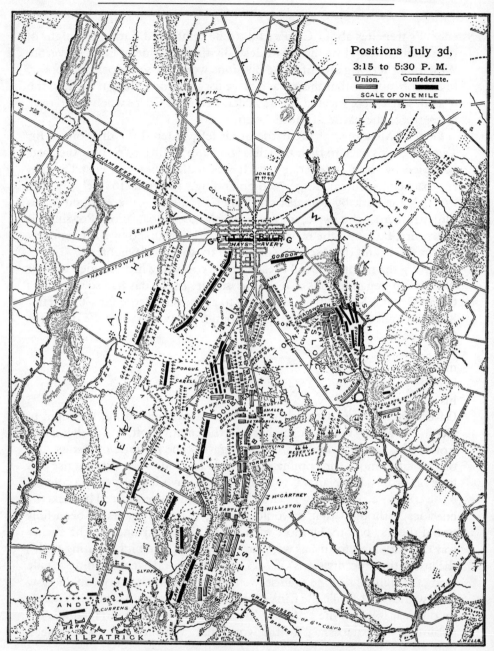

The third day at Gettysburg, July 3, 1863

close cooperation on other parts of the line; that the column as he proposed to organize it would have only thirteen thousand men (the divisions having lost a third of their numbers the day before); that the column would have to march a mile under concentrating battery fire, and a thousand yards under long-range musketry; that the conditions were different from those in the days of Napoleon, when field batteries had a range of six hundred yards and musketry about sixty yards.

He said the distance was not more than fourteen hundred yards. . . . He then concluded that the divisions of McLaws and Hood could remain on the defensive line; that he would reinforce by divisions of the Third Corps and Pickett's brigades, and stated the point to which the march should be directed. I asked the strength of the column. He stated fifteen thousand. Opinion was then expressed that the fifteen thousand men who could make successful assault over that field had never been arrayed for battle; but he was impatient of listening, and tired of talking, and nothing was left but to proceed. General Alexander was ordered to arrange the batteries of the front of the First and Third Corps. . . .

At the time of the conversation and arrangement of the assault by the Confederate right, artillery fire was heard on our extreme left. It seems that General Lee had sent orders to General Ewell to renew his battle in the morning, which was intended, and directed, as a cooperation of the attack he intended to order on his right, but General Ruger, anticipating, opened his batteries against Ewell at daylight. The Union divisions—Ruger's and Gary's—were on broken lines, open towards the trenches held by the Confederates, so that assault by our line would expose the force to fire from the enemy's other line. Ruger had occupied the trenches left vacant on his right, and Gary reached to his left under Greene, who had held his line against the attack of the day before. . . .

As the Union batteries opened, Johnson advanced and assaulted the enemy's works on his right towards the center and adjacent front of the new line, and held to that attack with resolution, putting in fresh troops to help it from time to time. Ruger put in two regiments forward to feel the way towards Johnson's left. They got into hot engagement and were repulsed; Johnson tried to follow, but was in turn forced back. He renewed his main attack again, but unsuccessfully, and finally drew back to the trenches. Ruger threw a regiment forward from his left which gained the stone wall; his division was then advanced, and it recovered the entire line of trenches.

While this contention was in progress the troops ordered for the column of assault were marching and finding positions under the crest of the ridge, where they could be covered during the artillery combat.[10] Alexander put in a battery of nine guns under the ridge and out of the enemy's fire to be used with the assaulting column. . . .

As the commands reported, Pickett was assigned on the right, Kemper's and Garnett's brigades to be supported by Armistead's; Wilcox's brigade of the Third Corps in echelon and guarding Pickett's right; Pettigrew's division on Pickett's left, supported by the brigades of Scales and Lane, under command of General Trimble. . . . The ridge upon which the commands were formed was not parallel to that upon which the enemy stood, but bending west towards our left, while the enemy's line bore northwest towards his right, so that the left of the assaulting column formed some little distance farther from the enemy's line than the right. To put the troops under the best cover during the artillery combat they were thus posted for the march, but directed to spread their steps as soon as the march opened the field, and to gain places of correct alignment.

Meanwhile, the enemy's artillery on his extreme right was in practice more or less active, but its meaning was not known or reported, and the sharpshooters of the command on the right had a lively fusillade about eleven o'clock, in which some of the artillery took part. The order was that the right was to make the signal of battle. General Lee reported that his left attacked before due notice to wait for the opening could be given, which was a mistake, inasmuch as the attack on his left was begun by the Federals, which called his left to their work. General Meade was not apprehensive of that part of the field. . . . He knew by the Confederate troops on his right just where the strong battle was to be.

The director of artillery was asked to select a position on his line from which he could note the effect of his practice, and to advise General Pickett when the enemy's fire was so disturbed as to call for the assault. General Pickett's was the division of direction, and he was ordered to have a staff officer or courier with the artillery director to bear notice of the moment to advance.

The little affair between the skirmish lines quieted in a short time, and also the noise on our extreme left. The quiet filing of one or two of our batteries into position emphasized the profound silence that prevailed during our wait for final orders. Strong battle was in the air, and the veterans of both sides swelled their breasts to gather nerve and strength to meet it. Division commanders were asked to go to the crest of the ridge and take a careful view of the field, and to have their officers there to tell their

---

[10] "Under the ridge" means on the side away from the enemy.

men of it, and to prepare them for the sight that was to burst upon them as they mounted the crest . . .

When satisfied that the work of preparation was all that it could be with the means at hand, I wrote Colonel Walton, of the Washington Artillery—

> HEADQUARTERS, JULY 3, 1863
>
> COLONEL—Let the batteries open. Order great care and precision in firing. When the batteries at the Peach Orchard cannot be used against the point we intend to attack, let them open on the enemy's on the rocky hill.
>
> Most respectfully,
> JAMES LONGSTREET
> Lieutenant-General, Commanding

At the same time a note to Alexander directed that Pickett should not be called until the artillery practice indicated fair opportunity. Then I rode to a woodland hard by, to lie down and study for some new thought that might aid the assaulting column. In a few minutes report came from Alexander that he would only be able to judge the effect of his fire by the return of that of the enemy, as his infantry was not exposed to view, and the smoke of the batteries would soon cover the field. He asked, if there was an alternative, that it be carefully considered before the batteries opened, as there was not enough artillery ammunition for this and another trial if this should not prove favorable.

He was informed that there was no alternative; that I could find no way out of it; that General Lee had considered and would listen to nothing else; that orders had gone for the guns to give the signal for the batteries; that he should call the troops at the first opportunity or lull in the enemy's fire.

The signal-guns broke the silence, the blaze of the second gun mingling in the smoke of the first, and the salvoes rolled to the left and repeated themselves, the enemy's fine metal spreading its fire to the converging lines, plowing the trembling ground, plunging through the line of batteries, and clouding the heavy air. The two or three hundred guns seemed proud of their undivided honors and organized confusion. The Confederates had the benefit of converging fire into the enemy's massed position, but the superior metal of the enemy neutralized the advantage of the position. The brave and steady work progressed.

Before this the Confederates of the left were driven from their captured trenches, and the hope of their effective cooperation with the battle of the right was lost, but no notice of it was sent to the right of the battle. They made some further demonstrations, but they were of little effect. . . .

General Pickett rode to confer with Alexander, then to the ground upon which I was resting, where he was soon handed a slip of paper. After reading it he handed it to me. It read:

> If you are coming at all, come at once, or I cannot give you proper support, but the enemy's fire has not slackened at all. At least eighteen guns are still firing from the cemetery itself.
>
> ALEXANDER

Pickett said, "General, shall I advance?"

The effort to speak the order failed, and I could only indicate it by an affirmative bow. He accepted the duty with seeming confidence of success, leaped on his horse, and rode gaily to his command. I mounted and spurred for Alexander's post. He reported that the batteries he had reserved for the charge with the infantry had been spirited away by General Lee's chief of artillery; that the ammunition of the batteries of position was so reduced that he could not use them in proper support of the infantry. He was ordered to stop the march at once and fill up his ammunition chests. But, alas! there was no more ammunition to be had.

The order was imperative. The Confederate commander had fixed his heart upon the work. Just then a number of the enemy's batteries hitched up and hauled off, which gave a glimpse of unexpected hope. Encouraging messages were sent for the columns to hurry on—and they were then on elastic springing step. The officers saluted as they passed, their stern smiles expressing confidence. General Pickett, a graceful horseman, sat lightly in the saddle, his brown locks flowing quite over his shoulders. Pettigrew's division spread their steps and quickly rectified the alignment, and the grand march moved bravely on. As soon as the leading columns opened the way, the supports sprang to their alignments. General Trimble mounted, adjusting his seat and reins with an air and grace as if setting out on a pleasant afternoon ride. When aligned to their places solid march was made down the slope and past our batteries of position.

Confederate batteries put their fire over the heads of the men as they moved down the slope, and continued to draw the fire of the enemy until the smoke lifted and drifted to the rear, when every gun was turned upon the infantry columns. The batteries that had been drawn off were replaced by others that were fresh. Soldiers and officers began to fall, some to rise no more, others to find their way to the hospital tents. Single files were cut here and there, then the gaps increased, and an occasional shot tore wider openings, but, closing the gaps as quickly as made, the march moved on. The divisions of McLaws and Hood were ordered to move to closer lines for the enemy on their front, to spring to the charge as soon as the breach at the center could be made. The enemy's right overreached my left and gave serious trouble. Brockenbrough's brigade went down and Davis's in impetuous charge. The general order required further assistance from the Third Corps if needed, but no support appeared. General Lee and the corps commander were there, but failed to order help.

Colonel Latrobe was sent to General Trimble to have his men fill the line of the broken brigades, and bravely they repaired the damage. The enemy moved out against the supporting brigade in Pickett's rear. Colonel Sorel was sent to have that move guarded, and Pickett was drawn back to that contention. McLaws was ordered to press his left forward, but the direct fire of infantry and crossfire of artillery was telling fearfully on the front. Colonel Fremantle ran up to offer congratulations on the apparent success, but the big gaps in the ranks grew until the lines were reduced to half their length. I called his attention to the broken, struggling ranks. Trimble mended the battle of the left in handsome style, but on the right the massing of the enemy grew stronger and stronger. Brigadier Garnett was killed, Kemper and Trimble were desperately wounded; Generals Hancock and Gibbon were wounded. General Lane succeeded Trimble, and with Pettigrew held the battle of the left in steady ranks.

Pickett's lines being nearer, the impact was heaviest upon them. Most of the field officers were killed or wounded. Colonel Whittle, of Armistead's brigade, who had been shot through the left leg at Williamsburg and lost his left arm at Malvern Hill, was shot through the right arm, then brought down by a shot through his left leg.

General Armistead, of the second line, spread his steps to supply the places of fallen comrades. His colors cut down, with a volley against the bristling line of bayonets, he put his cap on his sword to guide the storm. The enemy's massing, enveloping numbers held the struggle until the noble Armistead fell beside the wheels of the enemy's battery. Pettigrew was wounded, but held his command.

General Pickett, finding the battle broken, while the enemy was still reinforcing, called the troops off. There was no indication of panic. The broken files marched back in steady step. The effort was nobly made, and failed from blows that could not be fended. Some of the files were cut off from retreat by fire that swept the field in their rear. Officers of my staff, sent forward with orders, came back with their saddles and bridles in their arms. Latrobe's horse was twice shot.

Looking confidently for the advance of the enemy through our open field, I rode to the line of batteries, resolved to hold it until the last gun was lost. As I rode, the shells screaming over my head and plowing the ground under my horse, an involuntary appeal went up that one of them might take me from scenes of such awful responsibility; but the storm to be met left no time to think of one's self. The battery officers were prepared to meet the crisis—no move had been made for leaving the field. My old acquaintance of Sharpsburg experience, Captain Miller, was walking up and down behind his guns, smoking his pipe, directing his fire over the heads of our men as fast as they were inside of the danger line; the other officers were equally firm and ready to defend to the last. A body of skirmishers put out from the enemy's lines and advanced some distance, but the batteries opened severe fire and drove it back. Our men passed the batteries in quiet walk, and would rally, I knew, when they reached the ridge from which they started.

General Lee was soon with us, and with staff officers and others assisted in encouraging the men and getting them together. . . . When engaged collecting the broken files after the repulse, General Lee said to an officer who was assisting, "It is all my fault." . . .[11]

As the attack failed, General Kilpatrick put his [Union] cavalry brigade under General Farnsworth on the charge through the infantry detachment in rear of my right division. . . . Farnsworth had a rough ride over rocks and stone fences, but bore on in spite of all, cutting and slashing when he could get at the skirmishers or detachments. . . . He fell, pierced, it is said, by five mortal wounds. . . .

A little while after the repulse of our infantry column, Stuart's cavalry advanced and was met by Gregg's, and made one of the severest and stubborn fights of cavalry on record. General Wade Hampton was severely wounded. The Union forces held the field.

When affairs had quieted a little, and apprehension of immediate counterattack had passed, orders were sent to the divisions of McLaws and Hood to draw back and occupy the lines from which they had advanced to engage the battle of the second. . . .

The army when it set out on the campaign was all that could be desired (except that the arms were not all of the approved pattern), but it was despoiled of two of its finest brigades, Jenkins's and Corse's of Pickett's

[11] This sentence has been moved for narrative continuity.

division, and [the battle] was fought out by detail. The greatest number engaged at any one time was on the first day, when twenty-six thousand engaged twenty thousand of the First and part of the Eleventh Corps. On the afternoon of the second day about seventeen thousand were engaged on the right, and at night about seven thousand on the left; then later at night about three thousand near the center. On the third day about twelve thousand were engaged at daylight and until near noon, and in the afternoon fifteen thousand—all of the work of the second and third days against an army of seventy thousand and more of veteran troops in strong position defended by fieldworks.

General Lee was on the field from about three o'clock of the afternoon of the first day. Every order given the troops of the First Corps on that field up to its march on the forenoon of the second was issued in his presence. If the movements were not satisfactory in time and speed of moving, it was his power, duty, and privilege to apply the remedy. . . .[12]

The armies rested on the "Fourth"—one under the bright laurels secured by the brave work of the day before, but in profound sorrow over the silent forms of the host of comrades who had fallen during those three fateful days, whose blood bathed the thirsty fields of Gettysburg, made classic by the most stupendous clash of conflict of that long and sanguinary war; while the gentle rain came to mellow the sod that marked the honored rest of friend and foe; the other, with broken spirits, turned from fallen comrades to find safety away from the fields that had been so promising of ennobling fruits. The enemy had cast his lines on grounds too strong for lead and steel, and, exhausted alike of aggressive force and the means of protracted defense, there was nothing left for the vanquished but to march for distant homeward lines. . . .

Pursuit was made by the enemy, led by cavalry and the Sixth Corps, and the rearguard had to deploy near Fairfield to check it. Rain was helping us. Before the enemy could get through the mud and push his batteries over the boggy fields, our trains had reached the mountain gorge, and the rearguard was on the march following. . . . On this retreat the army, already crippled of its pride, was met by the dispiriting news of another defeat at Vicksburg, which meant that the Mississippi was free to the Federals from its source to the Gulf. . . .

After the retreat, and when resting on the south bank of the Rapidan,

---

[12] In this paragraph Longstreet (who has been blamed for losing the battle for the South) defends himself by blaming Lee—with good reason, despite his own foot-dragging on July 2.

reading of the progress of the march of General Rosecrans's army towards Georgia, it seemed sinful to lie there idle while our comrades in the West were so in need of assistance, and I wrote the Secretary of War suggesting that a detachment should be sent West from the idle army. General Lee objected, but the suggestion was ordered to be executed.[13]

In the years after the Civil War came to a close, someone once asked General Pickett why the Confederates had lost the battle of Gettysburg. Was it Ewell's hesitation in seizing Culp's Hill, or Longstreet's tardiness in attacking on the second day? Pickett reportedly shrugged his shoulders and said, "I always thought the Yankees had something to do with it."

And so they did. Despite unsurpassed bravery, the soldiers of the Army of Northern Virginia could not shake the Yankees from their position. Skillful and resolute action from the private soldiers through regimental commanders to General Meade himself characterized the performance of the Army of the Potomac during those bitterly contested three days. At the end, the rebels had indeed been whipped, and crowds across the North celebrated the first clear victory over Robert E. Lee and his men, at the moment of the Union's greatest peril.

Lincoln, however, was left unsatisfied. He sat in frustration as Meade moved sluggishly to pursue the battered Southern forces, now denuded of one-third of their numbers. Instead of trapping and destroying the main Confederate army so far from its base, Meade moved cautiously, seemingly unable to believe his own victory over the famed Lee. The general kept command of the Army of the Potomac, but Lincoln was reduced to tears of rage as the rebels slipped away.

Upon returning to Virginia, the Southern commander promptly offered his resignation, which was of course denied by President Jefferson Davis. Despite the catastrophe, it was clear to all that no one could replace Lee. Longstreet, however, received a second hearing on his plan to reinforce Bragg and carry the war into Tennessee, and before long he took two divisions west as the Army of Northern Virginia fended off Meade's half-hearted thrusts. Even as Longstreet's men boarded trains to join Bragg, another war was raging deep behind Union lines—a shadowy, savagely fought guerrilla war.

[13] This paragraph has been moved for narrative continuity.

V

THE GUERRILLA
WAR

11
MOSBY'S CONFEDERACY

Even as the great maneuvers and clashes of the main armies captured the world's attention, another war raged behind Union lines from Missouri to Virginia: a guerrilla war of sudden ambushes and raids, fought between small bands of mounted men, armed mainly with revolvers. By the time of Lee's surrender, hit-and-run attacks by raiding Confederate cavalrymen and civilian partisans had forced Federal commanders to station tens of thousands of troops far from the main battlefronts to guard vulnerable railway lines and supply depots. Columns of Union cavalry chased about the country in search of the elusive enemy, who slipped away with the help of the local population.

In Missouri and northern Virginia in particular, Confederate guerrillas scored tremendous successes against Union forces. In both areas, most of the fighters were local men who preferred to fight the Yankee enemy in their own backyards rather than in the main Southern armies. In Virginia, the local partisans fought under the leadership of a regular officer in the Confederate army, a brave and cunning cavalryman named John Singleton Mosby. Mosby had been a scout for General J.E.B. Stuart, the legendary cavalry commander for the Army of Northern Virginia, and had participated in such exploits as Stuart's famous ride around the Army of the Potomac in the Peninsula campaign.

In 1863, acting under the Confederate Partisan Ranger Act and with Stuart's encouragement, Mosby set about raising a guerrilla outfit in Loudoun County, Virginia. He proved to be a genius at hit-and-run warfare, and before long his Rangers had hounded Union forces so successfully that large areas of the state became known as Mosby's Confederacy. In the pages that follow, Mosby recounts his start as a partisan commander, and his most famous exploit—the capture of a Union general in bed, deep behind Federal lines and barely ten miles from Washington.

The Capture of General Stoughton
By Colonel John S. Mosby

[In December 1862] McClellan and Pope had been driven from Virginia, and Burnside had met a bloody repulse at Fredericksburg. The two hostile armies were in winter quarters on the Rappahannock, and the pickets on the opposite banks had declared a truce and were swapping coffee and tobacco. Occasionally a band on the northern bank played a favorite Southern air and soon, in response, the strain of the Star Spangled Banner came from our side. The cavalry was not used for picketing and had been sent to the rear to be more convenient to forage.

To relieve the monotony Stuart resolved to take his cavalry on a Christmas raid to Dumfries on Burnside's line of communication with Washington. A good many wagons with supplies were captured, and we chased a cavalry regiment through their own camp and got all their good things. . . .

When he returned, Stuart let me stay behind a few days with six men to operate on the enemy's outposts. He was so satisfied with our success that he let me have fifteen men to return and begin my partisan life in northern Virginia—which closed with the war. That was the origin of my battalion. On January 24, 1863, we crossed the Rappahannock and immediately began operations in a country which Joe Johnston had abandoned a year before. It looked as though I was leading a forlorn hope, but I was never discouraged. In general my purpose was to threaten and harass the enemy on the border and in this way compel him to withdraw troops from his front to guard the line of the Potomac and Washington. . . .

Recruits came to us from inside the enemy's lines, and they brought valuable information. Then, I had picketed for some time in Fairfax the year before and I had acquired considerable local knowledge. The troops attached to the defense of Washington, south of the Potomac, were distributed in winter quarters through Fairfax County and extended in an arc of a circle from the upper to the lower Potomac. The headquarters of General Stoughton, who commanded them, were at the Court House. In a day or so after I arrived in Loudoun, we began operations on the outposts of Fairfax. The weak points were generally selected for attack. Up to that time the pickets had passed a quiet life in the camps or dozing on the picket posts, but now they were kept under arms and awake all night by a foe who generally assailed them where he was least expected. . . .

After a few weeks of partisan life, I meditated a more daring enterprise than any I had attempted and fortunately received aid from an unexpected quarter. A deserter from the 5th New York Cavalry, named Ames, came to me. He was a sergeant in his regiment and came in his full uniform. I never cared to inquire what his grievance was. The account he gave me of the distribution of troops and the gaps in the picket lines coincided with what I knew and tended to prepossess me in his favor. . . .

I now determined to execute my scheme to capture both General Stoughton and Wyndham at their headquarters. Ames . . . knew where their headquarters were, and the place was familiar to me as I had been in camp there. I also knew, both from Ames and the prisoners, where the gaps in the lines were at night. The safety of the enterprise lay in its novelty; nothing of the kind had ever been done before.

On the evening of March 8, 1863, in obedience to orders, twenty-nine men met me in Dover, in Loudoun County. None knew my objective point, but I told Ames after we started . . .

The weather conditions favored my success. There was a melting snow on the ground, a mist, and about dark, a drizzling rain. Our starting point was about twenty-five miles from Fairfax Court House. It was pitch dark when we got near the cavalry pickets at Chantilly—five or six miles from the Court House. At Centreville, three miles away on the Warrenton Pike and seven miles from the Court House, were several thousand troops. Our problem was to pass between them and Wyndham's cavalry without giving the alarm. Ames knew where there was a break in the picket lines between Chantilly and Centreville, and he led us through this without a vidette seeing us. After passing the outpost the chief point in the game was won. I think no man with me, except Ames, realized that we were inside the enemy's lines. But the enemy felt secure and was ignorant as my men. The plan had been to reach the Court House by midnight so as to get out of the lines before daybreak, but the column got broken in the dark and the two parts traveled around in a circle for an hour looking for each other. After we closed up, we started off and struck the pike between Centreville and the Court House. But we turned off into the woods when we got within two or three miles of the village, as Wyndham's cavalry camps were on the pike.

We entered the village from the direction of the railroad station. There were a few sentinels about the town, but it was so dark that they could not distinguish us from their own people. Squads were detailed to go around to the officers' quarters and to the stables for the horses. The court-house yard was the rendezvous where all were to report. As our great desire was to capture Wyndham, Ames was sent with a party to the house in which he knew Wyndham had his quarters. But fortune was in Wyndham's favor that time, for that evening he had gone to Washington by train. But

Ames got his two staff officers, his horses, and his uniform. One of the officers, Captain Barker, had been Ames's captain. Ames brought him to me and seemed to take great pride in introducing him to me as his former captain.

When the squads were starting around to gather prisoners and horses, Joe Nelson brought me a soldier who said he was a guard at General Stoughton's headquarters. Joe had also pulled the telegraph operator out of his tent; the wires had been cut. With five or six men I rode to the house . . . where the commanding general was. We dismounted and knocked loudly at the door. Soon a window above was opened, and someone asked who was there. I answered, "Fifth New York Cavalry with a dispatch for General Stoughton." The door was opened and a staff officer, Lieutenant Prentiss, was before me. I took hold of his nightshirt, whispered my name in his ear, and told him to take me to General Stoughton's room. Resistance was useless, and he obeyed. A light was quickly struck, and on the bed we saw the general sleeping as soundly as the Turk when Marco Bozzaris waked him up. There was no time for ceremony, so I drew up the bedclothes, pulled up the general's shirt, and gave him a spank on his bare back, and told him to get up. As his staff officer was standing by me, Stoughton did not realize the situation and thought that somebody was taking a rude familiarity with him. He asked in an indignant tone what all this meant. I told him that he was a prisoner, and that he must get up quickly and dress.

I then asked him if he had ever heard of "Mosby," and he said he had.

"I am Mosby," I said. "Stuart's cavalry has possession of the Court House; be quick and dress."

He then asked whether Fitz Lee[1] was there. I said he was, and he asked me to take him to Fitz Lee—they had been together at West Point. Two days afterwards I did deliver him to Fitz Lee at Culpepper Court House. My motive in trying to deceive Stoughton was to deprive him of all hope of escape and to induce him to dress quickly. We were in a critical situation, surrounded by the camps of several thousand troops with several hundred in the town. If there had been any concert between them, they could have easily driven us out; but not a shot was fired although we stayed there over an hour. As soon as it was known that we were there, each man hid and took care of himself. Stoughton had the reputation of being a brave soldier, but a fop. He dressed before a looking-glass as carefully as Sardanapalus did when he went into battle. He forgot his watch and left it on the bureau, but one of my men, Frank Williams, took it and gave it to him. Two men

---

[1] Fitzhugh Lee was Robert E. Lee's nephew and a Confederate cavalry commander.

had been left to guard our horses when we went into the house. There were several tents for couriers in the yard, and Stoughton's horses and couriers were ready to go with us, when we came out with the general and his staff.

When we reached the rendezvous at the courtyard, I found all the squads waiting for us with their prisoners and horses. There were three times as many prisoners as my men, and each was mounted and leading a horse. To deceive the enemy and baffle pursuit, the cavalcade started off in one direction and, soon after it got out of town, turned in another. We flanked the cavalry camps, and were soon on the pike between them and Centreville. As there were several thousand troops in that town, it was not thought possible that we would go that way to get out of the lines, so the cavalry, when it started in pursuit, went in an opposite direction. Lieutenant Prentiss and a good many prisoners who started with us escaped in the dark, and we lost a great many of the horses . . .

Our safety depended on our getting out of the Union lines before daybreak. We struck the pike about four miles from Centreville; the danger I then apprehended was pursuit by the cavalry, which was in camp behind us. When we got near the pike, I halted the column to close up. Some of my men were riding in the rear, and some on the flanks to prevent the prisoners from escaping. I left a sergeant, Hunter, in command and rode forward to reconnoiter. As no enemy was in front, I called to Hunter to come on and directed him to go forward at a trot and to hold Stoughton's bridle reins under all circumstances. Stoughton no doubt appreciated my interest in him.

With Joe Nelson I remained some distance behind. We stopped frequently to listen for the hoofbeats of cavalry in pursuit, but no sounds could be heard save the hooting of owls. My heart beat higher with hope every minute; it was the crisis of my fortunes.

Soon the camp fires on the heights around Centreville were in sight; my plan was to flank the position and pass between that place and the camps at Chantilly. But we soon saw that Hunter had halted, and I galloped forward to find out the cause. I saw a fire on the side of the road about a hundred yards ahead of us—evidently a picket post. So I rode forward to reconnoiter, but nobody was by the fire, and the picket was gone. We were now half a mile from Centreville, and the dawn was just breaking. It had been the practice to place a picket on our road every evening and withdraw it early in the morning. The officer in charge concluded that, as it was near daylight, there was no danger in the air, and he returned to camp and left the fire burning. That was the very thing I wanted him to do. I called Hunter to come on, and we passed the picket fire and turned off to go around the forts at Centreville. I rode some distance ahead of the column. The camps were quiet; there was no sign of alarm; the telegraph wires had been cut, and no news had come about our exploit at the Court House. We could see the cannon bristling through the redoubts and hear the sentinel on the parapet call to us to halt, but no attention was paid to him, and he did not fire to give the alarm. No doubt he thought that we were a body of their own cavalry going out on a scout.

But soon there was a shot behind me and, turning around, I saw Captain Barker dashing towards a redoubt and Jake, the Hungarian, close behind him and about to give him another shot, when Barker's horse tumbled and fell on him in a ditch. We soon got them out and moved on. All this happened in sight of the sentinels and in gunshot of their camps.

After we had passed the forts and reached Cub Run, a new danger was before us. The stream was swift and booming from the melting snow, and our choice was to swim, or to turn back. In full view behind us were the white tents of the enemy and the forts, and we were within cannon range. Without halting a moment, I plunged into the stream, and my horse swam to the other bank. Stoughton followed and was next to me. As he came up to the bank, shivering from his cold morning bath, he said, "Captain, this is the first rough treatment I have to complain of." . . .

I could not but feel deep pity for Stoughton when he looked back at Centreville and saw that there was no chance of his rescue. Without any fault of his own, Stoughton's career as a soldier was blasted.

There is an anecdote told of Mr. Lincoln that, when it was reported to him that Stoughton had been captured, he remarked, with characteristic humor, that he did not mind so much the loss of a general—for he could make another in five minutes—but he hated to lose the horses.

12

THE MISSOURI BUSHWHACKERS

Mosby's war, for all its hair-raising effects on the Union forces, was a relatively controlled, organized campaign on the fringes of the main battle-front in northern Virginia. In Missouri, however, spontaneous fighting broke out that soon flamed into the most savage warfare ever seen on this continent.

Missouri, though far from the heart of the South, was a slave state heavily populated by settlers from Kentucky and other Southern states. The Civil War itself was the result in part of fighting along the Missouri-Kansas border in the 1850s, when abolitionist "Jayhawker" settlers from New England and pro-slavery "Border Ruffians" from Missouri battled over whether Kansas was to be a slave or free state. Some of Missouri's most prominent civic leaders led bloody raids across the border.

When the Civil War finally came, Missouri almost fell into Confederate hands after a rebel army under General Sterling Price won a victory at Wilson's Creek in August 1861. Shortly afterward, however, the Confederates fell back to Arkansas, leaving behind hundreds of local Missouri recruits. In March 1862, the Southerners made one more attempt to recapture the state; the result was a Union triumph at the Battle of Pea Ridge, effectively locking the rebels below the border with Arkansas.

Missouri, however, was far from secure for Federal forces. The state was thick with Confederate sympathizers, who were driven to action by the depredations of the Kansas Jayhawkers—now organized into Union cavalry regiments. Led by Senator Jim Lane and Charles Jennison, these units crossed into Missouri from Kansas and took revenge for the fighting of the 1850s. The Jayhawkers looted and burned farms, freed slaves, arrested suspected Confederates, and sacked Missouri towns.

Pro-Confederate Missourians—aided by such daring agents from the rebel army as Joseph Shelby—took to guerrilla warfare to battle back. Known as "bushwhackers," these men fought in small, loose bands, riding the fastest horses they could steal, and carrying numerous Colt Navy revolvers, the lightweight favorite of the guerrillas. They set up ambushes, raided Federal posts, attacked neighbors who sympathized with the Union, and butchered blacks and German immigrants.

The most famous bushwhacker of all was William C. Quantrill, who emerged as a sort of evil genius of this sort of warfare—a dark counterpart to Mosby of Virginia. His band became a training ground for the most feared and effective guerrilla leaders, including George Todd, Cole Younger, and the most vicious of all, "Bloody Bill" Anderson.

A scout named John McCorkle rode with Quantrill, and he took part in the bushwhackers' most infamous act: the massacre at Lawrence, the heart of abolitionist Kansas, on August 21, 1863. Before the raid, the frustrated Union command in Kansas City had rounded up a number of female relatives of the most notorious guerrillas. The women's prison collapsed, killing and injuring several of them. Believing the tragedy to be deliberate murder, the guerrillas vowed revenge. McCorkle's account rings true— except that the Lawrence victims were all helpless civilians.

The Lawrence Massacre
By John McCorkle

This foul murder [the Kansas City prison collapse] was the direct cause of the famous raid on Lawrence, Kansas. We could stand no more. Imagine, if you can, my feelings. A loved sister foully murdered and the widow of a dead brother seriously hurt by a set of men to whom the name assassins, murderers, and cutthroats would be a compliment. People abuse us, but, my God, did we not have enough to make us desperate and thirst for revenge? We tried to fight like soldiers, but were declared outlaws, hunted under a black flag and murdered like beasts. The homes of our friends burned, our aged sires, who dared sympathize with us had been either hung or shot in the presence of their families and all their furniture and provisions loaded in wagons and with our livestock taken to the state of Kansas. The beautiful farming country of Jackson County, Cass County, and Johnson County[2] were worse than desert, and on every hillside stood lone blackened chimneys, sad sentinels and monuments to the memory of

---

[2] This trio of counties was immediately south of the Missouri River, along the Kansas border.

our once happy homes. And these outrages had been done by Kansas troops, calling themselves soldiers, but a disgrace to the name soldier. And now our innocent and beautiful girls had been murdered in a most foul, brutal, savage, and damnable manner. We were determined to have revenge, and so, Colonel Quantrill and Captain Anderson[3] planned a raid on Lawrence, Kansas, the home of the leaders, Jim Lane and Jennison.

We were all in camp in our headquarters on the banks of the Sni [River]. Colonel Quantrill and Captain Anderson were getting the boys together for the raid on Lawrence, Kansas. The day before they started to Lawrence, Colonel Quantrill sent Andy Blount with fifteen men down into Johnson County in order to attract the Federal forces in that direction. After the fifteen men left with Blount, there still remained with Colonel Quantrill and Anderson about 150 men.[4] On the morning of the twentieth of August, Quantrill gave the order to break camp and march in a southwesterly direction, and went over on the Big Blue[5] to a point south of Little Santa Fe, a town just on the Kansas line. His entire march until he reached the Kansas line was through smoking ruins and blackened fields. He halted in the woods all day and just about dark he gave the order to mount and crossed into Kansas at a point about ten miles south of Little Santa Fe and turned directly west toward the town of Lawrence, and, riding all night, the town was reached just at daylight. At the entrance to the town, there were a lot of tents in which were camped a detachment of negro soldiers and a few white men. The command halted there and someone fired a shot. Immediately the negroes and white men rushed out of their tents, the majority of them starting in the direction of the river and some going in the direction of the town. The command was given to break ranks, scatter, and follow them. A few of the negroes reached the river, plunging into it, but none succeeded in reaching the opposite shore. The troops dashed back up into the town, down the main street, shooting at every blue coat that came in sight. Just before entering the town Colonel Quantrill turned to his men and said, "Boys, this is the home of Jim Lane and Jennison; remember that in hunting us they gave no quarter. Shoot every soldier you see, but in no way harm a woman or a child." He dashed ahead of his command down Main Street, firing his pistol twice,

---

[3] The guerrilla commanders in Missouri affected formal Confederate rank, though unlike Mosby in Virginia they had no official position in the Southern army.

[4] Estimates for his force range up to 400 men.

[5] The Big Blue was a river east of Kansas City that flowed north, emptying into the Missouri.

dismounted from his horse and went into the hotel, where he was met by the landlord, whom he recognized as an old friend and immediately gave the orders for the landlord not to be molested and stayed in the hotel and guarded him.

During all this time, his command were busy hunting men with blue clothes and setting fire to the town.[6] Jim Lane and Jennison were the ones wanted and some of the boys dashed at once to Jim Lane's house, but, unfortunately for the world, did not find him. They found his saber, which was very handsome. . . . In the parlor of Lane's house, there were three pianos and the boys recognized two of them as having belonged to Southern people in Jackson County, and a great many other things belonging to Southern people were found in his house. Quantrill remained in Lawrence about two hours and when he left, the town was in ashes and 175 Jayhawkers were left dead. Lane and Jennison had made desolate the border counties of Missouri. . . . Quantrill and his command had come to Lawrence to be avenged and they were.

After the Lawrence raid, Quantrill and his men escaped back to Missouri with Union cavalry biting at their heels the entire way. The scene they left behind was sickening: in home after home in Lawrence, they had pulled men and boys from their homes and shot them, before setting fire to the town. The atrocity raised the already vicious fighting to a white heat felt nowhere else in the Civil War. The raiders and their hunters now flew black flags when they went into battle, a sign that they would take no prisoners. It became standing policy on both sides to shoot enemy prisoners and wounded; Union soldiers tortured the relatives of bushwhackers for information, often shooting them when they were finished; guerrillas burned out and murdered farmers they suspected of helping the Federals. The Union command ordered all families in three Missouri counties along the Kansas border to quit their farms, to deprive the guerrillas of material support. Northern forces wrought such destruction in this zone that it became known as the Burnt District.

Finding the pressure from the Union troops to be too great in Missouri, many of the bushwhackers trekked south to Texas for the winter, where they plundered the local population indiscriminately. There, Quantrill and

[6] In fact, the Missourians went from house to house killing unarmed men and boys in front of their families, often tipping their hats to the women afterward.

his lieutenants fell out among themselves. The slaughter at Lawrence, the local Texans whispered, had been too much for the bushwhackers. Bloody Bill Anderson returned to Missouri in the spring at the head of his own troop (which soon recruited the teenaged Jesse James), while George Todd took command of the core of Quantrill's old group—including McCorkle, who now commanded his own small squad, and Frank James.

In late September 1864, the two commands reunited outside the town of Centralia. There, in a classic example of guerrilla tactics, they then won a complete victory over a Union force of about the same size—after an equally typical atrocity by Anderson's men. McCorkle's account captures the essence of the hell-for-leather fighting, followed by dispersion and escape—and the frequent disputes between the commanders.

The Massacre and Battle of Centralia
By John McCorkle

The next day we went into the woods southeast of Centralia in Boone County. Captain Anderson wanted us to go into the town of Centralia, but Todd refused to do it, so Anderson took his own company, leaving us in the woods, and went into town. While he was there a passenger train came in on the North Missouri Railroad . . . with a number of Federal soldiers aboard. Anderson had all the passengers and soldiers get out on the platform and, separating the soldiers from the other passengers, he and his men shot and killed all the Federal soldiers.[7] He then commanded the engineer to start his train, having set fire to the coaches. The old engineer . . . when he started his engine, opened a valve, so that the water would soon run out of the boiler and the burning train soon stopped after running a few miles. Captain Todd nor none of our command were with Anderson at the time and knew nothing of the killing of the soldiers until Anderson returned to our camp and told us, when Captain Todd severely reprimanded Anderson for doing it, telling him he did not endorse such actions.

In the afternoon, our pickets came in and reported that there was a command of Federals coming with a black flag hoisted. Captain Todd ordered Dave Poole to go and see who they were. He returned and

[7] These soldiers, twenty-five in number, were returning home on leave and were unarmed. After the massacre, Anderson's men mutilated their victims' bodies.

reported that there were between two and three hundred of them. Todd then commanded us to form in line, telling us that he would ride ahead of us and for us to remain standing until he signaled for us to come forward. He took three men with him, leaving us behind the brow of the hill out of sight and when the Federals had gotten to the foot of the hill, he raised his hat and we loped to him.

Major Johnson was in command of the Federals and, while in Centralia, he was bragging about how he was going to extinguish our entire command, showing his black flag and saying that he would take no prisoners, but would kill us all . . .

When we reached Captain Todd after he had signaled to us he commanded us to dismount and tighten our girths. When we dismounted, the Federals yelled, "They are dismounting; they are going to fight us afoot." Johnson then gave the command for his men to dismount and every fourth man to hold horses. We stood by our horses until their horses had been led away, when Captain Todd said, "Remount. Charge and kill them." We sprang into our saddles and started after them, each one of us trying to get there first. They fired one volley and then, becoming utterly demoralized, stampeded in all directions, some of them running for their horses and some of them starting for Centralia afoot. We followed them into the town of Centralia, which was about three miles away, dealing death at every jump. Some of them went through the town of Centralia and Frank James, Bill Hulse, Pink Gibson, Lee McMurtry, three others whose names I have forgotten, and myself followed them to the edge of the town of Sturgeon, when we saw the Federal infantry stationed there forming into line to come out to meet us. Frank James then said, "Hold on, boys, we've killed enough of them; let's go back." When we turned to go back, I found my mare could not go out of a walk, I having run her for nearly eleven miles. Frank James said, "That's all right, John; we'll not leave you and, if necessary, we'll take you behind one of us." . . .

There were 206 men in Major Johnson's command when we met them, and there were fourteen of them escaped, two of the latter number badly wounded. We had one man killed, Frank Shepherd, who was shot in the head when they first fired. He was riding between Frank James and I when he was shot and the blood from his wound spurted on Frank's boot . . .[8]

When we had gotten back to our camp we only stayed a short time, going in a southeast direction to Big Cedar Creek in Boone County. We

---

[8] Reportedly the teenage Jesse James led the charge of Anderson's men and personally shot down Major Johnson of the Union command.

rode seven or eight miles and scattered, trying to find something to eat. We then secured a pilot, who said he knew the country well and could take us out of it. We turned west and crossed a big creek. It was dark as pitch and raining torrents and our pilot became lost. Captain Todd then commanded us to dismount and every man get under a tree and stay until daylight. When daylight came we went up to a cornfield and were getting corn to feed our horses, and hearing someone on the other side of the field, we sent a man to find out who it was and he returned and told us that it was General Guitar with his entire command of Federals getting corn for their horses. Captain Todd then said, "Boys, this country's full of Federals and they are all after us and we'll have to disband and scatter."

After the battle (and massacre), the bushwhackers' days rapidly dwindled. As they were fighting at Centralia, Confederate General Sterling Price invaded Missouri from northeastern Arkansas with a ragged army, hoping to march into St. Louis before the Union could react. Stoutly defended fortifications, however, forced him to turn west, up the Missouri River valley, where bushwhackers rode by the hundreds to join his army, expecting him to capture the state for the South. It was exactly the situation the Union command had wished for over the previous three years: all the elusive raiders concentrated into one group, where they could be defeated in a set-piece battle. In the end, this is exactly what happened: Price's army was defeated near Kansas City; many of the bushwhackers (including Bloody Bill Anderson) were killed; and the guerrillas were eliminated as an effective force. Quantrill himself took a small band on a march east, proclaiming his mission to be the assassination of Lincoln; instead, he was bushwhacked himself and killed by a Union force in Kentucky.

After the war, some of the bushwhackers turned to banditry, relying on their fighting skills and the active support of many old Southern sympathizers. Out of this vicious war, then, was born the legend of the "Robin Hood" Jesse James, who with his brother Frank, the Younger brothers, and other ex-guerrillas terrorized Missouri for another twenty years.

VI

DECISION
IN THE WEST

FROM CHATTANOOGA
TO ATLANTA

13

THE BATTLE OF CHATTANOOGA
November 24–25, 1863

No fighting in the entire war was as desperate as Missouri's battle of neighbor against neighbor, Kansan against Missourian; yet it raged in near isolation, a war within a war. After Pea Ridge in early 1862, the principal fighting shifted far from the banks of the Missouri River—and Grant's capture of Vicksburg moved the battlefront even farther south and east. Then came a brilliant campaign by General Rosecrans, in command of the Army of the Cumberland, thrusting General Braxton Bragg's Confederates completely out of Tennessee.

Spreading his corps out like a net, each marching through a different pass in the Appalachian Mountains, Rosecrans outflanked Bragg and forced him back, winning a tremendous and largely bloodless success. From June through mid-September, the Confederate Army of Tennessee fell back first to Chattanooga and then to northern Georgia. Richmond found the situation desperate: Lee had been defeated at Gettysburg; Vicksburg was lost; now Tennessee slipped into the Yankee grasp, and Atlanta threatened to fall as well. It was under these circumstances that Jefferson Davis finally approved Longstreet's plan to take his two-division corps to reinforce Bragg and drive the enemy back.

On September 19, the newly reinforced Army of Tennessee smashed into the bluecoats near the banks of West Chickamauga Creek. On the second day of the battle, Longstreet's men split the Union front in two; half (including General Rosecrans) fled, while General George H. Thomas maintained a stout last-ditch defense. After this Battle of Chickamauga, the Union army fell back to Chattanooga, where the rebels established a siege.

The situation now seemed as critical to Lincoln as it had to Davis just a few weeks before. The defeat at Chickamauga was mortifying enough, but

193

for the Army of the Cumberland to be trapped in Chattanooga and besieged—threatened with complete capture—was unacceptable. There was only one man the president trusted to set things right: General Ulysses S. Grant.

Lincoln named Grant the supreme commander of all Union forces in the West, and ordered him to go personally to Chattanooga and take charge of the situation. And the situation was indeed desperate. The Confederates were entrenched on commanding heights (Lookout Mountain and Missionary Ridge), and they tightly gripped the Army of the Cumberland's supply line.

One of the division commanders shut up in Chattanooga was Philip H. Sheridan, who with his men had retreated at Chickamauga. He watched as the outsiders arrived—Joseph Hooker with Eastern reinforcements, then Grant, then Sherman and his Army of the Tennessee. Grant relied on the new troops to open a supply route; he believed the Army of the Cumberland was spent, and he planned to give Sherman's army the key role in the battle to come. But the combative Sheridan and his men were eager for revenge; when the battle finally came, they showed how much Grant had underestimated them by delivering one of the most astonishing assaults of the entire war—obliterating the shame of Chickamauga.

Up Missionary Ridge
By General Philip H. Sheridan

On October 16, 1863, General Grant had been assigned to the command of the "Military Division of the Mississippi," a geographical area which embraced the Departments of the Ohio, the Cumberland, and the Tennessee, thus effecting a consolidation of divided commands which might have been introduced most profitably at an earlier date. The same order that assigned General Grant relieved General Rosecrans, and placed General [George H.] Thomas in command of the Army of the Cumberland. At the time of the reception of the order, Rosecrans was busy with preparations for a movement to open the direct road to Bridgeport. . . . On the nineteenth of October, after turning command over to Thomas, General Rosecrans quietly slipped away from the army. . . .

General Grant arrived at Chattanooga on October 23, and began at once to carry out the plans that had been formed for opening the shorter or river road to Bridgeport. This object was successfully accomplished. . . .

The four weeks which followed this cheering result were busy with the work of refitting and preparing for the offensive operations as soon as General Sherman should reach us with his troops from West Tennessee. During this period of activity the enemy committed the serious fault of detaching Longstreet's corps—sending it to aid in the siege of Knoxville in East Tennessee—an error which has no justification whatever. . . . Thus depleted, Bragg still held Missionary Ridge in strong force, but that part of his line which extended across the intervening valley to the northerly point of Lookout Mountain was much attenuated.

By the eighteenth of November General Grant had issued instructions covering his intended operations. They contemplated that Sherman's column, which was arriving by the north bank of the Tennessee, should cross the river on a pontoon bridge just below the mouth of Chick-amauga Creek and carry the northern extremity of Missionary Ridge as far as the railroad tunnel; that the Army of the Cumberland—the center—should cooperate with Sherman; and that Hooker with a mixed command should continue to hold Lookout Valley and operate on our extreme right as circumstances might warrant. Sherman crossed on the twenty-fourth to perform his allotted part of the program, but in the meantime Grant becoming impressed with the idea that Bragg was en-deavoring to get away, ordered Thomas to make a strong demonstration in his front, to determine the truth or falsity of the information that had been received. This task fell to the Fourth Corps, and at twelve o'clock on the twenty-third I was notified that Wood's division would make a reconnaissance to an elevated point in its front called Orchard Knob, and that I was to support it with my division. . . . Wood's [division] took possession of Orchard Knob easily, and mine was halted on a low ridge to the right of the knob. . . .

On the twenty-fourth General Sherman made an attack for the purpose of carrying the north end of Missionary Ridge. His success was not com-plete, although at the time it was reported throughout the army to be so. It had the effect of disconcerting Bragg, however, and caused him to strengthen his right by withdrawing troops from his left, which circum-stance led Hooker to advance on the northerly face of Lookout Mountain. At first, with good glasses, we could plainly see Hooker's troops driving the Confederates up the face of the mountain. All were soon lost to view in the dense timber, but emerged again on the open ground, across which the Confederates retreated at a lively pace, followed by the pursuing line, which was led by a color-bearer, who, far in advance, was bravely waving on his comrades. The gallantry of this man elicited much enthusiasm among

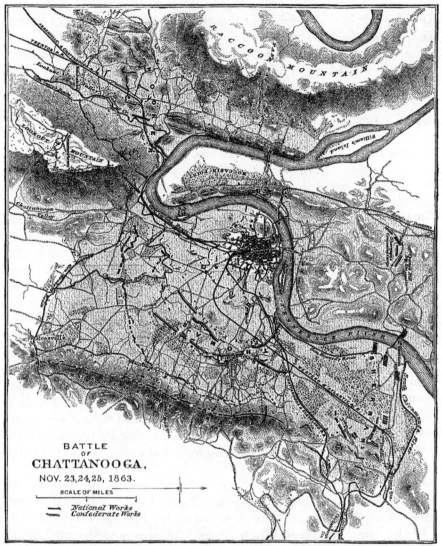

The Battle of Chattanooga, November 23–25, 1863

us all, but as he was a considerable distance ahead of his comrades I expected to see his rashness punished at any moment by death or capture. He finally got quite near the retreating Confederates, when suddenly they made a dash at him, but he was fully alive to such a move, and ran back, apparently uninjured, to his friends. About this time a small squad of men reached the top of Lookout and planted the Stars and Stripes on its very crest. Just then a cloud settled down on the mountain, and a heavy bank of fog obscured its whole face.

After the view was lost the sharp rattle of musketry continued some time, but practically the fight had already been won by Hooker's men, the enemy only holding on with a rear-guard to assure his retreat across Chattanooga Valley to Missionary Ridge. . . .

On the morning of the twenty-fifth of November Bragg's entire army was holding only the line of Missionary Ridge, and our troops, being now practically connected from Sherman to Hooker, confronted it with the Army of the Cumberland in the center bowed out along the front of Wood's division and mine. Early in the day Sherman, with great determination and persistence, made an attempt to carry the high ground near the tunnel, first gaining and then losing advantage, but his attack was not crowned with the success anticipated. Meanwhile Hooker and Palmer were swinging across Chattanooga Valley, using me as a pivot for the purpose of crossing Missionary Ridge in the neighborhood of Rossville. In the early part of the day I had driven in the Confederate pickets in my front, so as to prolong my line of battle on that of Wood, the necessity of continuing to refuse my right having been obviated by the capture of Lookout Mountain and the advance of Palmer.

About two o'clock orders came to carry the line at the foot of the ridge, attacking at a signal of six guns. I had few changes or new dispositions to make. Wagner's brigade, which was next to Wood's division, was formed in double lines, and Harker's brigade took the same formation on Wagner's right. Colonel F.T. Sherman's brigade came on Harker's right, formed in a column of attack, with a front of three regiments, he having nine. My whole front was covered with a heavy line of skirmishers. These dispositions made, my right rested a little south of Moore's road, my left joined Wood over toward Orchard Knob, while my center was opposite Thurman's house—the headquarters of General Bragg—on Missionary Ridge. A small stream of water ran parallel to my front, as far as which the ground was covered by a thin patch of timber, and beyond the edge of the timber was an open plain to the foot of Missionary Ridge, varying in width from four to nine hundred yards. At the foot of the ridge was the enemy's first line of rifle pits; at a point midway up its face, another line, incomplete; and on the crest was a third line, in which Bragg had massed his artillery.

The enemy saw we were making dispositions for an attack, and in plain view of my whole division he prepared himself for resistance, marching regiments from his left flank with flying colors, and filling up the spaces not already occupied in his entrenchments. Seeing the enemy thus strengthening himself, it was plain that we would have to act quickly if we expected to accomplish much, and I already began to doubt the feasibility of our remaining in the first line of rifle pits when we should have carried them. I discussed the order with Wagner, Harker, and Sherman, and they were similarly impressed, so while anxiously awaiting the signal I sent Captain Ransom of my staff to Granger, who was at Fort Wood, to ascertain if we were to carry the first line or the ridge beyond. Shortly after Ransom started the signal guns were fired, and I told the brigade commanders to go for the ridge.

Placing myself in front of Harker's brigade, between the line of battle and the skirmishers, accompanied by only an orderly so as not to attract the enemy's fire, we moved out. Under a terrible storm of shot and shell the line pressed forward steadily through the timber, and as it emerged on the plain took the double-quick and with fixed bayonets rushed the enemy's first line. Not a shot was fired from our line of battle, as it gained on my skirmishers they melted into and became one with it, and all three of my brigades went over the rifle pits simultaneously. They then lay down on the face of the ridge, for a breathing spell and for protection from the terrible fire of canister and musketry pouring over us from the guns on the crest. At the rifle pits there had been little use for the bayonet, for most of the Confederate troops, disconcerted by the sudden rush, lay close in the ditch and surrendered, though some few fled up the slope to the next line. The prisoners were directed to move out to our rear, and as their entrenchments had now come under fire from the crest, they went with alacrity, and without guard or escort, toward Chattanooga.

After a short pause to get breath, the ascent of the ridge began, and I rode into the ditch of the entrenchments to drive out a few skulkers who were hiding there. Just at this moment I was joined by Captain Ransom, who, having returned from Granger, told me that we were to carry only the line at the base, and that in coming back, when he struck the left of the division, knowing this interpretation of the order, he in his capacity as an aide-de-camp had directed Wagner, who was up the face of the ridge, to return, and that in consequence Wagner was recalling his men to the base. I could not bear to order the recall of troops now so gallantly climbing the hill step by step, and believing we could take it, I immediately rode to Wagner's brigade and directed it to resume the attack. In the meantime Harker's and F.T. Sherman's troops were approaching the partial line of works midway of the ridge, and as I returned to the center of their rear, they were being led by many stands of regimental colors. There seemed to be a rivalry as to which color should be farthest to the front; first one would go forward a few feet, then another would come up to it, the color-bearers vying with one another as to who should be foremost, until finally every standard was planted on the immediate works. The enemy's fire from the crest during the ascent was terrific in the noise made, but as it was plunging, it overshot and had little effect on those above the second line of pits, but was very uncomfortable for those below, so I deemed it advisable to seek another place, and Wagner's brigade having reassembled and again pressed up the ridge, I rode up the face to join my troops.

As soon as the men saw me, they surged forward and went over the works on the crest. The parapet of the entrenchments was too high for my horse to jump, so, riding a short distance to the left, I entered through a low place in the line. A few Confederates were found inside, but they turned the butts of their muskets toward me in token of surrender, for our men were now passing beyond them on both their flanks.

The right and right center of my division gained the summit first, they being partially sheltered by a depression in the face of the ridge, the Confederates in their immediate front fleeing down the southern face. When I crossed the rifle pits on the top the Confederates were still holding fast at Bragg's headquarters, and a battery located there opened fire along the crest, making things most uncomfortably hot. Seeing the danger to which I was exposed, for I was mounted, Colonel Joseph Conrad, of the Fifteenth Missouri, ran up and begged me to dismount. I accepted his excellent advice, and it probably saved my life, but poor Conrad was punished for his solicitude by being seriously wounded in the thigh at the moment he was thus contributing to my safety.

Wildly cheering, the men advanced along the ridge toward Bragg's headquarters, and soon drove the Confederates from this last position, capturing a number of prisoners, among them Breckinridge's and Bates's adjutant-generals, and the battery that had made such stout assistance on the crest—two guns which were named "Lady Breckinridge" and "Lady Buckner"—General Bragg himself having barely time to escape before his headquarters were taken.

My whole division had now reached the summit, and Wagner and Harker—the latter slightly wounded—joined me as I was standing in the battery just secured. The enemy was rapidly retiring, and though many of his troops, with disorganized wagon trains and several pieces of artillery, could be distinctly seen in much confusion about half a mile distant in the valley below, yet he was covering them with a pretty well organized line that continued to give us a desultory fire. Seeing this, I at once directed

Wagner and Harker to take up the pursuit along Moore's road, which led to Chickamauga Station—Bragg's depot of supply—and as they progressed, I pushed Sherman's brigade along the road behind them. Wagner and Harker soon overtook the rear guard, and a slight skirmish caused it to break, permitting nine guns and a large number of wagons which were endeavoring to get away in the stampede to fall into our hands. . . .

Although it cannot be said that the result of the two days' operations was reached by the methods which General Grant had indicated in his instructions preceding the battle, yet the general outcome was unquestionably due to his genius, for the maneuvering of Sherman's and Hooker's commands created the opportunity for the Army of the Cumberland to carry the ridge at the center. In directing Sherman to attack the north end of the ridge, Grant disconcerted Bragg—who was thus made to fear the loss of his depot of supplies at Chickamauga Station—and compelled him to resist stoutly; and stout resistance to Sherman meant the withdrawal of the Confederates from Lookout Mountain. While this attack was in process of execution advantage was taken of it by Hooker in a well-planned and well-fought battle. . . . The assault on Missionary Ridge by Granger's and Palmer's corps was not premeditated by Grant, he directing only the line at its base to be carried, but when this fell into our hands the situation demanded our getting the one at the top also.

14

GRANT'S GRAND STRATEGY

The smashing success of the Army of the Cumberland's attack up the steep, heavily fortified Missionary Ridge astounded everyone—including Grant. He watched in astonishment as the limited holding attack he had ordered turned into a devastating romp through the heart of the Confederate line. Battered and broken, the gray-clad men of the Army of Tennessee fell back to Dalton, a strategic rail junction in mountainous northwestern Georgia.

Once again, Bragg had turned victory into defeat. Jefferson Davis reluctantly gave in to the demand of Bragg's corps commanders and dismissed his friend, appointing Joseph E. Johnston to take his place. Meanwhile, Longstreet failed in his assault on Knoxville, and he gradually retreated through the mountains, back to Virginia to rejoin Robert E. Lee.

Lincoln was now convinced that he had, at last, found the man to win the war. By special act of Congress, the grade of Lieutenant General—a title only George Washington had ever formally held—was reactivated, and Grant was named general-in-chief of the Union armies. From now on there would be a single mind guiding the Federal military machine, coordinating its widespread forces (Halleck, who had never truly acted as a supreme commander, now became chief of staff). As 1864 dawned, Grant took his post and confidently straightened out the tangle of strategies driving the Union effort. His first concern: the last, decisive campaign in the West, to be directed by his old friend, William T. Sherman.

The Plans for 1864
By General U.S. Grant

The bill restoring the grade of lieutenant-general of the army had passed through Congress and became a law on the twenty-sixth of February [1864]. My nomination had been sent to the Senate on the first of March and confirmed the next day (the second). I was ordered to Washington on the third to receive my commission, and started the day following that. The commission was handed to me on the ninth. It was delivered to me at the Executive Mansion by President Lincoln in the presence of his cabinet, my eldest son, those of my staff who were with me, and a few other visitors. . . .

It had been my intention before this to remain in the West, even if I was made lieutenant-general; but when I got to Washington and saw the situation it was plain that here was the point for the commanding general to be. No one else could, probably, resist the pressure that would be brought to bear upon him to desist from his own plans and pursue others. I was determined, therefore, before I started back to have Sherman advanced to my late position, McPherson to Sherman's in command of the department [of the Tennessee], and Logan to the command of McPherson's corps. These changes were all made on my recommendation and without hesitation. . . .

On the eleventh I returned to Washington [after visiting General Meade] and, on the day after, orders were published by the War Department placing me in command of all the armies. I had left Washington the night before to return to my old command in the West and to meet Sherman whom I had telegraphed to join me in Nashville.[1]

Sherman assumed command of the military division of the Mississippi on the eighteenth of March, and we left Nashville together for Cincinnati. I had Sherman accompany me that far on my way back to Washington so that we could talk over the matters about which I wanted to see him, without losing any more time from my new command than was necessary. The first point which I wished to discuss was particularly about the cooperation of his command with mine when the spring campaign should commence. . . .

My general plan now was to concentrate all the force possible against the Confederate armies in the field.[2] There were but two such, as we have seen, east of the Mississippi River and facing north. The Army of Northern Virginia, General Robert E. Lee commanding, was on the south bank of the Rapidan, confronting the Army of the Potomac; the second, under General Joseph E. Johnston, was at Dalton, Georgia, opposed to Sherman

---

[1] Sherman had just completed a key raid from Vicksburg to Meridian, Mississippi, which created a swath of devastation that limited the Confederates' ability to mass an army in the state.

[2] This paragraph has been moved for narrative continuity.

[whose army] was still at Chattanooga. Besides these main armies the Confederates had to guard the Shenandoah Valley, a great storehouse to feed their armies from, and their line of communications from Richmond to Tennessee. Forrest, a brave and intrepid cavalry general, was in the West with a large force, making a larger command necessary to hold what we had gained in Middle and West Tennessee. We could not abandon any territory north of the line held by the enemy because it would lay the Northern States open to invasion. But as the Army of the Potomac was the principal garrison for the protection of Washington even while it was moving on Lee, so all the forces to the west, and the Army of the James, guarded their special trusts when advancing from them as well as when remaining at them. Better indeed, for they forced the enemy to guard his own lines and resources at a greater distance from ours, and with a greater force. Little expeditions could not so well be sent out to destroy a bridge or tear up a few miles of railroad track, burn a storehouse, or inflict other little annoyances. Accordingly I arranged for a simultaneous movement all along the line. Sherman was to move from Chattanooga, Johnston's army and Atlanta being his objective points. . . .

Some time in the winter of 1863–64 I had been invited by the general-in-chief [Halleck] to give my views of the campaign I thought advisable for the command under me—now Sherman's. General J.E. Johnston was defending Atlanta and the interior of Georgia with an army, the largest part of which was stationed at Dalton, about thirty-eight miles south of Chattanooga. Dalton is at the junction of the railroad from Cleveland with the one from Chattanooga to Atlanta.

There could have been no difference of opinion as to the first duty of the armies of the military division of the Mississippi. Johnston's army was the first objective, and that important railroad center, Atlanta, the second. At the time I wrote General Halleck giving my views of the approaching campaign, and at the time I met General Sherman, it was expected that General Banks [on the Red River, in western Louisiana] would be through with the campaign which he had been ordered upon before my appointment to the campaign of all the armies, and would be ready to cooperate with the armies east of the Mississippi, his part in the program being to move upon Mobile by land while the navy would close the harbor and assist to the best of its ability. The plan therefore was for Sherman to attack Johnston and destroy his army if possible, to capture Atlanta and hold it, and with his troops and those of Banks to hold a line through to Mobile, or at least to hold Atlanta and command the railroad running east and west, and the troops from one or other of the armies to hold important points on the southern road,[3] the only east and west road that would be left in the possession of the enemy. This would cut the Confederacy in two again, as our gaining possession of the Mississippi River had done before. Banks was not ready in time for the part assigned to him, and circumstances that could not be foreseen determined the campaign which was afterwards made, the success and grandeur of which has resounded throughout all lands.

[3] "Road" was often used to mean *railroad*, as it is here.

15

THE ATLANTA CAMPAIGN

Grant and Sherman understood each other as few fellow commanders ever have. While other generals quarreled over rank and glory, these two devoted themselves first and foremost to defeating the Confederacy by any means necessary; though Sherman had once been superior to Grant in responsibility and prestige, he worked eagerly as Grant's subordinate. Grant, in turn, trusted no one else to carry out the grand plan he now assigned to Sherman.

Grant's grand plan for the spring of 1864 was aptly summed up by Lincoln's famous expression, "Those not skinning can hold a leg." The simultaneous advance of Grant, Sherman, and their subordinates would deny the Confederates the use of their interior lines (exploited previously by Longstreet in the Chickamauga campaign), forcing them onto the horns of a dilemma: where to sacrifice, and what to protect?

As it turned out, the "leg holders," as James McPherson calls them, failed in their tasks, leaving Lee and Johnston with greater flexibility and more reinforcements. To meet the challenge, Sherman embarked on a campaign of wide flanking maneuvers, avoiding direct assaults and entrenching at every stop. His first such maneuver (taken from an idea by George H. Thomas) came within an inch of shattering the enemy army; as it was, he sent the rebels on the first of many hurried retreats. Sherman's opponent has often been criticized for retreating too hastily; but Joseph Johnston was a cool professional, and he kept his army intact and in hand, ready for a chance to strike back.

From Dalton to Cassville
By *General William T. Sherman*

On the eighteenth day of March, 1864, at Nashville, Tennessee, I relieved Lieutenant-General Grant in command of the Military Division of the Mississippi, embracing the Departments of the Ohio, Cumberland,

205

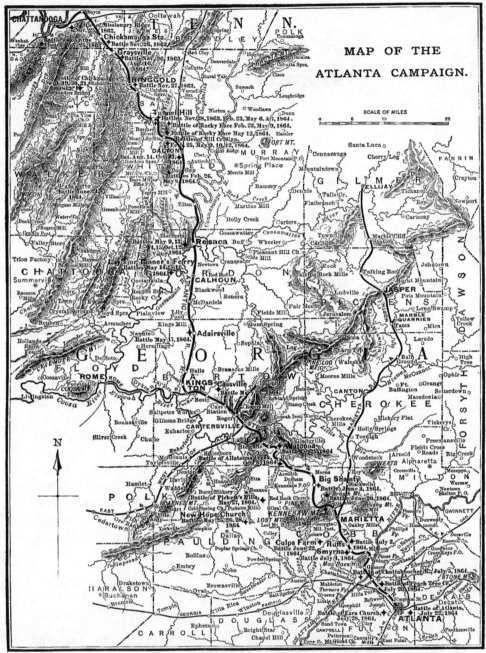

The Atlanta Campaign, May to September 1864

Tennessee, and Arkansas, commanded respectively by Major-Generals Schofield, Thomas, McPherson, and Steele. . . .

After my return to Nashville I addressed myself to the task of organization and preparation, which involved the general security of a vast region of the South which had already been conquered, more especially the several routes of supply and communication with the active armies at the front, and to organize a large army to move into Georgia, coincident with the advance of the Eastern armies against Richmond. . . .

The great question of the campaign was one of supplies. Nashville, our chief depot, was itself partially in a hostile country, and even the routes of supply from Louisville to Nashville by rail, and by way of the Cumberland River, had to be guarded. Chattanooga (our starting-point) was one hundred and fifty miles in front of Nashville, and every foot of the way, especially the many bridges, trestles, and culverts, had to be strongly guarded against the acts of a hostile population and of the enemy's cavalry. Then, of course, as we advanced into Georgia, it was manifest that we should have to repair the railroad, use it, and guard it likewise. . . . [General George H.] Thomas's spies brought him frequent and accurate reports of Joseph Johnston's army at Dalton, giving its strength at anywhere between forty and fifty thousand men, and these were being reinforced by troops from Mississippi, and by the Georgia militia, under General G.W. Smith. General Johnston seemed to be acting purely on the defensive, so that we had time and leisure to take all our measures deliberately and fully. I fixed the date of May 1st, when all things should be in readiness for the grand movement forward. . . .

We could not attempt an advance into Georgia without food, ammunition, etc.; and ordinary prudence dictated that we should have an accumulation at the front, in case of interruption to the railway by the act of the enemy, or by common accident. Accordingly, on the sixth of April, I issued a general order, limiting the use of the railroad cars to transporting only the essential articles of food, ammunition, and supplies for the army proper, forbidding any further issues to citizens, and cutting off all civil traffic. . . .

About this time, viz., the early part of April, I was much disturbed by a bold raid made by the rebel General Forrest up between the Mississippi and the Tennessee Rivers. He reached the Ohio River at Paducah, but was handsomely repulsed by Colonel Hicks. He then swung down toward Memphis, assaulted and carried Fort Pillow, massacring a part of its garrison, composed wholly of negro troops. . . .

I also had another serious cause of disturbance about that time. I wanted badly the two divisions of troops which had been loaned to General Banks

in the month of March previously, with the express understanding that
their absence was to endure only one month, and that during April they
were to come out of Red River, and be again within the sphere of my
command. . . . Rumors were reaching us thick and fast of defeat and
disaster in that quarter; and I feared then, what afterward actually happened, that neither General Banks nor Admiral Porter could or would
spare those two divisions. On the twenty-third of April . . . I saw that I
must go on without them. . . .

In Generals Thomas, McPherson, and Schofield, I had three generals of
education and experience, admirably qualified for the work before us. . . .
The departmental and army commanders had to maintain strong garrisons
in their respective departments, and also to guard their respective lines of
supply. I therefore, in my mind, aimed to prepare out of these armies, by
the first of May, 1864, a compact army for active operations in Georgia, of
about the following numbers:

Army of the Cumberland	50,000	Men
Army of the Tennessee	35,000	
Army of the Ohio	15,000	
TOTAL	100,000	

and, to make these troops as mobile as possible, I made the strictest
possible orders in relation to wagons and all species of encumbrances and
impedimenta whatever. Each officer and soldier was required to carry on
his horse or person food and clothing enough for five days. To each
regiment was allowed but one wagon and one ambulance, and to the
officers of each company one pack-horse or mule. . . .

These orders were not absolutely enforced, though in person I set the
example, and did not have a tent, nor did any officer about me have one;
but we had wall tent-flies, without poles, and no tent-furniture of any kind.
We usually spread our flies over saplings, or on fence-rails or posts improvised on the spot. Most of the general officers, except Thomas, followed
my example strictly; but he had a regular headquarters-camp. I frequently
called his attention to the orders on this subject, rather jestingly than
seriously. He would break out against his officers for having such luxuries,
but, needing a tent himself, and being good-natured and slow to act, he
never enforced my orders perfectly. . . .

On the tenth of April I received General Grant's letter of April 4th from
Washington, which formed the basis of all the campaigns of the year
1864. . . . [My] armies were to be directed against the rebel army com-

manded by General Joseph E. Johnston, then lying on the defensive, strongly entrenched at Dalton, Georgia; and I was required to follow it up closely and persistently, so that in no event could any part be detached to assist General Lee in Virginia; General Grant undertaking in like manner to keep Lee so busy that he could not respond to any calls of help by Johnston. Neither Atlanta, nor Augusta, nor Savannah, was the objective, but the "army of Joseph Johnston," go where it might. . . .

On the sixth of May was given to Schofield and McPherson to get into position, and on the seventh General Thomas moved in force against Tunnel Hill, driving off a mere picket-guard of the enemy, and I was agreeably surprised to find that no damage had been done to the tunnel or the railroad. From Tunnel Hill I could look into the gorge by which the railroad passed through a straight and well-defined range of mountains, presenting sharp palisade faces, and known as "Rocky Face." The gorge itself was called the "Buzzard Roost." We could plainly see the enemy in this gorge and behind it, and Mill Creek which formed the gorge, flowing toward Dalton, had been dammed up, making a sort of irregular lake, filling the road, thereby obstructing it, and the enemy's batteries crowned the cliffs on either side. The position was very strong, and I knew that such a general as my antagonist (Joseph Johnston), who had been there six months, had fortified it to the maximum. Therefore I had no intentions to attack the position seriously in front, but depended on McPherson to capture and hold the railroad to its rear, which would force Johnston to detach largely against him, or rather, as I expected, to evacuate his position at Dalton altogether. My orders to Generals Thomas and Schofield were merely to press strongly at all points in front, ready to rush in on the first appearance of "let go," and, if possible, to catch our enemy in the confusion of retreat.

All the movements of the seventh and eighth were made exactly as ordered, and the enemy seemed quiescent, acting purely on the defensive.

I had constant communication with all parts of the army, and on the ninth McPherson's head of column entered and passed through Snake Creek [Gap], perfectly undefended, and accomplished a complete surprise to the enemy. At its farther debouch he met a cavalry brigade, easily driven, which retreated hastily north toward Dalton, and doubtless carried to Johnston the first serious intimation that a heavy force of infantry and artillery was to his rear and within a few miles of his railroad. I got a short note from McPherson that day (written at 2 P.M., when he was within a mile and a half of the railroad, above and near Resaca), and we all felt jubilant. I renewed orders to Thomas and Schofield to be ready for the

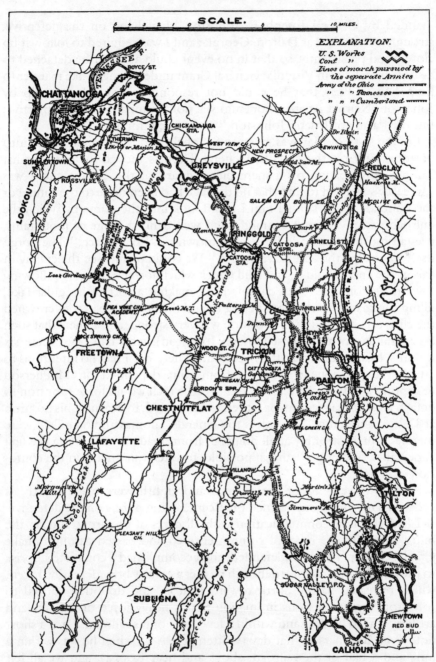

The Atlanta Campaign: the movement against Resaca

instant pursuit of what I expected to be a broken and disordered army, forced to retreat by roads to the east of Resaca, which were known to be very rough and impracticable.

That night I received further notices from McPherson that he had found Resaca too strong for a surprise; that in consequence he had fallen back three miles to the mouth of Snake Creek Gap, and there fortified. . . .

McPherson had startled Johnston in his fancied security, but had not done the full measure of his work. He had in hand twenty-three thousand of the best men of the army, and could have walked into Resaca (then held only by a small brigade), or he could have placed his whole force astride the railroad above Resaca, and there have easily withstood the attack of all of Johnston's army, with the knowledge that Thomas and Schofield were on his heels. Had he done so, I am certain that Johnston would not have ventured to attack him in position, but would have retreated eastward by Spring Place, and we should have captured half his army and all his artillery and wagons at the very beginning of the campaign.

Such an opportunity does not occur twice in a single life, but at the critical moment McPherson seems to have been a little cautious. Still, he was perfectly justified by his orders, and fell back and assumed an unassailable defensive position in Sugar Valley, on the Resaca side of Snake Creek Gap. As soon as informed of this, I determined to pass the whole army through Snake Creek Gap, and to move on Resaca with the main army.

But during the tenth, the enemy showed no signs of evacuating Dalton, and I was waiting for the arrival of Garrard's and Stoneman's cavalry, known to be near at hand, so as to secure the full advantages of victory, of which I felt certain. Hooker's 20th Corps was at once moved down to within easy supporting distance of McPherson; and on the eleventh, perceiving signs of evacuation at Dalton, I gave all the orders for the general movement, leaving the 4th Corps (Howard) and Stoneman's cavalry in observation in front of Buzzard Roost Gap, and directing all the rest of the army to march through Snake Creek Gap, straight on Resaca. The roads were only such as the country afforded, mere rough wagon-ways, and these converged to the single narrow track through Snake Creek Gap; but during the twelfth and thirteenth, the bulk of Thomas's and Schofield's armies were got through, and deployed against Resaca, McPherson on the right, Thomas in the center, and Schofield on the left. Johnston, as I anticipated, had abandoned all his well-prepared defenses at Dalton, and was found inside of Resaca with the bulk of his army, holding his divisions well in hand, acting purely on the defensive, and fighting well at all points of conflict. A complete line of entrenchments was found covering the place, and this was strongly manned at all points. On the fourteenth we closed in, enveloping the town on its north and west, and during the fifteenth we had a day of continual battle and skirmish. At the same time I caused two pontoon bridges to be laid across the Oostanaula River at Lay's Ferry, about three miles below the town, by which we could threaten Calhoun, a station on the railroad seven miles below Resaca. At the same time, May 14th, I dispatched General Garrard, with his cavalry division, down the Oostanaula by the Rome road, with orders to cross over, if possible, and to attack or threaten the railroad at any point below Calhoun and above Kingston. . . .

On the night of the fifteenth Johnston got his army across the bridges, set them on fire, and we entered Resaca at daylight. Our loss up to that time was about 600 dead and 3,375 wounded—mostly light wounds that did not necessitate sending the men to the rear for treatment. That Johnston had deliberately designed in advance to give up such strong positions as Dalton and Resaca, for the purpose of drawing us farther south, is simply absurd. Had he remained in Dalton another hour, it would have been his total defeat, and he only evacuated Resaca because his safety demanded it. The movement by us through Snake Creek Gap was a total surprise to him. My army about doubled his in size, but he had all the advantages of natural positions, of artificial forts and roads, and of concentrated action. We were compelled to grope our way through forests, across mountains, with a large army, necessarily more or less dispersed. Of course, I was disappointed not to have crippled his army more at that particular stage of the game; but, as it resulted, these rapid successes gave us the initiative, and the usual impulse of a conquering army.

Johnston having retreated in the night of May 15th, immediate pursuit was begun. A division of infantry (Jeff. C. Davis's) was at once dispatched down the valley toward Rome, to support Garrard's cavalry, and the whole army was ordered to pursue, McPherson by Lay's Ferry, on the right, Thomas directly by the railroad, and Schofield by the left, by the old road that crossed the Oostanaula above Echota or Newtown. We hastily repaired the railroad bridge at Resaca, which had been partially burned, and built a temporary floating bridge out of timber and materials found on the spot; so that Thomas got his advance corps over during the sixteenth, and marched as far as Calhoun, where he came into communication with McPherson's troops, which had crossed the Oostanaula at Lay's Ferry by our pontoon bridges, previously laid. . . .

On the seventeenth, toward evening, the head of Thomas's column, Newton's division, encountered the rear guard of Johnston's army near

Adairsville. I was near the head of the column at the time, trying to get a view of the position of the enemy from an elevation in an open field. My party attracted the fire of a battery; a shell passed through the group of staff officers and burst just beyond, which scattered us promptly. The next morning the enemy had disappeared, and our pursuit was continued to Kingston, which we reached during Sunday forenoon, the nineteenth.

From Resaca the railroad runs nearly due south, but at Kingston it makes junction with another railroad from Rome, and changes direction due east. At that time McPherson's head of column was about four miles to the west of Kingston, at a country place called "Woodlawn"; Schofield and Hooker were on the direct roads leading from Newtown to Cassville, diagonal to the route followed by Thomas. Thomas's head of column, which had followed the country roads alongside of the railroad, was about four miles east of Kingston, toward Cassville, when about noon I got a message from him that he had found the enemy, drawn up in line of battle, on some extensive, open ground, about halfway between Kingston and Cassville, and that appearances indicated a willingness and preparation for battle.

Aborted Counterattack
By General Joseph E. Johnston

My own operations, then and subsequently, were determined by the relative forces of the armies, and a higher estimate of the Northern soldiers than our Southern editors and politicians were accustomed to express, or even the Administration seemed to entertain. . . . It was not to be supposed that such troops, under a sagacious and resolute leader, and covered by entrenchments, were to be beaten by greatly inferior numbers. I therefore thought it our policy to stand on the defensive, to spare the blood of our soldiers by fighting under cover habitually, and to attack only when bad position or division of the enemy's forces might give us advantages counterbalancing that of superior numbers. So we held every position occupied until our communications were strongly threatened; then fell back only far enough to secure them, watching for opportunities to attack, keeping near enough to the Federal army to assure the Confederate Administration that Sherman could not send reinforcements to Grant, and hoping to reduce the odds against us by partial engagements. A material reduction of the Federal army might also be reasonably expected before the end of June, by the expiration of the terms of service of the regiments that had not reenlisted. I was confident, too, that the Administration would see the expediency of employing Forrest and his cavalry to break the enemy's railroad communications, by which he could have been defeated. . . .

Two roads lead southward from Adairsville—following the railroad through Kingston, and, like it, turning almost at right angles to the east at that place; the other, quite direct to the Etowah railroad bridge, passing through Cassville, where it is met by the first. The probability that the Federal army would divide—a column following each road—gave me a hope of engaging and defeating one of them before it could receive aid from the other. In that connection the intelligent engineer officer who had surveyed that section, Lieutenant Buchanan, was questioned minutely over the map as to the character of the ground, in the presence of Lieutenant-Generals Polk and Hood,[4] who had been informed of my object. He described the country on the direct road as open, and unusually favorable for attack. It was evident, from the map, that the distance between the two Federal columns would be greatest when that following the railroad should be near Kingston. Lieutenant Buchanan thought that the communications between the columns at this part of their march would be eight or nine miles, by narrow and crooked country roads.

In the morning of the eighteenth, Hardee's corps marched to Kingston; and Polk's and Hood's, following the direct road, halted within a mile of Cassville—the former deployed in two lines, crossing the road and facing Adairsville; the latter halted on its right. Jackson's division observed the Federal column on the Kingston road, and Wheeler's [the cavalry commander] troops that were moving toward Cassville. Those two officers were instructed to keep me accurately informed of the enemy's progress.

French's division of Polk's corps joined the army from Mississippi in the afternoon.

Next morning, when Brigadier-General Jackson's reports showed that the head of the Federal column following the railroad was near Kingston, Lieutenant-General Hood was directed to move with his corps to Adairsville, and parallel to it, and to march northward on that road, right in front. Polk's corps, as then formed, was to advance to meet and engage the enemy approaching from Adairsville; and it was expected that Hood's would be in position to fall upon the left flank of these troops as soon as

[4] Hardee, Polk, and Hood were Johnston's three corps commanders. Hood had come from the Army of Northern Virginia, where he had commanded a division in Longstreet's corps; Polk had just come from Mississippi with his troops.

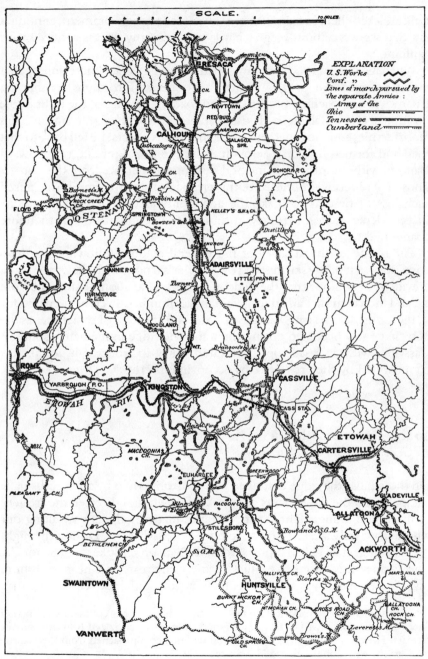

The Atlanta Campaign: the aborted Confederate counterattack at Cassville

Polk attacked them in front. An order was read to each regiment, announcing that we were about to give battle to the enemy. It was received with exultation.

When General Hood's column had moved two or three miles, that officer received a report from a member of his staff, to the effect that the enemy was approaching on the Canton road, in the rear of the right of the position from which he had just marched. Instead of transmitting this report to me, and moving on in obedience to his orders, he fell back to that road and formed his corps across it, facing to our right and rear, toward Canton, without informing me of this strange departure from the instructions he had received. I heard of this erratic movement after it had caused such loss of time as to make the attack intended impracticable; for its success depended on accuracy in timing it. The intention was therefore abandoned.[5]

The sound of the artillery of the Federal column following Hardee's corps, and that of the skirmishing of Wheeler's troops with the other, made it evident in an hour that the Federal forces would soon be united before us, and indicated that an attack by them was imminent. To be prepared for it, the Confederate army was drawn up in a position that I remember as the best that I saw occupied during the war—the ridge immediately south of Cassville, with a broad, open, elevated valley in front of it completely commanded by the fire of troops occupying its crest.

To the Gates of Atlanta
By General William T. Sherman

On these hills [the ridge described by Johnston] could be seen fresh-made parapets, and the movements of men, against whom I directed the artillery to fire at long range. The stout resistance made by the enemy along our whole front indicated a purpose to fight at Cassville. . . . During the night [of the nineteenth] I had reports from McPherson, Hooker, and Schofield. The former was about five miles to my right rear, and near the "nitre caves"; Schofield was about six miles north, and Hooker between us,

---

[5] Johnston blames Hood for ruining his best chance for a counterattack against Sherman—an ironic twist of fate, since Hood strenuously criticized Johnston's many retreats. However, a Union cavalry division *had* in fact approached from the Canton road, to the east, coming up on Hood's rear.

within two miles. All were ordered to close down on Cassville at daylight, and to attack the enemy wherever found. Skirmishing was kept up all night, but when day broke the next morning, May 20th, the enemy was gone, and our cavalry was sent in pursuit.[6] These reported him beyond the Etowah River. We were then well in advance of our railroad trains, on which we depended for supplies; so I determined to pause for a few days to repair the railroad, which had been damaged but little, except at the bridge at Resaca, and then to go on. . . .

I found at Cassville many evidences of preparation for a grand battle, among them a long line of entrenchments on the hill beyond the town, extending nearly three miles to the south, embracing the railroad crossing. I was also convinced that the whole of Polk's corps had joined Johnston's from Mississippi, and that he had in hand three full corps, viz. Hood's, Polk's, and Hardee's, numbering about sixty thousand men, and could not then imagine why he had declined battle, and did not learn the real reason till after the war, and then from General Johnston himself. . . . The telegraph . . . brought us the news of the bloody and desperate battles of the Wilderness, in Virginia, and that General Grant was pushing his operations against Lee with terrific energy. I was therefore resolved to give my enemy no rest.

In early days (1844), when a lieutenant of the Third Artillery, I had been sent from Charleston, South Carolina, to Marietta, Georgia. . . . I had ridden the distance on horseback, and noted well the topography of the country, especially that about Kennesaw, Allatoona, and the Etowah River. . . . I therefore knew that the Allatoona Pass was very strong, and would be hard to force, and resolved not even to attempt it, but to turn the position, by moving from Kingston to Marietta via Dallas; accordingly I made orders on the twentieth to get ready for the march to begin on the twenty-third. The Army of the Cumberland was ordered to march for Dallas, by Euharlee and Stilesboro; Davis's division, then in Rome, by Van Wert; the Army of the Ohio to keep on the left of Thomas, by a place called Burnt Hickory; and the Army of the Tennessee to march for a position a little to the south, so as to be on the right of the general army, when grouped about Dallas.

The movement contemplated leaving our railroad, and to depend for twenty days on the contents of our wagons; and as the country was very

[6] Sherman's artillery, which generally had a longer range than Johnston's, made the ridge untenable.

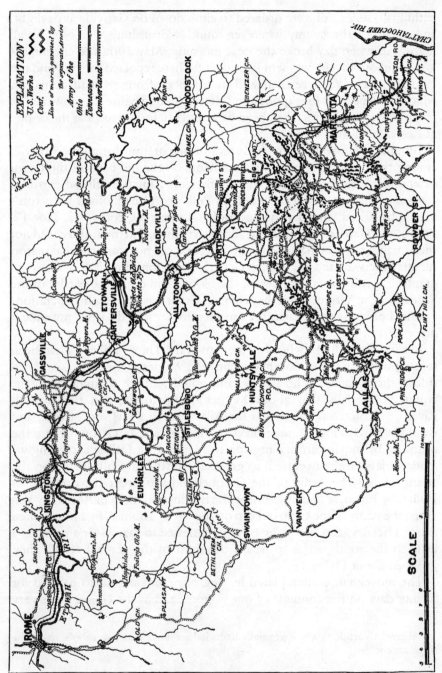

The Atlanta Campaign: from Cassville to Marietta

obscure, mostly in a state of nature, densely wooded, and with few roads, our movements were necessarily slow. We crossed the Etowah by several bridges and fords, and took as many roads as possible, keeping up communications by cross-roads, or by couriers through the woods. . . . Dallas, the point aimed at . . . was the point of concentration of a great many roads that led in every direction. Its possession would be a threat to Marietta and Atlanta, but I could not then venture to attempt either, till I had regained the use of the railroad, at least as far down as its debouch from the Allatoona range of mountains. Therefore, the movement was chiefly designed to compel Johnston to give up Allatoona.

On the twenty-fifth all the columns were moving steadily on Dallas— McPherson and Davis away off to the right, near Van Wert; Thomas on the main road in the center, with Hooker's 20th Corps ahead, toward Dallas; and Schofield to the left rear. For the convenience of the march, Hooker had his three divisions on separate roads, all leading toward Dallas, when, in the afternoon, as he approached a bridge across Pumpkin Vine Creek, he found it held by a cavalry force, which was driven off, but the bridge was on fire. This fire was extinguished, and Hooker's leading division (Geary's) followed the retreating cavalry on a road leading due east toward Marietta, instead of Dallas. This leading division, about four miles out from the bridge, struck a heavy infantry force, which was moving down from Allatoona toward Dallas, and a sharp battle ensued. I came up in person soon after, and as my map showed that we were near an important crossroad called New Hope, from a Methodist meeting house there of that name, I ordered General Hooker to secure it if possible that night. He asked for a short delay, till he could bring up his other two divisions, viz., of Butterfield and Williams, but before these divisions had got up and were deployed, the enemy had also gained corresponding strength. The woods were so dense, and the resistance so spirited, that Hooker could not carry the position, though the battle was noisy, and prolonged far into the night. This point, New Hope, was the accidental intersection of the road leading from Allatoona to Dallas with that from Van Wert to Marietta, was four miles northeast of Dallas, and from the bloody fighting there for the next week was called by the soldiers "Hell Hole."

The night was pitch-dark, it rained hard, and the convergence of our columns toward Dallas produced much confusion. I am sure similar confusion existed in the army opposed to us, for we were all mixed up. I slept on the ground, without cover, alongside of a log, got little sleep, resolved at daylight to renew the battle, and to make a lodgment on the Dallas and Allatoona road if possible, but the morning revealed a strong line of entrenchments facing us, with a heavy force of infantry and guns. The battle was renewed, and without success. McPherson reached Dallas that morning, viz., the twenty-sixth, and deployed his troops to the southeast and east of the town, placing Davis's division of the 14th Corps, which had joined him on the road from Rome, on his left; but this still left a gap of at least three miles between Davis and Hooker. Meantime, also, General Schofield was closing up on Thomas's left.

Satisfied that Johnston in person was at New Hope with all his army, and that it was so much nearer my "objective," the railroad, than Dallas, I concluded to draw McPherson from Dallas to Hooker's right, and gave orders accordingly; but McPherson was also confronted with a heavy force, and, as he began to withdraw according to his orders, on the morning of the twenty-eighth he was fiercely assailed on his right; a bloody battle ensued, in which he repulsed the attack, inflicting heavy loss on his assailants, and it was not until the first of June that he was enabled to withdraw from Dallas, and to effect a close junction with Hooker in front of New Hope. Meantime Thomas and Schofield were completing their deployments, gradually over-lapping Johnston on his right, and thus extending our left nearer and nearer to the railroad, the nearest point of which was Acworth, about eight miles distant. All this time a continual battle was in progress by strong skirmish-lines, taking advantage of every species of cover, and both parties fortifying each night by rifle trenches, with head logs, many of which grew to be as formidable as first-class works of defense. Occasionally one party or the other would make a dash in the nature of a sally, but usually it sustained a repulse with great loss of life. I visited personally all parts of our lines nearly every day, and was constantly within musket range, and though the fire of musketry and cannon resounded day and night along the whole line, vary-ing from six to ten miles, I rarely saw a dozen of the enemy at any one time; and these were always skirmishers dodging from tree to tree, or behind logs on the ground, or who occasionally showed their heads above the hastily constructed but remarkably strong rifle trenches. . . .

On the fourth of June I was preparing to draw off from New Hope Church, and to take position on the railroad in front of Allatoona, when, General Johnston himself having evacuated his position, we effected the change without further battle, and moved to the railroad, occupying it from Allatoona and Acworth forward to Big Shanty, in sight of the famous Kennesaw Mountain. . . .

With the drawn battle of New Hope Church, and our occupation of the natural fortress of Allatoona, terminated the month of May, and the first stage of the campaign.

Heavy rains set in about the first of June, making the roads infamous; but our marches were short, as we needed time for the repair of the railroad, so as to bring supplies forward to Allatoona Station. On the sixth I rode back to Allatoona, seven miles, found it all that was expected, and gave orders for its fortification and preparation as a "secondary base." General Blair arrived at Acworth on the eighth with his two divisions of the 17th Corps—the same which had been on veteran furlough—had come up from Cairo by way of Clifton, on the Tennessee River, and had followed our general route to Allatoona, where he had left a garrison of about fifteen hundred men. His effective strength, as reported, was nine thousand. These, with new regiments and furloughed men who had joined early in the month of May, equaled our losses from battle, sickness, and by detachments; so that the three armies still aggregated about one hundred thousand effective men.

On the tenth of June the whole combined army moved forward six miles, to Big Shanty, a station on the railroad, whence we had a good view of the enemy's position, which embraced three prominent hills, known as Kennesaw, Pine Mountain, and Lost Mountain. On each of these hills the enemy had signal stations and fresh lines of parapets. Heavy masses of infantry could be distinctly seen with the naked eye, and it was manifest that Johnston had chosen his ground well, and with deliberation had prepared for battle; but his line was at least ten miles in extent—too long, in my judgment, to be held successfully by his force, then estimated at sixty thousand. As his position, however, gave him a perfect view over our field, we had to proceed with due caution. McPherson had the left, following the railroad, which curved around the north base of Kennesaw; Thomas the center, obliqued to the right, deploying below Kennesaw and facing Pine Hill; and Schofield, somewhat refused, was on the general right, looking south, toward Lost Mountain.

The rains continued to pour, and made our developments slow and dilatory, for there were no roads, and these had to be improvised by each division for its own supply train from the depot in Big Shanty to the camps. Meantime each army was deploying carefully before the enemy, entrenching every camp, ready as against a sally. The enemy's cavalry was also busy in our rear, compelling us to detach cavalry all the way back as far as Resaca, and to strengthen all the infantry posts as far as Nashville. . . .[7]

---

[7] Through June and July, Sherman's subordinates in Memphis fought a frustrating struggle against Confederate cavalry under General Nathan Bedford Forrest. General A.J. Smith finally defeated Forrest at Tupelo, Mississippi, July 13–15, 1864.

By the fourteenth the rain slackened, and we occupied a continuous line of ten miles, entrenched, conforming to the irregular position of the enemy, when I reconnoitered, with a view to make a break in their line between Kennesaw and Pine Mountain. When abreast of Pine Mountain I noticed a rebel battery on its crest, with a continuous line of fresh rifle trench about halfway down the hill. Our skirmishers were at the time engaged in the woods about the base of this hill between the lines, and I estimated the distance to the battery on the crest at about eight hundred yards. Near it, in plain view, stood a group of the enemy, evidently observing us with glasses.[8] General Howard, commanding the Fourth Corps, was nearby, and I called his attention to this group, and ordered him to compel it to keep behind its cover. He replied that his orders from General Thomas were to spare artillery ammunition. This was right, according to the general policy, but I explained to him that we must keep up the morale of a bold offensive, that he must use his artillery, force the enemy to remain on the timid defensive, and ordered him to cause a battery close by to fire three volleys. I continued to ride down our line, and soon heard, in quick succession, the three volleys. The next division in order was Geary's, and I gave him similar orders. General Polk, in my opinion, was killed by the second volley fired from the first battery referred to . . .

On the fifteenth we advanced our general lines, intending to attack at any weak point discovered between Kennesaw and Pine Mountain; but Pine Mountain was found to be abandoned, and Johnston had contracted his front somewhat, on a direct line, connecting Kennesaw with Lost Mountain. . . . On the sixteenth, the general movement was continued, when Lost Mountain was abandoned by the enemy. Our right naturally swung around, so as to threaten the railroad below Marietta, but Johnston had still further contracted and strengthened his lines, covering Marietta and all the roads below.

On the seventeenth and eighteenth the rain again fell in torrents, making army movements impossible, but we devoted the time to strengthening our positions, more especially the left and center, with a view gradually to draw from the left to add to the right; and we had to hold our lines on the left extremely strong, to guard against a sally from Kennesaw against our depot at Big Shanty. . . .

On the nineteenth of June the rebel army again fell back on its flanks, to such an extent that for a time I supposed it had retreated to the

---

[8] This group was composed of General Johnston himself along with corps commanders Hardee and Polk.

Chattahoochee River, fifteen miles distant; but as we pressed forward we were soon undeceived, for we found it still more concentrated, covering Marietta and the railroad. . . .

While we were thus engaged about Kennesaw, General Grant had his hands full with Lee, in Virginia. General Halleck was the chief of staff at Washington, and to him I communicated almost daily. I find from my letter-book that on the twenty-first of June I reported to him tersely and truly the condition of facts on that day: "This is the nineteenth day of rain, and the prospect of fair weather is as far off as ever. The roads are impassable; the fields and woods become quagmires after a few wagons have crossed over. . . ."

During the twenty-fourth and twenty-fifth of June General Schofield extended his right as far as prudent, so as to compel the enemy to thin out his lines correspondingly, with the intention to make two strong assaults at points where success would give us the greatest advantage. I had consulted Generals Thomas, McPherson, and Schofield, and we all agreed that we could not with prudence stretch out any more, and therefore there was no alternative but to attack fortified lines, a thing carefully avoided up to that time. I reasoned, if we could make a breach anywhere near the rebel center, and thrust in a strong head of column that with the one moiety of our army we could hold in check the corresponding wing of the enemy, and with the other sweep in flank and overwhelm the other half. The twenty-seventh of June was fixed as the day for the attempt, and in order to oversee the whole, and to be in close communication with all parts of the army, I had a place cleared on the top of a hill to the rear of Thomas's center, and had the telegraph wires laid to it. The points of attack were chosen, and the troops were all prepared with as little demonstration as possible. About 9 A.M. of the day appointed, the troops moved to the assault, and all along our lines for ten miles a furious fire of artillery and musketry was kept up. At all points the enemy met us with determined courage and in great force. McPherson's attacking column fought up the face of the lesser Kennesaw, but could not reach the summit. About a mile to the right (just below the Dallas road), Thomas's assaulting column reached the parapet, where Brigadier-General Harker was shot down mortally wounded, and Brigadier-General McCook (my old law partner) was desperately wounded, from the effects of which he afterward died. By 11:30 the assault was in fact over, and had failed. We had not broken the rebel line at either point, but our assaulting columns had held their ground within a few yards of the rebel trenches, and there covered themselves with parapet. McPherson lost about five hundred men and several valuable officers, and Thomas lost nearly two thousand men. This was the hardest fight of the campaign up to that date. . . .

While the battle was in progress at the center, Schofield crossed Olley's Creek on the right, and gained a position threatening Johnston's line of retreat; and, to increase the effect, I ordered Stoneman's cavalry to proceed rapidly still farther to the right, to Sweetwater. Satisfied of the bloody cost of attacking entrenched lines, I at once thought of moving the whole army to the railroad at a point (Fulton) about ten miles below Marietta, or to the Chattahoochee River itself, a movement similar to the one afterward so successfully practiced at Atlanta. All the orders were issued to bring forward supplies enough to fill our wagons, intending to strip the railroad back to Allatoona, and leave that place as our depot, to be covered as well as possible by Garrard's cavalry. General Thomas, as usual, shook his head, deeming it risky to leave the railroad; but something had to be done, and I resolved on this move. . . .

McPherson drew out of his lines during the night of July 2nd, leaving Garrard's cavalry, dismounted, occupying his trenches, and moved to the rear of the Army of the Cumberland, stretching down the Nickajack; but Johnston detected the movement and promptly abandoned Marietta and Kennesaw. I expected as much, for, by the earliest dawn of the third of July, I was at a large spyglass mounted on a tripod. . . . I directed the glass on Kennesaw, and saw some of our pickets crawling up the hill cautiously; soon they stood upon the very top, and I could plainly see their movements as they ran along the crest just abandoned by the enemy. In a minute I roused my staff, and started them off with orders in every direction for a pursuit of every possible road, hoping to catch Johnston in the confusion of retreat, especially at the crossing of the Chattahoochee River. . . .

Of course, he chose to let go Kennesaw and Marietta, and fall back on an entrenched camp prepared by his orders in advance on the north and west of the Chattahoochee, covering the railroad crossing and several pontoon bridges. I confess I had not learned beforehand of the existence of this strong place, in the nature of a *tete-du-pont*, and had counted on striking him an effectual blow in the expected confusion of his crossing the Chattahoochee, a broad and deep river then to his rear. . . .

During the night [of July 4th] Johnston drew back all his army and trains inside the *tete-du-pont* at the Chattahoochee, which proved one of the strongest pieces of field fortification I ever saw. We closed up against it, and were promptly met by a heavy and severe fire. Thomas was on the main road in immediate pursuit; next on his right was Schofield; and McPherson on the extreme right, reaching the Chattahoochee River below Turner's

Ferry. Stoneman's cavalry was still farther to the right, along down the Chattahoochee River as far as opposite Sandtown; and on that day I ordered Garrard's division of cavalry up the river eighteen miles, to secure possession of the factories at Roswell, as well as to hold an important bridge and ford at that place.

About three miles out from the Chattahoochee the main road forked, the right branch following substantially the railroad, and the left one leading straight for Atlanta, via Paice's Ferry and Buckhead. We found the latter unoccupied and unguarded, and the 4th Corps (Howard's) reached the river at Paice's Ferry. The right-hand road was perfectly covered by the *tete-du-pont* before described, where the resistance was very severe, and for some time deceived me, for I was pushing Thomas with orders to fiercely assault his enemy, supposing that he was merely opposing us to gain time to get his trains and troops across the Chattahoochee; but, on personally reconnoitering, I saw the abatis and the strong redoubts, which satisfied me of the preparations that had been made by Johnston in anticipation of this very event. While I was with General Jeff. C. Davis, a poor negro came out of the abatis, blanched with fright, said he had been hidden under a log all day, with a perfect storm of shot, shells, and musket balls, passing over him, till a short lull had enabled him to creep out and make himself known to our skirmishers, who in turn had sent him back to where we were. This negro explained that he with about a thousand slaves had been at work a month or more on these very lines, which, as he explained, extended from the river about a mile above the railroad bridge to Turner's Ferry below, being in extent from five to six miles. . . .

I knew that Johnston would not remain long on the west bank of the Chattahoochee, for I could easily practice on that ground to better advantage our former tactics of entrenching a moiety in his front, and with the rest of our army cross the river and threaten either his rear or the city of Atlanta itself, which city was of vital importance to the existence not only of his own army, but of the Confederacy itself. . . .

At this time Stoneman was very active on our extreme right, pretending to be searching the river below Turner's Ferry for a crossing, and was watched closely by the enemy's cavalry on the other side. McPherson, on the right, was equally demonstrative at and near Turner's Ferry. Thomas faced substantially the entrenched *tete-du-pont*, and had his left on the Chattahoochee River, at Paice's Ferry. Garrard's cavalry was up at Roswell, and McCook's small division of cavalry was intermediate, above Soap's Creek. Meantime, also, the railroad-construction party was hard at work, repairing the railroad up to our camp at Vining's Station.

Of course, I expected every possible resistance in crossing the Chattahoochee River, and had made up my mind to feign on the right, but actually to cross over by the left. We had already secured a crossing-place at Roswell, but one nearer was advisable; General Schofield had examined the river well, found a place just below the mouth of Soap's Creek which he deemed advantageous, and was instructed to effect an early crossing there, and to entrench a good position on the other side, viz., the east bank. . . .

Schofield effected his crossing at Soap's Creek very handsomely on the ninth, capturing the small guard that was watching the crossing. By night he was on the high ground beyond, strongly entrenched, with two good pontoon bridges finished, and was prepared, if necessary, for an assault by the whole Confederate army. The same day Garrard's cavalry also crossed over at Roswell, drove away the cavalry pickets, and held its ground till relieved by Newton's division of Howard's corps, which was sent up temporarily, till it in turn was relieved by Dodge's corps (Sixteenth) of the Army of the Tennessee, which was the advance of the whole of that army.

That night Johnston evacuated his trenches, crossed over the Chattahoochee, burned the railroad bridge and his pontoon and trestle bridges, and left us in full possession of the north or west bank—besides which, we had already secured possession of the two good crossings at Roswell and Soap's Creek. I have always thought Johnston neglected his opportunity there, for he had lain comparatively idle while we got control of both banks of the river above him. . . .

By crossing the Chattahoochee above the railroad bridge, we were better placed to cover our railroad and depots than below, though a movement across the river below the railroad, to the south of Atlanta, might have been more decisive. But we were already so far from home, and would be compelled to accept battle whenever offered, with the Chattahoochee to *our* rear, that it became imperative for me to take all prudential measures the case admitted of, and I therefore determined to pass the river above the railroad bridge—McPherson on the left, Schofield in the center, and Thomas on the right. . . .

On the seventeenth we began the general movement against Atlanta, Thomas crossing the Chattahoochee at Powers's and Paice's, by the pontoon bridges; Schofield moving out toward Cross Keys, and McPherson toward Stone Mountain. We encountered but little opposition except by cavalry. On the eighteenth all the armies moved on a general right wheel, Thomas to Buckhead, forming a line of battle facing Peachtree Creek; Schofield was on his left, and McPherson well over toward the railroad between Stone Mountain and Decatur, which he reached at 2 P.M. of that day, about four miles from Stone Mountain, and seven miles east of Decatur, and there he turned toward Atlanta, breaking up the railroad as he progressed, his advance guard reaching Decatur about night, where he came into communication with Schofield's troops, which had also reached Decatur. About 10 A.M. of that day (July 18th), when the armies were all in motion, one of General Thomas's staff officers brought me a citizen, one of our spies, who had just come out of Atlanta, and had brought a newspaper of the same day, or of the day before, containing Johnston's order relinquishing the command of the Confederate forces in Atlanta, and Hood's order assuming command. I immediately inquired of General Schofield, who was his classmate at West Point, about Hood, as to his general character, etc., and learned that he was bold even to rashness, and courageous in the extreme; I inferred that the change of commanders meant "fight." Notice of this important change was at once sent to all parts of the army, and every division commander was cautioned to be always prepared for battle in any shape. This was just what we wanted, viz., to fight in open ground, on anything like equal terms, instead of being forced to run up against prepared entrenchments; but, at the same time, the enemy having Atlanta behind him, could choose the time and place of attack, and could at pleasure mass a superior force on our weakest points. Therefore, we had to be constantly ready for sallies.

On the nineteenth the three armies were converging toward Atlanta, meeting such feeble resistance that I really thought the enemy intended to evacuate the place. McPherson was moving astride the railroad, near Decatur; Schofield along a road leading toward Atlanta, by Colonel Howard's house and the distillery; and Thomas was crossing Peachtree in line of battle, building bridges for nearly every division as he deployed. There was quite a gap between Thomas and Schofield, which I endeavored to close by drawing two of Howard's divisions nearer Schofield. On the twentieth I was with General Schofield near the center, and soon after noon heard heavy firing in front of Thomas's right, which lasted an hour or so, and then ceased. I soon learned that the enemy had made a furious sally. . . .

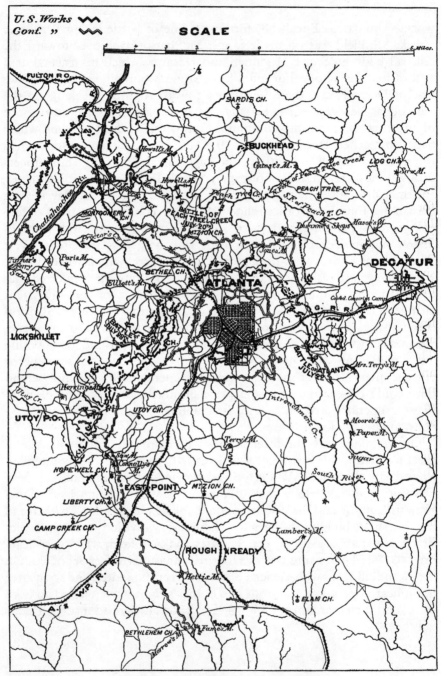

The Siege of Atlanta, July to September 1864

Counterattack: From Peachtree Creek to the Battle of Atlanta
By General John B. Hood

It is difficult to imagine a commander placed at the head of an army under more embarrassing circumstances than those against which I was left to contend on the evening of the eighteenth of July, 1864. I was, comparatively, a stranger to the Army of Tennessee. Moreover, General Johnston's mode of warfare formed so strong a contrast to the tactics and strategy which were practiced in Virginia, where far more satisfactory results were obtained than in the West, that I have become a still more ardent advocate of the Lee and Jackson school. The troops of the Army of Tennessee had for such a length of time been subjected to the ruinous policy pursued from Dalton to Atlanta that they were unfitted for united action in pitched battle. They had, in other words, been so long habituated to the security behind breastworks that they had become wedded to the "timid defensive" policy, and naturally regarded with distrust a commander likely to initiate offensive operations. . . .[9]

On the night of the eighteenth and morning of the nineteenth, I formed line of battle facing Peachtree Creek; the left rested near Pace's Ferry road, and the right covered Atlanta. I was informed on the nineteenth that Thomas was building bridges across Peachtree Creek, and that McPherson and Schofield were well over toward, and even on, the Georgia Railroad, near Decatur. I perceived at once that the Federal commander had committed a serious blunder in separating his corps, or armies, by such distance as to allow me to concentrate the main body of our army upon his right wing, whilst his left was so far removed as to be incapable of rendering timely assistance. General Sherman's violation of the established maxim that an army should always be well within hand, or its detachments within easy supporting distance, afforded one of the most favorable occasions for complete victory which could have been offered; especially as it presented an opportunity, after crushing his right wing, to throw our entire force upon his left. In fact, such a blunder affords a small army the best, if not the sole, chance of success when contending with a vastly superior force.

Line of battle having been formed, Stewart's corps was in position on the left, Hardee's in the center, and Cheatham's on the right.[10] Orders were given to Generals Hardee and Stewart to observe closely and report

[9] In this passage, Hood has followed the time-honored policy of defeated generals and blames his troops, who in fact fought very bravely in the days that followed.

[10] Stewart and Cheatham were serving as corps commanders after Polk's death and Hood's elevation to army command.

promptly the progress of Thomas in the construction of bridges across Peachtree Creek and the passage of troops. General Cheatham was directed to reconnoiter in front of his left; to erect, upon that part of his line, batteries so disposed to command the entire space between his left and Peachtree Creek, in order to completely isolate McPherson's and Schofield's forces from those of Thomas; and, finally, to thoroughly entrench his line. This object accomplished, and Thomas having partially crossed the creek and made a lodgment on the east side within the pocket formed by Peachtree Creek and the Chattahoochee River, I determined to attack him with two corps—Hardee's and Stewart's, which constituted the main body of the Confederate army—and thus, if possible, crush Sherman's right wing, as we drove it into the narrow space between the creek and the river.[11]

Major-General G.W. Smith's Georgia State troops were posted on the right of Cheatham, and it was impossible for Schofield or McPherson to assist Thomas without recrossing Peachtree Creek in the vicinity of Decatur, and making on the west side a detour which necessitated a march of not less than ten or twelve miles, in order to reach Thomas's bridges across this creek. I immediately assembled the three corps commanders, Hardee, Stewart, and Cheatham, together with Major-General G.W. Smith, commanding Georgia State troops, for the purpose of giving orders for battle on the following day, the twentieth of July. . . .

I also deemed it of equal moment that each should fully appreciate the imperativeness of the orders then issued, by reason of the certainty that our troops would encounter hastily constructed works thrown up by the Federal troops, which had been foremost to cross Peachtree Creek. Although a portion of the enemy would undoubtedly be found under cover of temporary breastworks it was equally certain a larger portion would be caught in the act of throwing up such works, and just in that state of confusion to enable our forces to rout them by a bold and persistent attack. With these convictions I timed the assault at 1 P.M., so as to surprise the enemy in their unsettled condition.

As stated in my official report, the charge was unfortunately not made till about four o'clock P.M., on account of General Hardee's failure to obey my specific instructions in regard to the extension of the one-half division front to the right, in order to afford General Cheatham an advantageous

---

[11] Hood's plan, to attack a fraction of Sherman's force with almost all of his own, was flawed by the fact that Thomas's army was about as large as his own—the very largest fraction of Sherman's legions.

position to hold in check McPherson and Schofield. The result was not, however, materially affected by this delay, since the Federals were completely taken by surprise.

General Stewart carried out his instructions to the letter; he moreover appealed in person to his troops before going into action, and informed them that orders were imperative they should carry everything, at all hazards, on their side of Peachtree Creek; he impressed upon them that they should not halt before temporary breastworks, but charge gallantly every obstacle and rout the enemy. . . . General Stewart and his troops nobly performed their duty in the engagement of the twentieth. At the time of their attack, his corps moved boldly forward, drove the enemy from his works, and held possession of them until driven out by an enfilade fire of batteries placed in position by General Thomas. . . .

Unfortunately, the corps on Stewart's right, although composed of the best troops in the army, virtually accomplished nothing. In lieu of moving the half division promptly to the right, attacking as ordered, and supporting Stewart's gallant assault, the troops of Hardee—as their losses on that day indicate—did nothing more than skirmish with the enemy. Instead of charging down upon the foe as Sherman represents Stewart's men to have done, many of the troops, when they discovered that they had come into contact with breastworks, lay down and, consequently, this attempt at pitched battle proved abortive. . . .

The failure on the twentieth rendered urgent the most active measures in order to save Atlanta even for a short period. Through the vigilance of General Wheeler [the cavalry commander], I received information, during the night of the twentieth, of the exposed position of McPherson's left flank; it was standing out in air near the Georgia Railroad between Decatur and Atlanta, and a large number of the enemy's wagons had been parked in and around Decatur. The roads were in good condition, and ran in the direction to enable a large body of our army to march, under cover of darkness, around this exposed flank and attack in rear.

I determined to make all necessary preparations for a renewed assault; to attack the extreme left of the Federals in rear and flank, and endeavor to bring the entire Confederate army into united action. . . .

General Hardee, who commanded the largest corps and whose troops were comparatively fresh, as they had taken but little part in the attack of the previous day, was ordered to hold his forces in readiness to move promptly at dark that night—the twenty-first. I selected Hardee for this duty, because Cheatham had, at that time, but little experience as a corps commander, and Stewart had been heavily engaged the day previous.

The position of the enemy during the twenty-first remained, I may say, unchanged, with the exception that Schofield and McPherson had advanced slightly toward Atlanta. To transfer after dark our entire line from the immediate presence of the enemy to another line around Atlanta, and to throw Hardee, the same night, entirely to the rear and flank of McPherson—as Jackson was thrown, in a similar movement, at Chancellorsville and Second Manassas—and to initiate the offensive at daylight, required no small effort upon the part of the men and officers. I hoped, however, that the assault would result not only in a general battle, but in a signal victory to our arms. . . .

The demonstrations of the enemy upon our right, and which threatened to destroy the Macon Railroad—our main line for receiving supplies—rendered it imperative that I should check, immediately, his operations in that direction; otherwise Atlanta was doomed to fall at a very early day. . . .

Stewart, Cheatham, and G.W. Smith were ordered to occupy soon after dark the positions assigned them in the new line round the city, and to entrench as thoroughly as possible. General Shoupe, chief of artillery, was ordered to mass artillery on our right. General Hardee was directed to put his corps in motion soon after dusk; to move south on the McDonough road, across Entrenchment Creek at Cobb's Mills, and to *completely* turn the left of McPherson's army and attack at daylight, or as soon thereafter as possible. He was furnished guides from Wheeler's cavalry, who were familiar with the various roads in that direction; was given clear and positive orders to detach his corps, to swing away from the main body of the army, and to march entirely around and to the rear of McPherson's left flank, even if he was forced to go to or beyond Decatur, which is only about six miles from Atlanta.

Major-General Wheeler was ordered to move on Hardee's right with all the cavalry at his disposal, and to attack with Hardee at daylight. General Cheatham, who was in line of battle on the right and around the city, was instructed to take up the movement from his right as soon as Hardee succeeded in forcing back, or throwing into confusion, the Federal left, and to assist in driving the enemy down and back upon Peachtree Creek, from right to left. General G.W. Smith would, thereupon, join in the attack. General Stewart, posted on the left, was instructed not only to occupy and keep a strict watch upon Thomas, in order to prevent him from giving aid to Schofield and McPherson, but to engage the enemy the instant the movement became general, i.e., as soon as Hardee and Cheatham succeeded in driving the Federals down Peachtree Creek and near his right. . . .

Thus orders were given to attack from right to left, and to press the Federal army down and against the deep and muddy stream in their rear. These orders were carefully explained again and again, till each officer present gave assurance that he fully comprehended his duties. . . . At dawn on the morning of the twenty-second Cheatham, Stewart, and G.W. Smith had, by alternating working parties during the night previous, not only strongly fortified their respective positions, but had kept their men comparatively fresh for action, and were in readiness to act as soon as the battle was initiated by Hardee who was supposed to be at that moment in the rear of the adversary's flank.

I took my position at daybreak near Cheatham's right, whence I could observe the left of the enemy's entrenchments which seemed to be thrown back a short distance on their extreme left. After waiting nearly the entire morning, I heard, about ten or eleven o'clock, skirmishing going on directly opposite the left of the enemy, which was in front of Cheatham's right and Shoupe's artillery. A considerable time had elapsed when I discovered, with astonishment and bitter disappointment, a line of battle composed of one of Hardee's divisions advancing directly against the entrenched flank of the enemy.[12]

The Capture of Atlanta
By General William T. Sherman

During the night [before Hardee's attack], I had full reports from all parts of our line, most of which was partially entrenched as against a sally, and finding that McPherson was stretching out too much on his left flank, I wrote him a note early in the morning not to extend so much by his left; for we had not troops enough to completely invest the place, and I intended to destroy utterly all parts of the Augusta Railroad to the east of Atlanta, then to withdraw from the left flank and add to the right. . . . In the morning we found the strong line of parapet, "Peachtree line," to the front of Schofield and Thomas, abandoned, and our lines were advanced rapidly close up to Atlanta. For some moments I supposed the enemy intended to evacuate, and in person was on horseback at the head of Schofield's troops, who had

[12] Historian Albert Castel has shown that Hardee's men, who had struggled through thick woods all night, emerged in the morning to find the Union flank was guarded after all.

advanced in front of the Howard House to some open ground, from which we could plainly see their men dragging up from the intervening valley, by the distillery, trees and saplings for abatis. . . . Schofield was dressing forward his lines, and I could hear Thomas farther to the right engaged, when General McPherson and his staff rode up. We went back to the Howard House, a double frame-building with a porch, and sat on the steps, discussing the chances of a battle, and of Hood's general character. McPherson had also been of the same class at West Point with Hood, Schofield, and Sheridan. We agreed that we ought to be unusually cautious and prepared at all times for sallies and hard fighting, because Hood, though not deemed much of a scholar, or of great mental capacity, was undoubtedly a brave, determined, and rash man. . . .

McPherson was in excellent spirits, well pleased at the progress of events so far, and had come over purposely to see me about the order I had given him to use Dodge's corps to break up the railroad, saying that the night before he had gained a position on Leggett's Hill[13] from which he could look over the rebel parapet, and see the high smokestack of a large foundry in Atlanta; that before receiving my order he had diverted Dodge's two divisions (then in motion) from the main road, on a diagonal one that led to his extreme left flank . . . for the purpose of strengthening that flank. . . . He said that he could put all his pioneers [a type of engineers] to work, and do with them in the time indicated all I had proposed to do with General Dodge's two divisions. Of course I assented at once, and we walked down the road a short distance, sat down by the foot of a tree where I had my map, and on it pointed out to him Thomas's position and his own. I then explained minutely that, after we had sufficiently broken up the Augusta road, I wanted to shift his whole army around by the rear to Thomas's extreme right, and hoped to reach the other railroad at East Point. While we sat there we could hear lively skirmishing going on near us (down about the distillery) . . . and then we heard an occasional gun back toward Decatur. I asked him what it meant. We took my pocket compass (which I always carried), and by noting the direction of the sound, we became satisfied that the firing was too far to our rear to be explained by known facts, and he hastily called for his horse, his staff, and his orderlies.

McPherson was then in his prime (about thirty-four years old), over six feet high, and a very handsome man in every way, was universally liked, and had many noble qualities. He had on his boots outside his pantaloons,

---

[13] Sherman calls this hill (locally called Bald Hill) after the General Mortimer Leggett, the Union officer whose men held it.

gauntlets on his hands, and had on his major-general's uniform, and wore a swordbelt, but no sword. He hastily gathered his papers (save one, which I now possess) into a pocketbook, put it in his breastpocket, and jumped on his horse, saying he would hurry down his line and send me back word what these sounds meant. His adjutant-general, Clark, Inspector-General Strong, and his aides, Captains Steele and Gile, were with him. Although the sound of musketry on our left grew in volume, I was not so much disturbed by it as the sound of artillery back toward Decatur. I ordered Schofield at once to send a brigade back to Decatur (some five miles) and was walking up and down the porch of the Howard House, listening, when one of McPherson's staff, with his horse covered with sweat, dashed up to the porch, and reported that General McPherson was either "killed or a prisoner." He explained that when they had left me a few minutes before, they had ridden rapidly across to the railroad, the sound of battle increasing as they neared the position occupied by General Giles A. Smith's division, and that McPherson had sent first one, then another of his staff to bring some of the reserve brigades of the Fifteenth Corps over to the exposed left flank; that he had reached the head of Dodge's corps (marching by the flank on the diagonal road as described), and had ordered it to hurry forward to the same point; that then, almost if not entirely alone, he had followed this road leading across the wooded valley behind the 17th Corps, and had disappeared in these woods, doubtless with a sense of absolute security. The sound of musketry was there heard, and McPherson's horse came back, bleeding, wounded, and riderless. I ordered the staff officer who brought this message to return at once, to find General Logan (the senior officer present with the Army of the Tennessee), to report the same facts to him, and to instruct him to drive back this supposed small force, which had evidently got around the 17th Corps through the blind woods in rear of our left flank. I soon dispatched one of my own staff (McCoy, I think) to General Logan with similar orders, telling him to refuse his left flank, and to fight the battle (holding fast to Leggett's Hill) with the Army of the Tennessee; that I would personally look to Decatur and to the safety of his rear, and would reinforce him if he needed it. I dispatched orders to General Thomas on our right, telling him of this strong sally, and my inference that the lines in his front had evidently been weakened by reason thereof, and that he ought to take advantage of the opportunity to make a lodgment in Atlanta, if possible.

Meantime the sounds of the battle rose on our extreme left more and more furious, extending to the place where I stood, at the Howard House. Within an hour an ambulance came in . . . bearing McPherson's body. . . .

The reports that came to me from all parts of the field revealed clearly what was the game of my antagonist, and the ground somewhat favored him. . . . The enemy was [due to the absence of the Union cavalry] enabled, under the cover of the forest, to approach quite near before he was discovered; indeed, his skirmish line had worked through the timber and got into the field to the rear of Giles A. Smith's division of the 17th Corps unseen, had captured Murray's battery of regular artillery, moving through these woods entirely unguarded, and had got possession of several of the hospital camps. The right of this rebel line struck Dodge's troops in motion, but, fortunately, this corps (16th) had only to halt, face to the left, and was in line of battle; and this corps not only held in check the enemy, but drove him back through the woods. About the same time this same force had struck General Giles A. Smith's left flank, doubled it back, captured four guns in position and the party engaged in building the very battery [on Leggett's Hill] which was the special object of McPherson's visit to me, and almost enveloped the entire left flank. The men, however, were skillful and brave, and fought for a time with their backs to Atlanta. They gradually fell back, compressing their own line, and gaining strength by making junction with Leggett's division of the 17th Corps, well and strongly posted on the hill. One or two brigades of the 15th Corps, ordered by McPherson, came rapidly across the open field to the rear, from the direction of the railroad, filled up the gap from Blair's new left to the head of Dodge's column—now facing to the general left—thus forming a strong left flank, at right angles to the original line of battle.

The enemy attacked, boldly and repeatedly, the whole of this flank, but met an equally fierce resistance; and on that ground a bloody battle raged from little after noon till into the night. A part of Hood's plan of action was to sally from Atlanta at the same moment; but this sally was not, for some reason, simultaneous, for the first attack on our extreme left flank had been checked and repulsed before the sally came from the direction of Atlanta. Meantime, Colonel Sprague, in Decatur, had got his teams harnessed up, and safely conducted his train to the rear of Schofield's position, holding in check Wheeler's cavalry till he had got off all his trains, with the exception of three or four wagons. I remained near the Howard House, receiving reports and sending orders. . . .

About 4 P.M. the expected sally came from Atlanta, directed mainly against Leggett's Hill and along the Decatur road. At Leggett's Hill they were met and bloodily repulsed. Along the railroad they were more successful. Sweeping over a small force with two guns, they reached our main line, broke through it, and got possession of De Gress's battery of four twenty-pound Parrotts [large artillery pieces], killing every horse, and turning the guns against us. General Charles R. Wood's division of the 15th Corps was on the extreme right of the Army of the Tennessee, between the railroad and the Howard House, where he connected with Schofield's troops. He reported to me in person that the line of his left had been swept back, and that his connection with General Logan, on Leggett's Hill, had been broken. I ordered him to wheel his brigades to the left, to advance in echelon, and to catch the enemy in flank. General Schofield brought forward all his available batteries, to the number of twenty guns, to a position to the left front of the Howard House, whence we could overlook the field of action, and directed a heavy fire over the heads of General Wood's men against the enemy; and we saw Wood's troops advance and encounter the enemy, who had secured possession of the old line of parapet which had been held by our men. His right crossed this parapet, which he swept back, taking it in flank; and, at the same time, the division which had been driven back along the railroad was rallied by General Logan in person, and fought for their former ground. These combined forces drove the enemy into Atlanta, recovering the twenty-pound Parrott guns. . . .

The battle of July 22nd is usually called the battle of Atlanta. It extended from the Howard House to General Giles A. Smith's position, about a mile beyond the Augusta Railroad, and then back toward Decatur, the whole extent of ground being fully seven miles. . . . The enemy had retired during the night inside of Atlanta, and we remained masters of the situation outside. . . .

But, about this time, I was advised by General Grant (then investing Richmond) that the rebel government had become aroused to the critical condition of things about Atlanta, and that I must look out for Hood being greatly reinforced. I therefore was resolved to push matters, and at once set about the original purpose of transferring the whole of the Army of the Tennessee to our right flank, leaving Schofield to stretch out so as to rest his left on the Augusta road, then torn up for thirty miles eastward; and, as auxiliary thereto, I ordered all the cavalry to be ready to pass around Atlanta on both flanks, to break up the Macon road at some point below, so as to cut off all supplies to the rebel army inside, and thus force it to evacuate, or come out and fight us on equal terms.

But first it became necessary to settle the important question of who should succeed General McPherson? . . . It was all-important that there should exist a perfect understanding among the army commanders, and at a conference with General George H. Thomas . . . we discussed fully the merits and qualities of every officer of high rank in the army, and finally settled on Major-General O.O. Howard as the best officer who was present. . . .

As soon as it was known that General Howard had been chosen to command the Army of the Tennessee, General Hooker applied to General Thomas to be relieved of the command of the 20th Corps, and General Thomas forwarded his application to me approved and *heartily* recommended. . . . [Henry Slocum replaced him.]

My plan of action was to move the Army of the Tennessee to the right rapidly and boldly against the railroad below Atlanta, and at the same time to send all the cavalry around by the right and left to make a lodgment on the Macon road about Jonesboro.

All the orders were given, and the morning of the twenty-seventh was fixed for commencing the movement. On the twenty-sixth I received from [cavalry commander] General Stoneman a note asking permission (after having accomplished his orders to break up the railroad at Jonesboro) to go on to Macon to rescue our prisoners of war known to be held there, and then to push on to Andersonville, where was the great depot of Union prisoners, in which were penned at one time as many as twenty-three thousand of our men, badly fed and harshly treated. I wrote him an answer consenting substantially to his proposition. . . .

Personally on the morning of the twenty-eighth I followed the movement, and rode to the extreme right, where we could hear some skirmishing and an occasional cannon shot. As we approached the ground held by the 15th Corps, a cannonball passed over my shoulder and killed the horse of an orderly behind; and seeing that this gun enfiladed the road by which we were riding, we turned out of it and rode down into a valley, where we left our horses and walked up to the hill held by Morgan L. Smith's division of the Fifteenth Corps. Near the house I met Generals Howard and Logan, who explained that there was an entrenched battery to their front, with the appearance of strong infantry support. I then walked up to the ridge, and found General Morgan L. Smith. His men were deployed and engaged in rolling logs and fence rails, preparing a hasty cover. From this ridge we could overlook the open fields near a meeting house known as Ezra Church, close by the Poor House. We could see the fresh earth of a parapet covering some guns (that fired an occasional shot), and there was also an appearance of activity beyond. . . .

As the skirmish fire warmed up along the front of Blair's corps, as well as along the 15th Corps (Logan's), I became convinced that Hood designed to attack this right flank, to prevent, if possible, the extension of our line in that direction. I regained my horse, and rode rapidly back to see that Davis's division had been dispatched as ordered [to take a wide march to the right and then loop back]. I found General Davis in person, who was unwell, and had sent his division that morning early, under the command of his senior brigadier, Morgan; but, as I attached great importance to the movement, he mounted his horse, and rode away to overtake and hurry forward the movement, so as to come up on the left rear of the enemy, during the expected battle.

By this time the sound of cannon and musketry denoted a severe battle in progress, which began seriously about 11:30 A.M., and ended substantially by four P.M. It was a fierce attack by the enemy on our extreme right flank, well posted and partially covered. . . .

At no time did I feel the least uneasiness about the result on the twenty-eighth, but wanted to reap fuller results, hoping that Davis's division would come up at the instant of defeat, and catch the enemy in flank; but the woods were dense, the roads obscure, and as usual this division got on the wrong road, and did not come into position until about dark. . . .

Our men were unusually encouraged by this day's work, for they realized that we could compel Hood to come out from behind his fortified lines and attack us at a disadvantage. In conversation with me, the soldiers of the 15th Corps, with whom I was on the most familiar terms, spoke of the affair of the twenty-eighth as the easiest thing in the world; that, in fact, it was a common slaughter of the enemy. . . .

The next morning the 15th Corps wheeled forward to the left over the battlefield of the day before, and Davis's division still farther prolonged the line, which reached nearly to the ever-to-be-remembered "Sandtown road."

Then, by further thinning out Thomas's line, which was well entrenched, I drew another division of Palmer's corps (Baird's) around to the right, to further strengthen that flank. I was impatient to hear from the cavalry raid, then four days out, and was watching for its effect, ready to make a bold push for the possession of East Point. . . .

CAPTURE OF ATLANTA

The month of August opened hot and sultry, but our position before Atlanta was healthy, with ample supply of wood, water, and provisions. The troops had become habituated to the slow and steady progress of the siege; the skirmish lines were held close up to the enemy, were covered by rifle trenches or logs, and kept up a continuous clatter of musketry. . . . The field batteries were in select positions, covered by handsome parapets, and occasional shots from them gave life and animation to the scene. The men loitered about the trenches carelessly, or busied themselves in constructing ingenious huts out of the abundant timber, and seemed as snug, comfortable, and happy, as though they were at home. General Schofield was still on the extreme left, Thomas in the center, and Howard on the right. . . .

I thus awaited the effect of the cavalry movement against the railroad about Jonesboro, and had heard from General Garrard that Stoneman had gone on to Macon. . . .[14]

During the second and third days of August . . . General McCook came in and reported the results of his cavalry expedition. . . . Finding his progress eastward, toward McDonough, barred by a superior force, he turned back to Newman, where he found himself completely surrounded by infantry and cavalry. He had to drop his prisoners and fight his way out, losing about six hundred men in killed and captured. . . . Meanwhile, rumors came that General Stoneman was down about Macon . . .

Stoneman had not obeyed his orders to attack the railroad *first* before going to Macon and Andersonville, but had crossed the Ocmulgee River high up near Covington, and had gone down that river on the east bank. . . . Stoneman shelled [Macon] across the river, but could not cross over by the bridge, and returned to Clinton, where he found his retreat obstructed, as he supposed, by a superior force. There he became bewildered, and sacrificed himself for the safety of his command. He occupied the attention of the enemy by a small force of seven hundred men, giving Colonels Adams and Capron leave, with their brigades, to cut their way back to me at Atlanta. The former reached us entire, but the latter was struck and scattered at some place farther north, and came in by detachments. Stoneman surrendered, and remained a prisoner until he was exchanged some time after, late in September, at Rough and Ready.

I now became satisfied that cavalry could not, or would not, make a sufficient lodgment on the railroad below Atlanta, and that nothing would suffice but for us to reach it with the main army. Therefore the most urgent efforts to that end were made, and Schofield, on the right, was committed the charge of this special object. He had his own corps (the 23rd) . . . with McCook's broken division of cavalry. . . . For this purpose I also placed the

[14] Macon is in central Georgia, not quite due south from Atlanta; Jonesboro sat on the key railroad running south from Atlanta to Macon. Andersonville was southwest of Macon, and Covington was southeast of Atlanta.

14th Corps (Palmer) under his orders. . . . I always expected to have a desperate battle to get possession of the Macon road,[15] which was the vital objective of my campaign. Its possession by us would, in my judgment, result in the capture of Atlanta, and give us the fruits of victory, although the destruction of Hood's army was the real object to be desired. Yet Atlanta was known as the "Gate City of the South," was full of foundries, arsenals, and machine shops, and I knew that its capture would be the death knell of the Confederacy.

On the fourth of August I ordered General Schofield to make a bold attack on the railroad, anywhere about East Point, and ordered General Palmer to report to him for duty. He [Palmer] at once denied General Schofield's right to command him. . . . He came on the sixth to my head-quarters, and insisted on his resignation being accepted, for which formal act I referred him to General Thomas. . . . General Thomas recommended that the resignation be accepted; that Johnson, the senior division commander of the corps, should be ordered back to Nashville as chief of cavalry, and that Brigadier-General Jefferson C. Davis, the next in order, should be promoted to major-general, and assigned to command of the corps. . . .

We could see . . . that the rebels were extending their lines, parallel with the railroad, about as fast as we could add to our lines of investment. On the tenth of August the Parrott thirty-pounders were received and placed in position; for a couple of days we kept up a sharp fire from all our batteries converging on Atlanta, and at every available point we advanced our infantry lines, thereby shortening and strengthening the investment; but I was not willing to order a direct assault, unless some accident or positive neglect on the part of our antagonist should reveal an opening. . . .

On the twelfth of August I heard of the success of Admiral Farragut in entering Mobile Bay, which was regarded as a most valuable auxiliary to our operations at Atlanta; and learned that I had been commissioned a major-general in the regular army, which was unexpected, and not desired until successful in the capture of Atlanta. These did not change the fact that we were held in check by the stubborn defense of the place, and a conviction was forced in my mind that our enemy would hold fast, even though every house in the town should be battered down by our artillery. It was evident that we must decoy him out to fight us on something like equal terms, or else, with the whole army, raise the siege and attack his communications. Accordingly, on the thirteenth of August, I gave general orders for

[15] This railroad ran south, through Rough and Ready.

the 20th Corps to draw back to the railroad bridge at the Chattahoochee, to protect our trains, hospitals, spare artillery, and the railroad depot, while the rest of the army should move bodily to some point on the Macon Railroad below East Point.

Luckily, I learned just then that the enemy's cavalry, under General Wheeler, had made a wide circuit around our left flank, and had actually reached our railroad at Tilton Station, above Resaca. . . . I became fully convinced that Hood had sent *all* of his cavalry to raid upon our railroads. . . . I at once ordered strong reconnaissances forward from our flanks on the left by Garrard and on the right by Kilpatrick. The former moved with so much caution that I was displeased; but Kilpatrick, on the contrary, displayed so much zeal and activity that I was attracted to him at once. . . . I summoned him to me, and was so pleased with his spirit and confidence, that I concluded to suspend the general movement of the main army, and to send him with his small division of cavalry to break up the Macon road about Jonesboro, in hopes that it would force Hood to evacuate Atlanta, and that I should thereby not only secure possession of the city itself, but probably catch Hood in the confusion of retreat. . . . Kilpatrick got off during the night of the eighteenth, and returned on the twenty-second, having made the complete circuit of Atlanta. He reported that he had destroyed three miles of the railroad about Jonesboro, which he reckoned would take ten days to repair. . . . On the twenty-third, however, we saw trains coming into Atlanta from the south, when I became more than ever convinced that cavalry could not or would not work hard enough to disable a railroad properly, and therefore resolved at once to proceed to the execution of my original plan. . . .

The real movement commenced on the twenty-fifth, at night. The 20th Corps drew back and took post at the railroad bridge, and the 4th Corps (Stanley) moved to his right rear, closing up with the 14th Corps (Jeff. C. Davis) near Utoy Creek; at the same time Garrard's cavalry, leaving their horses out of sight, occupied the vacant trenches, so that the enemy did not detect the change at all. The next night (twenty-sixth) the 15th and 17th Corps, composing the Army of the Tennessee (Howard), drew out of their trenches, made a wide circuit, and came up on the extreme right of the 4th and 14th Corps of the Army of the Cumberland (Thomas) along Utoy Creek, facing south. The enemy seemed to suspect something that night, using his artillery pretty freely . . . and the next morning some of his infantry came out of Atlanta and found our camps abandoned. It was afterward related that there was great rejoicing in Atlanta "that the Yankees were gone"; the fact was telegraphed all over the South, and several trains of cars (with ladies) came up from Macon to assist in the celebration of their grand victory.

On the twenty-eighth (making a general left-wheel, pivoting on Schofield) both Thomas and Howard reached the West Point Railroad, extending from East Point to Red Oak Station and Fairburn, where we spent the next day (twenty-ninth) in breaking it up thoroughly. The track was heaved up in sections the length of a regiment, then separated rail by rail; bonfires were made of the ties and of fence rails on which the rails were heated, carried to trees or telegraph poles, wrapped around and left to cool. Such rails could not be used again; and, to be still more certain, we filled up many deep cuts with trees, brush, and earth, and commingled with them loaded shells, so arranged that they would explode on an attempt to haul out the bushes. . . .

Meantime Schofield, with the 23rd Corps, presented a bold front toward East Point, daring and inviting the enemy to sally out and attack him in position. His first movement was on the thirtieth, to Mount Gilead Church, then to Morrow's Mills, facing Rough and Ready. Thomas was on his right, within easy support, moving by cross roads from Red Oak to the Fayetteville road, extending from Couch's to Renfrew's; and Howard was aiming for Jonesboro. . . .

The next morning (August 31st) all moved straight for the railroad. Schofield reached it near Rough and Ready, and Thomas at two points between there and Jonesboro. Howard found an entrenched foe (Hardee's corps) covering Jonesboro, and his men began at once to dig their accustomed rifle pits. Orders were sent to Generals Thomas and Schofield to turn straight for Jonesboro, tearing up the railroad track as they advanced. About 3 P.M. the enemy sallied from Jonesboro against the 15th Corps, but was easily repulsed, and driven back within his lines. All hands were kept busy tearing up the railroad, and it was not until toward evening of the first day of September that the 14th Corps (Davis) closed down on the north front of Jonesboro, connecting his right with Howard, and his left reaching the railroad, along which General Stanley was moving, followed by Schofield. General Davis formed his divisions in line about 4 P.M., swept forward over some old cotton fields in full view, and went over the rebel parapet handsomely, capturing the whole of Govan's brigade, with two field batteries of ten guns. Being on the spot, I checked Davis's movement, and ordered General Howard to send the two divisions of the 17th Corps (Blair) round by his right rear, to get below Jonesboro, and to reach the railroad, so as to cut off retreat in that direction. I also dispatched orders to hurry forward Stanley, so as to lap around Jonesboro on the east, hoping thus to capture the whole of Hardee's corps. I sent first Captain Audenreid (aide-de-camp), then Colonel Poe, of the Engineers, and lastly General Thomas himself (and that is the only time during the campaign I can recall seeing General Thomas urge his horse into a gallop). Night was approaching, and the country on the farther side of the railroad was densely wooded. General Stanley had come up on the left of Davis, and was deploying, though there could not have been on his front more than a skirmish line. Had he moved straight on by the flank, or by a slight circuit to his left, he would have enclosed the whole ground occupied by Hardee's corps, and that corps could not have escaped us; but night came on, and Hardee did escape. . . .[16]

The next morning General Hardee was gone, and we all pushed forward along the railroad south, in close pursuit, till we ran up against his lines at a point just below Lovejoy's Station. While bringing forward troops and feeling the new position of our adversary, rumors came from the rear that the enemy had evacuated Atlanta, and that General Slocum was in the city. Later in the day I received a note in Slocum's own handwriting, stating that he had . . . moved rapidly up from the bridge about daylight, and had entered Atlanta unopposed. His letter was dated inside the city, so there was not a doubt of the fact. General Thomas's bivouac was but a short distance from mine, and, before giving notice to the army in general orders, I sent one of my staff officers to show him the note. In a few minutes the officer returned, soon followed by Thomas himself, who again examined the note, so as to be perfectly certain that it was genuine. The news seemed to him too good to be true. He snapped his fingers, whistled, and almost danced, and, as the news spread to the army, the shouts that arose from our men, the wild hallooing and glorious laughter, were to us a full recompense for the labor and toils and hardships through which we had passed in the previous three months. . . .

The victory was most opportune; Mr. Lincoln himself told me afterward that even he had previously felt in doubt, for the summer was fast passing away; that General Grant seemed checkmated about Richmond and Petersburg, and my army seemed to have run up against an impassable barrier, when, suddenly and unexpectedly, came the news that "Atlanta was ours, and fairly won." . . . A presidential election then agitated the North. Mr. Lincoln represented the national cause, and General

---

[16] Hood, underestimating the force on the railroad south of Atlanta, had detached Hardee to protect it. Sherman almost succeeded in cutting Hardee off from the main army.

McClellan had accepted the nomination of the Democratic party, whose platform was that the war was a failure, and that it was better to allow the South to go free to establish a separate government, whose cornerstone would be slavery. Success to our arms at that instant was therefore a political necessity; and it was all-important that something startling in our interest should occur before the election in November. The brilliant success at Atlanta filled that requirement, and made the election of Mr. Lincoln certain.

The capture of Atlanta was the crowning glory of the long trail of maneuver and battle that began at Dalton in May. Grant, Lincoln, and most contemporaries and historians have judged Sherman's campaign to be one of the most brilliant of the war. Recently, however, historian Albert Castel has sharply criticized Sherman's performance in almost personally hostile terms, focusing in particular on Sherman's failure to utterly wipe out the Confederate army. And yet, the results speak for themselves. First, in the wooded mountains of northwest Georgia, Sherman repeatedly pinned Johnston with one part of his army, while outflanking him with the rest—and maintaining his own tenuous supply line the entire time. Upon reaching Atlanta, Sherman worked closely with his able subordinates to throw back every attack Hood made, with heavy Confederate losses. But his greatest stroke came from his realization that he could not completely encircle the city to besiege it, as Grant (aided by the Mississippi) had done at Vicksburg. Instead, in a tremendously daring move, Sherman took *almost his entire army* on a grand wheeling raid around Atlanta, laying waste to every possible rail link with the outside. Caught by surprise, Hood almost lost Hardee's corps before realizing that he had no choice—he had to withdraw from the city or face suffocation.

The Confederate Army of Tennessee might not have been destroyed, but it was now a shattered hulk, barely half its original size. The stage was set for Sherman's famous march to the sea, a campaign that would slice into the heart of the South.

VII

"DAMN THE TORPEDOES"

THE FINAL NAVAL BATTLES

16

THE CONFEDERATE CRUISERS

Ever since the battle between the *Monitor* and the *Merrimack*, the naval
war had seen a string of Union victories. In the West, Federal gunboat
fleets had seized command of the rivers as the armies captured such
strongpoints as Forts Henry and Donelson, Island No. 10, and Vicksburg.
By the summer of 1864, the main naval contest had shifted to the oceans
and coastlines, as the Confederates concentrated on slipping critical supply
ships through the Union blockade. From the date of Farragut's capture of
New Orleans, however, Yankee fleets and special army detachments had
captured one Southern port after another.

But it was on the open sea that the Confederates won a measure of naval
revenge. Unable to match the Union battle fleet, the South turned to
commerce raiding—a mission carried out brilliantly by a few remarkable
commanders in specially designed ships. A handful of these guerrilla
cruisers roamed the world's oceans, capturing and burning scores of Yankee commercial ships, permanently damaging the U.S. merchant and
whaling fleets.

The rebel most responsible for these successes was James D. Bulloch, an
ingenious, diplomatic man with eighteen years of experience in the U.S.
Navy. Under orders from Confederate Secretary of the Navy Stephen
Mallory, Bulloch went to England in mid-1861 and immediately set about
procuring ships from the yards of Liverpool for his fledgling fleet. He took
advantage of the tolerance of sympathetic British officials to subvert English neutrality laws, launching the *Florida* in 1862 before U.S. diplomats
could stop him; the ship went on to sink thirty-eight U.S. merchants
before being captured in Brazilian waters in late 1864.

It was the C.S.S. *Alabama*, however, that captured the imagination
of the world—and the consternation of Lincoln's administration. The
ship almost failed to get out of port; after the *Florida* sailed from the
Laird shipyards, the United States embassy had raised a furor in London.

Bulloch, however, rushed ahead the completion of the *Alabama*, and resorted to a trick to sneak it out of port. She was then taken over by Captain Raphael Semmes—like Franklin Buchanan of the *Merrimack*, a Marylander and an esteemed veteran of the U.S. Navy—who had already won fame as the skipper of a smaller commerce raider, the C.S.S. *Sumter*. Semmes's executive officer (the second in command) was John McIntosh Kell, another veteran of U.S. Navy service. The *Alabama* embarked on an epic voyage, which came to an end off the coast of France in the summer of 1864, where Semmes fought a climactic duel against the U.S.S. *Kearsarge*, under the command of John Winslow. The two commanders had once shared a cabin during the Mexican War; now they were determined rivals, each refusing to back down from the battle that loomed off the port of Cherbourg.

The Cruise of the C.S.S. *Alabama*
By John McIntosh Kell

The *Alabama* was built by the Lairds, of Birkenhead, England, for the Confederate States Government. . . . Captain James D. Bulloch, as agent for the Confederacy, superintended her construction. As a ruse, she was sent on a trial trip with a large party of ladies and gentlemen. A tug met the ship in the channel, and took off the guests, while the two hundred and ninetieth ship built in the Laird yard proceeded on her voyage to the island of Terceira, among the Azores, whither a transport had preceded her with war material. Captain Raphael Semmes, with his officers, carried by the *Bahama*, met her there. Under the lee of the island, outside the marine league, we lashed our ships together, and made the transfer of armament and stores.

Arriving on Wednesday, August 20th, 1862, by Saturday night we had completed the transfer, and on Sunday morning, under a cloudless sky, upon the broad Atlantic, a common heritage, we put in commission the *Alabama*, by the authority of the Confederate States Government. . . . We commenced our cruise of twenty-two months, which was the most successful accomplishment of the work for which she was constructed of any single ship of any nation in any age.

The *Alabama* was built for speed rather than battle. Her lines were symmetrical and fine; her material of the best. In fifteen minutes her propeller could be hoisted, and she could go through every evolution

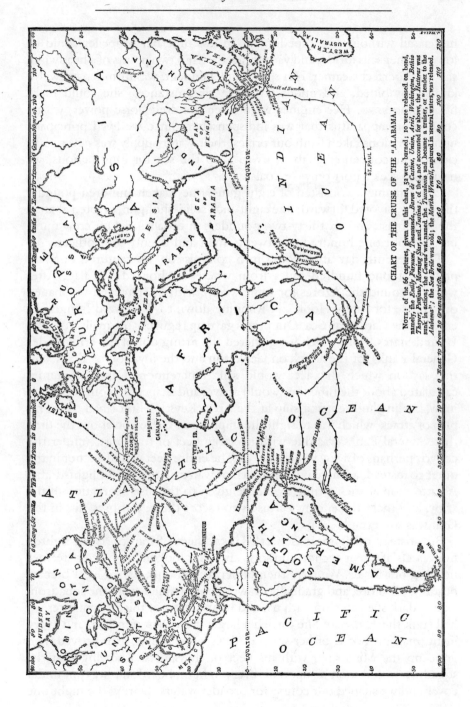

CHART OF THE CRUISE OF THE "ALABAMA."

NOTE: of the 66 captures, given on this chart, 52 were burned; 10 were released on bond, namely, the *Emily Farnum*, *Tonawanda*, *Baron de Castine*, *Union*, *Ariel*, *Washington*, *Bethia Thayer*, *Punjaub*, *Morning Star*, and *Justina*; 3 of the 4 not accounted for above, the *Hatteras* was sunk in action; the *Conrad* was named the *Tuscaloosa* and became a cruiser, or "tender to the *Alabama*"; the *Sea Bride* was sold; the *Martha Wenzell* captured in neutral waters, was released.

under sail without any impediment. In less time her propeller could be lowered; her sails furled, and yards braced within two points of a headwind, she was a perfect steamer. Her speed, independent, was from ten to twelve knots; combined, and under favorable circumstances, she could make fifteen knots. . . . Her engines were three hundred horse-power, with a condensing apparatus that was indispensable. Since we lived principally upon provisions taken from our prizes, their water-supply was never sufficient. Our condenser enabled us to keep the sea for long periods, we having to seek a port only for coals.

Our armament consisted of eight guns, one Blakely hundred-pounder rifled gun, pivoted forward; one eight-inch solid-shot gun, pivoted abaft in the mainmast; and six thirty-two pounders in broadside. Our crew numbered about one hundred and twenty men and twenty-four officers. . . .

The eleventh day after going into commission we captured our first prize, not one hundred miles from where we hoisted our flag. After working round the Azores for some weeks, with fine breezes, we shaped our course for Sandy Hook. . . . Running down to Windward Islands, we entered the Caribbean Sea. Our prizes gave up regularly the mails from the United States, from which we gathered the fitting out of the army under General Banks for the attack on Galveston and the invasion of Texas, and the day on which the fleet would sail. Whereupon, Captain Semmes calculated about the time they would arrive, and shaped his course accordingly, coaling and refitting ship at the Arcas Keys. He informed me of his plan of attack, which was to sight the shipping of Galveston about the time that General Banks was due with his large fleet of transports, under the convoy perhaps of a few vessels of war. The entire fleet would anchor in the outer roadstead, as there is only sufficient water on the bar for light-drafts. All attention at such a time would be given to the disembarkation of the army, and there the enemy's cruisers to escort them; our presence in the Gulf was not even known. . . .

But instead of sighting General Banks's fleet of transports we sighted five vessels of war at anchor, and soon after, our lookout reported a steamer heading out for us. We were then under topsail only, with a light breeze, heading off shore, and gradually drawing our pursuers from the squadron. About dark she came up with us, and in an action of thirteen minutes we had sunk the *Hatteras!* She carried a larger crew than our own, and every living man on board of her was saved. General Banks, as it proved, had gone up the Mississippi with his fleet of transports. Knowing that the squadron would soon be upon us, every light on board ship was put under cover and we shaped our course for broader waters. During the night one of those fearful northers came sweeping after us, and under the circumstances was a welcome gale. Hoisting our propeller, we crowded all the sail she could bear, and soon were out of harm's way. As Captain Blake of the *Hatteras* (whom I had known in the old service) came on deck, he remarked upon the speed we were making, and gracefully saluted me with, "Fortune favors the brave, sir!"

We patrolled then at Kingston, Jamaica, and after repairing a few shot-holes and coaling ship, we passed on to our work in the South Atlantic, taking our position at the crossroads of the homeward-bound East India and Pacific trade. . . . After a few weeks of good work in that locality and along the coast of Brazil, we crossed over to the Cape of Good Hope, where we played "hide and seek" with the United States steamer *Vanderbilt*. . . .

Our long stretch across the Indian Ocean placed us in the China Sea, where we were least expected, and where we soon fell in with the China trade. In a few weeks we had so paralyzed the enemy's commerce that their ships were absolutely locked up in port, and neutrals doing all the carrying trade. Having thus virtually cleared the sea of the United States flag, we ran down to Singapore, coaled ship, and then turned westward through the straits of Malacca, across to India, thence to the east coast of Africa. Passing through the Mozambique channel, we again touched in at the Cape of Good Hope, and thence crossed to the coast of Brazil.

Among the many prizes we captured and destroyed, we necessarily saw many varieties of the *genus homo* in the guise of the Yankee skipper. While taking the burning of their ships very philosophically as among the fortunes of war, some clung to "creature comforts" regardless of heavier losses. Upon one occasion, going aboard a fine ship, I told the captain "he might bring away his personal effects." He made a most ludicrous scene by earnestly appealing to me "to grant him one request," that he "might be permitted to take with him 'Spurgeon's Sermons' and a keg of very fine whisky." The sermons I granted, but told him the whisky must go overboard. . . .

Our little ship was now showing signs of the active work she had been doing. Her boilers were burned out, and her machinery sadly in want of repairs. She was loose at every joint, her seams were open, and the copper on her bottom was in rolls. Captain Semmes decided to seek a port in Europe, and to go into dock. . . .

We now set our course for Europe, and on the 11th day of June, 1864, entered the port of Cherbourg, and at once applied for permission to dock. There being none but national docks, the Emperor had first to be communicated with before permission could be granted, and he was absent from

Paris. It was during this interval of waiting, on the third day after our arrival, that the *Kearsarge* steamed into the harbor, for the purpose, as we learned, of taking on board the prisoners we had landed from our last two prizes. Captain Semmes, however, objected to this. . . . The authorities conceding this objection valid, the *Kearsarge* steamed out of the harbor, without anchoring. During her stay we examined her closely with glasses, but she was keeping on the opposite side of the harbor, out of the reach of a very close scrutiny, which accounts for our not detecting the boxing to her chain armor.[1] After she left the harbor Captain Semmes sent for me to his cabin, and said: "I am going out to fight the *Kearsarge*; what do you think of it?" We discussed the battery and especially the advantage the *Kearsarge* had over us in her eleven-inch guns. She was built for a vessel of war, and we for speed, and though she carried one gun less, her battery was more effective at point-blank range. While the *Alabama* carried one more gun, the *Kearsarge* threw more metal at a broadside; and while our heavy guns were more effective at long range, her eleven-inch guns gave her greatly the advantage at close range. She also had a slight advantage in her crew, she carrying one hundred and sixty-two all told, while we carried one hundred and forty-nine. Considering well these advantages, we nevertheless decided to engage her as soon as we could coal ship.

Captain Semmes communicated through our agent to the U.S. consul that if Captain Winslow would wait outside the harbor he would fight him as soon as we could coal ship. I at once proceeded to get everything snug for action, and by Saturday night we had finished taking in coals, and had scrubbed the decks. I reported to Captain Semmes that the ship was ready for battle.

The next morning, Sunday, June 19th, between the hours of nine and ten o'clock, we weighed anchor, and stood out of the western entrance of the harbor, the French ironclad frigate *Courenne* following us. The day was bright and beautiful, with a light breeze blowing. Our men were neatly dressed, and our officers in full uniform. The report of our going out to fight the *Kearsarge* had been circulated, and many persons from Paris and the surrounding country had come down to witness this engagement. . . . As we rounded the breakwater we discovered the *Kearsarge* about seven miles to the northward and eastward. We immediately shaped our course for her, called all hands to quarters, and cast loose the starboard battery.

---

[1] Captain Winslow of the *Kearsarge* had arranged a number of heavy iron chains across the sides of his ship for extra protection; they were concealed by a wooden sheath.

Upon reporting to the captain that the ship was ready for action, he directed me to send all hands aft, and mounting a gun-carriage, he made the following address:

OFFICERS AND SEAMEN OF THE *ALABAMA*: You have at length another opportunity of meeting the enemy—the first that has been presented to you since you sank the *Hatteras*. In the meantime you have been all over the world, and it is not too much to say that you have destroyed, and driven for protection under neutral flags, one half of the enemy's commerce, which at the beginning covered every sea. This is an achievement of which you may well be proud, and a grateful country will not be unmindful of it. The name of your ship has become a household word wherever civilization extends! Shall that name be tarnished by defeat? The thing is impossible! Remember that you are in the English Channel, the theater of so much of the naval glory of our race, and that the eyes of all Europe are at this moment upon you. The flag that floats over you is that of a young Republic, which bids defiance to her enemy's whenever and wherever found! Show the world that you know how to uphold it! Go to your quarters.

In about forty-five minutes we were somewhere over a mile from the *Kearsarge*, when she headed for us, presenting her starboard bow. At a distance of a mile, we commenced the action with our one-hundred pounder pivot-gun from our starboard bow. Both ships were now approaching each other at high speed, and soon the action became general with broadside batteries at a distance of about five hundred yards. To prevent passing, each ship used a strong port helm. Thus the action was fought around a common center, gradually drawing in the circle. At this range we used shell upon the enemy. Captain Semmes, standing on the horse-block abreast the mizzen-mast with his glass in hand, observed the effect of our shell. He called to me and said, "Mr. Kell, use solid shot; our shell strike the enemy's side and fall into the water." We were not at this time aware of the chain armor of the enemy and attributed the failure of our shell to our defective ammunition. After using solid shot for some time, we alternated shell and shot.

The enemy's eleven-inch shells were now doing severe execution upon our quarter-deck section. Three of them successively entered our eight-inch pivot-gun port: the first swept off the forward part of the gun's crew; the second killed one man and wounded several others; the third struck the base of the gun-carriage, and spun around on the deck, till one of the men picked it up and threw it overboard. Our decks were now covered with the dead and wounded, and the ship was careening heavily to starboard from the effects of the shot-holes to her waterline.

Captain Semmes ordered me to be ready to make all sail possible when the circuit of fight should put our head to the coast of France: then he would notify me at the same time to pivot to port and continue the action with the port battery, hoping thus to right the ship and enable us to reach the coast of France. The evolution was performed beautifully, righting the helm, hoisting the head-sails, hauling aft the fore try-sail sheet, and pivoting to port, the action continuing almost without cessation.

This evolution exposed us to a raking fire arc, but, strange to say, the *Kearsarge* did not take advantage of it. The port side of the quarterdeck was so encumbered with the mangled trunks of the dead that I had to have them thrown overboard, in order to fight the after pivot-gun. I abandoned the after thirty-two pounder, and transferred the men to fill up the vacancies to the pivot-gun under the charge of young Midshipman Anderson, who in the midst of the carnage filled his place like a veteran. At this moment the chief engineer came on deck and reported the fires put out, and that he could no longer work the engines. Captain Semmes said to me, "Go below, sir, and see how long the ship can float." As I entered the ward-room the sight was indeed appalling. There stood Assistant Surgeon Llewellyn at his post, but the table and the patient upon it were swept away from him by an eleven-inch shell, which opened in the side of the ship an aperture that was fast filling the ship with water.

It took me but a moment to return to the deck and report to the captain that "we could not float ten minutes." He replied to me, "Then, sir, cease firing, shorten sail, and haul down the colors; it will never do in this nineteenth century for us to go down, and the decks covered with our gallant wounded." The order was promptly executed.

17

THE BATTLE OF MOBILE BAY

August 5, 1864

The *Alabama*, despite her horrific suffering, had one more brief trial to endure: after her signal of surrender, a pair of defiant junior officers ran to a gun and fired at the Union ship, which then hit the *Alabama* with yet another broadside. Finally, with the surrender made clear, the *Alabama*'s crew took to the lifeboats and escaped the rapidly sinking ship. The *Kearsarge* set about gathering up her prisoners from the ocean—minus Captain Semmes and his executive officer, who were carried to safety at Southampton by an English yacht, the *Deerhound*.

The *Alabama* had destroyed an estimated sixty-four merchantmen and one U.S. Navy warship, but her destruction deepened the gloom in the South, struggling under the blows of Grant and Sherman that difficult summer of 1864. This loss was soon followed by an even greater Union victory—one that carried far greater strategic significance and gave rise to one of the richest legends in naval history: the Battle of Mobile Bay.

Mobile, Alabama, had troubled Grant for some time. It was an extremely well protected port, with two strong forts at the mouth of a vast bay, making it a key source of supplies smuggled in by blockade runners. After taking supreme command, Grant had ordered General Nathaniel Banks to march from New Orleans to capture the place. Banks, however, got bogged down in a campaign on the Red River, where, characteristically, he was defeated. Instead, it fell to the navy (and a small army detachment) to close Mobile down—specifically, it fell to David G. Farragut.

Farragut faced a formidable task at Mobile. First, he had to cope with a sandbar barrier across the mouth of the bay. Then, he had to battle the guns of Forts Morgan and Gaines. In addition, the Confederates had strung a line of mines—called "torpedoes" at the time (self-propelled torpedoes were yet to be invented)—across the bay, marking their location with a line of buoys. Finally, Farragut had to fight a squadron of Confederate gunboats, led by the powerful *Tennessee*, under the command of none other than Admiral Franklin Buchanan, the former commander of the ironclad C.S.S. *Virginia*, better known as the *Merrimack*.

Buchanan was determined to fight to the end; his flagship, after all, was the finest ironclad ever built by the South, far superior to the converted *Merrimack*—and most of the Union ships were made of wood, making the Yankee superiority in numbers count for far less. But Farragut carefully laid his plans: first he floated his fleet over the bar, then lashed the wooden vessels together in pairs for mutual protection during the great battle. That battle, described here in Farragut's own report, was won by the Union after he led his fleet through the mines, shouting from his place atop a mast on his flagship, "Damn the torpedoes! Full speed ahead!"

Detailed Report on the Battle of Mobile Bay
By Admiral David Glasgow Farragut

The result of the fight was a glorious victory, and I have reason to feel proud of the officers, seamen, and marines of the squadron under my command, for it has never fallen to the lot of an officer to be thus situated and sustained. Regular discipline will bring men to any amount of endurance, but there is a natural fear of hidden dangers, particularly when so awfully destructive of human life as the torpedo, which requires more than discipline to overcome.

Preliminary to a report of the action of the 5th, I desire to call attention . . . to the previous steps taken in consultation with Generals Canby and Granger. On the 8th of July I had an interview with these officers on board the *Hartford*, on the subject of an attack upon Forts Morgan and Gaines, at which it was agreed that General Canby would send all the troops he could spare to cooperate with the fleet. Circumstances soon obliged General Canby to inform me that he could not dispatch a sufficient number to invest both forts; and, in reply, I suggested that Gaines[2] should be first invested, engaging to have a force in the Sound ready to protect the landing of an army on Dauphin Island, in the rear of that fort, and I assigned Lieutenant-Commander De Krafft, of the *Conemaugh*, to that duty.

---

[2] Fort Gaines was located on Dauphin Island, which dominated the mouth of the bay. Fort Morgan was located across a channel, on the spit of land enclosing Mobile Bay.

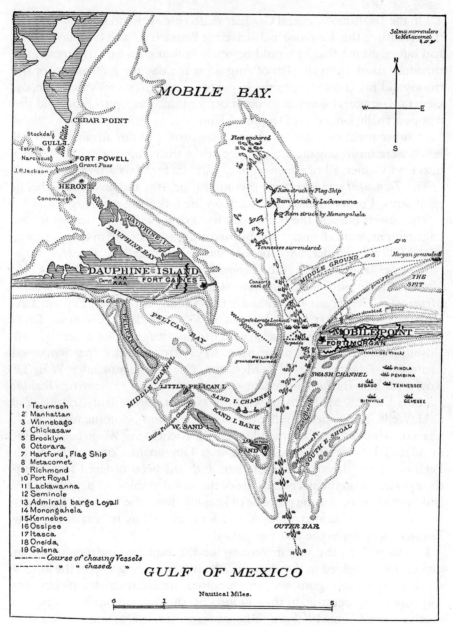

MOBILE BAY.

Selma surrenders
to Metacomet

CEDAR POINT

Stockdal
GULL I.
Estrella
Narcissus
J.P.Jackson

FORT POWELL
Grant Pass

HERON I.
Conomaugh

Fleet anchored

Ram struck by Flag Ship
Ram struck by Lackawanna
Ram struck by Monongahela

Tennessee surrendered

DAUPHINE I.

DAUPHINE BAY

Morgan grounded

MIDDLE GROUND

THE
SPIT

DAUPHINE ISLAND
Camp
FORT GAINES

Consorts
cast off

Pelican Channel

PELICAN BAY

PELICAN CHANNEL

Confederate Lookout
Station

Tennessee disabled

MOBILE POINT
FORT MORGAN
IVANHOE (Wreck)

PHILIPPI
grounded & burned

MIDDLE CHANNEL

LITTLE PELICAN I.

SAND I. CHANNEL

SWASH CHANNEL

PINOLA
PEMBINA
SEBAGO   TENNESSEE
BIENVILLE   GENESEE

SAND I. BANK

Little Pelican Channel

W. SAND I.

SAND I.

1 Tecumseh
2 Manhattan
3 Winnebago
4 Chickasaw
5 Brooklyn
6 Octorara
7 Hartford, Flag Ship
8 Metacomet
9 Richmond
10 Port Royal
11 Lackawanna
12 Seminole
13 Admirals barge Loyall
14 Monongahela
15 Kennebec
16 Ossipee
17 Itasca
18 Oneida
19 Galena

SOUTH E. SHOAL

OUTER BAR

————— Course of chasing Vessels
--------- "   " chased "

GULF OF MEXICO

Nautical Miles.

0   1   5

The Battle of Mobile Bay, August 5, 1864

On the 1st instant General Granger visited me again on the *Hartford*. In the meantime the *Tecumseh* had arrived at Pensacola,[3] and Captain Craven had informed me that he would be ready in four days for any service. We therefore fixed upon the 4th of August as the day for the landing of the troops and my entrance into the bay; but . . . the *Tecumseh* was not ready. General Granger, however, to my mortification, was up to time, and the troops actually landed on Dauphin Island.

As subsequent events proved, the delay turned to our advantage, as the rebels were busily engaged during the 4th in throwing troops and supplies into Fort Gaines, all of which were captured a few days afterward.

The *Tecumseh* arrived on the evening of the 4th, and, everything being propitious, I proceeded to the attack on the following morning. . . .

The vessels outside the bar, which were designed to participate in the engagement, were all under way by forty minutes past five in the morning, in the following order, two abreast, and lashed together: *Brooklyn*, Captain James Alden, with the *Octorora*, Lieutenant-Commander C.H. Green, on the port side; *Hartford*, Captain Percival Drayton, with the *Metacomet*, Lieutenant-Commander J. E. Jouett; *Richmond*, Captain T.A. Jenkins, with the *Port Royal*, Lieutenant-Commander B. Gherardi; *Lackawanna*, Captain J.B. Marchand, with the *Seminole*, Commander E. Donaldson; *Monongahela*, Commander J.H. Strong, with the *Kennebec*, Lieutenant-Commander W.P. McCann; *Ossipee*, Commander W.E. Le Roy, with the *Itasca*, Lieutenant-Commander George Brown; *Oneida*, Commander J.R.M. Mullany, with the *Galena*, Lieutenant-Commander C.H. Wells. The ironclads [all monitors]—*Tecumseh*, Commander T.A.M. Craven; *Manhattan*, Commander J.W.A. Nicholson; *Winnebago*, Commander T.H. Stevens; and *Chickasaw*, Lieutenant-Commander G.H. Perkins—were already inside the bar, and had been ordered to take up their positions on the starboard side of the wooden ships, or between them and Fort Morgan, for the purpose of keeping down the fire from the water battery and the parapet guns of the fort, as well as to attack the ram *Tennessee* as soon as the fort was passed.

It was only at the urgent request of the captains and commanding officers that I yielded to the *Brooklyn*'s being the leading ship of the line, as she had four chase-guns and an ingenious arrangement for picking up torpedoes, and because, in their judgment, the flagship ought not be too much exposed. This I believe to be an error; for, apart from the fact that

---

[3] Pensacola, Florida, remained in Union hands during the war, and was a major base for the blockade fleet.

exposure is one of the penalties of rank in the Navy, it will always be the aim of the enemy to destroy the flagship, and, as will appear in the sequel, such attempt was very persistently made, but Providence did not permit it to be successful.

The attacking fleet steamed steadily up the main ship-channel, the *Tecumseh* firing the first shot at forty-seven minutes past six o'clock. At six minutes past seven the fort opened upon us, and was replied to by a gun from the *Brooklyn*, and immediately after the action became general.

It was soon apparent that there was some difficulty ahead. The *Brooklyn*, for some cause which I did not then clearly understand, but which has since been explained by Captain Alden in his report,[4] arrested the advance of the whole fleet, while, at the same time, the guns of the fort were playing with great effect upon that vessel and the *Hartford*. A moment after I saw the *Tecumseh*, struck by a torpedo, disappear almost instantaneously beneath the waves, carrying with her her gallant commander and nearly all her crew. I determined at once, as I had originally intended, to take the lead; and, after ordering the *Metacomet* to send a boat to save, if possible, any of the perishing crew, I dashed ahead with the *Hartford*, and the ships followed on, their officers believing that they were going to a noble death with their commander-in-chief.[5]

I steamed through between the buoys, where the torpedoes were supposed to have been sunk. These buoys had been previously examined by my flag-lieutenant, J. Crittenden Watson, in several nightly reconnaissances. Though he had not been able to discover the sunken torpedoes, yet we had been assured, by refugees, deserters, and others, of their existence; but, believing that, from their having been some time in the water, they were probably innocuous, I determined to take the chance of their explosion.

From the moment I turned northward, to clear the Middle Ground, we were enabled to keep such a broadside fire upon the batteries of Fort Morgan, that their guns did us comparatively little injury.

Just after we passed the fort, which was about ten minutes before eight o'clock, the ram *Tennessee* dashed out at this ship, as had been expected, and in anticipation of which I had ordered the monitors on our starboard side. I took no further notice of her than to return her fire. [The *Tennessee* then temporarily retired from the battle.]

---

[4] It stopped short before the buoys marking the mines.

[5] It was at this moment that Farragut, lashed to the mast on his flagship, shouted "Damn the torpedoes! Full speed ahead!"

The rebel gunboats *Morgan*, *Gaines*, and *Selma* were ahead; and the latter particularly annoyed us with a raking fire, which our guns could not return. At two minutes after eight o'clock I ordered the *Metacomet* to cast off and go in pursuit of the *Selma*. Captain Jouett was after her in a moment, and in an hour's time he had her as a prize. She was commanded by P.V. Murphy, formerly of the United States Navy. He was wounded in the wrist, his executive officer, Lieutenant Comstock, and eight of the crew killed, and seven or eight wounded. Lieutenant-Commander Jouett's conduct during the whole affair commands my warmest commendations. The *Morgan* and *Gaines* succeeded in escaping under the protection of the guns of Fort Morgan, which would have been prevented had the other gunboats been as prompt in their movements as the *Metacomet*; the want of pilots, however, I believe, was the principal difficulty. The *Gaines* was so injured by our fire that she had to be run ashore, where she was subsequently destroyed; but the *Morgan* escaped to Mobile during the night, though she was chased and fired upon by our cruisers. . . .

With the exception of the momentary arrest of the fleet when the *Hartford* passed ahead,[6] to which I have already adverted, the order of battle was preserved, and the ships followed each other in close order past the batteries of Fort Morgan, and in comparative safety too, with the exception of the *Oneida*. Her boilers were penetrated by a shot from the fort, which completely disabled her; but her consort, the *Galena*, firmly fastened to her side, brought her safely through, showing clearly the wisdom of the precaution of carrying the vessels in two abreast. Commander Mullany, who had solicited eagerly to take part in the action, was severely wounded, losing his left arm. . . .

Having passed the forts and dispersed the enemy's gunboats, I had ordered most of the vessels to anchor, when I perceived the ram *Tennessee* standing up to this ship. This was forty-five minutes past eight. I was not long in comprehending Buchanan's intentions to be the destruction of the flagship. The monitors, and such of the wooden vessels as I thought best adapted for the purpose, were immediately ordered to attack the ram, not only with their guns, but bows on at full speed; and began one of the fiercest naval combats on record.[7]

The *Monongahela*, Commander Strong, was the first vessel that struck her, and in doing so carried away her own iron prow, together with the

---

[6] This paragraph has been moved for narrative continuity.

[7] Farragut intended to run a ship up on the low deck of the *Tennessee* and force her down until she sank.

cutwater, without apparently doing her adversary much injury. The *Lack-awanna*, Captain Marchand, was the next vessel to strike her, which she did at full speed; but though her stern was cut and crushed to the plank-ends for the distance of three feet above the water's edge to five feet below, the only perceptible effect on the ram was to give her a heavy list.

The *Hartford* was the third vessel which struck her, but, as the *Tennessee* quickly shifted her helm, the blow was a glancing one, and, as she rasped along our side, we poured our whole port broadside of nine-inch solid shot within ten feet of her casemate.

The monitors worked slowly, but delivered their fire as opportunity offered. The *Chickasaw* succeeded in getting under her stern, and a fifteen-inch shot from the *Manhattan* broke through her iron plating and heavy wooden backing, though the missile itself did not enter the vessel.

Immediately after the collision of the flagship, I directed Captain Drayton to bear down for the ram again. He was doing so at full speed, when, unfortunately, the *Lackawanna* ran into the *Hartford* just forward of the mizzen-mast, cutting her down to within two feet of the water's edge. We soon got clear again, however, and were fast approaching our adversary, when she struck her colors and ran up the white flag.

She was at this time sore beset; the *Chickasaw* was pounding away at her stern, the *Ossipee* was approaching her at full speed, and the *Monongahela*, *Lackawanna*, and this ship [*Hartford*] were bearing down upon her, determined upon her destruction. Her smokestack had been shot away, her steering chains were gone, compelling a resort to her relieving tackles, and several of her port shutters were jammed. Indeed, from the time the *Hartford* struck her until her surrender, she never fired a gun. As the *Ossipee*, Commander Le Roy, was about to strike her, she hoisted the white flag, and that vessel immediately stopped her engine, though not in time to avoid a glancing blow.

During this contest with the rebel gunboats and the ram *Tennessee*, which terminated in her surrender at ten o'clock, we lost many more men than from the fire of the batteries of Fort Morgan.

Admiral Buchanan was wounded in the leg; two or three of his men were killed, and five or six wounded. Commander Johnston, formerly of the United States Navy, was in command of the *Tennessee*, and came on board the flagship to surrender his sword, and that of Admiral Buchanan.

VIII

GRANT GOES EAST

THE LAST CAMPAIGNS

18

FROM THE WILDERNESS TO PETERSBURG
May and June 1864

A vast tangle of campaigns raged across the continent in 1864, from the waters of Mobile Bay to the lush Shenandoah Valley, from the swamps of Louisiana to the streets of Atlanta. Civilians in both the North and the South eagerly scanned the newspapers to make sense of these immense, simultaneous battles, as the hopes of the two sides were caught up in a rising crescendo of bloodshed. And yet, despite the scale and complexity of the fighting, one man towered over the events of 1864—one small, laconic, stoop-shouldered man.

Ulysses S. Grant dominated the campaigns of the last year of the war. It was his overarching vision, his understanding of the need for a truly coordinated effort, that changed the entire nature of Union strategy. Simultaneous pressure, he knew, would lead to a break in the Confederate defensive perimeter—a break that first opened when Sherman captured Atlanta.

Before Sherman started on his campaign, however, Grant had gone east to take charge of the most prominent—and politically sensitive—theater of all. As lieutenant general, he had overall command of the Union forces; but from the beginning it was understood that he would give personal direction to the Army of the Potomac, still under General Meade's command. Meade's role as an intermediate commander between Grant and the prime army soon proved an embarrassment, as Grant later admitted (in fact, Meade made serious mistakes in carrying out his orders), but it seemed the best compromise under the circumstances.

Grant's idea of concurrent attacks against the Confederacy extended to the local theater of northern Virginia. Southern writers and critical historians have created the picture of Grant as a bloody-minded butcher, a commander who had no better plan than to bludgeon the Army of Northern Virginia. He did, in fact, intend to strike heavy blows with his much larger force—but his strategy was much subtler than that. As Grant brought the Army of the Potomac to bear against the main rebel force, he planned for two smaller armies to advance toward vital strategic sites, the Shenandoah Valley and Richmond. Franz Sigel was assigned the job of cutting off Lee's supplies of food, animals, and recruits from the vital Shenandoah, while Benjamin Butler was to lead the Army of the James directly against the rebel capital. Faced with these forces and Grant's vast host, the Confederate high command would be faced with losing these invaluable places, or detaching troops to protect them—depleting the main army at the height of battle.

The outlook was bright, then, as Grant took his army across the Rapidan in early May 1864 (timed to coincide with Sherman's attack in Georgia). Unfortunately, three men ruined his plan: Sigel, Butler, and Robert E. Lee. Grant's subordinates (Sherman excepted) all failed, and the Union commander was left to fight Lee alone. With no strategic distractions, Lee was free to maneuver, and he displayed all his trademark daring and tactical skill in foiling Grant's flanking movements—first by attacking, then by slipping ahead of him and entrenching. Time and again, Grant was forced to either fight or retreat. He chose to fight.

From the Wilderness to Petersburg
By General U.S. Grant

By the twenty-seventh of April spring had so far advanced as to justify me in fixing a day for the great move. On that day Burnside left Annapolis [with a corps] to occupy Meade's position between Bull Run and the Rappahannock. Meade was notified and directed to bring his troops forward to his advance. On the following day Butler was notified of my intended advance on the fourth of May, and he was directed to move the night of the same day and get as far up the James as possible by daylight, and push on from there to accomplish the task given him. He was also notified that reinforcements were being collected in Washington city, which would be forwarded to him should the enemy fall back into the trenches at Richmond. The same day Sherman was directed to get his forces up ready to advance on the fifth. Sigel was in Winchester [in the Shenandoah] and was notified to move in conjunction with the others.

The criticism has been made by writers on the campaign from the Rapidan to the James River that all loss of life could have been obviated by moving the army there on transports. Richmond was fortified and

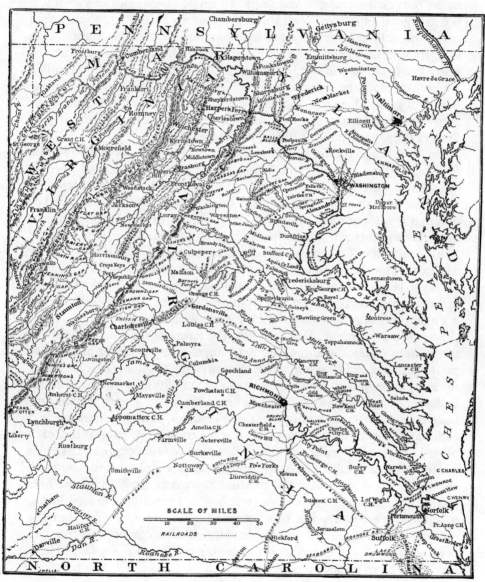

The Eastern Theater

entrenched so perfectly that one man inside to defend was more than equal to five outside besieging or assaulting. To get possession of Lee's army was the first great objective. With the capture of his army Richmond would necessarily follow. It was better to fight him outside of his stronghold than in it. If the Army of the Potomac had moved bodily to the James River by water Lee could have moved a part of his forces back to Richmond, called Beauregard from the south to reinforce it, and with the balance moved on to Washington. Then, too, I ordered a move, simultaneous with that of the Army of the Potomac, up the James River by a formidable army [under Butler] already collected at the mouth of the river. . . .

On [my last] visit to Washington I had my last interview with the President before reaching the James River. He had of course become acquainted with the fact that a general movement had been ordered all along the line, and seemed to think it a new feature in war. I explained to him that it was necessary to have a great number of troops to guard and hold the territory we had captured, and to prevent incursions into the Northern States. These troops could perform this service just as well by advancing as by remaining still; and by advancing they would compel the enemy to keep detachments to hold them back, or else lay his own territory open to invasion. His answer was: "Oh, yes! I see that. As we say out West, if a man can't skin he must hold a leg while someone else does." . . .

Soon after midnight, May 3rd–4th, the Army of the Potomac moved out from its position north of the Rapidan, to start upon that memorable campaign, destined to result in the capture of the Confederate capital and the army defending it. This was not to be accomplished, however, without as desperate fighting as the world has ever witnessed; not to be consummated in a day, a week, a month, or a single season. The losses inflicted, and endured, were destined to be severe; but the armies now confronting each other had already been in deadly conflict for a period of three years, with immense losses in killed, by death from sickness, captured, and wounded; and neither had made any real progress toward accomplishing the final end. . . . The campaign now begun was destined to result in heavier losses, to both armies, in a given time, than any previously suffered; but the carnage was to be limited to a single year, and to accomplish all that had been anticipated or desired at the beginning in that time. We had to have hard fighting to achieve this. . . .

The country over which the army had to operate, from the Rapidan to the crossing of the James River, is rather flat, and is cut by numerous streams which make their way to the Chesapeake Bay. The crossings of these streams by the army were generally made not far above tidewater, and where they formed a considerable obstacle to the rapid advance of troops even when the enemy did not appear in opposition. The country roads were narrow and poor. Most of the country is covered with a dense forest, in places, like the Wilderness and along the Chickahominy, almost impenetrable even for infantry except along the roads. All bridges were naturally destroyed before the National troops came to them.

The Army of the Potomac was composed of three infantry and one cavalry corps, commanded respectively by Generals W.S. Hancock, G.K. Warren, John Sedgwick, and P.H. Sheridan. The artillery was commanded by General Henry J. Hunt. . . .

The 5th Corps, General Warren commanding, was in advance on the right, and marched directly for Germania Ford, preceded by one division of cavalry, under General J.H. Wilson. General Sedgwick followed Warren with the 6th Corps. Germania Ford was nine or ten miles below the right of Lee's line. Hancock, with the 2nd Corps, moved by another road, farther east, directly upon Ely's Ford, six miles below Germania, preceded by Gregg's division of cavalry, and followed by the artillery. Torbert's division of cavalry was left north of the Rapidan, for the time, to picket the river and prevent the enemy from crossing and getting into our rear. The cavalry seized the two crossings before daylight, and drove the enemy's pickets guarding them away, and by six o'clock A.M. had the pontoon laid ready for the crossing of the infantry and artillery. This was undoubtedly a surprise to Lee. The fact that the movement was unopposed proves this.

Burnside, with the 9th Corps, was left back at Warrenton, guarding the railroad from Bull Run forward to preserve control of it in case our crossing the Rapidan should be long delayed. He was instructed, however, to advance at once on receiving notice that the army had crossed; and a dispatch was sent to him a little after one P.M. giving the information that our crossing had been successful.

The country was heavily wooded at all points of crossing, particularly on the south side of the river. The battlefield from the crossing of the Rapidan until the final movement from the Wilderness toward Spotsylvania was of the same character. There were some clearings and small farms within what might be termed the battlefield; but generally the country was covered with a dense forest. The roads were narrow and bad. All the conditions were favorable for defensive operations. . . .

There are two roads, good for that part of Virginia, running from Orange Court House [to the west] to the battlefield. The most southerly of these roads is known as the Orange Court House Plank Road, the northern one as the Orange Turnpike. . . .

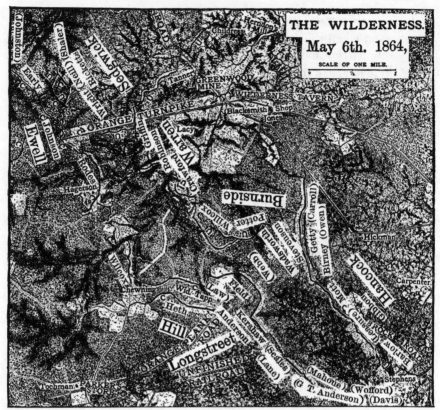

The Battle of the Wilderness, May 5–6, 1864

Lee's headquarters was at Orange Court House. From there to Fredericksburg he had the use of the two roads above described running nearly parallel to the Wilderness. This gave him unusual facilities, for that country, for concentrating his forces to his right. These roads strike the road from Germania Ford in the Wilderness. . . .

On discovering the advance of the Army of the Potomac, Lee ordered Hill, Ewell, and Longstreet, each commanding corps, to move to the right to attack us, Hill on the Orange Plank Road, Longstreet to follow on the same road. Longstreet was at this time—middle of the afternoon—at Gordonsville, twenty or more miles away. Ewell was ordered by the Orange Pike. He was nearby and arrived some four miles east of Mine Run before bivouacking for the night.

My orders were given through General Meade for an early advance on the morning of the fifth. Warren was to move to Parker's store, and

Wilson's cavalry—then at Parker's store—to move on to Craig's meeting house. Sedgwick followed Warren, closing in on his right. The Army of the Potomac was facing to the west, though our advance was made to the south, except when facing the enemy. Hancock was to move southwestward to join on the left of Warren, his left to reach Shady Grove Church.

At six o'clock, before reaching Parker's store, Warren discovered the enemy. He sent word back to this effect, and was ordered to halt and prepare to meet and attack him. Wright, with his division of Sedgwick's corps, was ordered, by any road he could find, to join on Warren's right, and Getty with his division, also of Sedgwick's corps, was ordered to move rapidly by Warren's rear and get on his left. This was the speediest way to reinforce Warren who was confronting the enemy on both the Orange Plank and Turnpike roads. . . .

Meade moved his headquarters on to Old Wilderness Tavern, four miles south of the river, as soon as it was light enough to see the road. I remained to hasten Burnside's crossing and to put him in position. Burnside at this time was not under Meade's command, and was his senior in rank. Getting information of the proximity of the enemy, I informed Meade, and without waiting to see Burnside, at once moved forward my headquarters to where Meade was.

It was my plan then, as it was on all other occasions, to take the initiative whenever the enemy could be drawn from his entrenchments if we were not entrenched ourselves. Warren had not yet reached the point where he was to halt, when he discovered the enemy nearby. Neither party had any advantage of position. Warren was, therefore, ordered to attack as soon as he could prepare for it. At nine o'clock Hancock was ordered to come up to the support of Getty. He himself arrived at Getty's front about noon, but his troops were yet far in the rear. Getty was directed to hold his position at all hazards until relieved. About this hour Warren was ready, and attacked with favorable though not decisive results. Getty was somewhat isolated from Warren and was in a precarious condition for a time. Wilson, with his division of cavalry, was farther south, and was cut off from the rest of the army. At two o'clock Hancock's troops began to arrive, and immediately he was ordered to join Getty and attack the enemy. But the heavy timber and narrow roads prevented him from getting into position for attack as promptly as he generally did when receiving such orders. At four o'clock he again received his orders to attack, and General Getty received orders from Meade a few minutes later to attack whether Hancock was ready or not. He met the enemy under Heth within a few hundred yards.

Hancock immediately sent two divisions, commanded by Birney and Mott, and later two brigades, Carroll's and Owen's, to the support of Getty. This was timely and saved Getty. During the battle Getty and Carroll were wounded, but remained on the field. One of Birney's most gallant brigade commanders—Alexander Hays—was killed.

I had been at West Point with Hays for three years, and had served with him through the Mexican War, a portion of the time in the same regiment. He was a most gallant officer, ready to lead his command whenever ordered. With him it was "Come, boys," not "Go."

Wadsworth's division and Baxter's brigade of the 2nd Division were sent to reinforce Hancock and Getty; but the density of the intervening forest was such that, there being no road to march upon, they did not get up with the head of column until night, and bivouacked where they were without getting into position.

During the afternoon Sheridan sent Gregg's division of cavalry to Todd's Tavern in search of Wilson. This was fortunate. He found Wilson engaged with a superior force under General Rosser, supported by infantry, and falling back before it. Together they were strong enough to turn the tables on the enemy and themselves become aggressive. They soon drove the enemy cavalry back beyond Corbin's bridge.

Fighting between Hancock and Hill continued until night put a close to it. Neither side made any special progress.

After the close of the battle of the fifth of May my orders were given for the following morning. We knew Longstreet with 12,000 men was on his way to join Hill's right, near the Brock Road, and might arrive during the night. I was anxious that the rebels should not take the initiative in the morning, and therefore ordered Hancock to make an assault at 4:30 o'clock. Meade asked to have the hour changed to six. Deferring to his wishes as far as I was willing, the order was modified and five was fixed as the hour to move.

Hancock had now fully one-half of the Army of the Potomac. Wadsworth with his division, which had arrived the night before, lay on a line perpendicular to that held by Hill, and to the right of Hancock. He was directed to move at the same time, and to attack Hill's left.

Burnside, who was coming up with two divisions, was directed to get in between Warren and Wadsworth, and attack as soon as he could get in position to do so. Sedgwick and Warren were to make attacks in their front, to detain as many of the enemy as they could and to take advantage of any attempt to reinforce Hill from that quarter. Burnside was ordered if he should succeed in breaking the enemy's center, to swing around to the left and envelop the right of Lee's army. Hancock was informed of all the movements ordered. . . .

Lee was evidently very anxious that there should be no battle on his right until Longstreet got up. This is evident from the fact that notwithstanding the early hour at which I had ordered the assault, both for the purpose of being the attacking party and to strike before Longstreet got up, Lee was ahead in his assault on our right. His purpose was evident, but he failed.

Hancock was ready to advance at the hour named, but learning in time that Longstreet was moving a part of his corps by the Catharpin Road, thus threatening his left flank, sent a division of infantry, commanded by General Barlow, with all his artillery, to cover the approaches by which Longstreet was expected. This disposition was made in time to attack as ordered. Hancock moved by the left of the Orange Plank Road, and Wadsworth by the right of it. The fighting was desperate for about an hour, when the enemy began to break up in great confusion.

I believed then, and see no reason to change that opinion now, that if the country had been such that Hancock and his command could have seen the confusion and panic in the lines of the enemy, it would have been taken advantage of so effectually that Lee could not have made another stand outside of his Richmond defenses.

Gibbon commanded Hancock's left, and was ordered to attack, but was not able to accomplish much.

On the morning of the sixth Sheridan was sent to connect with Hancock's left and attack the enemy's cavalry who were trying to get on our left and rear. He met them at the intersection of the Furnace and Brock roads and at Todd's Tavern, and defeated them at both places. Later he was attacked, and again the enemy was repulsed.

Hancock heard the firing between Sheridan and Stuart, and thinking that the enemy was coming by that road, still further reinforced his position guarding the entrance to Brock Road. Another incident happened during the day to further induce Hancock to weaken his attacking column. . . .

Hancock followed Hill's retreating forces, in the morning, a mile or more. He maintained this position until, along in the afternoon, Longstreet came upon him. The retreating column of Hill meeting reinforcements that had not yet been engaged, became encouraged and returned with them. They were enabled, from the density of the forest, to approach within a few hundred yards of our advance before being discovered. Falling upon a brigade of Hancock's corps thrown to the advance, they swept it away almost instantly. The enemy followed up his advantage and soon came upon Mott's division, which fell back in great confusion. Hancock made dispositions to hold his advanced position, but after holding it for a time, fell back into the position that he had held in the morning, which was strongly entrenched. In this engagement the intrepid Wadsworth while trying to rally his men was mortally wounded and fell into the hands of the enemy. The enemy followed up, but made no immediate attack.

The Confederate General Jenkins was killed and Longstreet seriously wounded in this engagement.[1] Longstreet had to leave the field, not to resume command for many weeks. His loss was a severe one to Lee, and compensated in a great measure for the mishap, or misapprehensions, which had fallen to our lot during the day.

After Longstreet's removal Lee took command of his right in person. He was not able, however, to rally his men to attack Hancock's position, and withdrew from our front for the purpose of reforming. Hancock sent a brigade to clear his front of all remnants that might be left of Longstreet's or Hill's commands. This brigade having been formed at right angles to the entrenchments held by Hancock's command, swept down the whole length of them from left to right. A brigade of the enemy was encountered in this move; but it broke and disappeared without a contest. . . .

At 4:15 Lee attacked our left. His line moved up to within a hundred yards of ours and opened a heavy fire. This status was maintained for about half an hour. Then a part of Mott's division and Ward's brigade of Birney's division gave way and retired in disorder. The enemy under R.H. Anderson took advantage of this and pushed through our line, planting their flags on a part of the entrenchments not on fire. But owing to the efforts of Hancock, their success was but temporary. Carroll, of Gibbon's division, moved at a double quick with his brigade and drove back the enemy, inflicting great loss. Fighting had continued from five in the morning sometimes along the whole line, at other times only in places. The ground fought over had varied in width, but averaged three-quarters of a mile. The killed, and many of the severely wounded, of both armies, lay within this belt where it was impossible to reach them. The woods were set on fire by the bursting shells, and the conflagration raged. The wounded who had not the strength to move themselves were either suffocated or burned to death. Finally the fire communicated with our breastworks, in places. Being constructed of wood, they burned with great fury. But the battle still

[1] Like Jackson at Chancellorsville, Longstreet was riding near his most advanced lines when his own men fired on him.

raged, our men firing through the flames until it became too hot to remain longer.

Lee was now in distress. His men were in confusion, and his personal efforts failed to restore order. These facts, however, were learned subsequently, or we would have taken advantage of his condition and no doubt gained a decisive success. His troops were withdrawn now, but I revoked the order, which I had given previously to this assault, for Hancock to attack, because his troops had exhausted their ammunition and did not have time to replenish from the train, which was at some distance.

Burnside, Sedgwick, and Warren had all kept up an assault during all this time; but their efforts had no other effect than to prevent the enemy from reinforcing his right from the troops in their front. . . .

The troops on Sedgwick's right had been sent to reinforce our left. This left our right in danger of being turned, and us of being cut off from all present base of supplies. Sedgwick had refused his right and entrenched it for protection against attack. But late in the afternoon of the sixth Early came out from his lines in considerable force and got in upon Sedgwick's right, notwithstanding the precautions taken, and created considerable confusion. Early captured several hundred prisoners, among them two general officers. The defense, however, was vigorous; and night coming on, the enemy was thrown into as much confusion as our troops, engaged, were. . . . Many officers, who had not been attacked by Early, continued coming to my headquarters even after Sedgwick had rectified his lines a little farther to the rear, with news of the disaster, fully impressed with the idea that the enemy was pushing on and would soon be upon me.

During the night all of Lee's army withdrew within their entrenchments. . . . Pickets and skirmishers were sent along our entire front to find the position of the enemy. Some went as far as a mile and a half before finding him. But Lee showed no disposition to come out of his works. There was no battle during the day, and but little firing. . . . This ended the Battle of the Wilderness.

More desperate fighting has not been witnessed on this continent than on the fifth and sixth of May. Our victory consisted in having successfully crossed a formidable stream, almost in the face of an enemy, and in getting the army together as a unit. We gained an advantage on the morning of the sixth, which, if it had been followed up, must have proven very decisive. In the evening the enemy gained an advantage; but was speedily repulsed. As we stood at the close, the two armies were relatively in the same condition to meet with each other as when the river divided them. But the fact of having safely crossed was a victory. . . .[2]

On the afternoon of the seventh I received news from Washington announcing that Sherman had probably attacked Johnston that day, and that Butler had reached City Point safely and taken it by surprise on the fifth. I had given orders for a movement by the left flank, fearing that Lee might move rapidly to Richmond to crush Butler before I could get there.

During the seventh Sheridan had a fight with the rebel cavalry at Todd's Tavern, but routed them, thus opening the way for the troops that were to go by that route at night. Soon after dark Warren withdrew from the front of the enemy, and was soon followed by Sedgwick. . . . With my staff and a small escort of cavalry I preceded the troops. Meade with his staff accompanied me. The greatest enthusiasm was manifested by Hancock's men as we passed by. No doubt it was inspired by the fact that the movement was south. It indicated to them that they had just passed through the "beginning of the end" in the battle just fought. . . .

My object in moving to Spotsylvania was twofold: first, I did not want Lee to get back to Richmond in time to attempt to crush Butler before I could get there; second, I wanted to get between his army and Richmond if possible; and, if not, to draw him into the open field. But Lee, by accident, beat us to Spotsylvania. Our wagon trains had been ordered easterly of the roads the troops were to march upon before the movement commenced. Lee interpreted this as a semi-retreat of the Army of the Potomac to Fredericksburg, and so informed his government. Accordingly he ordered Longstreet's corps—now commanded by Anderson—to move in the morning (the eighth) to Spotsylvania. But the woods being still on fire, Anderson could not go into bivouac, and marched directly on his destination that night. By this accident Lee got possession of Spotsylvania. It is impossible to say now what would have been the result if Lee's orders had been obeyed as given; but it is certain that we would have been in Spotsylvania, and between him and his capital. . . .

Anderson soon entrenched himself—if indeed the entrenchments were not already made—immediately across Warren's front. Warren was not aware of his presence, but probably supposed it was the cavalry which Merritt had engaged earlier in the day. He assaulted at once, but was repulsed. He soon organized his men, as they were not pursued by the

---

[2] Out of roughly 102,000 men, Grant lost over 17,000. Lee lost from his 61,000 troops more than 11,000 casualties. As a proportion of men in each army, these losses were about equal—but Lee was never able to take the offensive again.

enemy, and made a second attack, this time with his whole corps. This time he succeeded in gaining a position immediately in the enemy's front, where he entrenched. . . .

At this time my headquarters had been advanced to Piney Branch Church. I was anxious to crush Anderson before Lee could get a force to his support. To this end Sedgwick, who was at Piney Branch Church, was ordered to Warren's support. Hancock, who was at Todd's Tavern, was notified of Warren's engagement, and was directed to be in readiness to come up. Burnside, who was with the wagon trains at Aldrich's on our extreme left, received the same instructions. Sedgwick was slow in getting up for some reason—probably unavoidable, because he was never at fault when serious work was to be done—so that it was near night before the combined forces were ready to attack. Even then all of Sedgwick's command did not get into the engagement. Warren led the last assault, one division at a time, and of course it failed.

Warren's difficulty was twofold: when he received an order to do anything, it would at once occur to his mind how all the balance of the army should be engaged so as properly to cooperate with him. His ideas were generally good, but he would forget that the person giving him orders had thought of others at the time he had of him. In like manner, he did get ready to execute an order, after giving most intelligent instructions to division commanders, he would go in with one division, holding the others in reserve until he could superintend their movements in person also, forgetting that division commanders could execute their order without his presence. . . .

Lee had ordered Hill's corps—now commanded by Early—to move by the very road we had marched upon. This shows that even early in the morning of the eighth Lee had not yet become acquainted with the move, but still thought that the Army of the Potomac had gone to Fredericksburg. Indeed, he informed the authorities at Richmond that he had possession of Spotsylvania and thus was on my flank. . . .

On the eighth of May,[3] just after the Battle of the Wilderness and when we were moving on Spotsylvania, I directed Sheridan verbally to cut loose from the Army of the Potomac, pass around the left of Lee's army and attack his cavalry: to cut the two [rail]roads—one running west through Gordonsville, Charlottesville, and Lynchburg, the other to Richmond, and, when compelled to do so for want of forage and rations, to move on to the James River and draw these from Butler's supplies. This move took him past the entire rear of Lee's army. . . .

[3] This account of Sheridan's raid has been moved for narrative continuity.

The object of this move was threefold. First, if successfully executed, and it was, he would annoy the enemy by cutting his line of supplies and telegraphic communications, and destroy or get for his own use supplies in the rear and coming up. Second, he would draw the enemy's cavalry after him, and thus better protect our flanks, rear, and trains than by remaining with the army. Third, his absence would save the trains drawing his forage and other supplies from Fredericksburg, which had now become our base. He started at daylight the next morning, and accomplished more than was expected. It was sixteen days before he got back to the Army of the Potomac.

The course Sheridan took was directly to Richmond. Before night Stuart, commanding the Confederate cavalry, came on to the rear of his command. . . . Stuart, seeing that our cavalry was pushing toward Richmond, abandoned the pursuit on the morning of the tenth and, by a detour and an exhausting march, interposed between Sheridan and Richmond at Yellow Tavern, only about six miles north of the city. Sheridan destroyed the railroad and more supplies at Ashland, and on the eleventh arrived in Stuart's front. A severe engagement ensued in which the losses were heavy on both sides, but the rebels were beaten, their leader mortally wounded, and some guns and many prisoners captured. . . .

Sheridan on this memorable raid passed entirely around Lee's army; encountered his cavalry in four engagements, and defeated them in all; recaptured four hundred Union prisoners and killed and captured many of the enemy; destroyed and used many supplies and munitions of war; destroyed miles of railroad and telegraph; and freed us from annoyance by the cavalry of the enemy for more than two weeks. . . .

BATTLE OF SPOTSYLVANIA

By noon of the ninth the position of the two armies was as follows: Lee occupied a semicircle facing north, northwest and northeast enclosing the town [Spotsylvania]. Anderson was on his left extending to the Po, Ewell came next, then Early. Warren occupied our right, covered the Brock and other roads converging at Spotsylvania; Sedgwick was to his left and Burnside on our extreme left. Hancock was yet back at Todd's Tavern, but as soon as it was known that Early had left Hancock's front the latter was ordered up to Warren's right. He formed a line with three divisions on the hill overlooking the Po early in the afternoon, and was ordered to cross the

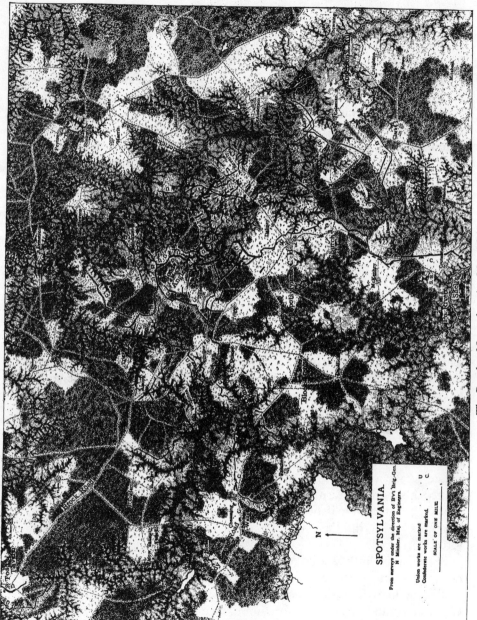

The Battle of Spotsylvania, May 1864

Po and get on the enemy's flank. The fourth division of Hancock's corps, Mott commanding, was left at Todd's when the corps first came up; but in the afternoon it was brought up and placed to the left of Sedgwick's—now Wright's—6th Corps. In the morning General Sedgwick had been killed near the right of his entrenchments by rebel sharpshooters. His loss was a severe one to the Army of the Potomac and to the nation. General H. G. Wright succeeded him in the command of his corps. . . .

The Po at the points Hancock's corps crossed runs nearly due east. Just below his lower crossing—the troops crossed at three points—it turns due south, and after passing under Wooden Bridge soon resumes a more easterly direction. During the night this corps built three bridges over the Po; but these were in the rear.

The position assumed by Hancock's corps forced Lee to reinforce his left during the night. Accordingly on the morning of the tenth, when Hancock renewed his effort to get over the Po to his front, he found himself confronted by some of Early's command, which had been brought from the extreme right of the enemy during the night. He succeeded in effecting a crossing with one brigade, however, but finding the enemy entrenched in his front, no more were crossed.

Hancock reconnoitered his front on the morning of the tenth, with the view of forcing a crossing, if it was found that an advantage could be gained. The enemy was found strongly entrenched on the high ground overlooking the river, and commanding the Wooden Bridge with artillery. Anderson's left rested on the Po, where it turns south; therefore, for Hancock to cross over—although it would bring him on to the same side of the stream with the rest of the army—would still further isolate him from it. The stream would have to be crossed twice in the face of the enemy to unite with the main body. The idea of a crossing was therefore abandoned.

Lee weakened the other parts of his line to meet this movement of Hancock's, and I determined to take advantage of it. Accordingly in the morning, orders were issued for an attack in the afternoon on the center by Warren's and Wright's corps, Hancock to command all the attacking force. . . .

Between the lines, where Warren's assault was to take place, there was a ravine grown up with large trees and underbrush, making it almost impenetrable by man. The slopes on both sides were also covered by a heavy growth of timber. Warren, before noon, reconnoitered his front twice, the first time with one and the second with two divisions. He was repulsed on both occasions, but gained such information of the ground as to induce him to report recommending the assault.

Wright also reconnoitered his front and gained a considerably advanced position from the one he started from. He then organized a storming party, consisting of twelve regiments, and assigned Colonel Emory Upton, of the 121st New York Volunteers, to the command of it. About four o'clock in the afternoon the assault was ordered, Warren's and Wright's corps, with Mott's division of Hancock's corps, to move simultaneously. The movement was prompt, and in a few minutes the fiercest of struggles began. The battlefield was so densely covered with forest that but little could be seen, by any one person, as to the progress made. Meade and I occupied the best position we could get, in the rear of Warren.

Warren was repulsed with heavy loss . . . To the left our success was decided, but the advantage was lost by the feeble action of Mott. Upton with his assaulting party pushed forward and crossed the enemy's entrenchments. Turning to the right and left he captured several guns and some hundreds of prisoners. Mott was ordered to his assistance but failed utterly. So much time was lost in trying to get up the troops which were in the right position to reinforce, that I ordered Upton to withdraw; but the officers and men of his command were so averse to giving up the advantage they had gained that I withdrew the order. To relieve them, I ordered a renewal of the assault. By this time Hancock, who had gone with Birney's division to relieve Barlow, had returned, bringing the division with him. His corps was now joined with Warren's and Wright's in this last assault. It was gallantly made, many men getting up to, and over, the works of the enemy; but they were unable to hold them. At night they were withdrawn. Upton brought his prisoners with him, but the guns he had captured he was obliged to abandon. Upton had gained an important advantage, but a lack in others of the spirit and dash possessed by him lost it to us. Before leaving Washington I had been authorized to promote officers on the field for special acts of gallantry. By this authority I conferred the rank of brigadier-general upon Upton on the spot, and this act was confirmed by the President. Upton had been badly wounded in this fight.

Burnside on the left had got up to within a few hundred yards of Spotsylvania Court House, completely turning Lee's right. He was not aware of the importance of the advantage he had gained, and I, being with the troops where the heavy fighting was, did not know of it at the time. He had gained his position with but little fighting, and almost without loss. Burnside's position now separated him widely from Wright's corps, the corps commander nearest to him. At night he was ordered to join on to this. This brought him back about a mile, and lost to us an important advantage. I attach no blame to Burnside for this, but

I do to myself for not having had a staff officer with him to report to me his position. . . .

On the eleventh there was no battle and but little firing; none except by Mott who made a reconnaissance to ascertain if there was a weak point in the enemy's line. . . .

I received information, through the War Department, from General Butler that his cavalry under Kautz had cut the railroad south of Petersburg, separating Beauregard from Richmond, and had whipped [D.H.] Hill, killing, wounding, and capturing many. Also that he was entrenched, and could maintain himself. On this same day came news from Sheridan to the effect that he had destroyed ten miles of the railroad and telegraph between Lee and Richmond, one and a half million rations, and most of the medical stores for his army.

In the reconnaissance made by Mott on the eleventh, a salient was discovered at the right center.[4] I determined that an assault should be made at that point. Accordingly Hancock was ordered to move his command by the rear of Warren and Wright, under cover of night, to Wright's left, and there form it for an assault at four o'clock the next morning. The night was dark, it rained heavily, and the road was difficult, so that it was midnight when he reached the point where he was to halt. It took most of the night to get the men in position for their advance in the morning. The men got but little rest. Burnside was ordered to attack on the left of the salient at the same hour. I sent two of my staff officers to impress upon him the importance of pushing forward vigorously. Hancock was notified of this. Warren and Wright were ordered to hold themselves in readiness to join in the assault if circumstances made it advisable. I occupied a central position most convenient for receiving information from all points. Hancock put Barlow on his left, in double column, and Birney to his right. Mott followed Birney, and Gibbon was held in reserve.

The morning of the twelfth opened foggy, delaying the start more than half an hour.

The ground over which Hancock had to pass to reach the enemy was ascending and heavily wooded to within two or three hundred yards of the enemy entrenchments. In front of Birney there was also a marsh to cross. But, notwithstanding all these difficulties, the troops pushed on in quick time without firing a gun, and when within four or five hundred yards of the enemy's line broke out in loud cheers, and with a rush went up to and over the breastworks. Barlow and Birney entered almost simultaneously.

[4] This soon became known as the Bloody Angle.

Here a desperate hand-to-hand conflict took place. The men of the two sides were too close together to fire, but used their guns as clubs. The hand conflict was soon over. Hancock's corps captured some four thousand prisoners—among them a division and a brigade commander—twenty or more guns with their horses, caissons, and ammunition, several thousand stand of arms, and many colors. Hancock, as soon as the hand-to-hand conflict was over, turned the guns of the enemy against him and advanced inside the rebel lines. About six o'clock I ordered Warren's corps to the support of Hancock's. Burnside, on the left, had advanced up the east of the salient of the very parapet of the enemy. Potter, commanding one of his divisions, got over but was not able to remain there. However, he inflicted a heavy loss upon the enemy; but not without loss in return.

This victory was important, and one that Lee could not afford to leave us in full possession of. He made the most strenuous efforts to regain the position he had lost. Troops were brought up from his left, and attacked Hancock furiously. Hancock was forced to fall back; but he did so slowly, with his face to the enemy, inflicting on him heavy loss, until behind the breastworks he had captured. These he turned, facing them the other way, and continued to hold. Wright was ordered up to reinforce Hancock, and arrived by six o'clock. He was wounded soon after coming up but did not relinquish the command of his corps, although the fighting lasted until one o'clock the next morning. At eight o'clock Warren was ordered up again, but was so slow in making his dispositions that his orders were frequently repeated, and with emphasis. At eleven o'clock I gave Meade written orders to relieve Warren from his command if he failed to move promptly. Hancock placed batteries on high ground in his rear, which he used against the enemy, firing over the heads of his own troops.

Burnside accomplished but little on our left of a positive nature, but negatively a great deal. He kept Lee from reinforcing his center from that quarter. . . .

Lee massed heavily from his left flank on the broken point of his line. Five times during the day he assaulted furiously, but without dislodging our troops from their new position. His losses must have been fearful. Sometimes the belligerents would be separated by but a few feet. In one place a tree, eighteen inches in diameter, was cut entirely down by musket balls. All the trees between the lines were very much cut to pieces by artillery and musketry. It was three o'clock next morning before the fighting ceased. Some of our troops had been twenty hours under fire. In this engagement we did not lose a single organization, not even a company. The enemy lost one division with its commander, one brigade, and

one regiment, with heavy losses elsewhere. Our losses were heavy, but, as
stated, no whole company was captured. At night Lee took a position in
rear of his former one, and by the following morning he was strongly
entrenched in it. . . .

On the fifteenth news came from Butler and Averill. The former
reported the capture of the outer works at Drewry's Bluff, on the James
River, and that this cavalry had cut the railroad and telegraph south
of Richmond on the Danville road; and the latter, the destruction of a
depot of supplies at Dublin, West Virginia, and the breaking of New
River Bridge on the Virginia and Tennessee Railroad. The next day
news came from Sherman and Sheridan. Sherman had forced Johnston
out of Dalton, Georgia, and was following him south. The report from
Sheridan embraced his operations up to his passing the outer defenses
of Richmond. The prospect must now have been dismal in Richmond.
The road and telegraph were cut between the capital and Lee. The
roads and wires were cut in every direction from the rebel capital. Temporarily that city was cut off from all communication with the outside
except by courier. This condition of affairs, however, was of but short
duration. . . .

News came that Sigel had been defeated at New Market, badly, and was
retreating down the [Shenandoah] valley. Not two hours before I had sent
the inquiry to Halleck whether Sigel could not get to Staunton to stop
supplies coming from there to Lee. I asked at once that Sigel might be
relieved, and someone else put in his place. Hunter's name was suggested,
and I heartily approved. Further news from Butler reported him driven
from Drewry's Bluff, but still in possession of the Petersburg road. Banks
had been defeated in Louisiana, relieved, and Canby put in his place. This
change of commander was not on my suggestion. All this news was very
discouraging. All of it must have been known by the enemy before it was by
me. In fact, the good news (for the enemy) must have been known to him
at the moment I thought he was in despair, and his anguish had already
been relieved when we were enjoying his supposed discomfiture. But this
was no time for repining. I immediately gave orders for a movement by the
left flank, on towards Richmond, to commence on the night of the nineteenth. . . .

In consequence of the disasters that had befallen us in the past few days,
Lee could be reinforced largely, and I had no doubt he would be. Beauregard had come up from the south with troops to guard the Confederate
capital when it was in danger. Butler being driven back, most of the troops
could be sent to Lee. Hoke was no longer needed in North Carolina; and

Sigel's troops having gone back to Cedar Creek, whipped, many troops could be spared from the valley. . . .

We were now to operate in a different country from any we had before seen in Virginia. The roads were wide and good, and the country well cultivated. No men were seen except those bearing arms, even the black man having been sent away. The country, however, was new to us, and we had neither guides nor maps to tell us where the roads were, or where they led to. Engineer and staff officers were put to the dangerous duty of supplying the place of both maps and guides. By reconnoitering they were enabled to locate the roads in the vicinity of each army corps. Our course was south, and we took all roads leading in that direction which would not separate the army too widely . . .

On the twenty-third Hancock's corps was moved to the wooden bridge which spans the North Anna River just west of where the Fredericksburg Railroad crosses. It was near night when the troops arrived. They found the bridge guarded, with troops entrenched, on the north side. Hancock sent two brigades, Egan's and Pierce's, to the right and left, and when properly disposed they charged simultaneously. The bridge was carried quickly, the enemy retreating over it so hastily that many were shoved in the river, and some of them were drowned. Several hundred prisoners were captured. The hour was so late that Hancock did not cross until morning. . . .

Lee now had his entire army south of the North Anna. Our lines covered his front, with the six miles separating the two wings guarded by but a single division. To get from one wing to the other the river would have to be crossed twice. Lee could reinforce any part of his line from all points of it in a very short march; or could concentrate the whole of it wherever he might choose to assault. We were, for the time, practically two armies besieging. . . .

On the twenty-fifth I gave orders, through Halleck, to Hunter, who had relieved Sigel, to move up the Valley of Virginia, cross over the Blue Ridge to Charlottesville, and go as far as Lynchburg if possible, living upon the country and cutting the railroads and canal as he went. After doing this he could find his way back to his base, or join me.

On the same day news was received that Lee was falling back on Richmond. This proved not to be true. But we could do nothing where we were unless Lee would assume the offensive. I determined, therefore, to draw out of our present position and make one more effort to get between him and Richmond. I had no expectation now, however, of succeeding in this; but I did expect to hold him far enough west to enable me to reach the

James River high up. Sheridan was now again with the Army of the Potomac. . . .

It was a delicate move to get the right wing of the Army of the Potomac from its position south of the North Anna in the presence of the enemy. . . . Wilson's division of cavalry was brought up from the left and moved by our right south to Little River. Here he maneuvered to give the impression that we were going to attack the left flank of Lee's army.

Under cover of night our right wing was withdrawn to the north side of the river, Lee being completely deceived by Wilson's feint. On the afternoon of the twenty-sixth Sheridan moved, sending Gregg's and Torbert's cavalry to Taylor's and Littlepage's fords towards Hanover. . . . Sheridan was followed by a division of infantry under General Russell. On the morning of the twenty-seventh the crossing was effected with but little loss, the enemy losing thirty or forty, taken prisoners. Thus a position was secured south of the Pamunkey. . . .

Hanover Town is about twenty miles from Richmond. There are two roads leading there; the most direct and shortest one crossing the Chickahominy at Meadow Bridge, near the Virginia Central Railroad, the second going by New and Old Cold Harbor. A few miles out from Hanover Town there is a third road by way of Mechanicsville to Richmond. New Cold Harbor was important to us because while there we both covered the roads back to White House (where our supplies came from), and the roads southeast over which we would have to pass to get to the James River below the Richmond defenses. . . .

BATTLE OF COLD HARBOR

On the thirty-first Sheridan advanced to near Old Cold Harbor. He found it entrenched and occupied by cavalry and infantry. A hard fight ensued but the place was carried. The enemy well knew the importance of Cold Harbor to us, and seemed determined that we should not hold it. He returned with such a large force that Sheridan was about withdrawing without making any effort to hold it against such odds; but about the time he commenced the evacuation he received orders to hold the place at all hazards, until reinforcements could be sent to him. He speedily turned the rebel works to face against them and placed his men in position for defense. Night came on before the enemy was ready for assault.

Wright's corps was ordered early in the evening to march directly to

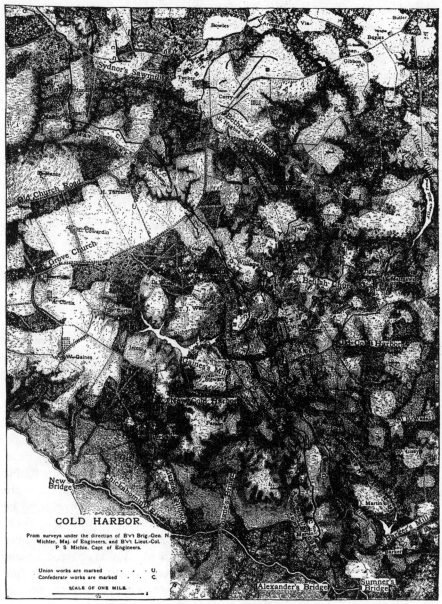

The Battle of Cold Harbor, June 3, 1864

Cold Harbor passing by the rear of the army. It was expected to arrive by daylight or before; but the night was dark and the distance great, so that it was nine o'clock of the first of June before it reached its destination. Before the arrival of Wright the enemy had made two assaults on Sheridan, both of which were repulsed with heavy loss to the enemy. Wrights's corps coming up, there was no further assault on Cold Harbor. . . .

By six o'clock in the afternoon Wright and Smith were ready to make an assault. In front of both the ground was clear for several hundred yards, and then became wooded. Both charged across the open space and into the wood, capturing and holding the first line of rifle pits of the enemy, and also capturing seven or eight hundred prisoners.

While this was going on, the enemy charged Wright three separate times with vigor, but were repulsed each time with loss. There was no officer more capable, nor one more prompt in acting, than Wright when the enemy forced him to it. . . . During the night the enemy made frequent attacks with the view of dispossessing us of the important position we had gained, but without effecting their object.

Hancock was moved from his place in line during the night and ordered to the left of Wright. I expected to take the offensive on the morning of the second, but the night was so dark, the heat and dust so excessive and the roads so intricate and hard to keep, that the head of column only reached Old Cold Harbor at six o'clock, but was in position at 7:30 A.M. Preparations were made for an attack in the afternoon, but did not take place until the next morning. . . . While Warren and Burnside were making . . . changes, the enemy came out several times and attacked them, capturing several hundred prisoners. The attacks were repulsed, but not followed up as they should have been. I was so annoyed at this that I directed Meade to instruct his corps commanders that they should seize all such opportunities when they occurred, and not wait for orders, all of our maneuvers being made for the very purpose of getting the enemy out of his cover. . . .

During the night Lee moved his left up to make his line correspond to ours. His lines extended now from the Totopotomy to New Cold Harbor. Mine from Bethesda Church by Old Cold Harbor to the Chickahominy, with a division of cavalry guarding our right. An assault was ordered for the third, to be made mainly by the corps of Hancock, Wright, and Smith; but Warren and Burnside were to support it by threatening Lee's left, and to attack with great earnestness if he should either reinforce more threatened points by drawing from that quarter or if a favorable opportunity should present itself.

The corps commanders were to select the points in their respective fronts where they would make their assaults. The move was to commence at half-past four in the morning. Hancock sent Barlow and Gibbon forward at the appointed hour, with Birney as a reserve. Barlow pushed forward with great vigor, under a heavy fire of both artillery and musketry, through thickets and swamps. Notwithstanding all the resistance of the enemy and the natural obstructions to overcome, he carried a position occupied by the enemy outside their main line where the road makes a deep cut through a bank affording as good a shelter for troops as if it had been made for that purpose. Three pieces of artillery had been captured here, and several hundred prisoners. The guns were immediately turned against the men who had just been using them. No assistance coming to him, he (Barlow) entrenched under fire and continued to hold his place. Gibbon was not so fortunate on his front. He found the ground over which he had to pass cut up with deep ravines, and a morass difficult to cross. But his men struggled on until some of them got up to the very parapet covering the enemy. Gibbon gained ground much nearer the enemy than that which he left, and here entrenched and held fast.

Wright's corps moving in two lines captured the outer rifle pits in their front, but accomplished nothing more. Smith's corps also gained the outer rifle pits in its front. The ground over which this corps (18th) had to move was the most exposed of any over which charges were made. An open plain intervened between the contending forces at this point, which was exposed both to a direct and a cross fire. . . .

This assault cost us heavily and probably without benefit to compensate; but the enemy was not cheered by the occurrence sufficiently to induce him to take the offensive. In fact, nowhere after the Battle of the Wilderness did Lee show any disposition to leave his defenses far behind.

Fighting was substantially over by half-past seven in the morning. . . .

I have always regretted the last assault at Cold Harbor was ever made. I might say the same thing of the assault of the twenty-second of May, 1863, at Vicksburg. At Cold Harbor no advantage whatever was gained to compensate for the heavy loss we sustained. Indeed, the advantages, other than those of relative losses, were on the Confederate side.[5] Before that, the Army of Northern Virginia seemed to have acquired a wholesome regard for the courage, endurance, and soldierly qualities generally of the Army of the Potomac. They no longer wanted to fight them "one Confederate to five Yanks." Indeed, they seemed to have given up any idea of

---

[5] The Confederates suffered fewer casualties in relative terms, in fact, as well as in absolute numbers.

gaining any advantage of their antagonist in the open field. They had come
to much prefer breastworks to revive their hopes temporarily; but it was of
short duration. The effect upon the Army of the Potomac was the reverse.
When we reached the James River, however, all effects of the battle of Cold
Harbor seemed to have disappeared. . . .[6]

THE MOVEMENT ON PETERSBURG

Lee's position was now so near Richmond, and the intervening swamps of
the Chickahominy so great an obstacle to the movement of an enemy, that
I determined to make my next left flank move carry the Army of the
Potomac south of the James River. Preparations for this were promptly
commenced. The move was a hazardous one to make: the Chickahominy
River, with its marshy and heavily timbered approaches, had to be crossed;
all the bridges over it east of Lee were destroyed; the enemy had a shorter
line and better roads to travel on to confront me in crossing; more than
fifty miles intervened between me and Butler, by the roads I should have to
travel, with both the James and the Chickahominy unbridged to cross; and
last, the Army of the Potomac had to be got out of a position but a few
hundred yards from the enemy at the widest place. Lee, if he did not
choose to follow me, might, with his shorter distance to travel and his
bridges over the Chickahominy and the James, move rapidly on Butler and
crush him before the army with me could come to his relief. Then too he
might spare troops enough to send against Hunter who was approaching
Lynchburg, living upon the country he passed through, and without
ammunition further than what he carried with him.

But the move had to be made, and I relied upon Lee's not seeing my
danger as I saw it. Besides we had armies on both sides of the James River
and not far from the Confederate capital. I knew that its safety would be a
matter of the first consideration with the executive, legislative, and judicial
branches of the so-called Confederate government, if it was not with the
military commanders. But I took all the precautions I knew of to guard
against all dangers.

Sheridan was sent with two divisions to communicate with Hunter and
to break up the Virginia Central Railroad and the James River Canal, and
on the seventh of June, taking instructions to Hunter to come back with

[6] In fact, some historians have attributed the failure of the later assault on Petersburg
to "Cold Harbor syndrome"—a fear of attacking fortified positions after the slaughter
at Cold Harbor.

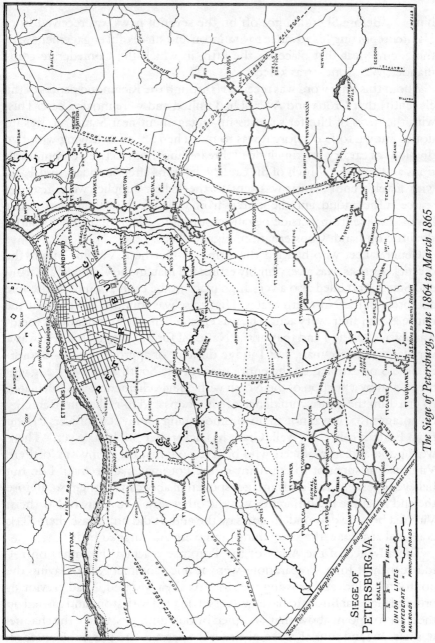

SIEGE OF
PETERSBURG, VA.

SCALE

1 MILE

UNION LINES
CONFEDERATE "
RAILROADS   PRINCIPAL ROADS

Note. This Map joins Map N° 3 by a similar diagonal line on the North east corner.

The Siege of Petersburg, June 1864 to March 1865

him. . . . Before Sheridan got off on the seventh news was received from Hunter reporting his advance to Staunton and successful engagement with the enemy near that place on the fifth, in which the Confederate commander, W.S. Jones, was killed. . . .

About this time word was received (through the Richmond papers of the eleventh) that Crook and Averell had united and were moving east. This, with the news of Hunter's successful engagement near Staunton, was no doubt known to Lee before it was to me. Then Sheridan leaving with two divisions of cavalry, looking indeed threatening, both to Lee's communications and supplies. Much of his cavalry was sent after Sheridan, and Early with Ewell's entire corps was sent to the Valley. Supplies were growing scarce in Richmond, and the sources from which to draw them were in our hands. People from outside began to pour into Richmond to help eat up the little on hand. Consternation reigned there. . . .

General Lee, who had led the Army of Northern Virginia in all [the recent] contests, was a very highly estimated man in the Confederate army and States, and filled also a very high place in the estimation of the people and press of the Northern States. His praise was sounded throughout the entire North after every action he was engaged in; the number of his forces was always lowered and that of the National forces exaggerated. He was a very large, austere man, and I judge difficult of approach to his subordinates. To be extolled by the entire press of the South after every engagement, and by a portion of the North with equal vehemence, was calculated to give him the entire confidence of his troops and to make him feared by his antagonists. It was not an uncommon thing for my staff officers to hear from Eastern officers, "Well, Grant has never met Bobby Lee yet." There were good and true officers who believe now that the Army of Northern Virginia was superior to the Army of the Potomac man to man. I do not believe so, except as the advantages spoken of above made them so. Before the end I believe the difference was the other way. The Army of Northern Virginia became despondent and saw the end. It did not please them. The National army saw the same thing, and were encouraged by it.

The advance of the Army of the Potomac reached the James on the fourteenth of June. Preparations were at once commenced for laying the pontoon bridges and crossing the river. As already stated, I had previously ordered General Butler to have two vessels loaded with stone and carried up the river to a point above that occupied by our gunboats, where the channel was narrow, and sunk there to obstruct the passage and prevent Confederate gunboats from coming down the river. Butler had these boats filled and put in position, but had not had them sunk before my arrival. I ordered this done, and also directed that he should turn over all material and boats not then in use in the river to be used in ferrying all the troops across.

I then, on the fourteenth, took a steamer and ran up to Bermuda Hundred to see General Butler for the purpose of directing a movement against Petersburg, while our troops of the Army of the Potomac were crossing.

I had sent General W.F. Smith back from Cold Harbor by the way of White House, thence on steamers to City Point for the purpose of giving General Butler more troops with which to accomplish this result. General Butler was ordered to send Smith with his troops reinforced, as far as that could be conveniently done, from other parts of the Army of the James. This gave Smith about six thousand reinforcements, including some twenty-five hundred cavalry under Kautz, and about thirty-five hundred colored infantry under Hinks.

This distance which Smith had to move to reach the enemy's lines was about six miles, and the Confederate advance line of works was but two miles outside of Petersburg. Smith was to move under cover of night, up close to the enemy's works, and assault as soon as he could after daylight. I believed then, and still believe, that Petersburg could have been easily captured at that time. It only had about 2,500 men in the defenses besides some irregular troops, consisting of citizens and employees in the city who took up arms in case of emergency. Smith started as proposed, but his advance encountered a rebel force entrenched between City Point and their lines outside of Petersburg. This position he carried, with some loss to the enemy; but there was so much delay that it was daylight before his troops really got off from there. While there I informed General Butler that Hancock's corps would cross the river and move to Petersburg to support Smith in case the latter was successful, and that I could reinforce there more rapidly than Lee could reinforce from his position.

I returned down the river to where the troops of the Army of the Potomac now were, communicated to General Meade, in writing, of the directions I had given to General Butler and directed him (Meade) to cross Hancock's corps over under cover of night, and push them forward in the morning to Petersburg; halting them, however, at a designated point until they could hear from Smith. . . .

Smith arrived in front of the enemy's lines early in the forenoon of the fifteenth, and spent the day until seven o'clock in the evening in reconnoitering what appeared to be empty works. The enemy's line consisted of redans [built-up fortifications] occupying commanding positions, with rifle pits connecting them. To the east side of Petersburg, from the

Appomattox back, there were thirteen of these redans extending a distance of several miles, probably three. If they had been properly manned they could have held out against any force that could have attacked them, at least until reinforcements could have got up from the north of Richmond.

Smith assaulted with the colored troops, and with success. By nine o'clock at night he was in possession of five of these redans and, of course, of the connecting line of rifle pits. All of them contained artillery, which fell into our hands. Hancock came up and proposed to take any part assigned to him; and Smith asked him to relieve his men who were in the trenches.

Next morning, the sixteenth, Hancock himself was in command, and captured another redan. Meade came up in the afternoon and succeeded Hancock, who had to be relieved, temporarily, from the command of his corps on accounting of the breaking out afresh of the wound he had received at Gettysburg. During the day Meade assaulted and carried one more redan to his right and two to his left. In all this we lost very heavily. The works were not strongly manned, but they all had guns in them which fell into our hands, together with the men who were handling them in the effort to repel these assaults.

Up to this time Beauregard, who had commanded south of Richmond, had received no reinforcements, except Hoke's division from Drewry's Bluff, which had arrived the morning of the sixteenth; though he had urged the authorities very strongly to send them, believing, as he did, that Petersburg would be a valuable prize which we might seek.[7]

During the seventeenth the fighting was very severe and the losses very heavy; and at night our troops occupied about the same position they had occupied in the morning, except that they held a redan which had been captured by Potter during the day. During the night, however, Beauregard fell back to the line which had been already selected, and commenced fortifying it. . . .

The Army of the Potomac was given the investment of Petersburg, while the Army of the James held Bermuda Hundred and all the ground we possessed north of the James River. The 9th Corps, Burnside's, was placed on the right of Petersburg; the 5th, Warren's, next; the 2nd, Birney's, next; then the 6th, Wright's, broken off to the left and south. Thus began the siege of Petersburg.

---

[7] Almost all the railroads connecting Richmond to the rest of the South went through Petersburg; its loss would force the Confederates to abandon their capital.

19
SHERIDAN IN THE VALLEY
September–October 1864

The movement to Petersburg was a grand stroke, foiled only by William F. Smith's timidity. Despite defeat at Cold Harbor, Grant had kept his cool, and managed to utterly surprise Lee—moving his entire army from immediately in front of the Confederate lines, across two rivers, to the gates of Petersburg, deep in Lee's rear. But Smith, the leader of the Yankee spearhead, had failed to take the city while it was almost empty.

Even so, Grant now had Lee pinned down in defense of Petersburg, the key to Richmond itself. With the Army of Northern Virginia locked in place, Sherman and Hunter could cut into the vulnerable, resource-rich regions of Georgia and the Shenandoah.

Unfortunately for Grant, Lee was not completely pinned, nor did Hunter finish cutting. As Grant noted above, Lee had dispatched an entire corps under Jubal Early in June to drive Hunter from the Valley. Early did so in fine style—then emerged from the Shenandoah in July for a quick raid on Washington.

Early and his 15,000 men were driven back, but Grant had had enough of the troubles in the Valley. With the army bogged down in besieging Petersburg, he dispatched Philip Sheridan to the region with orders to destroy Early and the Shenandoah with him. Mindful of the political necessity of complete success, the cavalry commander only skirmished for six weeks as he sounded out reports of heavy Confederate reinforcements. On September 19, satisfied of his advantage, Sheridan struck.

The Shenandoah Campaign
By General Philip H. Sheridan

When I took command of the Army of the Shenandoah its infantry force comprised the 6th Corps, one division of the Nineteenth Corps, and two divisions from West Virginia. The 6th Corps was commanded by Major-General Horatio G. Wright; its three divisions by Brigadier-Generals David A. Russell, George W. Getty, and James B. Ricketts. The single division of the 19th Corps had for its immediate chief Brigadier-General George Crook. . . . General Torbert's division, then arriving from the Cavalry Corps of the Army of the Potomac, represented the mounted arm of the service, and in the expectation that Averell would soon join me with his troopers, I assigned General Torbert as chief of cavalry, and General Wesley Merritt succeeded to the command of Torbert's division. . . .

In a few days after my arrival preparations were completed, and I was ready to make the first move for the possession of the Shenandoah Valley. For the next five weeks the operations on my part consisted almost wholly of offensive and defensive maneuvering for certain advantages, the enemy confining himself meanwhile to measures intended to counteract my designs. . . .

The difference of strength between the two armies at this date was considerably in my favor, but the conditions attending my situation in a hostile region so much detached service to protect trains, and to secure Maryland and Pennsylvania from raids, that my excess numbers was almost canceled by these incidental demands that could not be avoided, and although I knew that I was strong, yet, in consequence of the injunctions of General Grant, I deemed it necessary to be very cautious; and the fact that the presidential election was impending made me doubly so, the authorities at Washington having impressed upon me that the defeat of my army might be followed by the overthrow of the party in power, which event, it was believed, would at least retard the progress of the war, if, indeed, it did not lead to the complete abandonment of all coercive measures.[8] Under circumstances such as these I could not afford to risk disaster . . . so, notwithstanding my superior strength, I determined to take all the time necessary to equip myself with the fullest information,

---

[8] This is a rather artful and not entirely honest attempt at explaining why he was so slow to use his much larger force; his numerical advantage was hardly "almost canceled" by the need to protect his communications.

and then seize an opportunity under such conditions that I could not well fail of success. . . .

I felt the need of an efficient body of scouts to collect information regarding the enemy, for the defective intelligence establishment with which I started out from Harper's Ferry early in August had not proved satisfactory. I therefore began to organize my scouts on a system which I hoped would give better results than had the method hitherto pursued in the department, which was to employ in this service doubtful citizens and Confederate deserters. . . . Two of my scouts put me in the way of getting news conveyed from Winchester [where Early was encamped]. They had learned that just outside of my lines, near Millwood, there was living an old colored man, who had a permit from the Confederate commander to go into Winchester and return three times a week, for the purpose of selling vegetables to the inhabitants. . . . I hesitated at first, but finally deciding to try it, dispatched the two scouts to the old negro's cabin, and they brought him to my headquarters late that night. I was soon convinced of the negro's fidelity, and asking him if he was acquainted with Miss Rebecca Wright [a Union loyalist], of Winchester, he replied that he knew her well. Thereupon I told him what I wished to do, and after a little persuasion he agreed to carry a letter to her on his next marketing trip. . . .

Miss Wright's answer proved of more value to me than she anticipated, for it not only quieted the conflicting reports concerning Anderson's corps [formerly Longstreet's], but was most important in showing that Kershaw [with a Confederate division] was gone, and this circumstance led, three days later, to the battle of the Opequon, or Winchester as it has been unofficially called. . . .

My losses in the battle of the Opequon were heavy, amounting to about 4,500 killed, wounded, and missing. Among the killed was General Russell, commanding a division, and the wounded included Generals Upton, McIntosh, and Chapman, and Colonels Duval and Sharpe. The Confederate loss in killed, wounded, and prisoners about equaled mine, General Rodes being of the killed, while Generals Fitzhugh Lee and York were severely wounded.

We captured five pieces of artillery and nine battle flags. The restoration of the lower Valley—from the Potomac to Strasburg—to the control of the Union forces caused great rejoicing in the North, and relieved the Administration from further solicitude for the safety of the Maryland and Pennsylvania borders. . . .

The battle was not fought out on the plan with which marching orders were issued to my troops, for I then hoped to take Early in detail, and with

Crook's force cut off his retreat. I adhered to this purpose during the early start of the contest, but was obliged to abandon the idea because of the unavoidable delays from getting the 6th and 19th Corps through [a] narrow defile and into position early enough to destroy [Confederate General] Ramseur while still isolated. . . . I changed my plan as to Crook, and moved him from my left to my right. This I did with great reluctance, for I hoped to destroy Early's army entirely if Crook continued on his original line of march toward the Valley pike, south of Winchester; and although the ultimate results did in a measure vindicate the change, yet I have always thought that by adhering to the original plan we might have captured the bulk of Early's army.

The night of the nineteenth of September I gave orders for following Early up the Valley next morning—the pursuit to begin at daybreak. . . . The enemy, having kept up his retreat at night, presented no opposition whatever until the cavalry discovered him posted at Fisher's Hill, on the first defensive line where he could hope to make any serious resistance. . . .

A reconnaissance . . . convinced me that the enemy's position at Fisher's Hill was so strong that a direct assault would entail unnecessary destruction of life, and, besides, be of doubtful result. At the point where Early's troops were in position, between the Massanutten range and Little North Mountain, the Valley is only about three and a half miles wide. All along the precipitous bluff which overhangs Tumbling Run on the south side, a heavy line of earthworks had been constructed when Early retreated to this point in August, and these were now being strengthened so as to make them almost impregnable; in fact, so secure did Early consider himself that, for convenience, his ammunition chests were taken from the caisson and placed behind the breastworks. . . .

In consequence of the enemy's being so well protected from a direct assault, I resolved on the night of the twentieth to use again a turning column against his left, as had been done on the nineteenth at the Opequon. To this end I resolved to move Crook, unperceived if possible, over to the eastern face of Little North Mountain, whence he could strike the left and rear of the Confederate line, and as he broke it up, I could support him by a left half-wheel of my whole line of battle. The execution of this plan would require perfect secrecy, however, for the enemy from his signal station on Three Top could plainly see every movement of our troops in daylight. Hence, to escape such observation, I marched Crook during the night of the twentieth into some heavy timber north of Cedar Creek, where he lay concealed all day the twenty-first. This same day Wright and Emory were moved up closer to the Confederate works, and the 6th

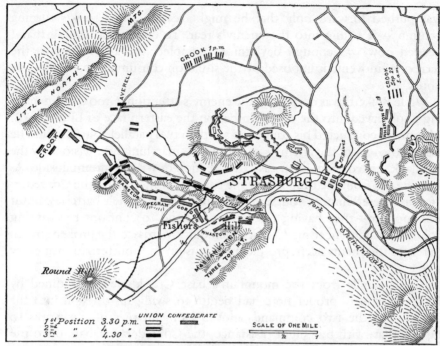

The Battle of Fisher's Hill, September 22, 1864

Corps, after a severe fight, in which Ricketts and Getty were engaged, took up some high ground on the right of the Manassas Gap railroad in plain view of the Confederate works, and confronting a commanding point where much of Early's artillery was massed. . . .

In the darkness of the night of the twenty-first, Crook was brought across Cedar Creek and hidden in a clump of timber behind Hupp's Hill till daylight of the twenty-second, when, under cover of the intervening woods and ravines, he was marched beyond the right of the 6th Corps and again concealed not far from the Back road. After Crook had got into this last position, Ricketts's division was pushed out until it confronted the left of the enemy's infantry, the rest of the 6th Corps extending from Ricketts's left to the Manassas Gap railroad, while the 19th Corps filled in the space between the left of the 6th and the North Fork of the Shenandoah.

When Ricketts moved out on this new line, in conjunction with Averell's cavalry on his right, the enemy surmising, from information secured from his signal station, no doubt, that my attack was to be made from Ricketts's front, prepared for it there, but no such intention ever existed. Ricketts's was pushed forward only that he might readily join Crook's turning column as it swung into the enemy's rear. To ensure success, all that I needed now was enough daylight to complete my arrangements, the secrecy of movement imposed by the situation consuming many valuable hours.

While Ricketts was occupying the enemy's attention, Crook, again moving unobserved into the dense timber on the eastern face of Little North Mountain, conducted his command south in two parallel columns until he gained the rear of the enemy's works, when, marching his divisions by the left flank, he led them in an easterly direction down the mountainside. As he emerged from the timber near the base of the mountain, the Confederates discovered him, of course, and opened fire with their batteries, but it was too late—they having few troops at hand to confront the turning column. Loudly cheering, Crook's men quickly crossed the broken stretch in rear of the enemy's left, producing confusion and consternation at every step.

About a mile from the mountain's base Crook's left was joined by Ricketts, who in proper time had begun to swing his division into the action, and the two commands moved along in rear of the works so rapidly that, with but slight resistance, the Confederates abandoned the guns massed near the center. The swinging movement of Ricketts was taken up successively from right to left throughout my line, and in a few minutes the enemy was thoroughly routed, the action, though brief, being none the less decisive. Lomax's dismounted cavalry gave way first, but was shortly followed by all the Confederate infantry in an indescribable panic, precipitated doubtless by fears of being caught and captured in the pocket formed by Tumbling Run and the North Fork of the Shenandoah River. The stampede was complete, the enemy leaving the field without semblance of organization, abandoning nearly all his artillery and such other property as was in the works, and the rout extending through the fields and over the roads toward Woodstock, Wright and Emory in hot pursuit. . . .

The battle of Fisher's Hill was, in measure, a part of the battle of the Opequon; that is to say, it was an incident of the pursuit resulting from that action. In many ways, however, it was much more satisfactory, and particularly so because the plan arranged on the evening of the twentieth was carried out to the very letter. . . .

The failure of Averell to press the enemy the evening of the twenty-third [for which Sheridan replaced him with Colonel William Powell] gave Early time to collect his scattered forces. . . . The enemy rapidly retreated in line of battle up the Valley through New Market, closely followed by Emory, their artillery on the pike and their columns on its right and left. Both sides moved with celerity, the Confederates stimulated by the desire to escape, and our men animated by the prospect of wholly destroying Early's army. . . . The chase was kept up on the Keezeltown road till darkness overtook us, when my weary troops were permitted to go into camp; and as soon as the enemy discovered by our fires that the pursuit had stopped, he also bivouacked some five miles farther south. . . . His whole army then fell back to the mouth of Brown's Gap to await Kershaw's division and Cutshaw's artillery, now on their return. . . .

While we lay in camp at Harrisonburg it became necessary to decide whether or not I would advance to Brown's Gap, and, after driving the enemy from there, follow him through the Blue Ridge into eastern Virginia. . . . I . . . advised that the Valley campaign be terminated north of Staunton, and I be permitted to return [to join the Army of the Potomac], carrying out on the way my original instructions for desolating the Shenandoah country so as to make it untenable for permanent occupation by the Confederates. . . . I was in hopes that General Grant would take the same view of the matter; but just at this time he was so pressed by the government and by public opinion in the North, that he advocated the wholly different conception of driving Early into eastern Virginia, and adhered to this plan with some tenacity. . . . I being on the ground, General Grant left to me the final decision of the question, and I solved the first step by determining to withdraw down the valley at least as far as Strasburg, which movement was begun on the sixth of October.

The cavalry as it retired was stretched across the country from the Blue Ridge to the eastern slope of the Alleghenies, with orders to drive off all [live]stock and destroy all supplies as it moved northward. The infantry preceded the cavalry, passing down the Valley pike, and as we marched along the many columns of smoke from burning stacks, and mills filled with grain, indicated that the adjacent country was fast losing the features which hitherto had made it a great magazine of stores for the Confederate armies. . . .

On the tenth my army, resuming its retrograde movement, crossed to the north side of Cedar Creek. . . . I was . . . required by the following telegram from Secretary Stanton to repair to [Washington]:

WASHINGTON, OCTOBER 13, 1864

MAJOR-GENERAL SHERIDAN:

If you can come here, a consultation on several points is extremely
desirable. I propose to visit General Grant, and would like to see you
first.

EDWIN M. STANTON
SECRETARY OF WAR[9]

I got all ready to comply with the terms of Secretary Stanton's dispatch,
but in the meantime the enemy appeared in front in force, with infantry
and cavalry. . . . The day's events pointing to a probability that the enemy
intended to resume the offensive, to anticipate such a contingency I
ordered the 6th Corps to return from its march toward Ashby's Gap [on its
way to rejoin the Army of the Potomac]. . . . Before leaving Cedar Creek I
had fixed the route of my return to be by rail from Washington to Martinsburg, and thence by horseback to Winchester and Cedar Creek, and
had ordered three hundred cavalry to Martinsburg to escort me from that
point to the front. . . .

I and my staff, without horses, took the cars for Washington, where we
arrived on the morning of the seventeenth at about eight o'clock. I proceeded at an early hour to the War Department, and as soon as I met
Secretary Stanton, asked him for a special train to be ready at twelve
o'clock to take me to Martinsburg, saying in view of existing conditions I
must get back to my army as quickly as possible. . . .

We arrived about dark at Martinsburg, and there found the escort of
three hundred men which I had ordered before leaving Cedar Creek. We
spent that night at Martinsburg, and early next morning mounted and
started up the Valley pike for Winchester. . . . We did not reach Winchester
till between three and four o'clock in the afternoon, though the distance is
but twenty-eight miles. As soon as we arrived at Colonel Edwards's headquarters in the town, where I intended stopping for the night, I sent a
courier to the front to bring me a report of the condition of affairs. . . . A
courier came in from Cedar Creek bringing word that everything was all
right, that the enemy was quiet at Fisher's Hill, and that a brigade of
Grover's division was to make a reconnaissance in the morning, the nine-

[9] This telegram resulted from the disagreement between Grant and Sheridan (largely
edited from this passage) over Grant's plan for Sheridan to move south and operate
against Gordonsville and Charlottesville.

teenth, so about ten o'clock I went to bed greatly relieved, and expecting to rejoin my headquarters at leisure the next day.

Toward six o'clock the morning of the nineteenth, the officer on picket duty at Winchester came to my room, I being yet in bed, and reported artillery firing from the direction of Cedar Creek. . . . A little later the picket officer came back and reported that the firing, which could be distinctly heard from his line on the heights outside of Winchester, was still going on. I asked him if it sounded like a battle, and as he again said that it did not, I still inferred that the cannonading was caused by Grover's division banging away at the enemy simply to find out what he was up to. . . .

We mounted our horses between half-past eight and nine, and as we were proceeding up the street which leads directly through Winchester, from the Logan residence, where Edwards was quartered, to the Valley pike, I noticed that there were many women at the windows and doors of the houses, who kept shaking their skirts at us and who were otherwise markedly insolent in their demeanor, but supposing this conduct to be instigated by their well-known and perhaps natural prejudices, I ascribed to it no unusual significance. On reaching the edge of the town I halted a moment, and there heard quite distinctly the sound of artillery firing in an unceasing roar. Concluding from this that a battle was in progress, I now felt confident that the women along the street had received intelligence from the battlefield by the "grapevine telegraph," and were in raptures over some good news, while I as yet was utterly ignorant of the actual situation. . . .

At Mill Creek my escort fell behind, and we were going ahead at a regular pace, when, just as we made the crest of the rise beyond the stream, there burst upon our view the appalling spectacle of a panic-stricken army—hundreds of slightly wounded men, throngs of others unhurt but utterly demoralized, and baggage wagons by the score, all pressing to the rear in hopeless confusion, telling only too plainly that a disaster had occurred at the front. On accosting some of the fugitives, they assured me that the army was broken up, in full retreat, and that all was lost; all this with a manner true to that peculiar indifference that takes possession of panic-stricken men. I was greatly disturbed by the sight, but at once sent word to Colonel Edwards, commanding the brigade at Winchester, to stretch his troops across the valley, near Mill Creek, and stop all fugitives, directing also that the transportation be passed through and parked on the north side of the town. . . .

I was fixing in my mind what I should do. My first thought was to stop the army in the suburbs of Winchester as it came back, form a new line, and

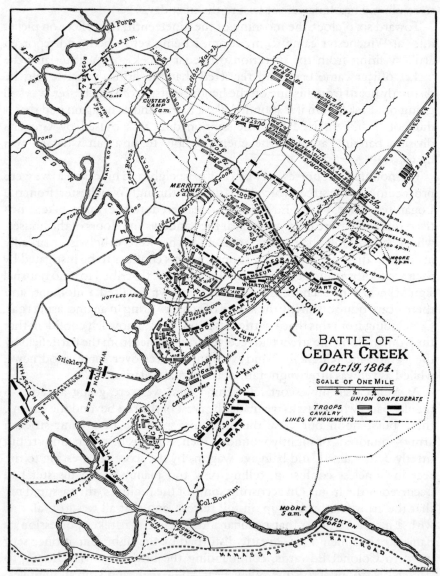

The Battle of Cedar Creek, October 19, 1864

fight there; but as the situation was more maturely considered a better conception prevailed. I was sure the troops had confidence in me, for heretofore we had been successful; and as at other times they had seen me present at the slightest sign of trouble or distress, I felt that I ought to try now to restore their broken ranks, or, failing in that, to share their fate because of what they had done hitherto. . . .

For a short distance I traveled on the road, but soon found it so blocked with wagons and wounded men that my progress was impeded, and I was forced to take to the adjoining fields to make haste. When most of the wagons and wounded men were past I returned to the road, which was thickly lined with unhurt men, who, having got far enough to the rear to be out of danger, had halted, without any organization, and begun cooking coffee, but when they saw me they abandoned their coffee, threw up their hats, shouldered their muskets, and as I passed along turned to follow with enthusiasm and cheers. To acknowledge this exhibition of feeling I took off my hat, and with [staff officers] Forsyth and O'Keefe rode some distance in advance of my escort, while every mounted officer who saw me galloped out on either side of the pike to tell the men at a distance that I had come back. In this way the news was spread to the stragglers off the road, when they, too, turned their faces to the front and marched toward the enemy, changing in a moment from the depths of depression to the extreme of enthusiasm. I already knew that even in the ordinary condition of mind enthusiasm is a potent element with soldiers, but what I saw that day convinced me that if it can be excited from a state of despondency its power is almost irresistible. I said nothing except to remark, as I rode among those on the road: "If I had been with you this morning this disaster would not have happened. We must face the other way; we will go back and recover our camp." . . .[10]

When nearing the Valley pike, just south of Newtown I saw about three-fourths of a mile west of the pike a body of troops, which proved to be Ricketts's and Wheaton's divisions of the 6th Corps, and then learned that the 19th Corps had halted a little to the right and rear of these; but I did not stop, desiring to get to the extreme front. Continuing on parallel with the pike, about midway between Newtown and Middletown I crossed to the west of it, and a little later came up in rear of Getty's division of the 6th Corps. When I arrived, this division and the cavalry were the only troops in the presence of and resisting the enemy; they were apparently acting as a rear guard at a point about three miles north of the line we held at Cedar Creek

[10] Sheridan also, apparently, cut loose with a string of words unfit for polite society.

when the battle began. General Torbert was the first officer to meet me, saying as he rode up, "My God! I am glad you've come." Getty's division, when I found it, was about a mile north of Middletown, posted on the reverse slope of some slightly rising ground, holding a barricade made with fence rails, and skirmishing slightly with the enemy's pickets. Jumping my horse over the line of rails, I rode to the crest of the elevation, and there taking off my hat, the men rose up from behind their barricade with cheers of recognition. . . . In a few minutes some of my staff joined me, and the first directions I gave were to have the 19th Corps and the two divisions of Wright's corps brought to the front, so they could be formed on Getty's division, prolonged to the right; for I had already decided to attack the enemy from that line as soon as I could get matters in shape to take the offensive. . . .

Between half-past three and four o'clock, I was ready to assail, and decided to do so by advancing my infantry line in a swinging movement, so as to gain the Valley pike with my right between Middletown and the Belle Grove House; and when the order was passed along, the men pushed steadily forward with enthusiasm and confidence. General Early's troops extended some little distance beyond our right, and when my flank neared the overlapping enemy, he turned on it, with the effect of causing a momentary confusion, but General McMillan quickly realizing the danger, broke the Confederates at the reentering angle by a countercharge with his brigade, doing his work so well that the enemy's flanking troops were cut off from their main body and left to shift for themselves. [George Armstrong] Custer, who was then moving in from the west side of Middle Marsh Brook, followed McMillan's timely blow with a charge of cavalry, but before starting out on it, and while his men were forming, riding at full speed himself, to throw his arms around my neck. By the time he had disengaged himself from this embrace, the troops broken by McMillan had gained some little distance to their rear, but Custer's troopers sweeping across the Middletown meadows and down toward Cedar Creek, took many of them prisoners before they could reach the stream—so I forgave the delay.

My whole line as far as the eye could see was now driving everything before it, from behind trees, stone walls, and all such sheltering obstacles. . . . Meanwhile Lowell's brigade of cavalry, which, it will be remembered, had been holding on, dismounted, just north of Middletown ever since the time I arrived from Winchester, fell to the rear for the purpose of getting their led horses. A momentary panic was created in the nearest brigade of infantry by this withdrawal of Lowell, but as soon as his men were mounted they charged the enemy clear up to the stone walls in the edge of Middletown; at sight of this the infantry brigade renewed its attack, and the enemy's right gave way. The accomplished Lowell received his death wound in this courageous charge.

All our troops were now moving on the retreating Confederates, and as I rode to the front Colonel Gibbs, who succeeded Lowell, made ready for another mounted charge, but I checked him from pressing the enemy's right, in the hope that the swinging attack from my right would throw most of the Confederates to the east of the Valley pike, and hence off their line of retreat through Strasburg to Fisher's Hill. The eagerness of the men soon frustrated this anticipation, however, the left insisting on keeping pace with the center and right, and all pushing ahead till we regained our old camps at Cedar Creek. . . . When news of the victory was received, General Grant directed a salute of one hundred shotted guns to be fired into Petersburg, and the President at once thanked the army. . . .

It was not till after the battle that I learned fully what had taken place before my arrival, and then found that the enemy, having gathered all the strength he could through the return of convalescents and other absentees, had moved quietly from Fisher's Hill, in the night of the eighteenth and early on the morning of the nineteenth, to surprise my army, which, it should be remembered, was posted on the north bank of Cedar Creek. . . .

Early's broken army practically made no halt in its retreat after the battle of Cedar Creek until it reached New Market. . . . Early got back to New Market on the fourteenth of November, and, from lack of subsistence, being unable to continue demonstrations to prevent my reinforcement of General Grant, began himself to detach to General Lee by returning Kershaw's division to Petersburg. . . . At this time General Grant wished me to send him the 6th Corps. . . . By the middle of [December] the whole of the 6th Corps was at Petersburg; simultaneously with its transfer to that line Early sending his 2nd Corps to Lee.

During the entire campaign I had been annoyed by guerrilla bands under such partisan chiefs as Mosby, White, Gilmore, McNeil, and others, and this had considerably depleted my line-of-battle strength, necessitating as it did large escorts for my supply trains. The most redoubtable of these leaders was Mosby, whose force was made up from the country around Upperville, east of the Blue Ridge, to which section he always fled for a hiding place when he scented danger. I had not directed any special operations against these partisans while the campaign was active, but as Mosby's men had lately killed, within my lines, my chief quartermaster, Colonel Tolles, and Medical Inspector Ohlenchlager, I concluded to

devote particular attention to these "irregulars" during the lull now occurred; so on the twenty-eighth of November, I directed General Merritt
to march to the Loudoun Valley and operate against Mosby, taking care to
clear the country of forage and subsistence, so as to prevent the guerrillas
from being harbored there in the future, their destruction or capture being
well nigh impossible, on account of their intimate knowledge of the mountain region. Merritt carried out his instructions with his usual sagacity and
thoroughness, sweeping widely over each side of his general line of march
with flankers, who burned the grain and brought in large herds of cattle,
hogs, and sheep, which were issued to the troops.

20

THE APPOMATTOX CAMPAIGN
March–April 1865

Sheridan's campaign in the Valley, though it involved only a fraction of the troops fighting in Georgia and before Petersburg, proved one of the most decisive of the war. The loss of the Shenandoah denied Lee critical supplies, and desertions by troops from the area increased; furthermore, Grant had succeeded in further extending his lines around Petersburg after Lee had sent reinforcements to help Early. Sheridan's victories, along with Sherman's capture of Atlanta, guaranteed Lincoln's reelection and the decisive conclusion of the war.

The Army of the Potomac, however, remained bogged down in its siege of Petersburg. In fighting that foreshadowed the trench warfare of World War I, the troops burrowed into the ground, hiding from shells and snipers' bullets. Just before Sheridan left for the Valley, Grant missed his best chance to break the Confederate lines in the famed Battle of the Crater. A regiment of Pennsylvania coal miners had dug the longest military tunnel in history under the rebel trenches—more than 500 feet—and had filled it with four tons of gunpowder. A division of black soldiers was specially trained to lead the assault; Meade, however, made a white division the spearhead, mistrusting the blacks' fighting abilities and fearing that they would be seen as sacrifices to save white lives. On July 30, 1864, the mine went off, blowing a huge hole in the Confederate defenses, sending rebel soldiers running in panic. But the untrained white troops failed to roll up the Southern line; instead, they milled about *inside* the crater, where they were butchered in a counterattack.

So the siege went on through the summer and winter, as events advanced elsewhere. In Georgia, Sherman chased for a time after Hood's much-reduced army as it moved west from Atlanta. Frustrated with the fruitless chase after a lighter, faster enemy, Sherman proposed to leave George H. Thomas behind (based at Nashville) to cope with anything Hood might try, while he himself took an army through the heart of Georgia to destroy the source of the Confederate supplies. The war would never end, Sherman wrote Grant, until the Southern civilians far behind the lines felt its hard hand. After some debate Grant approved, launching the campaign that devastated the Confederate will.

On November 15, 1864, Sherman destroyed the city of Atlanta and set out on his march to the sea, leaving behind a swath of destruction—torn-up railroads, burned mills and foundries, and scorched fields. He faced little opposition, because as he moved south Hood took his own army north, on an invasion of Tennessee.

As Thomas collected reinforcements at Nashville, General George Schofield with 30,000 men opposed the Confederates at Franklin. On November 30, Hood launched a head-on assault against the Union trenches, losing more than 7,000 casualties, including a dozen generals. Schofield retreated to join Thomas at Nashville, followed by the now desperately depleted Confederate Army of Tennessee. For two weeks, Thomas delayed his counterattack, as he made sure that everything was perfectly prepared for the assault. Grant grew so impatient that he made plans to go to Nashville in person to replace Thomas.

Fortunately, the Confederates did not slip away (an art they were skilled in) before the attack came. On December 15, 1864, Thomas's assault rolled over the battered, badly outnumbered rebels, virtually destroying the Army of Tennessee.

Farther east, Sherman reached Savannah by the end of the month, then turned north to march through South Carolina. Joseph Johnston took command of the 20,000 Confederates gathered to oppose him; but Sherman continually bewildered the Southern general about his intentions, moving north into North Carolina after leaving behind his trademark wake of destruction and demoralization. On January 15, 1865, the last blockade-running port was closed as General Alfred Terry and Admiral David Porter captured Fort Fisher, the bastion of Wilmington, North Carolina. Southern soldiers began to desert by the hundreds.

Spring drew near, and the days of the Confederacy rapidly dwindled. Once Sherman came north into Virginia, Lee would be surrounded, and the last army of the Confederacy would be captured. To avoid this fate, Lee planned to withdraw from Grant's grip at Petersburg, join Johnston in North Carolina, and overwhelm Sherman. In preparation, he launched an attack on Fort Steadman, the strongpoint of Grant's right, on March 24, 1865, but the assault was thrown back. Following up his advantage, Grant sent Sheridan on a wide swing to the left to complete the encirclement of the Army of Northern Virginia. It was the beginning of the end for the daring, aristocratic Virginian.

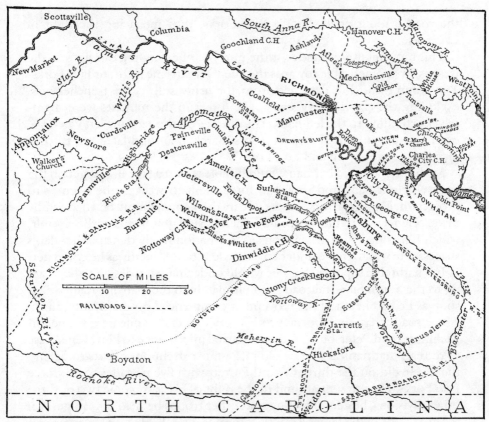

The region of the Appomattox Campaign, April 1865

From Five Forks to Lee's Surrender
By General U.S. Grant

Finally the twenty-ninth of March came, and fortunately there having been a few days free from rain, the surface of the ground was dry, giving indications that the time had come when we could move. On that date I moved out with all the army available after leaving sufficient force to hold the line about Petersburg. It soon set in raining again, however, and in a very short time the roads became practically impassable for teams, and almost so for cavalry.... The next day, March 30th, we had made sufficient progress to the southwest to warrant me in starting Sheridan with his cavalry over by Dinwiddie with instructions to then come up by the road leading northwest to Five Forks, thus menacing the right of Lee's line.

This movement was made for the purpose of extending our lines to the west as far as practicable towards the enemy's extreme right, or Five Forks. The column moving detached from the army still in the trenches was, excluding the cavalry, very small. The forces in the trenches were themselves extending to the left flank. Warren was on the extreme left when the extension began, but Humphreys was marched around later and thrown into line between him and Five Forks.

My hope was that Sheridan would be able to carry Five Forks, get on the enemy's right flank and rear, and force them to weaken their center to protect their right so that an assault in the center might be successfully made. General Wright's corps had been designated to make this assault, which I intended to order as soon as information reached me of Sheridan's success. He was to move under cover as close to the enemy as he could get.

It is natural to suppose that Lee would understand my design to be to get up to the South Side [railroad] and ultimately to the Danville Railroad, as soon as he had heard of the movement commenced on the twenty-ninth. These roads were so important to his very existence while he remained in Richmond and Petersburg, and of such vital importance to him even in case of retreat, that naturally he would make most strenuous efforts to defend them. He did on the thirtieth send Pickett with five brigades to reinforce Five Forks. He also sent around to the right of his army some two or three other divisions, besides directing that other troops be held in readiness on the north side of the James River to come over on call. He came over himself to superintend in person the defense of his right flank.

Sheridan moved back to Dinwiddie Court House on the night of the thirtieth, and then took a road leading northwest to Five Forks. He had only his cavalry with him. Soon encountering the rebel cavalry he met with very stout resistance. He gradually drove them back however until in the neighborhood of Five Forks. Here he had to encounter other troops besides those he had been contending with, and was forced to give way.

In this condition of affairs he notified me of what had taken place and stated that he was falling back toward Dinwiddie gradually and slowly, and asked me to send Wright's corps to his assistance.[11] I replied to him that it was impossible to send Wright's corps because that corps was already in line close up to the enemy, where we should want to assault when the

---

[11] This was the 6th Corps, which had fought so successfully with Sheridan in the Valley.

proper time came, and was besides a long distance from him; but the 2nd (Humphreys's) and 5th (Warren's) Corps were on our extreme left and a little to the rear of it in a position to threaten the left flank of the enemy at Five Forks, and that I would send Warren.

Accordingly orders were sent to Warren to move that night (the thirty-first) to Dinwiddie Court House and put himself in communication with Sheridan as soon as possible, and report to him. He was very slow in moving, some of his troops not starting until after five o'clock next morning. When he did move it was done very deliberately. . . . He was so late that Sheridan determined to move forward without him. However, Ayres's division of Warren's corps reached him in time to be in the fight all day, most of the time separated from the remainder of the 5th Corps and fighting directly under Sheridan.

Warren reported to Sheridan about eleven o'clock on the first, but the whole of his troops were not up so as to be much engaged until late in the afternoon. . . .

Sheridan succeeded in the middle of the afternoon or a little later, in advancing up to the point from which to make his designed assault upon Five Forks itself. He was very impatient to make the assault and have it all over before night, because the ground he occupied would be untenable for him in bivouac during the night. Unless the assault was made and was successful, he would be obliged to return to Dinwiddie Court House, or even further than that for the night.

It was at this junction of affairs that Sheridan wanted to get Crawford's division in hand, and he also wanted Warren. He sent staff officer after staff officer in search of Warren, directing that general to report to him, but they were unable to find him. At all events Sheridan was unable to get that officer to him. Finally he went himself. He issued an order relieving Warren and assigning Griffin to the command of the 5th Corps. The troops were then brought up and the assault successfully made. . . .

It was dusk when our troops under Sheridan went over the parapets of the enemy. The two armies were mingled together there for a time in such manner that it was almost a question of which one was going to demand the surrender of the other. Soon, however, the enemy broke and ran in every direction; some six thousand prisoners, besides artillery and small arms in large quantities, falling into our hands. The flying troops were pursued in different directions, the cavalry and 5th Corps under Sheridan pursuing the larger body which moved northwest.

This pursuit was continued until about nine o'clock at night, when Sheridan halted his troops, and knowing the importance to him of the part of the enemy's line which had been captured, returned, sending the 5th Corps across Hatcher's Run to the southwest of Petersburg, and facing them toward it. Merritt, with the cavalry, stopped and bivouacked west of Five Forks.

This was the condition which affairs were in on the night of the first of April. I then issued orders for an assault by Wright and Parke at four o'clock on the morning of the second. I also ordered the 2nd Corps, General Humphreys, and General Ord with the Army of the James, on the left, to hold themselves in readiness to take any advantage that could be taken from weakening in their front. . . .

I was afraid that Lee would regard the possession of Five Forks as of so much importance that he would make a last desperate effort to retake it, risking everything upon the cast of a single die. It was for this reason that I ordered the assault to take place at once, as soon as I had received the news of the capture of Five Forks. The corps commanders, however, reported that it was so dark that the men could not see to move, and it would be impossible to make the assault then. But we kept up a continuous artillery fire upon the enemy around the whole line including that north of the James River, until it was light enough to move, which was about a quarter to five in the morning.

At that hour Parke's and Wright's troops moved out as directed, brushed the abatis from their front as they advanced under a heavy fire of musketry and artillery, and went without flinching directly on till they mounted the parapets and threw themselves inside of the enemy's line. . . .

Wright swung around to his left and moved to Hatcher's Run, sweeping everything before him. . . . Both Parke and Wright captured a considerable amount of artillery and some prisoners—Wright about three thousand of them.

In the meantime Ord and Humphreys, in obedience to the instructions they had received, had succeeded by daylight, or very early in the morning, in capturing the entrenched picket lines in their front, and before Wright got up to that point, Ord had also succeeded in getting inside of the enemy's entrenchments. The 2nd Corps soon followed; and the outer works of Petersburg were in the hands of the National troops, never to be wrenched from them again. When Wright reached Hatcher's Run, he sent a regiment to destroy the South Side Railroad just outside of the city. . . .

Lee made frantic efforts to recover at least part of the lost ground. Parke on our right was repeatedly assaulted, but repulsed every effort. Before noon Longstreet [now recovered from his wound from the Wilderness] was ordered up from the north side of the James River, thus bringing the bulk of

Lee's army around to the support of his extreme right. As soon as I learned this I notified Weitzel and directed him to keep up close to the enemy and to have Hartsuff, commanding the Bermuda Hundred front, to do the same thing, and if they found any break to go in; Hartsuff especially should do so, for this would separate Richmond from Petersburg.

Sheridan, after he had returned to Five Forks, swept down to Petersburg, coming in on our left. This gave us a continuous line from the Appomattox River below the city to the same river above. . . .

The enemy had in addition to their entrenched line close up to Petersburg, two enclosed works outside of it, Fort Gregg and Fort Whitworth. We thought it had now become necessary to carry them by assault. About one o'clock in the day, Fort Gregg was assaulted by Foster's division of the 24th Corps (Gibbon's), supported by two brigades from Ord's command. The battle was desperate and the National troops repulsed several times; but it was finally carried, and immediately the troops in Fort Whitworth evacuated the place. . . .

During the night of April 2nd our line was entrenched from the river above to the river below. I ordered a bombardment to be commenced the next morning at five A.M., to be followed by an assault at six o'clock; but the enemy evacuated Petersburg early in the morning.

General Meade and I entered Petersburg on the morning of the third and took a position under cover of a house which protected us from the enemy's musketry which was flying thick and fast there. As we could occasionally look around the corner we could see the streets and the Appomattox bottom, presumably near the bridge, packed with the Confederate army. I did not have artillery brought up, because I was sure Lee was trying to make his escape, and I wanted to push immediately in pursuit. At all events I had not the heart to turn the artillery on such a mass of defeated and fleeing men, and I hoped to capture them soon. . . .

I had held most of the command aloof from the entrenchments, so as to start them out on the Danville Road early in the morning, supposing that Lee would be gone during the night. During the night I strengthened Sheridan by sending him Humphreys's corps.

Lee, as we now know, had advised the authorities at Richmond, during the day, of the condition of affairs, and told them it would be impossible for him to hold out longer than night, if he could hold out that long. Davis was at church when he received Lee's dispatch. The congregation was dismissed with the notice that there would be no evening service. The rebel government left Richmond about two o'clock in the afternoon of the second.

At night Lee ordered his troops to assemble at Amelia Court House, his object being to get away, join Johnston if possible, and to try to crush Sherman before I could get there. As soon as I was sure of this I notified Sheridan and directed him to move out on the Danville Railroad to the south side of the Appomattox River as speedily as possible. He replied that he already had some of his command nine miles out. I then ordered the rest of the Army of the Potomac under Meade to follow the same road in the morning. . . .

The next morning after the capture of Petersburg, I telegraphed Mr. Lincoln asking him to ride out there and see me, while I would await his arrival. . . . About the first thing that Mr. Lincoln said to me, after warm congratulations for the victory, and thanks both to myself and to the army which had accomplished it, was: "Do you know, general, that I have had a sort of sneaking idea for some days that you intended to do something like this." . . .

Mr. Lincoln knew that it had been arranged for Sherman to join me at a fixed time, to cooperate in the destruction of Lee's army. I told him that I had been very anxious to have the Eastern armies vanquish their old enemy who had so long resisted all their repeated and gallant attempts to subdue them or drive them from their capital. The Western armies had been in the main successful until they had conquered all the territory from the Mississippi River to the State of North Carolina, and were now almost ready to knock at the back door of Richmond, asking admittance. I said to him that if the Western armies should even be upon the field, operating against Richmond and Lee, the credit would be given to them for the capture, by politicians and the noncombatants from the section of the country which those troops hailed from. It might even lead to disagreeable bickerings between the members of Congress of the East and those of the West in some of their debates. . . .

Mr. Lincoln said he saw that now, but had never thought of it before, because his anxiety was so great that he did not care where the aid came from so the work was done. . . .

Soon after I left President Lincoln I received a dispatch from General Weitzel which notified me that he had taken possession of Richmond at 8:15 o'clock in the morning of that day, the third, and that he had found the city on fire in two places. The city was in the most utter confusion. . . .

Lee entrenched himself at Amelia Court House, and also his advance north of Jetersville, and sent his troops out to collect forage. The country was very poor and afforded but very little. His foragers scattered a great deal; many of them were picked up by our men, and many others never returned to the Army of Northern Virginia.

Griffin's corps was entrenched across the railroad south of Jetersville, and Sheridan notified me of the situation. I again ordered Meade up with all dispatch, Sheridan having but the one corps of infantry with a little cavalry confronting Lee's entire army. Meade, always prompt in obeying orders, now pushed forward with great energy, although he was himself sick and hardly able to be out of bed. Humphreys moved at two, and Wright at three o'clock in the morning, without rations, as I have said, the wagons being far in the rear.

I stayed that night at Wilson's Station on the South Side Railroad. On the morning of the fifth I sent word to Sheridan of the progress Meade was making, and suggested that he might now attack Lee. We had now no other objective than the Confederate armies, and I was anxious to close the thing up at once. . . .

Meade himself reached Jetersville about two o'clock in the afternoon, but in advance of all his troops. The head of Humphreys's corps followed in about an hour afterwards. Sheridan stationed the troops as they came up, at Meade's request, the latter still being very sick. He extended two divisions of this corps off to the west of the road to the left of Griffin's corps, and one division to the right. The cavalry by this time had also come up, and they were put still farther off to the left, Sheridan feeling certain that there lay the route by which the enemy intended to escape. He wanted to attack, feeling that if the time was given, the enemy would get away; but Meade prevented this, preferring to wait till his troops were all up. . . .

I then started with a few of my staff and a very small escort of cavalry, going directly through the woods, to join Meade's army. The distance was about sixteen miles; but the night being dark our progress was very slow through the woods in the absence of direct roads. However, we got to the outposts about ten o'clock in the evening, and after some little parley convinced the sentinels of our identity and were conducted in to where Sheridan was bivouacked. We talked over the situation for some little time, Sheridan explaining to me what he thought Lee was trying to do, and that Meade's orders, if carried out, moving to the right flank, would give him the coveted opportunity of escaping us and putting us in rear of him.

We then together visited Meade, reaching his headquarters about midnight. I explained to Meade that we did not want to follow the enemy; we wanted to get ahead of him, and that his orders would allow the enemy to escape, and besides that, I had no doubt that Lee was moving right then. Meade changed his orders at once. They were now given for an advance on Amelia Court House, at an early hour in the morning. . . .

As expected, Lee's troops had moved during the night before, and our army in moving upon Amelia Court House soon encountered them. There was a good deal of fighting before Sailor's Creek was reached. Our cavalry charged in upon a body of theirs which was escorting a wagon train in order to get it past our left. A severe engagement ensued, in which we captured many prisoners, and many men were killed and wounded. There was as much gallantry displayed by some of the Confederates in these little engagements as was displayed at any time during the war, notwithstanding the sad defeats of the past week.

The armies finally met on Sailor's Creek, when a heavy engagement took place, in which infantry, artillery, and cavalry were all brought into action. Our men on the right, as they were brought against the enemy, came in on higher ground, and upon his flank, giving us every advantage to be derived from the lay of the country. Our firing was also very much more rapid, because the enemy commenced his retreat westward and in firing as he retreated had to turn around every time he fired. The enemy's loss was very heavy, as well in killed and wounded as in captures. Some six general officers fell into our hands in this engagement, and seven thousand men were made prisoners. This engagement was commenced in the middle of the afternoon of the sixth, and the retreat and pursuit was continued until nightfall, when the armies bivouacked upon the ground where the night had overtaken them. . . .

Lee himself pushed on and crossed the wagon road bridge [over the Appomattox] near the High Bridge, and attempted to destroy it. He did set fire to it, but the flames had made but little headway when Humphreys came up with his corps and drove away the rearguard which had been left to protect it while it was being burned up. Humphreys forced his way across with some loss, and followed Lee to the intersection of the road crossing at Farmville with the one from Petersburg. Here Lee held a position which was very strong, naturally, besides being entrenched. Humphreys was alone, confronting him all through the day, and in a very hazardous position. He put on a bold face, however, and assaulted with some loss, but was not assaulted in return. . . .

I rode in to Farmville on the seventh, arriving there early in the day. Sheridan and Ord were pushing through, away to the south. Meade was back towards the High Bridge, and Humphreys confronting Lee as before stated. After having gone into bivouac at Prince Edward's Court House, Sheridan learned that seven trains of provisions and forage were at Appomattox, and determining to start at once and capture them; and a forced march was necessary in order to get there before Lee's army could secure them. He wrote me a note telling me this. This fact . . . gave me the idea of opening correspondence with General Lee on the subject of the surrender of his army. I therefore wrote to him on this day, as follows:

HEADQUARTERS ARMIES OF THE U.S.
APRIL 7, 1865, 5 P.M.

GENERAL R.E. LEE,
Commanding C.S.A.

The results of the last week must convince you of the hopelessness of further resistance on the part of the Army of Northern Virginia in this struggle. I feel that it is so, and regard it as my duty to shift from myself the responsibility of any further effusion of blood, by asking of you the surrender of that portion of the Confederate States army known as the Army of Northern Virginia.

U.S. GRANT,
LIEUT.-GENERAL

Lee replied on the evening of the same day as follows:

APRIL 7, 1865

GENERAL: I have received your note of this day. Though not entertaining the opinion you express on the hopelessness of further resistance on the part of the Army of Northern Virginia, I reciprocate your desire to avoid useless effusion of blood, and therefore before considering your proposition, ask the terms you will offer on condition of its surrender.

R.E. LEE,
GENERAL

LIEUT.-GENERAL U.S. GRANT
COMMANDING ARMIES OF THE U.S.

This was not satisfactory, but I regarded it as deserving another letter and wrote him as follows:

APRIL 8, 1865

GENERAL R.E. LEE,
Commanding C.S.A.

Your note of last evening in reply of same date, asking the condition on which I will accept the surrender of the Army of Northern Virginia is just received. In reply I would say that, peace being my great desire, there is but one condition I would insist upon, namely: that the men and officers surrendered shall be disqualified for taking up arms again against the Government of the United States until properly exchanged. I will meet you, or will designate officers to meet any officers you may name for the same purpose, at any point agreeable to you, for the purpose of arranging definitely the terms upon which the surrender of the Army of Northern Virginia will be received.

U.S. GRANT,
LIEUT.-GENERAL

Lee's army was rapidly crumbling. Many of his soldiers had enlisted from that part of the State where they now were, and were continually dropping out of the ranks and going to their homes. . . .

Although Sheridan had been marching all day, his troops moved with alacrity and without any straggling. They began to see the end of what they had been fighting four years for. Nothing seemed to fatigue them. They were ready to move without rations and travel without rest until the end. Straggling had entirely ceased, and every man was now a rival for the front. The infantry marched about as rapidly as the cavalry could.

Sheridan sent Custer with his division to move south of Appomattox Station, which is about five miles southwest of the Court House, to get west of the trains and destroy the roads to the rear. They got there the night of the eighth, and succeeded partially; but some of the train men had just discovered the movement of our troops and succeeded in running off three of the trains. The other four were held by Custer.

The head of Lee's column came marching up there on the morning of the ninth, not dreaming, I suppose, that there were any Union soldiers near. The Confederates were surprised to find our cavalry in possession of the trains. However, they were desperate and at once assaulted, hoping to recover them. In the melee that ensued they succeeded in burning one of the trains, but not in getting anything from it. Custer then ordered the other trains run back on the road towards Farmville, and the fight continued.

So far, only our cavalry and the advance of Lee's army were engaged. Soon, however, Lee's men were brought up from the rear, no doubt expecting they had nothing to meet but our cavalry. But our infantry had pushed forward so rapidly that by the time the enemy got up they found Griffin's corps and the Army of the James confronting them. A sharp engagement ensued, but Lee quickly set up a white flag.

LEE'S SURRENDER

On the eighth I had followed the Army of the Potomac in rear of Lee. I was suffering severely with a sick headache, and stopped at a farmhouse on the road some distance in rear of the main body of the army. I spent the night in bathing my feet in hot water and mustard, and putting mustard plasters on my wrists and the back part of my neck, hoping to be cured by morning. During the night I received Lee's answer to my letter of the eighth, inviting an interview between the lines on the following morning. But it was for a different purpose from that of surrendering his army. . . . [Grant then sent a note in reply.]

Lee, therefore, sent an escort with the officer bearing this message through his lines to me.

APRIL 9, 1865

GENERAL: I received your note of this morning on the picket line whither I had come to meet you and ascertain definitely what terms were embraced in your proposal of yesterday with reference to the surrender of this army. I now request an interview in accordance with the offer contained in your letter of yesterday for that purpose.

R.E. LEE
GENERAL

LIEUTENANT-GENERAL U.S. GRANT
COMMANDING U.S. ARMIES

When the officer reached me I was still suffering with the sick headache; but the instant I saw the contents of the note I was cured. . . .

I was conducted at once to where Sheridan was located with his troops drawn up in line of battle facing the Confederate army nearby. They were very much excited, and expressed their view that this was all a ruse employed to enable the Confederates to get away. . . . But I had no doubt about the good faith of Lee, and pretty soon was conducted to where he was. I found him at the house of a Mr. McLean, at Appomattox Court House, with Colonel Marshall, one of his staff officers, awaiting my arrival. . . .

I had known General Lee in the old army, and had served with him in the Mexican War; but did not suppose, owing to the difference in our age and rank, that he would remember me; while I would more naturally remember him distinctly, because he was the chief of staff of General Scott in the Mexican War.

When I had left camp that morning I had not expected so soon the result that was then taking place, and consequently was in rough garb. I was without sword, as I usually was when on horseback in the field, and wore a soldier's blouse for a coat, with the shoulder straps of my rank to indicate to the army who I was. When I went into the house I found General Lee. We greeted each other, and after shaking hands took our seats. I had my staff with me, a good portion of whom were in the room during the whole of the interview.

What General Lee's feelings were I do not know. As he was a man of much dignity, with an impassable face, it was impossible to say whether he felt inwardly glad that the end had finally come, or felt sad over the result, and was too manly to show it. Whatever his feelings, they were entirely concealed from my observation; but my own feelings, which had been quite jubilant on the receipt of his letter, were sad and depressed. I felt like anything rather than rejoicing at the downfall of a foe who had fought so long and valiantly, and had suffered so much for a cause, though that cause was, I believe, one of the worst for which a people ever fought, and one for which there was the least excuse. I do not question, however, the sincerity of the great mass of those who were opposed to me.

General Lee was dressed in a full uniform which was entirely new, and was wearing a sword of considerable value, very likely the sword which had been presented by the State of Virginia; at all events, it was an entirely different sword from the one that would ordinarily be worn in the field. In my rough traveling suit, the uniform of a private with the straps of a lieutenant-general, I must have contrasted very strangely with a man so handsomely dressed, six feet high and of faultless form. But this was not a matter that I thought of until afterwards.

We soon fell into a conversation about old army times. He remarked that he remembered me very well in the old army; and I told him that as a matter of course I remembered him perfectly, but from the difference in our rank and years (there being about sixteen years' difference in our ages),

I had thought it very likely that I had not attracted his attention sufficiently to be remembered by him after such a long interval. Our conversation grew so pleasant that I almost forgot the object of our meeting. After the conversation had run on in this style for some time, General Lee called my attention to the object of our meeting, and said that he had asked for this interview for the purpose of getting from me the terms I proposed to give his army. I said that I meant merely that his army should lay down their arms, not to take them up again during the continuance of the war unless duly and properly exchanged. He said that he had so understood the letter.

Then we gradually fell off again into conversation about matters foreign to the subject which had brought us together. This continued for some little time, when General Lee again interrupted the course of the conversation by suggesting that the terms I proposed to give his army ought to be written out. I called to General Parker, secretary on my staff, for writing materials. . . .

When I put my pen to the paper I did not know the first word that I should make use of in writing the terms. I only knew what was in my mind, and I wished to express it clearly, so that there could be no mistaking it. As I wrote on, the thought occurred to me that the officers had their own private horses and effects, which were important to them, but of no value to us; also that it would be unnecessary humiliation to call upon them to deliver their sidearms.

No conversation, not one word, passed between General Lee and myself, either about private property, sidearms, or kindred subjects. He appeared to have no objections to the terms first proposed; or if he had a point to make against them he wished to wait until they were in writing to make it. When he read over that part of the terms about sidearms, horses, and private property of the officers, he remarked, with some feeling, I thought, that this would have a happy effect upon his army.

Then, after a little further conversation, General Lee remarked to me again that their army was organized a little differently from the army of the United States (still maintaining by implication that we were two countries); that in their army the cavalrymen and artillerists owned their own horses; and he asked if he was to understand that the men who so owned their horses were to be permitted to retain them. I told him that as the terms were written they would not; that only the officers were permitted to take their private property. He then, after reading over the terms a second time, remarked that that was clear.

I then said to him that I thought this would be about the last battle of the war—I sincerely hoped so; and I said further I took it most of the men

in the ranks were small farmers. The whole country had been so raided by
the two armies that it was doubtful whether they would be able to put in a
crop to carry themselves and their families through the next winter without the aid of the horses they were riding. The United States did not want
them and I would, therefore, instruct the officers I left behind to receive
the paroles of his troops to let every man of the Confederate army who
claimed to own a horse or mule take the animal to his home. Lee remarked
again that this would have a happy effect. . . .

General Lee, after all was completed and before taking his leave, remarked that his army was in a very bad condition for want of food, and that
they were without forage; that his men had been living for some days on
parched corn exclusively, and that he would have to ask me for rations and
forage. I told him "certainly," and asked for how many men he wanted
rations. His answer was "about twenty-five thousand": and I authorized
him to send his commissary and quartermaster to Appomattox Station,
two or three miles away, where he could have, out of the trains we had
stopped, all the provisions wanted. . . .

Generals Gibbon, Griffin, and Merritt were designated by me to carry
into effect the paroling of Lee's troops before they should start for their
homes—General Lee leaving Generals Longstreet, Gordon, and Pen-
dleton for them to confer with in order to facilitate this work. Lee and I
then separated as cordially as we had met, he returning to his own lines,
and all went into bivouac for the night at Appomattox. . . .

When news of the surrender first reached our lines our men commenced
firing a salute of a hundred guns in honor of the victory. I at once sent
word, however, to have it stopped. The Confederates were now our
prisoners, and we did not want to exult over their downfall.

Lee's surrender proved what most observers had long suspected: Robert
E. Lee *was* the Confederacy. Perhaps this states the case too strongly; but
in the last phase of the war, the hopes of the South increasingly rested in
the person of its most successful commander. Grant, too, declared that his
war-winning object was Lee and his army, not the Confederate capital.
Indeed, once the proud Virginian succumbed, his cause collapsed: Joseph
Johnston and the other rebel commanders quickly surrendered, and even
the wild guerrillas of Missouri rode to the nearest Union posts and gave
themselves up.

At the moment of triumph, Lincoln fell victim to John Wilkes Booth's pistol. In short order, Booth was cornered in a barn and killed; Jefferson Davis (also on the run) was captured and imprisoned, to be held for two years without trial; and Congress began its tormented struggle with President Andrew Johnson over reconstructing the vanquished Southern states.

Historians have argued over the causes of the Confederate defeat, often emphasizing population, economics, political will, and the public morale. James McPherson, however, has aptly expressed the recent shift in historical thinking to a new emphasis on battlefield events. At numerous points in the war, he notes, the tide of events could easily have turned the other way; at each point, key victories gave the respective combatants the will to continue in the face of rising casualties. In the end, the successes of Sherman and Sheridan gave Grant the public support he needed to see his strategy through to victory.

In cities and towns throughout the eastern half of the United States, public memorials stand in tribute to the Civil War dead. Many were erected twenty or thirty years after the conflict came to a close, testifying to how deeply the nation felt its loss. More than 620,000 combatants fell from wounds and disease in the war: 360,000 Union casualties and 260,000 Confederate, more than all our other wars combined. The South suffered untold damage. Places like the Shenandoah Valley and the city of Atlanta had been utterly destroyed. In Missouri alone, historian Michael Fellman tells us, the population fell by 300,000 people (almost one in three): they fled for their lives, were driven out by one side or the other, or died.

On the other hand, the signal conflict in American history was resolved. Four million slaves emerged from the war into freedom. Sectionalism was soundly defeated; the United States stood as a nation, not a voluntary association of states. At war's end, Northern industries were booming and immigration leaped ahead. Meanwhile, the new Homestead Act released a fresh flood of settlers—Yankees and Southerners alike—into the West, leading to the nation's next great conflict. For even as the political battles of Reconstruction raged and industrialization roared ahead, the nation's imagination was caught up in that massive, diffuse drama—the struggle for the frontier.